THE WEARING OF THE GREEN

A History of St Patrick's Day

— ⚮ —

Mike Cronin and Daryl Adair

Routledge
Taylor & Francis Group

LONDON AND NEW YORK

First published 2002 by Routledge

First published in paperback in 2006
by Routledge
2 Park Square, Milton Park, Abingdon, Oxon, OX14 4RN

Simultaneously published in the US
by Routledge
270 Madison Avenue, New York, NY 10016

Routledge is an imprint of the Taylor & Francis Group

© 2002, 2006 Mike Cronin and Daryl Adair

Typeset in Garamond by Wearset Ltd, Boldon, Tyne and Wear
Printed and bound in Great Britain by MPG Books Ltd, Bodmin,
Cornwall

British Library Cataloguing in Publication Data
A catalogue record for this book is available from the British
Library

Library of Congress Cataloging in Publication Data

ISBN 0-415-18004-X (cased)
ISBN 0-415-35912-0 (limp)

In memory of my grandfather, Geoffrey Davies, and for my
nephew and niece, James and Nicola Cronin (MC)
For my family, Cheryl and Kane Adair (DA)

Beannacht Dé agus Naomh Padraig oraibh go léir
(The blessing of God and St Patrick on you all)

CONTENTS

— ∽ —

ILLUSTRATIONS

— ⁂ —

FOREWORD

— ⦇∞⦈ —

Just what is it about a parade, whether martial, triumphal or carnival that delights the senses and never fails to draw a crowd? Reading the fascinating story of the evolution of St Patrick's Day Parades as told by Cronin and Adair, I couldn't help but wonder if the words 'pride' and 'parade' were not somehow derived from each other. In fact, it seems that the only common denominator between the extremely diverse parades of modern times is the pride they exude, be that pride in a glorious past as most commonly manifested in diaspora communities such as in North America, or pride in a glorious future as witnessed in recent years on the streets of Dublin.

It seems quite fitting that the celebration of St Patrick's Day has finally come full circle, arriving 'back home' just in time to conclude this first-ever study of 17 March and its significance. When St Patrick's Festival was established as Ireland's National Festival, it faced the challenge of bringing the celebration of St Patrick's Day back home, at a time when Irish society had undergone such rapid and radical change, and when the celebration of our national holiday could easily have lost its relevance. This challenge was met by placing the emphasis on making St Patrick's Day an invitation to celebrate Irishness and on prioritizing the entertainment value of the event above all else – the imagery and symbolism were driven by celebratory themes and artistic values rather than by tradition or custom.

We have come a long way, and the picture-postcard image of Ireland has changed beyond all recognition. The images of Ireland that are beamed across the world on St Patrick's weekend reflect the vibrant, confident and creative identity of contemporary Ireland. The festival aims to be a participatory, community event, accessible to all, and to embrace both the age-old traditions of St Patrick's Day and the new ways in which we celebrate it with pride and diversity. The transition of St Patrick's Day celebrations from their early religious origins, through to the secularized festivals of the twenty-first century is a key component of the history presented in this book.

The full extent to which St Patrick's Festival reflects the spirit of the Irish nation is evidenced by the 1.3 million people who attend and the 970,000 domestic TV viewers. The success of the concerted national effort to prevent a foot and mouth epidemic (which saw the postponement of the 2001 Festival) yielded a surge of national pride which translated into an atmosphere of joyous celebration on the streets of Dublin when the Festival finally happened in May. That to me is what St Patrick's Day is all about – truly having something to celebrate and be proud of.

Cronin and Adair help us to see that St Patrick's Day celebrations have been, and always will be, a reflection of their time. By tracking the evolution of St Patrick's Day celebrations they have actually succeeded in illustrating the development of the concepts of Irish identity at home and abroad. By this process, the concept of Irishness has moved from simplistic, romantic, singular ideals to the more complicated amalgam of cultural, economic, demographic and pragmatic factors. Just as St Patrick's Day has become all things to all people, so too has the notion of 'Irishness'.

So whatever your own concept of Irishness may be, St Patrick's Day affords you an opportunity to celebrate it in your own personal way. Perhaps, if the closing aspiration of this book is to be fully realized, it should never be taken more seriously than that.

Maria Moynihan
Chief Executive
St Patrick's Festival Dublin

ACKNOWLEDGEMENTS

— ⚬⚬ —

All books are the result of long hours and hard work. As authors, we have also relied heavily on the advice and assistance of a wide variety of people and institutions. In a study such as this, whose subject matter was spread across the globe, the contributions of time, effort and advice from a wide range of people were invaluable.

The authors would like to thank the British Academy, the Scouloudi Foundation, De Montfort University and the University of Canberra for essential financial assistance towards travel and consumables. Such funding allowed us to undertake research in archives that would have otherwise been closed to us.

William Cobert and Phyllis Towey Brugnolotti at the American Irish Historical Society provided great help, with courtesy and friendship, to an Englishman in New York. In Dublin, the staff of the St Patrick's Festival, most notably its two directors, Marie Claire Sweeney (1994–2000) and Maria Moynihan (2000–), were a mine of information and provided a real understanding of the workings of a contemporary Patrician celebration. They have both provided a huge amount of help, assistance and introductions throughout the project, even at those pressing times when they had a festival to run. The staff of various libraries and archives have been wonderful in providing materials to researchers who seemed to demand everything quickly and at short notice. These include the National Library, National Archives and Guinness Archives in Dublin; the Public Record Office and Linen Hall Library in Belfast; the Public Record Office and British Library in London; the Library of the American Irish Historical Society in New York; the Burns Library at Boston College; the Mitchell Library in Sydney; the Melbourne City Council Archives; the Public Record Office of Victoria, the National Library of Australia, the Australian Capital Territory Library Service, the Australian National University Library, and the University of Canberra Library.

Wherever this book has been discussed it has provoked comment and, as is normal for the academic community, there followed a welter of helpful suggestions, references to be followed up, and papers found. There are a host of people around the world that provided us with academic and intellectual assistance, but special thanks go to: Paul Bew, David Cannadine, Bruce Coe, William Corcoran, Daniel Craddock, Jay P. Dolan, Roy Foster, Ray Gillespie, Richard Holt, Ian Jackson, Kevin James, Michael Kenneally, Donald

MacRaild, Elizabeth Malcolm, Tony Mason, Carl Milofsky, Gerry Moran, Eunan O'Halpin, Teresa O'Donnell, Gary Owens, Ronald Patkus, John Regan, Peggy Regan, Ronald Rudin, David Ryan, Amanda Smith, Johanne Trew, Murray Turner and Emma Wensing.

The penultimate chapter could not have been written without the time taken by many people to respond to our requests for information. Logistically, not all of the data could be included in our study. Yet the totality of responses provided the book with an understanding of how individuals across the world have related to St Patrick's Day and what it means to them. To each of those people, our profound thanks for their time and engagement with the project. We must also acknowledge a host of newspapers, most notably the *Irish Post* and the *Irish Emigrant*, for their efforts in promoting our endeavour to locate people willing to assist the research by offering personal reminiscences.

Finally, there is the belief in, and the final production of, a book such as this. At Routledge we wish to acknowledge the encouragement and assistance of Victoria Peters, and her patience in dealing with co-authors who live at opposite ends of the world. At home, that most important environment for completing a book, we both have to say a completely inadequate thank you to Julie Anderson, and Cheryl and Kane Adair, for their love, patience, support and understanding.

Mike Cronin and Daryl Adair
Leicester and Canberra
March 2001

The Wearing of the Green

O Paddy dear, and did you hear the news that's going round?
The shamrock is forbid by law to grow on Irish ground;
St Patrick's Day no more we'll keep, his colours can't be seen,
For there's a bloody law against the wearing of the green.
I met with Napper Tandy and he took me by the hand,
And he said, 'How's poor old Ireland, and how does she stand?'
She's the most distressful counterie that ever yet was seen,
And they're hanging men and women for the wearing of the green.

Then since the colour we must wear is England's cruel red,
Sure Ireland's sons will ne'er forget the blood that they have shed.
You may take a shamrock from your hat and and cast it on the sod,
It will take root and flourish there though underfoot it's trod.
When law can stop the blades of grass from growing as they grow,
And when the leaves in summer-time their verdure dare not show,
Then will I change the colour that I wear in my caubeen,
But 'til that day, please God, I'll stick to wearing of the green.

But if at last our colour should be torn from Ireland's heart,
Our sons with shame and sorrow from this dear old isle will part;
I've heard a whisper of a land that lies beyond the sea
Where rich and poor stand equal in the light of freedom's day.
O Erin, must we leave you driven by a tyrant's hand?
Must we ask a mother's blessing from a strange and distant land?
Where the cruel cross of England shall nevermore be seen,
And where, please God, we'll live and die still wearing of the green!

Dion Boucicault (1822–90)

INTRODUCTION

— ༀ —

SAINT PATRICK'S DAY. A holiday based on the work of an Irish holy man whose main miracle was chasing the snakes out of Ireland. The facts? There were no snakes. The country had been on a century-long bender born of British oppression, they all had the D.T.'s and thought they saw snakes. Patrick came in, made seven thousand kegs' worth of coffee, and five hours later the sober, snake-free masses declared him a hero, a real saint.[1]

The 17 of March – St Patrick's Day – evokes powerful emotions and sentiments among the Irish and their diaspora around the world. It is *the* day for the Irish wherever they may be, and, just as importantly, whoever they are. St Patrick's Day is observed by Irish nationals, those who claim an Irish heritage, those who purport to be Irish and further still by many non-Irish. By the turn of the twenty-first century, therefore, St Patrick's Day does not appear particularly tribal. For many people, it is a day of celebration in the company of family and friends – whether in church, at the pub, or in the family home. Annual festive customs, such as lunches of cabbage and corned beef, the wearing of green clothing and exchange of greetings cards take centre stage. Beyond this, St Patrick's Day is a public demonstration of 'Irishness', with marchers parading in distinctive regalia, displays of Irish dancing and performances of Irish music. At yet another level, St Patrick's Day is a 'mainstream' event involving various civic groups, schools, religious sodalities, commercial enterprises and the media. Whatever the mode of remembrance or manner of observance, St Patrick's Day is fundamentally *about* the Irish: their sense of self, their ties to home, their place in the world, their views of the past and their claims to the future. These issues are both complex and complicated; the Irish do, after all, vary considerably in terms of their geographic location, social background, religious belief and political affiliation. Despite its many meanings, why do millions of Irish and non-Irish celebrate the life of a 1,500-year-old saint in an annual display of parading and revelry, festooned with the symbolism of the shamrock and emerald green while drinking beer?

In answering this most basic of questions we turn our attention to the historical development of St Patrick's Day and its observance in key parts of the world today. We will use 17 March as a metaphorical window through which to gain insights into the Irish and their diaspora. On one level our purpose is to reveal multiple experiences and representations of St Patrick's

Day – from claims of commonality and solidarity, to expressions of difference and dissent. An underlying premise here is that commemoration of St Patrick's Day has changed considerably over time, and will continue to do so. On a second level our book proposes to do more: to contribute to Irish historiography by asserting the importance of St Patrick's Day as an arbiter, and thus not merely a barometer, of the 'progress' and 'destiny' of the Irish. In this view, 17 March has not simply reflected or mirrored the position of the Irish, it has also provided them with annual opportunities for advocacy – even activism – on various social and political issues in their given location. Yet, on a third level, St Patrick's Day may present a distorted impression of the Irish; instead of putting a mirror to how the Irish *were*, it depicts them as they *wished* to be seen – congenial, convivial, public-spirited and united. Green clothes, shamrocks and vast parades suggest uniformity of sentiment and purpose, but they may also conceal long-standing divisions within the Irish community, or between the Irish diaspora and other groups in a host society. As historians, then, we are concerned principally with power relationships, with St Patrick's Day as a theatre for expression of community and negotiation of difference. We are, nonetheless, mindful that for many people St Patrick's Day has long been a time of mirth and merriment with no obvious 'agenda' beyond the romance of Ireland and the recognition of its patron saint.

INVESTIGATING ST PATRICK'S DAY

In preparing this study we devised four key questions. First, how and why did St Patrick's Day become such an important occasion in the Irish calendar? What, in other words, is known about the origins and early development of Patrician observance of 17 March? A second, and related question, is why has St Patrick's Day been celebrated with more fanfare among Irish emigrants and their descendants than in Ireland itself? Why, in short, has the diaspora tried to appear 'more Irish' than the Irish? Third, St Patrick's Day is often associated with conviviality and revelry, but does that mean wider political, sectarian and regional divides within the Irish 'community' have been overlooked, or even overcome, on 17 March? How, in other words, has St Patrick's Day been accepted (or otherwise) in places where Irish people are under particular stress, such as via Catholic–Protestant and Unionist–Nationalist divides in Belfast and Liverpool? And how does that experience compare with Irish groups that have become relatively comfortable in a broader, mainstream culture, such as those in New York or Sydney? Fourth, has the commemoration of St Patrick's Day been open to all, or have some forms of Patrician observance been the preserve of specific groups within the Irish community? What, in short, does St Patrick's Day reveal about differences of class, status and gender within Ireland and among its diaspora? Our overall aim, then, is to unveil competing representations

[handwritten: what the essays festivals about the Irish migrant experience]

[handwritten margin: Historiography]

and divergent experiences of St Patrick's Day and to use 17 March as a way
of interrogating key aspects of Irish and diaspora history. *[handwritten: ✱]*

Given our claim about the long-term significance of St Patrick's Day it is
a puzzle why it has received so little attention from prominent writers and
publishers.[2] Academic studies of Irish culture abound, but there are only a
few articles dedicated to the history of St Patrick's Day,[3] and just a handful
of relatively unheralded books and manuscripts.[4] Curiously, leading historians of Ireland and the diaspora have paid little more than lip-service to St
Patrick's Day. It seems odd that eminent analysts of Irish history, who if not
annually celebrating, would be fully aware of St Patrick's Day, have not considered the importance and meaning of 17 March in their research. Admittedly, the political history of Ireland and the theme of emigration have been
the central concerns of many scholars, but the history of Patrician observance
of 17 March has much to contribute to these stories, as this book will show.

[handwritten margin: little attention from writers / historians]

Academic reluctance to take St Patrick's Day seriously may also be a reaction to stereotypes that trivialize the Irish and diaspora's observance of this
anniversary. Seamus Metress, for example, in his survey, *The American Irish
and Irish Nationalism*, lists several Irish-American groups that, as he puts it,
have contributed heroically towards 'the struggle in Northern Ireland'. He
then stresses that 'the average activist is not a sloppy, sentimental St
Patrick's Day Irishman that loves the blarney stone, leprechauns and Danny
boy'.[5] While there is some credence to this caricature, Metress's dismissal of
Patrician observance as comical overlooks the historical significance of Irish
politics in the American commemoration of St Patrick's Day – in particular
the role of 17 March as a fund-raiser for nationalist causes in Northern
Ireland.

[handwritten: can't just dismiss the celebrations as farce]

Meanwhile, the general reader is likely to have trouble uncovering re-
liable information about the evolution of St Patrick's Day. *The Oxford Companion to Irish History* does not include a listing for St Patrick's Day, which
receives just three lines under the category 'anniversaries', and five lines
under 'calendar custom'.[6] Similarly, *The Blackwell Companion to Modern Irish
Culture* contains a total of five lines about both St Patrick and observance of
17 March.[7] Neither of these texts claim to be encyclopaedias, but the *Oxford
Companion* found space for a comprehensive entry on 'banking', as did the
Blackwell Companion on 'sculpture': it is difficult to see how these generic
topics rate more prominence than the subject of St Patrick's Day, which is
peculiar to the Irish.

Considering the prominence of St Patrick's Day in the Irish social calendar, and the popularity of associated celebrations, it is intriguing that 17
March barely rates a mention among great figures of Irish literature – notably
Jonathan Swift, Oscar Wilde, James Joyce and W.B. Yeats.[8] This is particularly puzzling because each of these writers, with the exception of Yeats, was
Dublin-born, and that city has long been associated with St Patrick's Day festivities in Ireland. Even Joyce's *Dubliners*, a collection of tales about the

vivacity of life in Dublin around the turn of the twentieth century, makes no mention of 17 March as special.[9] Yeats made public appearances and speeches on St Patrick's Day itself, but to the best of our knowledge his great span of work does not dwell on the anniversary celebrations themselves. This all seems to suggest that 'serious' writers have not viewed St Patrick's Day as worthy of reflection, though the religious solemnity and spiritual iconography of the anniversary could hardly have been lost on such astute observers. Perhaps they have dismissed St Patrick's Day as a farcical concern of the lower orders – a day steeped in drunken revelry. Indeed, one of the few writers to turn his attention to St Patrick's Day, Sean O'Casey, begins his short essay, 'St Pathrick's Day in the Morning', in the pub:

> Sean and Mick McChree ... stood at the counter of the Four-Leaved Clover, drinking in Ireland's National Day, he with claret, McChree with a pint of double stout. 'Ay,' said Mick, 'St Pathrick's Day in the morning Sean. All of us are Irish for that day, anyhow; the holy-day and holiday of us Irish wherever we may be – at home, on the sea, in the deep Canadian woods, or pushing along the crowd-clustered avenues of New York City; a sprig of the dear little plant in every cap, in every bodice, in every blouse. Symbol of our faith in the Holy Trinity, and of – what's this Moore the poet said? Oh, yes: of love and valour of wit, to' ... He drank the last of his pint, and ordered another.[10]

O'Casey's essay is actually a lament for the Irish diaspora across history. The speech of Mick McChree distils a key theme in St Patrick's Day celebrations: remembrance and celebration of the Irish, and their lives, across the globe.

If we consider the genre of 'popular' Irish literature, here too St Patrick's Day has often been noticeable by its absence. Recently published memoirs, such as Patrick Galvin's *Song for a Raggy Boy*, and Dermot Healey's *The Bend for Home*, dwell on the transition from youth to adulthood in Ireland, but in neither case does St Patrick's Day feature.[11] Even the now famous Frank McCourt, who narrates a colourful life in Limerick in his best-selling novel *Angela's Ashes*, is silent about St Patrick's Day in the city of his childhood. McCourt does, however, reveal some amusing aspects of 17 March in New York – particularly as he was expected to teach class on a day when students looked for any excuse to be away and watch the parade.[12] In addition, another big-selling autobiography about Irish-America, *A Song for Mary*, written by Dennis Smith, is silent about St Patrick's Day. This trend is repeated in Australia: Bill Wannan's literary companions *Wearing of the Green: The Lore, Literature, Legend* and *Balladry and The Folklore of the Irish in Australia* both overlook St Patrick's Day within Irish-Australian popular culture.[13]

Despite such omissions, there are works of literature that mention or are set on St Patrick's Day. Such texts, though varying widely in their literary merit, often feed off images and situations that are keys to understanding St Patrick's Day and its history. In 1831, Richard Brinsley Sheridan's play, *St Patrick's Day or the Scheming Lieutenant*, was first performed at Covent Garden. This short piece, which concentrates on relationships within a socially elite group, has little to do with St Patrick's Day, but is, however, set on 17 March. In this respect the story reveals two important historical themes. First, the relationship between drink and St Patrick's Day celebrations. The Lieutenant, the main character of the play, offers his men money to enjoy St Patrick's Day, but implores them not to spend it on beer. In response, a Sergeant informs the Lieutenant that they must 'drink St Patrick's and your honour's health', while a soldier encourages his comrades to 'come along, St Patrick, his honour and strong beer for ever'.[14] The soldiers, having taken their drink, parade outside the house of the local magistrate, in honour of King George. Such loyalty to the Crown does not endear the soldiers to the magistrate, who complains of the soldiers, 'O the villans [sic]! This is St Patrick's Day and the rascals have been parading my house all the morning'.[15] The two scenes, written in the first half of the nineteenth century, demonstrate that the hierarchy, represented by the Lieutenant, were already concerned about the level of drinking associated with St Patrick's Day, and that the lower orders saw such consumption as part and parcel of the day. The play also locates the Patrician parading tradition as one that was championed, prior to the famine years at least, by members of the British army – which is an important clue to understanding the early origins of St Patrick's Day parades.

On a different level to the work of Sheridan, and some 150 years later, the novelist Nelson de Mille produced *Cathedral*. The sleeve note of 1982 promised the reader:

> The Epic Siege Novel of Our Time: St Patrick's Day when everyone, everywhere, is an honorary Irishman, a day of celebration and good cheer ... but which this year explodes into a nightmare of bloody violence.[16]

The marketing of de Mille's book was designed to convince the prospective reader to part with their money in the airport bookshop, yet it also reveals a key theme in the history of St Patrick's Day. The 17 March anniversary is understood as a day of celebration that is open to everyone, yet over the years it has often been linked with the violent politics of Northern Ireland. A related St Patrick's Day theme, especially at the diplomatic and governmental level, is the opportunity the anniversary affords Irish politicians to access the Irish-American public and US politics. This theme was recognized by the novelist Frank Delaney in *Desire and Pursuit*. This story, set in 1972, features a British journalist who has been granted an interview with the Taoiseach. The journalist's editor reminds him that 'tomorrow is St Patrick's Day. He'll [the Taoiseach] be playing to the American gallery.'[17]

Despite the important themes illustrated by these works of fiction, it is still surprising how few texts actually reflect on St Patrick's Day. There is no simple answer as to why those producing literature and memoirs have overlooked the most Irish of days — whether in terms of discussing the behaviour of the Irish, or as a setting for writing about the Irish. By contrast, there is an abundance, especially in North America, of 'juvenile' texts about St Patrick's Day; that is, books written on this topic for children and adolescents. These publications are, of course, rather straightforward. They tend to focus on the romance of 17 March, notably the glamour of parades and the use of Irish symbols, such as the shamrock and the leprechaun.[18] But they at least acknowledge the significance of St Patrick's Day in popular culture, and, just as importantly, its festive appeal to children. Such books emerge from a larger focus, within the North American school system, on the history, function and symbolism of various national and religious festival days. As a result, the awareness among many young people of what St Patrick's Day is about, is matched by their knowledge of an array of other national and ethnic group celebrations.

The largest assortment of material about St Patrick's Day can now be found online; there are literally hundreds of Internet web sites dedicated to the life of St Patrick and commemoration of 17 March. These resources are principally the work of individual enthusiasts, so they tend to be lighthearted celebrations of St Patrick's Day traditions — entertaining but not particularly informative. A few sites, such as www.st-patricks-day.com/ and www.stpatricksday.com/, provide basic details of key St Patrick's Day celebrations in Ireland and the diaspora, but there is no definitive online source.[19] Indeed, Suzanne Barrett, who edits the web site Ireland for Visitors, suggests 'there are more than 120 St. Patrick's Day parades organized throughout the United States', but laments that 'only a handful have web addresses'. That may explain why key Irish and diaspora web resources, such as Irelandbynet, Ireland On-Line, Irishnet, Local Ireland, Irish Abroad, Irish America Net, and USA Irish Network, provide little information or discussion about the observance of St Patrick's Day in different places.[20] An encouraging sign, though, is that online newspapers, most notably the *Irish Times*, are increasing their annual coverage of St Patrick's Day, with some offering stories and images that can be viewed all year round. The ever-increasing use of the Internet as a way of promoting and celebrating St Patrick's Day demonstrates the communal and localized nature of many celebrations. These local parades and identity ties then become, once they are available on the Internet, another aspect of the globalization of 17 March celebrations.

Our overriding message, then, is that St Patrick's Day, although not immediately visible in historical and literary works need not be invisible. It is evident across the Internet and, as the remainder of our book will show, it holds a key place within Irish and diaspora newspapers, in government archives and within the archival holdings of various Irish institutions. St Patrick's Day, we will argue, is far from invisible. In the same way as the desert flower awaits the annual rains before it can bloom, albeit briefly, St Patrick's Day lurks in the Irish popular subconscious, waiting for an opportunity to spring forth every year.

PATTERNS AND PURPOSES OF OBSERVANCE

Like other saints' days and national anniversaries, the evolution of 17 March as a special day can be understood as an 'invented tradition' with a particular starting point, the evolution of distinct patterns of observance, and their annual repetition.[21] As this book will show, though, it was not a simple process, nor was it uniform. St Patrick's Day was not only invented in Ireland; it was (re)discovered and shaped anew among the diaspora abroad.[22] Moreover, the observance of St Patrick's Day varied considerably according to social group, geographic location and historical period. While acknowledging such difference and diversity, our book will show that St Patrick's Day has been a major contributor to the rise of a global 'imagined community' of otherwise disparate Irish people.[23]

St Patrick's Day is, of course, only one of numerous saints' days, national commemorations and ethnic celebrations the world over. What do scholars tell us about the nature and purpose of civic anniversaries, ceremonies, parades and the like? And how might this inform our analysis of St Patrick's Day? Early research by anthropologists emphasized the integrative function of collective rituals in 'pre-modern' tribal settings; they were described as evidence of a community's need to regularly display 'the collective sentiments and collective ideas which make its unity and personality'.[24] Modern societies could also be harmonious, it was thought, if members were given opportunities to reaffirm in unison the beliefs and values that held them together.[25] Critics have since flipped this argument on its head, as if it were a coin. They have stressed that collective ceremonial, rather than being evidence of consensus, is actually propaganda – a 'mobilization of bias' in the interests of a dominant social and political order. In this view, civic rituals in modern societies have been tools of a ruling class, with inequalities in power, status and privilege legitimized by the symbolic appearance of consensus through spectacle. Public support of such 'ruling class' ceremonies is dismissed by critics as either stage-managed or a product of the 'false consciousness' of subordinated groups – thus, certainly not a genuine expression of general harmony.[26]

Recent research has disputed both 'consensus' and 'propaganda' views, showing instead that what seems an agreeable community-wide ceremony 'may in fact be interpreted by different social groups in a variety of different ways'.[27] Those who lead a parade, preside at a dais, or make speeches obviously experience the occasion in a very different way to those among the audience. Just as significantly, those at the margins of pomp and pageantry may not be content with a ruling order: indeed, some collective public rituals have offered little more than a temporary reprieve from long-standing conflicts over national allegiances, political representation, the status of women, and so on.[28] Moreover, if we again flip our metaphorical coin, it is clear that some civic events, such as anniversaries of colonization or nation-hood, have themselves been the subject of considerable debate, even outright opposition, on the part of minority groups, thereby moving much of the public focus away from consensus and towards conflict during ceremonial.[29] Perhaps the biggest flip of all, however, has been civic rituals involving sym-bolic forms of role reversal. This was particularly common in pre-industrial Britain and Europe where, for instance, mock effigies of political leaders were carried in procession, the local elite provided food and drink, and the 'village idiot' was crowned king for a day. This was carnival, not a *coup d'état*, so there was generally a prompt return to conventional social roles for both gentry and peasants.[30]

Most of the scholarship has contended with civic occasions of a 'universal' or community-wide character, with an emphasis on how ceremonies within this genre, such as monarchs' birthdays, national commemorations and mili-tary parades, have been used to symbolically exert or reinforce power.[31] Some researchers have also stressed the importance of a second genre of collective public performance – group-centred civic ritual. This has been apparent in Labor Day and May Day processions, where the mass movement of marchers symbolizes worker solidarity and the political significance of trade unionism within industrial society.[32] Similarly, in societies dominated by a particular religious tradition, minority church groups have marched in the streets to signal the legitimacy and vitality of their beliefs. Salvation Army parades and Corpus Christi processions have, albeit in different ways, publicly offered alternative forms of worship.[33] There are two key forms of investiga-tion that emerge from this group-centred approach. First, it prompts research on marginal or subordinate groups that have used their traditional civic rituals to express a 'common consciousness . . . and their place within the dominant, melting-pot ideology'.[34] Second, this strategy focuses atten-tion on the equally important issue of how minority groups have used their own anniversaries and street parades to voice disapproval of an established order, thus publicly signalling a need for change.[35]

This overview of research into civic ritual suggests that it would be sim-plistic to speak of an 'essential' St Patrick's Day; it fits into either of the above genres of civic ritual, and perhaps even both concurrently. At times, St Patrick's Day has seemed a community-wide celebration in Ireland, though less so in the north-east where sectarian and political tensions have made the very notion of shared celebration problematic. In some places it has seemed more of a group-centred 'ethnic' festival, with Irish migrants marching proudly in unison to demonstrate their historic links with Ireland *use*

and their place in a new society. Yet the observance of St Patrick's Day by the Irish diaspora need not follow assimilationist or melting-pot tendencies. As this book will show, there have been numerous examples of Irish dissent on 17 March, and these expressions of disquiet – whether about diaspora issues or the politics of Ireland – have been readily apparent during St Patrick's Day parades and speeches.

It is also too simple to speak of an 'essential' St Patrick's Day in terms of observance. There are, we accept, archetypal customs, ceremonies and festivities associated with St Patrick's Day worldwide. These include the Irishness of St Patrick's Day, the wearing of green clothing,[36] popular attachment to the shamrock, and so on. But caveats must be made. For example, the colour originally associated with St Patrick is blue,[37] while the cross of St Patrick, which forms part of the Union flag of Britain, is red and white.[38] The *distinctly Irish* 'wearing of the green' on St Patrick's Day has ecumenical origins and was evident as early as the seventeenth century. However, by the second half of the nineteenth century, green-coloured symbols and clothing on 17 March were increasingly associated with Catholic and nationalist traditions. Moreover, while there is a long Irish tradition of parading on key dates in the political and religious calendar (particularly among the Protestant and Unionist community), the custom of staging street parades for St Patrick's Day seems to have been a North American invention.[39] The twentieth-century commercialization and secularization of 17 March also complicate the notion of a uniform commemoration of St Patrick's Day. Our study will show that sponsors have assumed greater influence over the manner in which festivities are conducted. Concurrently, the preponderance of secular floats and figures in parades, as well as the institutionalization of drinking marathons at pubs, implies a diminishing religious observance of St Patrick's Day. Our message, then, is that the historical study of St Patrick's Day requires an awareness of the particular context in which a commemoration took place, as well as an appreciation of changing patterns of observance over time.[40] A marriage of the particular and general is never smooth, but it offers a framework for interpretation.

WRITING ST PATRICK'S DAY

We make no claim about having produced a conclusive or even comprehensive historical analysis of St Patrick's Day. We have taken the unusual step of producing a wide-ranging, general overview as a precursor to a portfolio of detailed local studies and case analysis. As indicated previously, although anniversaries, commemorations and parades have been of great interest to social and cultural historians, this has not been true of St Patrick's Day, which, despite its familiarity to Irish and diaspora scholars, has never been researched systematically.

Our contribution, in what follows, has two main thrusts. First, while

St Patrick's Day has been observed in numerous ways, such as by church services, banquets, dances, sporting activities and drinking sessions, we will focus mainly on street parades – the collective public face of St Patrick's Day. The performance of parades on (or near) 17 March has, since the mid-nineteenth century, been central to the observance of St Patrick's Day in many parts of the world. All manner of Irish and allied groups have marched together annually, by this process displaying their connection with Ireland and, in the case of the diaspora, their position in a newer society. The parade is, more than any other St Patrick's Day activity on 17 March, an 'out-of-the-ordinary-event',[41] whereas church attendance, dinners and dances, sporting activities and drinking are carried on routinely throughout the year. Parading is also distinctive in that it is attention-seeking collective behaviour carried out in communal space. In the case of St Patrick's Day, this has meant occupation of public thoroughfares for a brief time annually, during which the parade offers spectacle and movement via ornate dress, colours, banners and the like in procession, together with sounds of music, singing and feet marching in unison. The lure of the parade is, therefore, both public and aesthetic – the transitory nature of bodily movement through distance and over time. As two Canadian writers have reflected: 'The magic of parades stems from the movement of its elements ... We see things in a parade only briefly; they approach, they are suddenly and vividly before us, and then they are gone.'[42]

Yet the parade not only stimulates the senses, it endeavours to communicate by providing images, symbols and messages to observers. In this sense, the lure of the parade is narrative, not simply artistic.[43] Parades can therefore be said to have their own 'ceremonial language', with troupes of marchers 'impressing their group identities on the minds of countless bystanders'.[44]

This leads us to the second thrust of our study: the politics of performance and representation through St Patrick's Day parading. The performance of a parade is political in a basic sense in that permission is generally needed from civic authorities before the streets can be used for the purposes of processing. This is an obvious logistical requirement because the route of a march and the time at which it proceeds must take into account disruption to traffic, management of crowds, adequate public transportation and the like. But it is also an issue of political rights and ideology. In seeking permission to use the streets, organizers are typically required to convince municipal authorities that they have a rightful claim to parade publicly, and, just as importantly, that the nature of their procession will be both lawful and unlikely to cause offence.[45] Performance is, therefore, linked inextricably to the politics of representation – which are conveyed via the images, symbols and messages on public parade. Processional icons, signs and texts may be dramatic or humorous, celebratory or critical, but they are always political in the sense of claiming to represent the loyalties, identities, traditions and aspirations of a particular group. Importantly, then, whether a parade is considered patriotic, seditious, or innocuous will depend, as much as anything else, on the ideological perspective of the observer.

Our overall mission, then, is threefold: to demonstrate the significance of St Patrick's Day as a subject for historical inquiry; to outline the evolution of St Patrick's Day in Ireland and the diaspora; and, by focusing on St Patrick's Day parades, to reveal key aspects about the politics of performance and representation in public space.

↳ ▽ USE

LOCATING ST PATRICK'S DAY

Given the formidable size and scope of our project, we have selected key localities in both Ireland and abroad for analysis. In Ireland we are interested principally in Dublin and Belfast: they are major population areas, centres of government and sites of great significance to Irish history. Just as important-antly, they epitomize fundamental contrasts in religious affiliation, with Dublin eventually dominated by Catholics and Belfast by Protestants. Also, from 1922 onwards, they have been capitals of the Irish Free State (later Republic) and Northern Ireland respectively. This 'tale of two cities' has obvious limitations, so where suitable we make observations and compari-sons about St Patrick's Day elsewhere in Ireland.

Our story then moves abroad to areas where Irish migration has been most significant. The largest Irish diasporas are found in predominantly English-speaking regions – the United States, Canada, Britain and Aus-tralia. This is no coincidence: the vast bulk of Irish migration took place in the context of, and thus parallel with, British settlement worldwide. This developmental nexus enables us to make 'broad-brush' comparisons about the status of Irish settlers in different parts of the colonies (or former colonies) of the British Empire. Within these countries there are centres of Irish 'community' that will be our principal focus for discussion. In the United States these are New York, Boston and Chicago, where large numbers of Irish immigrants settled, and where an urbanized Irish-American diaspora has since flourished. Our focus in other places is based on a similar premise. The Irish in England have been especially visible in London and Liverpool, while the Irish in Australia have been prominent in Sydney and Melbourne. In Canada both Toronto and Montreal have been significant sites for British and Irish settlement, but the latter has also featured, along with Quebec City, a preponderance of French migrants. This has resulted in distinct linguistic communities in the province of Quebec; and, since the French have been principally Catholic, the evolution of identities based on a combination of ethnicity, religion and language.

Again, this city-centred approach has limitations. First, a focus on the east coasts of the United States, Canada or Australia tells the reader nothing about the diversity of the Irish community across America, or the variety of ways that St Patrick's Day has been celebrated in rural areas. For although the Irish settled in eastern cities in considerable numbers, a significant volume also moved west, seeking land on which to graze or farm. Second, although a survey of 17 March across the vast Irish diaspora allows for international comparisons, it is hardly self-evident that the London experience is typical of England generally, or that Sydney and Melbourne encapsulate the rest of Australia. There are always caveats to be made about the particular versus the general.

There is, however, much to be gained by comparing the demographic, social and political environments in which the Irish have located, as well as differences within these diaspora regions. The Irish abroad typically faced restrictions on religious faith, suffrage, access to parliament and ownership of property. Anti-Catholicism was often a key factor in this, but many Irish Protestants were also 'on the margins' of British-dominated societies. This reminds us that pejorative attitudes towards ethnic and national differences may override other areas of commonality, such as religion and language.

An underlying premise of this book is that the Irish, both at home and abroad, have been a *colonized* people. Yet they have also been highly resistant to colonization. In the British Isles the English wielded political sovereignty, which enabled them to exert influence over language and religion. Much of Wales and Scotland was Anglicized, with Anglicanism and Protestantism becoming the dominant forms of religious practice across Britain. But the Irish clung tenaciously to their Gaelic language and Catholic religion, whether the invaders were Vikings, Normans or English. Indeed, a major theme of Irish history is the *incompleteness* of conquest by other peoples.[46] Furthermore, as we will show, the Irish abroad have sometimes felt little urgency about resisting British colonial rule, instead adapting themselves into a 'mainstream' culture, or co-opting elements of a dominant order to suit their own needs. Having said that, the extent to which an ethnic group is labelled as, or sees itself as, marginal depends very much also on the policy of a host society towards minorities – whether that be isolation, assimilation, or pluralism.

It is also important to remember that the Irish have not simply been colonized, they have been part of a system that has dominated indigenous 'others' – from Aboriginal peoples in Australia and Canada to native Americans and African Americans in the United States. In this respect the Irish have themselves been colonizers. So when nationalistic historians speak triumphally about the creation of an 'empire' of Irish abroad, they should remember that this ascendancy of Irish (and other European) settlers has much to do with the subjugation and demise of indigenous communities. Curiously enough, among those persecuted by the Irish was a young Roman-Briton named Succat. He is better remembered today as St Patrick, Apostle of Ireland; a man celebrated across the world in a variety of ways every 17 March.

ST PATRICK THE APOSTLE

There has long been dispute between scholars about the life and lore of St Patrick. Twenty years ago, an academic sub-discipline 'Patrician Studies' crystallized in the wake of debates among historians and theologians. This is not the place to rehearse the finer points of such arguments; our intention here is to briefly overview the 'cult' of St Patrick, his elevation to the Apostle of Ireland, and the early memorialization of Patrick on 17 March.[47] We begin with a synopsis of the life of Maewyn Succat, and his transformation into Patricius the cleric.

There is spirited debate about basic aspects of Succat's existence. His birthplace was probably Roman Britain – most likely Wales, but perhaps Scotland or even France – and his birth date around AD 416, though some writers suggest as early as AD 387. His father was a Roman-Christian civil servant, Calpurnius, and his grandfather a Catholic priest. From Patricius's *Confessio* we are informed retrospectively that he was about sixteen years old when abducted by Irish marauders and enslaved. He worked as a shepherd on the slopes of Slemish (now part of County Antrim), praying to a Christian God while captive in a pagan land. After six years an angel came to him in a dream, prompting him to escape and seek out his homeland. After travelling more than 200 miles by foot, he was eventually given passage on a boat travelling east across the Irish Sea. His destination was Britain, but he settled soon after in France – most likely in the Tours region. Local tradition has it that Succat was the nephew of St Martin of Tours and spent twenty years of his life as a monk in Marmoutier Abbey.[48] There he again received a celestial visitation, this time calling him to return to the land where he had been enslaved, though now with a mission as a priest and convertor. Upon ordination he was given the title Patricius. Whether he travelled to Ireland under the direct order of Pope Celestine or not is still debated.[49]

It is often assumed that Patricius was the first to bring Christianity to Ireland in *c.* AD 432, but Pope Celestine had already sent Palladius in AD 431, while other priests also appear to have been in Ireland around this time. Of them, we only have documentary evidence for the experiences of Patricius, through his *Confessio* and *Letter to Coroticus*.[50] His life has therefore been of great interest to religious scribes who, subsequently, elevated Patricius to the status of 'founding father' of Irish Christianity. A single figure with historical credentials was attractive as a birth story.[51] However, according to critics, the 'historical' Patrick has been misrepresented: instead of the humility and piety evident in the *Confessio*, biographers have invested him with an imposing presence and mystical powers – the St Patrick of 'legend'.[52] Hagiographers, those who specialize in writing about saints' lives, have gone beyond Patrick the Christian missionary who learned to speak Gaelic and converted many natives, to invent Patrick the ancient superhero – replete with Christ's staff and the ability to perform miracles. This same

Patrick was also said to be fearsome: able to put curses on enemies, turn men into animals, and purge rivers of fish.[53]

Patrick is thought to have died sometime between AD 463 and AD 493, with 17 March the most likely day. There is dispute about his place of burial. The site with the strongest claim seems to be Down Cathedral, where 'the grave' of St Patrick is protected by a large slab of rock on which the word *Patric* is inscribed.[54] Veneration of Patrick gradually assumed the status of a local cult; he was not simply remembered in Saul and Downpatrick, he was worshipped. Around AD 688, the church federation in Armagh engaged a biographer in what now seems a propaganda role: to reposition Armagh as the centre of the cult of St Patrick. Muirch, a skilful scribe, not only achieved this, he also 'ensured that the cult was elevated to that of a "national" apostle'.[55] Indeed, homage to Patrick as *Ireland's* saint was apparent in the eighth century AD, when a 'Prayer to Saint Patrick' included lines (composed originally in Gaelic) such as 'We invoke holy Patrick, Ireland's chief apostle', and 'We pray to Patrick chief apostle; his judgement hath delivered us in Doom from the malevolence of dark devils'.[56] At this time Patrick's status of national apostle was made independently of Rome: he was claimed locally as a saint before the practice of canonization was introduced by the Vatican.[57] McCormack argues that Patrick's sainthood was distinctive because he was considered 'the convertor of all the Irish . . . the banisher of all evil and the ultimate judge of the Irish . . . which gave him a national role'.[58] The cult also held that Patrick continued intercession in heaven on behalf of the Irish people.[59] The veneration in which the Irish have held St Patrick is evidenced by the salutation, still common today, 'May God, Mary, and Patrick bless you'.

The St Patrick of legend has, according to some scholars, fused more than one person's life into the same story. A theory of two St Patricks has in turn been supplanted by three and even five St Patricks, while some researchers have concluded that 'there had never been a Saint Patrick at all'.[60] Differences between the Patrick of history and legend can also be attributed to political strategies on the part of the churches. In the seventeenth century, for example, the Church of Ireland attempted to trace its local origins to Patrick. The Catholic Church, too, made a concerted effort to link the achievements of Patrick with the sanction of Rome. The Pope's consecration of Patricius as a saint confirmed what Celtic Catholics already accepted, but it re-established the idea of Patrick as a servant of the church of Rome.[61] This initiative was, in part, a matter of Vatican protocol, but the *Irishness* of Patrick was undiminished even though he was, of course, born elsewhere. This remains so via Celtic churches in Patrick's name (both Catholic and Protestant), religious sites in Ireland attributed to particular stages of his life, and pilgrimages up the Reek (Croaghpatrick) in memory of his piety and personal commitment to the Irish people. There are, nonetheless, those who view St Patrick not as someone who brought a divine light to Ireland, but rather as a colonizing agent for the erosion of pagan customs and belief systems.

Within the Christian calendar, though, Patrick has long been remembered with fondness. This began as early as the ninth century AD with the feast of St Patrick's 'falling asleep' – in other words his passing on 17 March. The *Book of Armagh* included a note directing all monasteries and churches in Ireland to honour the memory of the saint by 'the celebration, during three days and three nights in mid-spring, with every kind of good food except flesh, of the festival of his "falling asleep" '.[62] This ritual was a religious occasion, 'with a lengthy sermon on the saint's glorious deeds as the highlight of each day's celebrations'.[63] By the seventeenth century (and perhaps earlier) the nomenclature of the 17 March anniversary had changed. It was now St Patrick's Day, with continued religious importance but rising secular significance as an occasion for drinking and revelry.[64] It is here, too, that Patrick of ancient legend was revisited annually. As this book will show, fables about Patrick ridding Ireland of snakes or his use of the shamrock to explain the Trinity, still endure as part of modern St Patrick's Day folklore and custom. Myth is more fun than truth.

CHAPTER 1

THE EVOLUTION OF
ST PATRICK'S DAY

— ℘ℐℴ —

Here were thousands of persons congregated together peaceably and orderly, a considerable number of whom had on many former festivals of Saint Patrick deemed it an honour to celebrate it by the commission of the most odious and detestable properties – drunkenness, riot and disorder prevailed to an extent which was frightful to contemplate; but happily those exhibitions have passed away, never again we trust to be repeated.[1]

ST PATRICK'S DAY IN IRELAND: *c.*1600–1790

While the 'cult of St Patrick' has received considerable attention by historians, the origins of 'St Patrick's Day' – the popular rite of observance – are less clear. In Ireland, the feast day of various saints often involved pilgrimage to a sacred site, followed by robust celebrations.[2] These 'patterns', as they were called, included recognition of 17 March as the anniversary of Patrick's death. But the evolution of St Patrick's Day as a widely recognized 'holy day' in Ireland is not certain. As early as 1607 it was listed as a saint's day in the Irish legal calendar; hence by then it had assumed 'official' recognition as a religious occasion.[3] After that Patrick was elevated to the status of patron saint of Ireland, 17 March assumed much greater importance: the memory of St Patrick was now linked inextricably to a commemoration of Ireland's Christian roots. Yet it appears that the early saints, including Patrick, were first acclaimed locally (in his case, very soon after his death) rather than centrally by Rome. The Vatican later supported the cult of Patrick because his episcopal appointment strengthened the Popes' claim to jurisdiction over the Celtic Church.[4] Pope Urban VIII added the feast of St Patrick to the calendar of the Church in 1631, and in 1687, Pope Innocent XI made 17 March a 'double rite with nine lessons'.[5] Thus the decision to embrace St Patrick's Day was not simply a response to local enthusiasm for Patrick. Although the Vatican proclaimed Patrick as a Catholic saint, 17 March remained an important date within the Irish Ascendancy calendar, and it was celebrated by Protestants well into the seventeenth century.[6] It should be noted, though, that there were some thirty-five officially recognized Church feast and fasting days in Ireland.[7] This means that St Patrick was not alone as a spiritual icon. He was, however, apostle of Ireland, so he soon overshadowed all others. Essentially, St Patrick had established himself, by the seventeenth century at least, as a popular saint who was celebrated as part of a consensual festival.[8]

Patrician observance of 17 March, while religious, also became an opportunity for civic celebration in the seventeenth century. This stemmed from the tradition of the Irish 'pattern', but it was also linked to the Irish custom of staging fairs and markets. St Patrick's Day, in that sense, accommodated features from both pattern and popular festival: religious observance followed by plenty of food and drink, Irish music and dance, and playful physical activities.[9] By this process, it seems, 17 March eventually became recognized as both a Patrician and civic occasion. Such a mix of religious devotion and conviviality was not controversial: in Armagh, for instance, a 'St Patrick's Day Fair' was supported by Archbishop Hamilton during the early 1600s.[10] Eighty years later, an English visitor to Ireland, Thomas Dineley, noted the widespread acceptance of St Patrick's Day:

> the 17th day of March yeerly [*sic*] is St Patrick's, an immovable feast when ye Irish of all stations and condicions were crosses in their hats, some of pins, some of green ribbon, and the vulgar superstitiously wear shamroges [*sic*], 3-leaved grass, which they likewise eat (they say) to cause a sweet breath.[11]

By the late seventeenth century, then, 17 March in Ireland was renowned as a 'day of celebration for all ranks of society with established customs and emblems'.[12] Public awareness of St Patrick was, of course, not restricted to the annual anniversary. The image of the Apostle of Ireland, replete with shamrock, even appeared on Irish coinage in the 1760s.[13]

Was St Patrick's Day as inherently agreeable and inclusive as these comments suggest? To pursue that question effectively we need to look first at the nature of Irish society in the seventeenth century. Two subjects, in particular, require review – religion, and its sibling, politics. Ireland was staunchly Catholic: compared to countries to its east, such as England and France, the effect of the Protestant Reformation was felt rather late. The Reformation was consolidated in Ireland during the reign of England's Protestant King James I (1603–25): this was when the officially sanctioned Church of Ireland (the Irish equivalent of the Church of England) 'finally established a presence throughout Ireland'.[14] However, widespread Irish conversion from Catholicism to Anglicanism did not follow. Few Church of Ireland clergy were fluent in Irish-Gaelic language, so they ministered principally to English-speaking flocks in Ireland, most of whom were Protestant settlers from England and Scotland and their descendants in Ulster and areas surrounding Dublin. The resilience of Irish Catholicism also had much to do with the administrative weakness of Dublin Castle: in effect, it ruled only a small section of Ireland with authority, so decrees establishing the Church of Ireland were loosely enforced, if at all, in far-flung places like Galway or Killarney.[15] This meant that an edict requiring all Irish clergy to use the Protestant English Prayer Book (1559), and fines for laity who did not attend a Church of Ireland service, had a disproportionate regional impact. These types of factors enabled the non-recognized Catholic Church to maintain a strong following among Irish natives, but also within parts of the Anglo-Irish community that had long-standing allegiances to Catholicism. By the second half of the seventeenth century, then, Ireland's religious culture featured a key division along Catholic–Protestant lines: the former was unofficial and illegal; the latter was sanctioned officially and, therefore, deemed legal. Rather than instilling uniformity of worship, the Reformation had brought about diversity of religion in Ireland.[16]

Since the Anglo-Norman invasion in the twelfth century, Ireland had been a 'feudal lordship' of England; this effectively meant indirect English influence rather than direct rule. The subsequent rise of an Irish parliament actually fostered a colonial relationship because Dublin became answerable to Westminster. As far as British Protestants were concerned, this power had unforeseen consequences. By the late seventeenth century, the illegitimacy of Catholicism in the British Isles was under review. This was because in 1685, a self-declared Catholic, King James II, succeeded his Protestant brother, Charles II, to the throne of England. The new monarch suspended several anti-Catholic laws, thereby providing hope for religious autonomy among Catholics in Britain and Ireland. Crucially, though, these initiatives were short-lived. Under threat from militant Protestants, King James II fled to Catholic France. Thereafter he made a 'triumphal' appearance in Catholic-dominated Dublin, but his defeat in the Battle of the Boyne at the hands of the Protestant William of Orange effectively ended his reign. The victor, a Dutch royal, was now King William III of England. This changing of the guard allowed Protestants to re-establish punitive legislation against Catholics across the British Isles. In Ireland this meant both renewed and additional restrictions on Catholic religious practice, property holdings and voting rights.[17]

Such reinforcement of a sectarian climate complicated the observance of St Patrick's Day hereafter. The anniversary was a long-standing commemoration of Ireland's patron saint, yet it had a particularly strong emotional pull for Catholics whose religious tradition recognized and celebrated saints' days more readily than the non-Catholic churches. The Williamite parliament of 1695 outlawed many of the saints' days that had previously been celebrated by Catholics, instituting instead a list of twenty-nine holidays based on the Anglican tradition of the Church of Ireland.[18] St Patrick's Day was not recognized by the new parliament; consequently, observance of the apostle's anniversary was unofficial during the late seventeenth and early eighteenth centuries. However, during the course of the eighteenth century this situation changed so that, eventually, 'among traditional anniversaries, the state recognized St Patrick's Day as the day customarily associated with Ireland's patron saint'.[19] Nonetheless, Patrician observance of 17 March was but one of a number of traditional anniversaries honoured by the Irish state in the eighteenth century, with many of these events involving parades.[20]

Despite the questioning of the place of St Patrick's Day within the religious calendar, it seemed in little danger of disappearing from public memory. Irish Catholics in both Ireland and Britain continued to celebrate 17 March as special. Equally, for the Protestant population in Ireland, particularly during the era of the eighteenth-century Ascendancy, when a discernible Protestant-based Irish nationalism evolved, the patron saint still generated significant emotional attachment. A notable development in marking St Patrick's Day as a time of celebration was the decision of King George III to introduce, from 1783, an honours system for the 'Knights of the most illustrious Order of St Patrick'. In creating such an Order, the King linked the Irish vice-regal court with St Patrick, and with the day of his national festival.[21]

The Dublin-born Protestant writer Jonathan Swift observed eighteenth-century Patrician celebration in his diaries and letters. In 1713, when visiting London, he wrote: 'The Irish folks were disappointed that the parliament did not meet today, because it was St Patrick's Day, and the mall was so full of crosses, that I thought all the world was Irish.'[22] Swift, who was Dean of St Patrick's Cathedral (1713–45), later complained to a correspondent of the 'deafening' he suffered as a result of the bell-ringing that had taken place during the St Patrick's Day celebration of 1729 at St Patrick's Cathedral in Dublin.[23] This ringing of bells at St Patrick's Cathedral and other Protestant churches in Ireland, formed a regular part of celebrating St Patrick's Day among the Protestant Ascendancy population.

By the last quarter of the eighteenth century, St Patrick's Day events were hosted annually by Dublin Castle.[24] They were largely private and genteel affairs, such as dinners and 'fancy balls' for the 'upper crust' of Anglo-Irish society. In 1784, St Patrick's Day in the Castle began with the investiture of a new member of the Illustrious Order of St Patrick. This was followed by a lavish banquet, featuring an orchestra, country dances and supper at three in the morning. Many of the guests were in fancy dress, including a number dressed as 'Paddies: by now paddywhackery was becoming part of the repertoire of Castle entertainments'.[25] But these grand occasions were not always held on the day of 17 March. In 1785, for example, Castle authorities delayed their St Patrick's Day celebration to enable Irish nobles and gentlemen, who were hampered by assizes elsewhere in the country, extra time to arrive in Dublin. Organizers linked this decision to financial imperatives: a slightly later date would allow tradesmen and manufacturers to cater for a larger group of wealthy customers, while Irish charitable societies, who relied on donations from the Anglo-Irish elite, also benefited from the initiative.[26] Hence St Patrick's Day, even at this comparatively early stage, was economically significant. Tailors and craftsmen earned income from making costumes and decorations, caterers provided food and drink, while musicians plied their trade as entertainers. Just five years later, though, Dublin Castle's 'fancy ball' was dispensed with and replaced by a 'ball and supper', a much more mundane affair. The *Dublin Evening Post* complained that the move did not reflect the significance of the Irish saint's day; and, just as importantly, it did not recognize commercial opportunities stemming from costume design and manufacture of apparel.[27] In addition to Dublin Castle, Irish fraternal societies staged private functions to observe St Patrick's Day. The aptly named Sons of the Shamrock, for instance, arranged a dinner for members at a Dublin hall in 1785, with each gentleman expected to arrive dressed formally, wearing the insignia of the society. But St Patrick's Day celebrations were not confined to the elite; they were part and parcel of working-class popular culture. In the process, various hotels and inns around Dublin expected to make a handsome, albeit once a year, return on food, drink and entertainment.[28]

The delay in the Dublin Castle celebrations in 1785 may have caused, by default, one of the early St Patrick's Day parades to take place in Ireland.[29] Due to the postponement of the Castle event, a group of self-declared 'true patriots' gathered together at the Rotunda in Dublin. Prior to a banquet they had organized, the gentlemen in attendance 'marched in a grand procession round the garden, dressed in true blue, and carrying along with them a number of curious pageants'.[30] While this procession was in no way similar to the mass parades of the nineteenth and twentieth centuries, it anticipated a significant aspect of St Patrick's Day traditions in later times.

ST PATRICK'S DAY IN IRELAND: *c.*1790–1845

During the 1790s, the Irish political landscape became increasingly unstable. The independent parliament of Ireland, led by Henry Grattan, was causing disquiet in London as a result of its constant administrative challenges to the overriding power of Westminster. Also, in the wake of the American and French revolutions, ideas of militant republicanism had taken root in Ireland, exemplified by the rise of the United Irishmen. Led by Wolfe Tone, the United Irishmen sought to create, through force of arms, a free Ireland. In 1798, they struck out against the British in Ireland and rebellion followed. The rebellion was a bloody affair which, despite the United Irishmen's stated non-sectarian aims, denigrated into an orgy of intercommunity religious violence. The British regained control of the country, executed the leaders of the rebellion, including Wolfe Tone, and enforced an Act of Union (1801) on Ireland. The Act was an attempt to curtail the political freedom of constitutionalists such as Grattan, and to reduce the risks from insurgents such as Tone.

In the wake of the Act of Union, St Patrick's Day again became a key

5

date in Dublin Castle's annual social calendar. The Castle celebrations were revived by John Russell, 6th Duke of Bedford in 1806. This decision was, in light of the Act of Union, 'a popular initiative with the Catholics'.[31] Yet, by this time, the commemoration of the patron saint posed problems for the Anglo-Irish in terms of their sense of identity and belonging. The *Freeman's Journal* described the Castle's colour and ceremony:

> The assemblage of the nobility and persons of distinction upon this occasion was numerous and brilliant, and presented a blaze of beauty, rank and fashion truly delightful ... departure was protracted until an advanced hour in the morning by the engaging manners and amiable condescension of our present illustrious Representatives of Majesty. The imperial standard was displayed from the top of Bedford Tower in the upper Castle yard during the whole of the day ... Her Grace, the Duchess of Richmond's dress on St Patrick's Day, was clearly of Irish manufacture. The body and sleeves ornamented with the star of the Order of St Patrick, the shamrock and other devices appropriate to the day.[32]

The flags and regalia of the British royal family were evident, yet the whole scene was underscored by a distinctive sense of Irishness. In 1834 the report on the annual festivities noted that in the Castle's St Patrick's Hall, where the event was staged, there were 'tapestry and hangings [that] were new – rich and of Irish manufacture. The floor was neatly chalked and figured with the Royal arms.'[33] For the Anglo-Irish elite, then, St Patrick's Day was something they wished to embrace so that they could celebrate the patron saint of the country in which they lived and where their financial or business interests lay. Yet, at the same time, they wanted to perpetuate their loyalty to the Crown and their sense of difference from the Irish. The Dublin Castle celebration of St Patrick's Day was a state-organized event, played out within the walls of the home of the vice-regent. The events held within the Castle thus formally excluded the Catholic population, but the spectacle of such an event of finery and show was irresistible to onlookers. Whether through fascination, or as part of their St Patrick's Day celebrations, it is apparent that the Castle events attracted a big crowd that would wait outside the gates to catch a glimpse of the evening's happenings.[34]

Considering the subsequent nationalist connotations of St Patrick's Day, it may appear incongruous that Dublin Castle, the very heart of British authority in Ireland, should celebrate the country's patron saint, especially in view of increasing links between Patrician observance and Catholicism. Such celebration should be understood only partially as evidence of the ongoing religious dispute as to who 'owned' St Patrick. In the context of the administrative independence of Ireland, as stressed by the Anglo-Irish elite through Grattan's parliament, as well as the practical embodiment of an

Irish identity that was enshrined in the Act of Union, many of the Ascendancy, though fiercely Protestant, also saw themselves as Irish. To celebrate their national saint was, in this sense, only natural. It is clear that in the pre-famine decades there were services to honour St Patrick in both Protestant and Catholic churches, and that members of both faiths, as well as the different social orders, held various forms of non-religious celebrations. The duality of Patrician observance is most clearly illustrated in the work of Hill, who has argued that in the pre-famine decades:

> St Patrick became an object of contention between the Anglican and Catholic churches in Ireland. By the mid-nineteenth century both were claiming him as the precursor of their own communion ... the state ... by transferring focus of its attention from Williamite to St Patrick's Day festivals ... was tacitly endorsing the 'national' status being sought by the liberals [both Catholic and Protestant] for the Patrician tradition.[35]

In the early decades of the nineteenth century, the celebration of St Patrick's Day became a permanent fixture for all social and religious groups within Ireland, and this process was fully supported by Dublin Castle. Yet the Castle festivities themselves were essentially closed celebrations, with the local populace only offered fleeting glimpses of the Lord Lieutenant when he appeared on the Castle balcony. Indeed, in 1844, the Lord Lieutenant, Thomas Philip, made his appearance, 'swathed in shamrocks', but his presence was not greeted by 'a single cheer'.[36] While the crowds were undoubtedly attracted away from the Castle by a large St Patrick's Day Temperance march through the city, the lack of reaction to Philip's appearance offers evidence for the increased divide between Castle and public. As we shall show, the years that followed the famine would see an erosion of such shared veneration for the day, and this made parading in Ireland a contentious issue.[37]

A DIASPORA IN THE MAKING: *c.*1600–1845

Emigration from Ireland has a lengthy history, which predates the mass emigration of the mid-nineteenth-century famine period. The travels of Irish missionaries and the seasonal migration to Britain by Irish agricultural workers have the longest history, but the years of increased industrialization in Britain proved a great pull factor in the steady numerical increase in permanent emigration from the late eighteenth century onwards. With the growing development of Britain's overseas possessions, the Irish travelled to America, Canada, Australia, South Africa and elsewhere. As Akenson has pointed out:

The Irish did not go in significant numbers anywhere that the British had not gone first. From the eighteenth century onward, the Irish mingled with the British flow. Frequently they were on the same ships. They passed through the same foreign ports and went on to settlements in the same New Worlds. It is hardly an accident that the overwhelming bulk of the Irish diaspora went to points in the English-speaking world.[38]

But what was the experience of the Irish once they had settled in a new country? And how was St Patrick's Day and its accompanying celebrations moved across the globe? In early nineteenth-century Britain, the Irish population, which was overwhelmingly working class, faced economic hardship and problems of social acceptance.[39] Life spent working as a navvy in Glasgow or a textile worker in Liverpool meant little time to commemorate St Patrick's Day, and few resources with which to make it special. Patrician observance was, therefore, largely small scale, ad hoc, and localized. British cities with a large Irish presence did stage formal and public St Patrick's Day events. In 1841, for instance, the St Patrick's Day parade in Liverpool attracted over 5,000 marchers and several times as many spectators from within the local Irish diaspora. However, the 'legitimacy' of this type of public performance was questioned in an increasingly sectarian political climate. In the wake of anti-Catholic 'No Popery' campaigns in Britain during the early 1840s, the Orange Order had been revived. Protestant 12th of July parades and associated 'party processions' had been banned in Britain since the 1830s.[40] Yet St Patrick's Day, which was deemed an Irish national rite, but not a party political occasion, still featured a parade. The ire of Orangemen towards St Patrick's Day in Liverpool was, therefore, predictable. Rumours spread quickly that the annual Irish parade would come under violent attack from Protestants. However, the marches were heavily policed in the 1840s, which may explain why the *Liverpool Standard*, which had feared ugly clashes, went on to report otherwise.[41]

ST PATRICK'S DAY IN COLONIAL AMERICA:
*c.*1700–88

The Irish were not alone as an ethnic or immigrant group in celebrating feast and saints' days in colonial America. The variety and frequency of various types of celebrations within that fledgling society were impressive.[42] In America today, the celebration of St Patrick's Day is associated most strongly with the Irish-Catholic diaspora. However, the origins of Patrician observance in America lie with Irish Protestants and, in the first instance, with the Charitable Irish Society of Boston. John D. Crimmins, who in 1902 published a chronology of St Patrick's Day celebrations in America, claims that the first formal St Patrick's Day celebration in the colonies took place in the early eighteenth century. He informs us that Catholics were not part of this rite:

> The Irish gentlemen and merchants who met convivially in Boston on March 17, 1737, to honour St Patrick, and founded a benevolent society with quaint officials bearing silver keys described themselves as Irish or of Irish extraction and of Protestant faith.[43]

As incongruous as it may seem to Irish Catholics today, the first St Patrick's Day celebration in colonial Boston had been transplanted via Ulster Protestants. Yet this is really no surprise: Protestants had dominated Irish migration to North America in the early eighteenth century, and those who arrived at Boston were already familiar with Patrician observance of 17 March by the Anglo-Irish Ascendancy.

Although the Charitable Irish Society of Boston paid homage to St Patrick at its inaugural meeting, its purpose was to meet the welfare needs of newly arrived Irish emigrants. In the early 1730s Boston had a population of some 15,000, many of whom claimed Irish descent. By 1737 Boston was suffering from a double scourge of high inflation and successive bad winters. As a result, poverty became a feature of Bostonian life. Reacting to such distress, 'several gentlemen and others of the Irish nation residing in Boston' agreed to form a society for the relief of 'those of the Irish nation who might be reduced by sickness, age or other infirmities and accidents or distress'.[44] This vision of charity to Irish comrades portrays an inclusive picture, but the structure of the association itself was elitist. Its rules stated that the managers of the charity fund and officers of the society would have to be 'Protestants and inhabitants of Boston'.[45] The 'respectable' social cache of the society was circumscribed in a by-law stating that all members had to be clean and decently dressed, 'not in cap or apron'.[46] Curiously, for the next fifty-seven years the society did not formally observe St Patrick's Day, meeting instead in April every year. Not until 1794 was 17 March restored as the group's major date of assembly.

It was with other Irish charitable organizations that the observance of St Patrick's Day became institutionalized in Boston. During the second half of the eighteenth century, many Irish charitable societies were created by Irish Protestants, several of whom observed St Patrick's Day as a key rite of fellowship. It soon became customary for them to organize a dinner and special religious service to commemorate St Patrick's Day. In 1775, for instance, the officers of the Sons of St Patrick, some seventy in all, marched in unison to King's Chapel to hear a special sermon, after which they assembled for dinner at 'Mr Ingersoll's in King Street'.[47] The officers in question comprised Irish members of the 47th regiment of the Most Ancient and Benevolent Order of the Friendly Brothers of St Patrick. It appears, therefore, that an Irish contingent of the British army may have staged the first St Patrick's

Day parade through the streets of Boston. Exactly one year later, though, Boston-based Crown soldiers were marching hastily in retreat. On St Patrick's Day, 1776, General Sullivan, an Irish-born soldier serving the Continental forces, led George Washington into Boston, thereafter assuming military control of the city after British forces evacuated.[48] Since then 17 March has been remembered as 'Evacuation Day' in Boston. Yet the significance of St Patrick's Day in Boston remained. Irish Americans who celebrated the 'liberation' of Boston on 17 March could boast Irish leadership of that process. Hence they took part in a dual celebration – local independence from British rule, and, by remembrance of St Patrick, their connection with the Emerald Isle.

Early commemorations of St Patrick's Day in New York followed a similar pattern to that of Boston. The first recorded Patrician festivities took place on 17 March 1762 in the house of John Marshall, an Irish Protestant.[49] Such localized St Patrick's Day observances soon became customary in New York, with 'Irish residents of the city' meeting on 17 March each year 'in loving remembrance of the parent land'.[50] It is impossible to say how widespread Patrician commemorations were in late eighteenth-century New York, but two main forms of observance seem to have emerged in the years before the American Revolution.[51] The first was Protestant based and an elite occasion, while the latter was part and parcel of working-class immigrant Catholic life in the city. Irish charitable societies that celebrated St Patrick's Day in New York had invariably been founded by Protestants. They tended to see both Ireland and the American colonies as parts of the British Empire; hence they were loyal to the English monarch. Their St Patrick's Day celebrations were characterized by dinners, speeches and formal gatherings, often with charitable purposes, aimed at their countrymen who had fallen on hard times. Such assemblies are relatively easy to understand, as they feature most commonly in newspaper reports of the period, and are the product of an elite and literate social grouping. The second form of St Patrick's Day celebration was largely Catholic, public and unpretentious. It featured family gatherings, church services and imported Patrician customs such as drowning the shamrock. This social group was highly mobile, transient and often illiterate; it is therefore difficult to establish precisely its St Patrick's Day observances.

What appears to be the first St Patrick's Day parade in North America, a military procession, took place in New York in 1766 when, 'the day of St Patrick, tutelar Saint of Ireland, was ushered in at dawn, with Fifes and Drums, which produced a very agreeable harmony before the doors of many Gentlemen of the nation and others'.[52] The duality of religious affiliation within Irish America was apparent in the colonial military, and the St Patrick's Day parade offered evidence of this. For Irish-Catholic immigrants, enlistment in the British army was one of the careers open to them in colonial America. Catholic soldiers were, however, rarely found beyond the rank and file of the military, while Irish-born army officers were overwhelmingly of Protestant faith. So despite sharing ancestry, Irish Catholics and Protestants in the British army were effectively divided in terms of career opportunity and military status. This schism was reflected in observance of St Patrick's Day, even though rank and file Irish-Catholic soldiers, as well Irish-Protestant officers, looked to commemorate the patron saint of their homeland.

On 17 March 1779, a march of the 'Volunteers', which consisted of rank and file Catholics in the British army, was led by its Protestant leader Colonel Lord Rawdon, who presented the troops to his Excellency General Knyphausen.[53] The march drew honour to the patron saint of Ireland, but it had a broader purpose in encouraging Irish-American recruits to join the British army. New York's *Weekly Mercury* reported that 'the Volunteers of Ireland, preceded by their band of music', marched out to the Bowery, where a St Patrick's Day dinner was held for 500 people.[54] Elsewhere in America, the British army provided similar encouragement for Irish troops to commemorate their patron saint. Hence there were military parades on St Patrick's Day at Fort William on Lake George in 1757 and at Fort Pitt (now Pittsburgh) in 1763.[55] Subsequently, during the 1770s, there were also military parades to commemorate St Patrick's Day in South Carolina, Maryland, Kentucky, Baltimore and Charleston.[56] However, as we will show, though Irish Americans were welcome to parade, they were obliged to do so on terms that were acceptable to Protestants.[57]

ST PATRICK'S DAY IN THE AMERICAN REPUBLIC: 1788–1845

The American War of Independence (1775–83) included Irish soldiers in both Loyalist and American camps. Hence St Patrick's Day in revolutionary America was observed separately by groups of Irishmen committed to killing each other.[58] The heroics of Irish soldiers in the victorious Continental army suggested that the Irish 'people' in America – despite many of them having supported Crown forces – had earned themselves a 'place' in the new republic. This heightened sense of profile and purpose was reflected, in part, by the key role of several Irish immigrants in the political culture of the new nation. Irish Americans soon featured prominently in Fourth of July parades, symbolizing by this process their sense of citizenship in a wider polity. St Patrick's Day, too, gained impetus as Irish people took to the streets in parade on 17 March. As part of an independent American Republic they were effectively announcing pride in an Irish heritage while also committing themselves to a new land. This duality about Irish-American observance of St Patrick's Day continued in the decades to follow, and, as we discuss in Chapter 7, is still evident today.[59]

The Charitable Irish Society of Boston, in a break with tradition, began to meet again on St Patrick's Day in the mid-1790s. This reflected a change in policy: the society's by-laws were altered so that all annual meetings would now take place on 17 March. This allowed the society to assemble formally while also recognizing St Patrick's Day as special. The format established from 1795 onwards was a formal dinner for society members, a tradition that continues today. In the late eighteenth century, the Charitable Irish Society of Boston, while benevolent, was both paternalistic and elitist. When the 1797 St Patrick's Day Dinner was attended by twenty-four members, including former Secretary of War, General Henry Knox, they each paid US\$5 for the privilege – a hefty sum for the time.[60] The cost of such a salubrious banquet on St Patrick's Day enabled social vetting of participants. Members of the Charitable Irish Society of Boston were gentlemen of status and means; they assembled together in a manner that reflected this power. They certainly supported initiatives to cater for the welfare needs of the Irish poor, but they were hardly rubbing shoulders with them. So while the society raised large sums for charity on 17 March each year, it did so in a cultural environment that effectively excluded 'ordinary' Irish people. St Patrick's Day, in that sense, was not a time of fellowship for all Irish immigrants.

After the turn of the century, Boston attracted increasing numbers of emigrants from Ireland, particularly from its southern regions. This rising presence of Irish Catholics in Boston was, in part, a consequence of new-found religious freedoms for American Catholics. In the state of Massachusetts, the constitution of 1780 allowed Catholics liberty of public worship as well as rights of citizenship, such as voting and eligibility to hold public office. In Ireland, by contrast, Catholics continued to face restrictions on religious practice, suffrage and political representation. No wonder Irish-Catholic emigration to America rose between 1780–1825. This change had implications for the membership structure of the Charitable Irish Society of Boston. Between 1800 and 1825 some three-quarters of all Irish migrants joining the society were from southern Irish counties. The religious affiliation of the Charitable Society's members was, therefore, increasingly Catholic.[61] The rising demographic presence of Catholics soon resulted in their increased influence within Irish-American charitable societies: for many years such associations had either barred Catholics from membership or curtailed their right to executive office. This uncharitable attitude was no longer possible in an environment where Irish Americans of Catholic extraction outnumbered those of a Protestant background. Eventually, Irish Catholics assumed greater influence, even control, over Irish charitable societies with a history of Protestant domination. This transformation had implications for the manner in which St Patrick's Day was celebrated in America: Catholics, as we will now see, tended to commemorate 17 March in a more public manner than had Protestants.

The Charitable Irish Society of Boston celebrated its centenary year on St Patrick's Day, 1837. This occasion reveals much about membership changes within the society, and more generally about the evolving nature of St Patrick's Day celebrations.[62] The society, now dominated by Catholics, had carried a motion that the centennial observance should consist of a public procession, exercises and a formal dinner. The scale of the undertaking and the wealth of the society's membership can be gauged by the budgeted cost of the occasion – a hefty US$115. The influence of Catholics within the society was evident by an approach to the Catholic Bishop of Boston to sanction the festivities. As St Patrick's Day in 1837 fell on a Friday, Catholics within the society required special dispensation from the bishop in order to feast outside the usual confines of Lenten observance. The permission was granted on the proviso that all diners gave a small sum to charity. The profile of Catholics within the society was also reflected in the Patrician parade and exercises. Most notably, the society was joined in procession by the religious sodality Young Catholic Friends. Together they marched before dignitaries that included the Governor of Massachusetts, the Mayor of Boston, the City Marshal, the Secretary of State and several members of the State Senate and House of Representatives. Such esteemed company signalled the importance of St Patrick's Day within Boston's social calendar, as well as the legitimate place of both Irish Protestants and Catholics in society generally. Such ecumenical reform was also apparent within the Charitable Irish Society of Boston. During St Patrick's Day exercises at the city's Masonic Temple, the president of the society, Mr Boyd, spoke for two hours. He concluded that while he was a Protestant and that the society's original rules had excluded Catholics from office and membership, he was happy to report that for the previous twenty-five years a majority of the group's members had been Catholic.[63] This open embrace of the Catholic membership was a tacit admission that the charitable society, and along with it St Patrick's Day, had ceased to be an enclave of Irish Protestantism.

Elsewhere in America, St Patrick's Day celebrations initially waned in the decades following the founding of the nation, with many Irish celebrating 4 July rather than 17 March. Indeed, leading Irish-American groups, such as the Shamrock Friendly Association and the Republican Greens, paraded in honour of American independence on 4 July, yet on 17 March they did not march in honour of the Irish patron saint. Irish-American newspapers, such as the *Shamrock* and the *Hibernian Chronicle*, nonetheless reported an annual round of dinners and evening meetings on 17 March in the early 1800s.

The need for organizations that catered for, represented, and gave a voice to the wider Irish community in America, was heightened from 1827. Prior to that date the British had restricted the number of Irish who were allowed to emigrate to a new life in America. With the lifting of such restrictions the number of Irish arrivals to America grew rapidly. By 1835 over 30,000 Irish emigrants were landing in New York annually.[64] The influx of such large numbers gave an added boost to the membership of Irish organizations and involvement in St Patrick's Day. A growing number of Irish Catholics had migrated to America, and, as they had done back home, took an interest in the observance of St Patrick's Day in a new land. They neither rejected nor withdrew from 4 July celebrations, instead making commemoration of 17 March and its parades 'their own'. As a result, St Patrick's Day processions began to take on an overtly Catholic character. This meant that they flaunted Catholic symbols of Irishness, and generally rejected British rule over Ireland.

Organizations involved in the planning of St Patrick's Day festivities in America were usually charitable in nature. According to Crimmins, the Friendly Sons of St Patrick made 2,850 charitable donations to individuals in New York between 1805 and 1829.[65] The most prominent Irish organization was the Hibernian Universal Benevolent Society. With this group's support the annual St Patrick's Day parade in New York grew in importance, becoming an ever more ostentatious display of the Irish presence. In 1831 it was reported that members of the society carried 'the richest and most splendid banners we have ever witnessed, with other appropriate insignia of the Emerald Isle and mottoes of most of the revolutionary characters'.[66] In keeping with the society's aim of benevolence, US$94 was collected for the St Mary's Institute for Orphans. It was obvious, however, that charity was but one function of the parade; another was to promote the Catholic faith in America and republican sentiments towards Ireland. In the two decades before the onset of the Irish famine, St Patrick's Day parades in New York celebrated the Irish-Catholic presence in America; Irish Protestants, though dominant in the eighteenth century, were now on the margins. Concurrently, 17 March was a time to parade republican symbols through the streets of New York, such as with banners depicting the deceased Irish revolutionaries Wolfe Tone and Robert Emmett.

American celebrations of Ireland's patron saint had begun as formal events controlled and organized by socially elite Irish organizations. The shift to public marches by members of the lower classes, many of whom were Catholic, both transformed and divided St Patrick's Day celebrations. Irish-American groups, such as the Hibernians, though led by small-scale business operators and artisans, brought about an openness of celebration that allowed their community 'to develop an identity that contrasted sharply with the more exclusive dinners held by the Friendly Sons of St Patrick'.[67] The development of celebrating 17 March through parading, which included a wide social mix, can be seen in the origins of the parade in Lowell, Massachusetts. The first took place in 1830; it included all groups within the town, and was organized specifically to mark the opening of the local St Patrick's Church. This special event subsequently became an annual 17 March custom.[68]

In 1835 a series of St Patrick's Day dinners and events took place across

New York that illustrate how important the day had become to the city's Irish population. On 17 March that year the following gatherings took place: the Society of the Friendly Sons of St Patrick dinner, the Hibernian Provident Society dinner at Chamber's Sixth Ward Hotel, the O'Connell House dinner, and the Sons and Friends of the Green Isle dinner at Jefferson House.[69] According to press reports, the elite of New York's Irish-American society was in attendance. The format of each dinner was remarkably similar, as were the sentiments expressed in speeches and toasts. Common themes included reverence for St Patrick's Day, the social and political liberties offered by America, the beauty of Ireland, the campaigns of Daniel O'Connell, the longed for 'freedom of Ireland', and the patriots of '98. Such dinners offer a window into the otherwise exclusive lives of well-to-do Irish Americans. The diners at such events were clearly both American and Irish patriots, believed wholeheartedly in Irish independence through various means, supported the central place of the Catholic Church within Irish immigrant life, and were socially benevolent in collecting money for Irish less fortunate than themselves. What such gatherings also illustrated, though it was never explicit, was that Irish-American life consisted of two key strands. There were those of wealth, power and influence who dressed for their St Patrick's Day dinner in the city's exclusive hotels and restaurants, and those of lower social standing, resident in areas like the Bowery, who paraded and celebrated St Patrick's Day like the Irish at home. Such a social division within St Patrick's Day celebrations was common in other parts of America in the first half of the nineteenth century, and became entrenched in the decades following the Irish famine.

The central themes of charity, Catholicism and nationalism, which dominated pre-famine American St Patrick's Day celebrations, can all be found in the coverage of the day in the leading local Irish newspaper of the time, the *Truth Teller*. In 1836, the newspaper constantly reiterated the importance of charity within the St Patrick's Day celebrations. In that particular year, the chosen charity was the Orphan Asylum on Prince Street. Readers were reminded that 'while Irishmen, and the friends of Ireland are preparing to participate in the wonted festivities, they should remember the poor orphans whose little hands are extended towards them in earnest supplication'.[70] In the week before St Patrick's Day, 1836, the newspaper appealed to its readers' sense of Irishness and its understanding of their homeland, as well as making clear statements in support of the nationalist movement in Ireland. The newspaper informed its readers of the social nature of the day that caused such pride:

> The native of the Green Isle and all who honour its natural beauty, its fertility, its poetic character, its hardy sons and its fair daughters, meet this day to down the soamrock [*sic*] in the flowin [*sic*] bowl, and to give way to the warm feelings gushing from the heart.[71]

The paper also expressed its support for Daniel O'Connell and his campaign for repeal of the Act of Union, applauding his success in bringing about Catholic Emancipation:

> Ireland's sun is soon to beam with effulgent brilliancy upon a regenerated nation. Ireland's star is soon to culminate resplendent in the heaven's never more obscured. The Agitator is rapidly approaching the goal at which he is to pause – a Liberator aided by him, advised by him, the people have already loosened the fetters by which they have been shackled, and in but a short time, they must feel themselves free, prosperous and happy.[72]

On St Patrick's Day, 1836, the Hibernian Universal Benevolent Society marched in parade from the Sixth Ward Hotel to the Catholic church in Chamber Street for a service. In the evening, the Hibernian Provident Society met for dinner at McMahon's long room on Broadway. Thomas Trainor, 'a true worthy of [17]98' attended.[73] The toasts at such dinners, always recorded verbatim by the newspapers, gave readers an impression of the central purposes of St Patrick's Day for the society: the life and lore of St Patrick, Ireland's freedom from British rule, opportunities for Irish emigrants in America and the importance of Catholic charity to those in need.

The custom of dining on St Patrick's Day was repeated elsewhere in America. In 1821 the Hibernian Society of New Orleans met for dinner at Mr Beale's Hotel, and was honoured by 'the company of the Governor of the State, the Senior Officers of the Army in this city, and the Commanding Officer of the Navy on the New Orleans station'. The dinner concluded with the usual round of toasts to 'the day we celebrate', and a rendition of a specially composed song, 'Erin tho' lost, still dear to all'.[74]

But why was St Patrick's Day, and the parades that took place on this day, so readily accepted by the Irish as a method of celebrating their sense of collective identity? One of the most important events for migrants, prior to leaving Ireland, was the Irish wake. These were emotional gatherings of families and communities so that they could bid farewell to an emigrant whom they would, in all likelihood, never see again.[75] The ready embrace of St Patrick's Day celebrations by the immigrant Irish in America may be understood, in part, as a resurrection after the wake. Leaving Ireland, especially in the decades after the famine, was a painful experience that led to the severing of family and community ties. Arrival in America, though often difficult, was marked by opportunities for integration into a new Irish community. By parading or dining with other Irish on 17 March, the migrant was able to reconfirm their identity, nullify the painful memories of the wake, and embrace the power and celebration of the Irish on St Patrick's Day. The parades and banquets also allowed Irish nationalists, the vast majority of whom were Catholic, an opportunity to vent the antagonism that many of them felt towards Britain's Irish policy, and to create loyalties and ties based on intense local Irish-American patriotism. Their new communities and organizations were centred on religion, family and regional ties with others from the same areas of Ireland.[76]

As the western frontiers of America opened up during the early nineteenth century, so the Irish transported St Patrick's Day. By 1820 in St Louis, which was then a small log town, the local Irish population gathered to celebrate St Patrick's Day with a dinner, where they toasted the prospects of statehood for their region.[77] The formalization of St Patrick's Day by the different dining or parading organizations was highly structured. The need for controlled forms of celebration was a product of the deep suspicion of the Irish (and Catholics) held by Anglo-Americans, and a popular literary depiction of the Irish as perpetual failures destined for an early grave. By showing themselves as sober, orderly and hard working, both in their lives and during St Patrick's Day celebrations, the Irish demonstrated that they were successful.[78] In New York, for instance, Patrician street parades and formal dinners offered the Irish an opportunity to declare publicly their legitimate place in what was 'a basically unsympathetic city'.[79] In particular the parade, especially when it was orderly, won praise for the Irish. In 1838, for example, the *Herald* remarked on the absence of 'beautiful broken heads, picturesque bloody noses and enchanting shillelaghs'.[80]

The potency of St Patrick's Day parades in the big American cities, while powerful, was always tempered by the control exerted by organizations that ran the events. Throughout the nineteenth century there was an understanding that while 17 March was an important day for the Irish as a day of leisure, enjoyment and remembrance, it was also essential that celebrations were respectable and presented officially sanctioned messages.[81]

OBSERVANCE OF ST PATRICK'S DAY IN CANADA: c.1765–1845

Irish migration to British North America was, as previously explained, significant well before the mass exodus of the famine. In 1825, some 80 per cent of all transatlantic passengers from Ireland arrived in Canada.[82] It appears that a considerable volume of Irish migrants then made their way to the United States; Canada was, for them, a first port of call. Yet there remained a significant presence of Irish settlers in these British colonies, the vast majority of whom – like other locals – inhabited rural areas.[83] Our interest, with respect to St Patrick's Day, is nonetheless with cities in Canada, for this is where events on 17 March were most likely to be recorded. Our focus on three cities, in particular, is intended to unravel both Catholic and Protestant observances of St Patrick's Day in the early nineteenth century. Toronto was the major city of the largely Protestant and English-speaking province of Ontario, which featured a population around one-third Irish (migrants and descendants), comprising some two-thirds of the total Irish cohort in Canada.[84] Montreal and Quebec City were key urban sites within the largely Catholic and French-speaking province of Quebec: by 1825 the Irish comprised some 12 per cent of Montreal's 25,000 residents, and over 21 per cent of Quebec City's 32,000 inhabitants.[85] Irish Catholics in Canada were, therefore, a 'double minority'.[86] The vast majority of English and Scottish migrants to Canada were Protestant; so too were most of the early Irish migrants. Not until the second quarter of the nineteenth century did Irish Catholics make a significant impact as a settlement group. Irish Catholics were thus in a minority among groups who spoke the same language, while as worshippers they were outnumbered by French-speaking Catholics.[87] Eventually the labels 'Protestant Ontario and Popish Quebec' emerged,[88] suggesting that these regions were separated more along the lines of religion than language. The presence of the Irish in both places certainly contributed to this perception: there was a preponderance of Irish Protestants in Toronto, while in Montreal and Quebec City Irish Catholics were demographically significant.[89]

The first mention of a Patrician ceremony in British North America was at Quebec City in 1765, where Irish Protestant officers in the Quebec Garrison of the British Army celebrated the saint's anniversary.[90] The key ceremony of the day was a Divine Service at the Recollet Church, where the Reverend Doctor Brooke, Protestant chaplain of the Quebec Garrison, gave blessings and offered a sermon 'suitable to the day'. Subsequently, worshippers proceeded to the local 'Sun-Tavern' where 'many Loyal and Patriotic Toasts were drank'. The social climax of the festivities was a dinner and ball at the city's concert hall.[91] Like the early observances of St Patrick's Day in Boston and New York, the first recorded Patrician event in Quebec was commemorated by Irish-Protestant soldiers in the standing British army. Intriguingly, this celebration took place in a city dominated by Catholics, but since the local Catholic population was French rather than Irish, the day had no local significance for them.

The Quebec City celebration of St Patrick's Day, 1765 took place in a triumphal context: the British Army had overwhelmed New France just five years earlier, claiming this territory for the Crown. It was a British imperial victory, but since the empire was Protestant it also had major religious implications. In Canada, anti-Catholicism was the official policy of the new ruling administration, and this was 'expressed in legal restrictions on the religious and political freedom of Catholics'.[92] Yet caveats must be made. Both the Treaty of Paris (1763) and the Quebec Act (1774) contained initiatives allowing French Catholics religious and political autonomy in Canada. This group was, as Terence Murphy has put it, 'simply too numerous to suppress, and as the tide of [anti-British] rebellion rose to the south it became an urgent necessity to foster loyalty in British North America'.[93] Religious reform was, in this regard, an intelligent strategy; the American colonies had been settled by Protestants and, despite their rhetoric about religious freedom, were stridently anti-Catholic. The application of liberalizing measures in Canada was, however, uneven. The French-Catholic population of Quebec was the group under focus, yet reform naturally also applied to English-speaking Catholics in that region. In other parts of Canada though, residents who were either French or Catholic were a small minority, so there was less political urgency to remove anti-Catholic sanctions. Not until 1830 was 'official anti-Catholicism' removed from statute books across Canada.[94] This was timely as far as many Irish migrants were concerned; a significant number of arrivals from Ireland over the following thirty years were indeed Catholic.[95]

In the early 1800s, however, Irish Protestants were more numerous and vocal than their Irish-Catholic counterparts in British North America. The Orange Order, which had been formed in Ireland in 1795, soon found wide support in English-speaking Canada. As in the Irish homeland, these local Orangemen stood for 'community defence, Protestant solidarity, and colonial loyalty to the British Crown'.[96] They had, it seemed, much to be wary about politically: expansionist Americans to the south, a politically nascent French community in their midst, and a gradual increase of Catholic immigrants from the Irish homeland. Little wonder, then, that the Orange Order paraded with gusto on 12 July; their orange sashes and associated regalia were worn proudly as markers of loyalty to empire and Protestant faith.[97] St Patrick's Day was, by comparison, less politically charged in the early nineteenth century. The anniversary had ecumenical origins in the homeland, and since there were comparatively few Canadian Irish Catholics at the turn of the nineteenth century, no demographic impetus towards sectarianism. St Patrick's Day was, however, controversial in a basic sense; that is, it tended to be a raucous celebration of Irishness prompted by heavy drinking and brawling. For example, in the timber-producing region of Ottawa Valley, annual St Patrick's Day celebrations provided a welcome distraction from hard labour for immigrant Irish woodcutters. They immersed themselves fully in the festivities, sometimes with hilarious results, such as the occasion when 'burly young lumbermen were seen buying up all the green silk parasols in town and mincing around the streets in a parody of the local ladies of fashion'.[98] According to MacKay, however, such high spirits just as often ended in trouble, as in 1828 when the St Patrick's Day parade, consisting of '200 men "drunk, dancing and fighting", degenerated into a riot in which one man was killed and several injured'.[99]

The rise of various Irish societies and associations in Canada brought order, context and continuity to the observance of St Patrick's Day. In 1824 the Hibernian Society of Montreal organized a formal dinner to recognize 'this auspicious day for the Emerald Isle'.[100] Thirty guests met at the Mansion House, each of whom, the *Gazette* newspaper reported glowingly, were 'brought together on a joyous occasion, united by one liberal feeling, untainted by either religious or national prejudices . . . all seemed united in brotherly love'.[101] In these formative years neither membership nor office in the Hibernian Society was restricted to a specific religious group; non-Irishmen were even welcomed into the fold, such was the emphasis on the Hibernian 'connection' with an essentially non-Irish Montreal society. St Patrick's Day toasts were nonetheless partisan in that they lionized British imperial rule. As expected, glasses were raised first for Ireland's patron saint, but this was followed by sixteen 'loyal' toasts, including 'The King – with 4 times four', which included the anthem 'God Save the King'; various toasts to the British Army, British Navy, and its distinguished leaders; raised glasses to the British royal family with a rendition of 'Rule Britannia', and so on.[102] There were no 'Erin go Bragh' salutations: aside from the title 'Hibernian', the Montreal society's St Patrick's Day dinner seemed reminiscent of Anglo-Irish and Protestant observances of 17 March. The local Irish-Catholic cohort was, of course, neither demographically significant nor politically influential in the early 1800s. Only thirty men attended the Hibernians' St Patrick's Day dinner of 1824; no wonder they invited allcomers to join them. The cheers for Britain, and implicitly Ireland's ongoing place within the Union and the empire, reflected the dominance of loyalist sentiments in Canada. The British colonies had been won from France and retained in the north despite the American Revolution. From a local perspective there was much to toast.

By the 1830s there were dedicated St Patrick's societies in Toronto, Montreal and Quebec City, each of which undertook responsibility for staging Patrician commemorations.[103] They had much in common. They were Irish 'national' societies, but hardly nationalist; Irishmen from both Protestant and Catholic backgrounds were welcome, and there were rules or conventions that constrained the discussion of religious and political matters. Kevin James, in his study of the St Patrick's Society of Montreal, contends that 'the implicit criterion for membership at this time was class . . . the men who assembled for the Society's founding were an impressive lot, representing the high and middling echelons of capital and civic power'.[104] Societies of an elite nature had also been formed to represent other national groups in Montreal: Scotsmen met under the banner of the St Andrew's Society, Englishmen did the same in the name of St George, while French, German and Dutch immigrants each formed their own fraternal associations. The 'Tory' British and Irish societies shared a vision of Canada under the Union flag; they were, indeed, united from 1835 by a common commitment to the Constitutional Association. This conservative political organization was a counterpoint to the liberal–radical *patriote* movement. The latter was a French-inspired lobby group: together with activists from other ethnic minorities, the *patriote* movement agitated for reforms to the government of Canada, hoping to make the political order ethnically plural. Opponents to the Canadian 'establishment' included the Irish liberal newspaper the *Vindi-*

cator, which was allied politically with the French reformist organ, *La Minerve*. Perhaps the most vocal critic was the Irishman Edmund Bailey O'Callaghan: during the early 1830s he was editor of the *Vindicator* and went on to be a key participant in the failed anti-government rebellions in Montreal during 1837–8. James emphasizes that 'O'Callaghan also used the *Vindicator* as an organ to oppose the conservative orientation of the St Patrick's Society, which in 1835 was under the presidency of the Tory Councillor John Donnellan.'[105] Both the *Vindicator* and *La Minerve* expressed their 'condemnation of the Saint Patrick's Society as an Orange organ'.[106]

Montreal's Patrician parades of the 1830s, led by the St Patrick's Society, featured collaboration between national groups representing the union of England, Scotland and Ireland. Both the St George's Society and the St Andrew's Society were deemed 'sister societies' to the St Patrick's fraternity, each agreeing to celebrate in unison the anniversary of their respective patron saint. So the English, the Scots, and even the Germans marched on St Patrick's Day, then retired to a formal dinner where loyal toasts were offered and national airs played. This was very much a Tory celebration: although Irish cultural traditions were central to the commemoration of St Patrick's Day, 'toasts were offered up to the Saint George's Society, whereupon "Britons, Strike Home" was sung, followed by the Saint Andrew's Society (to the tune of "Auld Lang Syne" and "Here's a Health, Bonnie Scotland")'.[107] It was also a martial occasion: membership of the St Patrick's Society and that of the Loyal Volunteer and Queen's Volunteer Militias often crossed over, a connection that was made obvious on 17 March. During the 1835 dinner, Michael O'Sullivan, president of the St Patrick's Society, 'noted that he was surrounded by a large number of men clad in the uniforms of the 18th Royal Irish Regiment'.[108] The 1836 procession featured the Standard of Ireland alongside of which marched soldiers 'with battle-axe', followed by Irish pipers and the band of the 32nd Royal Irish Regiment.[109]

The St Patrick's Societies in Toronto and Quebec City were, like that of Montreal, largely Protestant and Tory. There were no rules barring Catholics, but there were too few such Irishmen among their membership to be influential. Michael Cotterell points out that there were 'a few small scale and generally disorganized parades' in Toronto by the late 1840s, but it was not until the 1850s that the march became a regular part of St Patrick's Day – and this coincided with the Catholic Church assuming organizational responsibility for the procession.[110] The St Patrick's Society of Quebec was, by comparison, better prepared for 17 March. Despite an embarrassing opening in 1837, when the society had no banners or badges with which to parade – which left the St George's Society and the Caledonian Society as the main contributors to the Patrician procession from the Albion Hotel to St Patrick's Church – the following year saw vast improvements on the part of local Irishmen. On 17 March 1838 the Saint Patrick's Society led the parade, which was headed by two marshals with white wands, followed by the Union Jack carried by twelve society members, the Irish flag with similar bearers, then the St George's, St Andrew's and Caledonian societies bringing up the rear.[111]

ST PATRICK'S DAY IN AUSTRALIA: *c.*1788–1845

Habitation of Australia by whites began when convicts from Britain and Ireland were transported to New South Wales in 1788. A penal colony, as the name suggests, was supposed to *penal*ize interns. But the settlements on the Australian east coast did not become gulags. It was strategically import-ant for Britain to establish permanent colonies in the Antipodes, this proving difficult in an unfamiliar environment, so the principal concern of early governors was economic survival, not penal discipline. Convicts were not simply prisoners for they were the main labour source and responsible to several masters, from civic authorities to landowners. Indeed, although a penal status presupposed strong discipline, including the inglorious specta-cle of flogging, many convicts were allowed specific liberties, such as mar-riage, cohabitation, free time each week to spend with children, and tickets of leave. The later arrival of shiploads of free settlers, particularly from the 1830s onwards, suggested that the Australian colonies were destined to become more than simply dumping grounds for felons.[112] Land grants, lease-hold properties and sale of Crown territory enabled fledgling agricultural and mining industries to begin; and, with government or parish-assisted passage available to 'respectable and industrious' emigrant labourers, a work force on the move from various parts of the British Isles.[113]

By 1836, however, convicts still constituted 36 per cent of the population of New South Wales – which was 77,096.[114] Among this demographic group, the Irish were significant: they included prisoners transported from Ireland, as well as Irish-born prisoners from Britain. Overall, the Irish com-prised about 25 per cent of the convict population between 1788–1853; this involved some 29,000 males and 9,000 females.[115] Among the overall convict population, male felons outnumbered their female counterparts by 10 to 1 in 1836.[116] In that same year the overall male population of the colony was 55,539 compared with the female population of 21,557. This gender imbalance narrowed significantly during the next two decades, particularly as an increasing number of single female free settlers were granted assisted passage to the colonies – many of them from Ireland.[117] The proportion of Irish felons in Australia's eastern colonies was similar to that of the general population breakdown in the white settlements. It is under-stood that by the mid-nineteenth century 'between a quarter and a third of the population of NSW was of Irish birth and Catholic faith – a proportion more than twice that of Catholics, both English and Irish, in England'. The percentage in Victoria was thought to be smaller, between one quarter and a fifth of that colony's population.[118] These estimates are supported by subsequent census figures. In the NSW census of 1861, for example, 30 per cent of people declared themselves Catholic, while 34 per cent of respondents were of Irish birth.[119] A crucial point, which is not spelled out in these statistics, is that the vast majority of Catholics in Australia were of Irish descent, while most Irish Australians were Catholics.

Indeed, what distinguished the Irish collectively from other immigrants was that they were the sole settlement group that was overwhelmingly of Catholic faith. This had very significant social and political ramifications. A majority of the Irish immigrants' fellow settlers were either Anglican or Protestant; for many of them, Catholicism was a dubious, even un-British, Romanist creed. Irish-Catholic colonists, being religious fringe dwellers, were well advised not to openly revisit Orange–Green divides, however much embers of mistrust or unease burned away inside some Irish nationalist hearts. For, by contrast to Irish Catholics in post-revolutionary America, Australia's Irish Catholics had to come to terms with the social and political reality of being part of a colonial outpost that *coveted* British imperial rule.[120] That said, Australia's Irish Catholics were comparatively free to practise their religious faith. NSW had led ecumenical reform by abandoning the British model of an established Church of England and Ireland. Michael Hogan explains that the NSW Church Act of 1836 introduced the principle of 'legal equality of the major churches and state support for their activities', and 'this established equality between the four main churches – Anglican, Catholic, Presbyterian and Methodist – but excluded [state funding for] smaller groups such as the Jews'.[121] In this respect, the Catholic Church was offered greater official recognition in the Australian colonies than it had received previously in the Anglican or Presbyterian strongholds of England, Scotland and Wales.[122] Australian Catholics were also in a better position than many American colonists of the same faith; Protestant-dominated legislatures often prevented or curtailed Catholic religious practice in the United States. Freedom of Catholic worship in Australia, coupled with the fact that Irish Australians had rights to property and the franchise akin to other emigrant groups from the British Isles, meant that Irish-Catholic settlers were not defined in colonial law as second-class British subjects. However, as we will see in Chapters 4 and 5, they were still susceptible to being treated as such, particularly during times of social and political crisis.

For the Irish, whether they were convicts, emancipists, or free settlers, St Patrick's Day was a time of merriment. The Judge-Advocate of NSW, Englishman David Collins, an ecumenical observer, recorded in his journal in March 1795: 'On the 17th St Patrick found many votaries in the settlement ... libations to the saint were so plentifully poured that at night the cells were full of prisoners'.[123] In a similar vein, Irishman Joseph Holt, a landowner and farmer, wrote in 1803: 'my usual time to commence sow was the first Monday after St Patrick's Day: it requiring a few days to get my

23

men sober'.[124] By 1810 the Governor of NSW, Lachlan Macquarie, had given formal recognition to St Patrick's Day. As the *Sydney Gazette* reported:

> His EXCELLENCY was this day pleased to give an entertainment to a number of the Government artificers and labourers, in honor of the day, being Saint Patrick's; on which occasion British hospitality displayed itself; and every heart was filled with sentiments of respect and gratitude.[125]

Patrick O'Farrell suggests two reasons for this official sanction. First, it was a time for the colonial elite to feast together on a day that, although having patriotic connections to the Emerald Isle, was in no way considered subversive to the union of Britain and Ireland. It was deemed as a nostalgic and innocuous ritual that simply warmed the hearts of Irish emigrants; the support of the English colonial establishment, therefore, was a goodwill strategy. Even the Bank of NSW was closed specifically in honour of St Patrick's Day.[126] Second, Macquarie saw St Patrick's Day as an opportunity to bring Catholics and Protestants together in a common cause. And celebrate they did. O'Farrell explains that the phrase 'keeping up St Patrick' became 'a euphemism for getting blind drunk'. This behaviour, he adds, 'had no necessary boundaries on the saint's day'.[127] Indeed, for some revellers, it was a case of St Patrick's *week*. A Bathurst farmer complained to his Catholic priest that his labourers were incapable of work at this time: 'They have been keeping St Patrick's Day since the 12th inst. and not ended it yet.'[128]

National boundaries may well have been absent on St Patrick's Day, but class boundaries were reinforced. By the 1830s, Patrician banquets and balls catered annually for the colonial elite of NSW. The aptly named Sons of St Patrick had assumed organizational responsibility; this group comprised 'Irish Gentlemen'. Members were entitled to nominate guests to attend the Society's official functions, which enabled vetting of those in attendance.[129] It was very important to the Irish elite – and doubtless most of all the Anglo-Irish elite – that St Patrick's Day involved the 'well-to-do' of Sydney, such as the governor, the treasurer and ministers of religion.[130] The *Australian* newspaper of March 1840 reported that the new court house was the site for a 'gay and festive' St Patrick's night function, which involved 'three and four hundred persons of the highest rank and distinction in the colony'.[131] The ballroom and supper rooms were decorated with 'wreaths of green shrubs and flowers' which were formed into 'elegant festoons' by the superintendent of Sydney's Botanic Gardens. Military bands of the 28th and 50th Regiments 'played quadrilles, waltzes, and country dances'. The movement and renditions had little connection to traditional Irish dance and music, but they kept the guests entertained until the festivities ended just before dawn.[132] The social elite of Sydney had done their part, it seemed, in 'keeping up St Patrick'.

24

In 1841, the St Patrick's Society was formed under clerical leadership; it now took over the reins as organizer of the 17 March festivities. The churches, as self-declared moral guardians of the penal colony, wanted to make the celebration more devout and less drunken. They staged a procession of schoolchildren on St Patrick's Day, followed by High Mass, then a formal dinner in the evening for 'a hundred gentlemen'. O'Farrell explains that this range of events was intended 'to demonstrate the respectability, loyalty and community spirit of affluent Irish emancipists [ex-convicts], both Protestant and Catholic'.[133] But local press reactions varied. The *Australian* of March 1842 reported favourably on the St Patrick's Day procession, mass and dinner: 'All the proceedings of the day went off with order and harmony.'[134] On the previous year, the *Sydney Morning Herald* was less charitable in its assessment. The paper considered that the Irish at the St Patrick's Day dinner of 1841 'were not "gentlemen" as they claimed, but "respectable citizen-artisans"'.[135] These Irishmen were, by the *Herald*'s reckoning, of a lower status than the British rulers of the colony. Even in a penal setting, snobbery worked to establish pecking orders. A highlight of the 1843 festivities was an exhibition of aeronautics: on the evening of 17 March two 'Montgolfier Balloons' took to the air from the grounds of the Stonemason's Arms in Parrammatta Street. Entrance to see the filling of the balloon and its setting off was one shilling per person.[136] But there was plenty more hot air in Sydney that night: a split along class lines had emerged in the Irish community, with the result that 'there were two simultaneous St Patrick's Day dinners ... one for the top of the Irish Australian pyramid, the other for those less well placed'.[137] This class consciousness was, of course, not only apparent among Irish colonists. It had much to do with 'free settlers' wanting to distance themselves socially from emancipists and convicts.

ST PATRICK'S DAY: NATURE OF CEREMONIES

As the celebration of St Patrick's Day spread across Ireland and into Britain, North America and Australia, what format did such celebrations take? In 1681, the English traveller, Thomas Dineley noted a series of St Patrick's Day practices which, in one form or another, became standard markers for those celebrating the day.[138] Dineley observed that the Irish wore Celtic crosses, had green ribbon in their hats, pinned shamrock to their clothes, and, after demanding St Patrick's groat from their masters, drank so that 'very few of the zealous are found sober at night'.[139] Dineley had observed three long-standing components of St Patrick's Day – wearing the colour green, adorning the shamrock and indulging liberally in alcohol.

The crosses mentioned by Dineley were a common feature of St Patrick's Day celebration that only began to disappear from Irish celebrations in the post-First World War era. The crosses, which were predominantly made and worn by children, consisted of a paper or card backing and featured coloured ribbons as decoration, all of which were centred around a Celtic cross. In 1895, the 'little girl's St Patrick's Day Cross' was described as a cross of paper 'wrapped or covered with silk or ribbon of different colours, and a bunch or rosette of green silk in the centre'.[140] The St Patrick's Day crosses have been replaced by the wearing of shamrock, a tradition that dates back to the sixteenth century.[141] The shamrock has taken its place as a symbol of St Patrick's Day because of its supposed links with the saint himself. In his teachings St Patrick commonly referred to the Holy Trinity, and it is claimed that he used the humble shamrock, a plant that has always grown freely across Ireland, to illustrate the symmetry of the Trinity. As early as 1727, the botanist Caleb Threlkeld wrote that the plant

> is worn by people in their hats on the 17th day of March yearly, which is called St Patrick's Day, it being a current tradition that, by this three-leaved grass, he emblematically set forth to them the mystery of the Holy Trinity.[142]

In 1920, the Reverend J.A. Dowling argued in the *Irish Independent* that while there was no documentary evidence for the consecration of the shamrock by St Patrick, 'a tradition which has developed into a national belief cannot be lightly discredited'.[143] As a result of its connection with St Patrick's Day, the shamrock also became a symbol of Irish national self-image and, in some cases, national self-determination.[144]

A common St Patrick's Day custom was the 'wetting' or 'drowning' of the shamrock. The tradition of wetting the shamrock was referred to by Dineley in 1681 and Threlkeld in 1727, and appears regularly in Irish literature and engravings during the nineteenth century.[145] At the close of the festive day, the piece of shamrock, which had resided upon the wearer's clothing, was placed in the bottom of a glass or cup, then covered with punch, whiskey, or any other available alcohol. Liberal indulgence of food and drink was a central component of St Patrick's Day celebrations. The 17 March usually falls within the period of Lenten abstinence, but Patrician tradition has decreed that the faithful are, for that special day, free from this constraint. Hence they could eat meat and drink freely as they commemorated the life of the apostle of Ireland.

There was a welter of other customs connected with St Patrick's Day, most of which have their origins in the pre-famine period. The genesis of such traditions is difficult to trace, but the presence of a lively set of beliefs, practices and superstitions connected with 17 March was uncovered in the 1920s by the interviewers of the Irish Folklore Commission. Many of those interviewed in Ireland during the 1920s recalled that on the morning of St Patrick's Day:

A cross is made on the right arm with a burned sally rod, in a family the cross is usually made on all the members by the father.[146]

It was the custom of the father of the family to burn a sally rod and with the charred end of it to make the sign of the cross on the left shoulder of each member of the family, repeating at the same time, 'May the sign of the Holy Cross of Christ be about you and may you always keep the faith that St Patrick brought us.'[147]

As Ireland was, even at the time of the Folklore Commission interviews, a predominantly rural society, many of the traditions associated with St Patrick's Day related to the land and the process of farming. There was a belief, probably because of the proximity of 17 March to the start of spring and its use as a marker of the changing seasons, that grain 'should be sown as near as possible to St Patrick's Day'.[148] Concerns were expressed over the welfare of animals on 17 March, as there was a commonly held belief that dogs cried on St Patrick's eve,[149] and that the day itself was a dangerous time for cows. As a result, 'people always watched them on that day, lest they would go in a bog hole and be drowned'. There was a belief that cows drowned on 17 March because 'they might go for their Patrick's pot'.[150]

Whatever the truth or otherwise of these customs and superstitions, they reveal much about the importance of St Patrick's Day within the Irish calendar. While those who lived in larger towns could engage in public activities on 17 March, the majority of Irish people, based as they were within rural areas, experienced St Patrick's Day as a local and family event dominated by their faith and rural occupations.

In the decade prior to the Irish famine, St Patrick's Day traditions were well established in Ireland and the United States, and partly established in England, Canada and Australia. Protestant control of St Patrick's Day celebrations had been overturned by an influx of Catholic migrants who infiltrated Irish charitable societies and established Catholic benevolent groups of their own. In the process they virtually took over the management and promotion of St Patrick's Day in Dublin, Liverpool, Boston and New York, with parading established as a key form of observance.

Particularly in the United States, organizations to co-ordinate and sustain St Patrick's Day parades across the country were in place by the 1840s. Divisions, largely of a class nature, between charitable collectives of gentlemen who dined formally on St Patrick's Day and the more populist parade goers, were also entrenched. In Ireland the nature of St Patrick's Day observance was more fluid, though as we discuss in Chapter 2, temperance societies began to provide a 'respectable' model for future Patrician celebrations. Above all, as we see next, the famine fundamentally changed Irish society and its diasporic communities, and this had a significant effect on the nature of St Patrick's Day observances.

CHAPTER 2

FAMINE AND EXODUS

— ලාර —

It is often said, by the opponents of the anti-slavery cause, that the condition of the people of Ireland is more deplorable than that of the American slaves. Far be it from me to underrate the sufferings of the Irish people ... Yet I must say that there is no analogy between the two cases. The Irishman is poor, but he is not a slave. He may be in rags, but he is not a slave ... The Irishman has not only the liberty to emigrate from his country, but he has liberty at home. He can write, and speak, and cooperate for the attainment of his rights and the redress of his wrongs.[1]

CAUSES OF THE IRISH FAMINE

The Irish famine, which lasted from 1845 to 1851, was a pivotal turning point in Irish history. Both the famine and its legacy had an extraordinary impact on the Irish economy, and, because of the ensuing wave of Irish emigration, produced major changes in the diaspora abroad.[2] The original catalyst for the famine was a fungal disease within the potato, a crop that many of the poorer Irish had become reliant upon. The effects of the potato blight, while devastating enough, were exacerbated by long-standing structural problems within Irish agriculture, land ownership and government. In essence, too many people were dependent on a single crop, and farmers having to subside on very small plots of land exaggerated the risks of this reliance on potatoes. That said, the famine was an unforeseen disaster which neither Irish nor British civic leaders were equipped to tackle. The British government's response to the blight was inadequate: various public works and food importation schemes were attempted, but with poor planning and co-ordination such schemes were abject failures. Various charitable bodies in Britain and North America sent food and money to Ireland for famine relief, but they could not make an impact, given the scale of the catastrophe. In addition, infectious diseases now spread rapidly across Ireland, which devastated people who were undernourished and, in many cases, starving. The inadequacy of outside responses to the famine, coupled with its sheer size and longevity, resulted in terrible loss of life. It has been conservatively estimated that in the decade after 1845 some 1.5 million Irish people died from starvation and disease, while over 2 million more emigrated.

The memory of the famine exerted a powerful influence on Irish political life, both at home and among the diaspora. First-hand reports of the tragedy appeared the world over, recorded by diarists and travellers, while emigrants carried their own stories of hardship to new lands. Many Irish people blamed the British for the famine. They pointed to the weakness of the government response to the famine and its consequence for Irish people. They raised the issue of land ownership in Ireland, which the British government had failed to address adequately, and which was seen as a major factor in the virulence of the famine. Most distressingly for many of the Irish, and one of the most enduringly powerful images of the famine, was the series of evictions that became common in Ireland in the decade from 1845. It has been estimated that as many as half a million tenant farmers who fell behind with their rent, principally because of the failure of their crop and the collapse of seasonal employment, were forcibly evicted by agents of the landowners. Tales and images of agents, assisted by a British police force, acting in many cases for absentee landlords in England, contributed to a widespread belief that the famine and its suffering were a deliberate strategy on the part of the British government. Such apportioning of blame, while simplistic, was understandable in circumstances of distress. There were, indeed, precedents which cast doubt on British motives in Ireland, from the Anglo-Norman invasion to the reign of terror under Oliver Cromwell. Since the time of the famine there have been potent debates among political observers and historians as to the causes of this catastrophe. Two key divisions have emerged: the first supports an interpretation that the famine was an act of British genocide, the second points to long-term structural causes for the mid-nineteenth-century hunger.[3] A legacy of the famine, therefore, has been its stimulus to Irish separatist politics, or, at the very least, claims that the Irish ought to be self-governing. How, then, was the observance of St Patrick's Day affected by the famine? And how were the famine and its dire consequences depicted during subsequent Patrician parades?

THE FAMINE IRISH: 1845–60

St Patrick's Day in Ireland during the period 1845–60 is difficult to reconstruct. There has been an understandable focus by historians on the tragedy of the famine and its economic and social effects. The study of popular culture or leisure time in this era has, therefore, received little attention from scholars. There are also problems pursuing such an inquiry: newspapers, diaries and memoirs focus almost solely on the impact of the famine. Press reports of the time, if they mentioned St Patrick's Day at all, did so in recognition of its traditional place in the calendar; there was, understandably, little to celebrate on 17 March and few resources by which to do so. In 1846, neither the *Cork Examiner* nor the *Dublin Evening Post* mentioned St Patrick's Day, suggesting that public forms of observance had ceased, or, in view of the famine, were judged too trivial to report.

That said, the uneven manner in which the famine affected Irish society is apparent by the fact of St Patrick's Day festivities in some parts of Ireland. In Drogheda, for example, located roughly midway between Belfast and Dublin, the town's customary St Patrick's Race Day was staged in 1846, with Dublin and Drogheda Railways offering two shilling third-class return tickets specially for the meeting.[4] This demonstrates, albeit in a small way, that the effects of the famine varied considerably, and that in some areas of Ireland social customs continued without obvious signs that a tragedy was unfolding elsewhere. The major Irish upper-class celebration of St Patrick's Day was Dublin Castle's Ball. This was a prestigious event open only to Irish 'high' society, which in this case meant the aristocratic bureaucrats who presided over Ireland from the confines of the Castle. During the years of the famine the Castle Ball continued as per usual, which was important symbolically because 'the elegance and implicit wealth' of the formalities 'suggested that all was well with the ruling class in Ireland'.[5] Ireland's national festival would be celebrated in style, despite local circumstances, with its Dublin-centred 'loyal leadership . . . represented as being on a par with social high life in England'.[6]

St Patrick's Day had occasionally been a forum for social protest prior to the famine, but strong emotions aroused by the effects of starvation and mass emigration, together with the crystallization of nationalist sentiment, engendered a situation where 17 March became a regular focus for claims about a separatist Irish identity. On St Patrick's Day, 1846, two ships, the *Thatis* and the *Borneo*, harboured in Limerick, illegally hoisted the green flag of Ireland in 'honour of the national festival'. The flags were quickly removed on the orders of the British war steamer, the *Pinto*, but not before 'the feelings of the multitude' watching and cheering the flag from the harbour wall, 'were desperately excited'.[7] This demonstration, while illegal, was ultimately an unimportant affair, but it did demonstrate how nationalist feelings could find a voice on 17 March. During the 1850s, the expression of such sentiments became far more vocal, and, for British authorities in Ireland, increasingly threatening. This related, largely, to the vexed issue of land ownership in Ireland. In the wake of the famine, the Tenant Right Movement emerged to champion the cause of the tenant and to campaign against high rents, insecure tenure of land and summary eviction. The movement held its key public meetings on St Patrick's Day: it was an occasion on which many people were granted a holiday by their employers in honour of the day's religious significance, so were free to attend. On St Patrick's Day in 1850 the Tenant Right Movement staged mass meetings in Donhill, Co. Tipperary and Castlecomber, Co. Kilkenny, which attracted crowds of some 30,000 and 20,000 people respectively.[8] Generally, though, dislocation caused by famine and emigration meant that St Patrick's Day was not, at this stage, an important vehicle for major public gatherings — whether in celebration or protest.

THE GROWING IRISH DIASPORA: 1845–60

Problems caused by the famine – poverty, death and mass emigration – prompted a search for solutions. This included, more than ever, demands that the Irish be in control of their own destiny instead of being accountable to British rule under the Act of Union. In this context nationalism became a major force in Irish political culture, and was expressed in movements like the Young Irelanders and the Fenians. Such separatist ideology was reflected among the Irish abroad by the Fenians and by those Irish gatherings that paid homage to political figures like Wolfe Tone and Daniel O'Connell. This concern with the 'Irish question' in the diaspora drew attention to political links with the homeland each St Patrick's Day. Yet the festivities associated with 17 March usually focused much more on the place of the Irish community in a 'new' land. On St Patrick's Day in North America, parades featured distinctive Irish symbols and well-known Irish music, which reminded spectators of the 'uniqueness' of this growing ethnic community. It was also a political statement in that marchers were expressing the 'legitimacy' of the Irish stake in host nations – which was all the more important given that, upon arrival, the famine Irish had often been treated with disdain. Subsequent feelings of exclusion or marginalization encouraged Irish immigrants to develop social networks based on ethnic background (or a combination of ethnicity and religious affiliation). Traditional symbols, songs and stories of the Irish homeland were, in that sense, revisited with clan-like intensity on 17 March.

That said, the use of St Patrick's Day to cultivate an Irish sense of belonging in the midst of a host community is only one side of the emigrant story. While there is abundant evidence that migrants developed self-conscious Irish affiliations, expressed in part by St Patrick's Day celebrations, other members of the Irish diaspora 'quickly dropped out of ethnic networks, or exploited them only as a transitory tool for self-advancement'.[9] For many Irish migrants, St Patrick's Day was a once-a-year symbol of their place within a host society and a reminder of their links with 'home', but the decision of some Irish expatriates to reject such ties should not be overlooked. The story of the 'active' Irish diaspora can be traced through its own societies, clubs, rituals and churches that represented the public face of collective Irishness. But the story of Irish migrants or their descendants who withdrew from ethnic networks, or distanced themselves completely, is far more difficult to uncover.

ST PATRICK'S DAY IN BRITAIN: 1845–60

In Britain the celebration of St Patrick's Day during the famine was a muted affair. The Irish who had recently migrated tried to find factory work in mill towns, or else travelled across the country following the ever-diminishing supply of seasonal work.[10] Many of the Irish who travelled to Britain found their first homes among their fellow Irish in the back streets and ghettos of industrial towns. Trapped as they were in such appalling conditions, the Irish were seen by many of the host population as problematic – lawless, drunken and carriers of disease. Such anti-Irish feeling was widespread in the immediate post-famine years, and often found expression on St Patrick's Day when the Irish-Catholic community came under attack from opponents – most notably the Orange Order. In 1839, for example, the *Liverpool Standard* stated that:

> if the 'Papists' were allowed to parade through the town on St Patrick's Day ... all we can say is that the public authorities of the town are willing to be considered conniving at treason and the Protestant inhabitants of the town have consented to place their necks under the yoke of Popish tyranny.[11]

By the mid-1840s the local press had a new tack; it criticized St Patrick's Day parades as being an unwelcome excess in a time of famine. This view was, to some degree, shared by Catholic clergy, who advised against festivities during a time of crisis in the homeland. In March 1848 the *Liverpool Mercury* reported, acrimoniously:

> St Patrick's Day was celebrated on Wednesday last by a public procession – at a time when a large number of the people of Ireland are plunged into the deepest distress by poverty, famine and fever, and when the resources of the benevolent people of England and America are taxed to the utmost in endeavouring to mitigate ... this dreadful state of things. Hundreds of pounds, which could have otherwise been so desireably [sic] appropriated, have been wasted in the geegaw tomfooleries of a procession.

The celebration of St Patrick's Day by the Irish in Britain took two main forms during the famine years: first, self-indulgent enjoyment; second, the promotion of Irish nationalism. For working-class Irish immigrants, located in the many Irish districts of British cities and reliant on manual labour for a living, St Patrick's Day was an opportunity for celebration centred on drink and convivial self-indulgence.[12] Such revelry was frowned upon by the Catholic Church, which saw them as destructive to the faith and moral fibre of the Irish. British authorities were also concerned that St Patrick's Day might be used as a rallying point for Irish nationalism. In the years of heightened Fenian activity – most notably 1848, 1867 and 1868 – British authorities were particularly interested in public gatherings of the Irish, so watched them vigilantly for signs of trouble. Liverpool was a particular focus because it had a large Irish population.[13] Police were so concerned that the city's St Patrick's Day parade might lead to violence and insurrection, that 3,455 'special constables' were sworn in to police the 1848 parade. Fears of public disorder were also expressed by Liverpool's Irish groups: the Catholic Church appealed to its flock to stay away from the parade, while Irish leaders within the labour movement dissuaded their members from marching. Adding fuel to the fire were worrying 'intelligence' reports received by Liverpool police: Dublin Castle informed them that Irish dissidents were planning to set fire to both Liverpool and Manchester on St Patrick's Day. Another informant from Glasgow warned authorities that 17 March would be used for the launch of a rebellion in Ireland, coinciding with similar moves by the Irish in Liverpool, Manchester and Glasgow. Despite these apocalyptic warnings, St Patrick's Day 1848 passed off more quietly than usual.[14] Despite occasional political threats associated with the Irish on St Patrick's Day, intemperance and disorder were annual issues that concerned British police on 17 March. The famine and its terrible impact on Ireland were reported widely and often compassionately in British newspapers, this helping to create local sympathy for immigrant Irish. Such humanitarian feelings were, however, always tempered by assumptions about the 'drunken' and 'sedentary' Irish which had long been reflected in cartoons and commentary about the Irish appearing in newspapers and magazines.[15]

St Patrick's Day celebrations were muted affairs during the decade after the famine. Although there had been a huge influx of Irish migrants into Britain, the nature of the diaspora, and the general condition of the Irish, were markedly different to that which traversed the Atlantic. Britain was geographically closer to Ireland, and so tended to attract those who were unable to afford the more expensive, though possibly more fruitful, journey to North America. Anti-Irish prejudice had long been a feature of British society; an unprecedented volume of Irish immigrants now exacerbated such feelings. This movement of people across the Irish Sea exaggerated wider fears of imported 'Irish' diseases, proselytizing Catholics, and expectations of 'Irish' drunken and lawless behaviour. The Irish, even when their numbers were boosted by famine emigration, were not in a position to celebrate St Patrick's Day in large-scale public demonstrations such as parades. Hence Patrician celebrations in this period were very low-key affairs, surrounded by the air of the genteel. They were non-threatening, and in many ways gatherings subservient to the ideal of assimilation within British life. The St Patrick's Day dinner held at the Theatre Royal in Liverpool in 1846,[16] and the gathering of the Catholic Literary Society in Birkenhead in 1854 to celebrate the 'national festival' and enjoy 'excellent tea ... enlivened by Mr Monkhouse's band',[17] both demonstrate the low-key nature of St Patrick's Day in Britain during the famine and the years immediately after.[18]

Concurrently, Irish organizations, such as the Hibernians, had become influential within migrant communities, particularly in terms of kinship networks and social welfare. Their mentoring role included increased influence over the nature of St Patrick's Day celebrations in Britain. Encouraged by the Church, which supported schemes to draw people away from drunken revelry, Irish societies organized various social activities. Balls and banquets were key events, featuring traditional displays of Irish-Gaelic culture, including, singing, music and dance. These events were held in 'most centres of Irish settlement – whether in the archetypal cities of Glasgow or Liverpool or in the smaller outposts such as Whitehaven'.[19] This suggested a move away from public displays, such as parades, on St Patrick's Day.)not neccisarily.

ST PATRICK'S DAY IN AMERICA: 1845–60

By the early 1840s, many working-class Irish Americans had established respectable roles in 'mainstream' society, most notably through jobs in the police force, fire department and the railways. The Irish-American elite had also made its presence felt in municipal government and small business. All this created a gradual self-confidence among Irish Americans that was reflected, in part, by the rising significance of St Patrick's Day. The Irish were, by this time, numerically significant in the United States, but the famine accelerated the Irish presence way beyond expectations. For resident Irish Americans, the mass arrival of impoverished immigrants from Ireland during the late 1840s and 1850s eroded their localized sense of progress in the host community. The Irish were, yet again, stereotyped as economically backward and socially dysfunctional. Despite this fall from grace, there was a determination by many Irish Americans to declare their 'rightful place' in a so-called free society. Henceforth, the commemoration of St Patrick's Day became a once-a-year vehicle for the Irish to symbolically claim their 'stake' in the United States, and to declare their allegiance to a homeland vividly remembered.

In Boston in 1841, the first populist Patrician parade was staged. This public assembly was a response to the social elitism of Irish-American organizations, such as the Charitable Irish Society of Boston, which assembled to dine and honour the Saint in self-glorifying isolation. The increasingly large number of Irish residents in Boston meant that 'no banquet room was broad enough to comprehend all the sons of Eire, even had they the price of the dinner'.[20] The Shamrock Society was formed as a defiantly inclusive alternative for the Boston Irish. This group was soon influential, with membership rising strongly from the time of its foundation in 1830. Here emerged a new commitment to celebrate St Patrick's Day in public and, most notably, by the staging of a street parade in Boston – the first of which, in 1841, involved 2,000 marchers. St Patrick's Day parades in both Boston and New York were, however, still relatively minor affairs during the 1840s. They tended to be organized around specific urban neighbourhoods and were the work of local, and thus comparatively small-scale, Irish-American societies. By 1849, the New York parade, while still modest in size, was at least an accepted fixture on the city's calendar. The *New York*

Herald reported that the occasion would be celebrated 'in the usual manner by the various Irish societies in the city ... [who] will march in procession through Prince Street, Bowery, Third avenue, Twenty-third street, Eight avenue, Hudson street, Broadway, Chambers and other streets'.[21]

The rise of parades notwithstanding, the observance of St Patrick's Day in the United States was otherwise constrained during the famine years. In 1847 the Charitable Irish Society of Boston elected not to hold its annual St Patrick's dinner, deeming that expenses associated with this event 'be applied to the relief of the suffering'.[22] In that spirit, US$56 was collected and dispatched to Ireland. In the same year, Irish-American societies and organizations involved in the New York parade agreed to forego their annual dinner, thereby sending money to Ireland for famine relief. Reports of the suffering in Ireland had, by 1847, been widely circulated in the American press, and these stories were given greater impact by the arrival of masses of undernourished immigrants at Ellis Island. As a result of a rising awareness among Irish Americans about the scale of the famine and its dire effects, charitable funds were raised on St Patrick's Day across America, with the Hibernian Burial Benevolent Society donating over US$1,500 towards famine relief in Ireland.[23] The American experience of St Patrick's Day during the famine years suggests that while 17 March was important for promoting an Irish identity within America, it was also a celebration that was expendable. More credibility could be gained, and vital charitable work carried out, if parades and other costly exercises were cancelled.

The growing number of Irish in America affected both the scale and nature of St Patrick's Day observances. The sheer volume of immigrants, though not welcomed by all sections of the host society, gave the Irish constituency within America a numerical boost. The Irish became a significant population group in major cities such as New York, Boston and Chicago, and were becoming prominent elsewhere, such as in Savannah and New Orleans. The St Patrick's Day parade became an annual barometer of how potentially powerful (or at least numerous) Irish Americans were in such places. The parades also allowed Irish Americans to project a set of beliefs and aspirations to both their cohorts and other Americans generally. In that regard, a key aim of Patrician processions, particularly in the wake of the 1848 rebellion in Ireland, was not simply to celebrate Ireland and the place of the Irish in America, but to affirm a dual sense of loyalty to both homeland and adopted society. Patriotism of this kind intended to win the confidence of Anglo-Protestant Americans who found the growing local Irish presence both threatening and unnerving. These themes were apparent during the 1852 St Patrick's Day parade in New York:

This delight in display, a reminder of the recruiting drives of 1848 with their fife and drum bands, pikes and tricolours, was soon to be formalized in annual procession, on the one day of the year when Irish

35

Americans took control of public ceremonial space. The pattern was established in 1852: at the first massed St Patrick's Day procession in New York, pride of place went to the military companies, followed by benevolent, temperance, burial and other forms of Irish associational culture, with the women in carriages bringing up the rear.[24]

That said, the sheer weight of Irish numbers in major American cities, reflected in their mass assembly on St Patrick's Day, was also a show of latent force. The parade aimed to impress upon politicians seeking re-election that the Irish were now a powerful interest group that could not be ignored. Irish-American civic leaders quickly realized that if their urban ethnic population could be brought together politically, socially and culturally, they might form a significant voting bloc within the body politic. Influential members of the Irish-American community, such as newspaper editors, entrepreneurs and politicians, envisaged a shared 'Irish-American perspective' on key issues of the day. In that regard, 'the annual St Patrick's Day parade became a visible symbol of the bonds of Irish communal solidarity'; it was the one day of the year when 'the Irish took over the streets of New York and announced to its non-Irish residents that they were a force to be contended with'.[25] The symbolic cohesion of the parade was evident by the disparate range of organizations that took part. From the late 1840s, marchers included the Operative Masons, the Quarrymen's United Protective Society, the Labourer's United Benevolent Society, and fourteen other labour organizations. This social mix, dominated by the working classes, provided clear evidence of the broad class appeal of the Irish cause.[26]

The St Patrick's Day parade in New York, which had been driven by the enthusiasm of the Labourer's United Benevolent Association, came under the organizational control of an umbrella group from 1851. The newly formed Convention of Irish Societies was professional in outlook, meeting every Friday throughout the year to plan and stage the parade; the organization of the 17 March street procession was, indeed, the sole function of this body. Centralization of the parade management meant that localized, neighbourhood marches were now less likely, with interested parties invited to parade in unison down Fifth Avenue. A single march of impressive scale and colour was likely to capture more public attention than a series of smaller neighbourhood parades on St Patrick's Day. The profile of the Fifth Avenue parade was also heightened by the appointment of a 'grand marshal' to head the march. The first of these was Captain Patrick Kerrigan, a coal merchant and commander of the civilian cavalry unit of the Irish Dragoons. According to a report in the *New York Times*, the parade he led was viewed by a large crowd 'with hearts throbbing and eyes delighted, having their own native land brought so vividly before their memory'.[27]

With improved organization the modern St Patrick's Day parade was becoming an important occasion for many Irish Americans; this was reflected in an increased number of marching groups and a sizeable crowd presence each year. As the spectacle and hype of the parade grew, so greater publicity followed in the daily press; St Patrick's Day was emerging as a social 'event' in New York City. This transformation was reflected, as much as anything, by the active involvement of non-Irish politicians on St Patrick's Day; they paid attention to the parade so as to ingratiate themselves with their Irish constituency. In order to win Irish-American votes, they 'attended diligently to immigrant sensitivities; green flags and much bombast flew from the steps of Tammany Hall on St Patrick's Day'.[28] By 1853, the annual parade included enough marchers to bring traffic in New York to a standstill; this sign of growing ethnic presence and power could not have been lost on those of an anti-Irish and anti-Catholic persuasion. In the same year, the city's mayor and council elected to review the parade from a specially constructed stand. This established a precedent for subsequent years, elevating further the significance of Irish Americans and their annual parade in New York City.[29]

The year 1853 was also significant in that the Ancient Order of Hibernians (AOH) took its place in the parade for the first time. This group was supported by a large local membership, and its leadership strove for prominence in the Irish-American community. Indeed, by the end of the 1850s the AOH dominated the organization of the New York parade, and has controlled it ever since. The modern organization of the AOH again raised the profile of St Patrick's Day: the group tapped into its growing national network of affiliated Irish clubs, prompting a marked upturn in the number of marchers on St Patrick's Day. By 1860, the New York parade included over 10,000 marchers, a number bolstered by the AOH's invitation to Irish groups outside the city to join in the procession. Another successful initiative was the welcome of various expatriate Irish County societies in the festivities; the first of these, the County Monaghan Social Club, marched in 1860.[30] A major impetus for the rise of the AOH, and the gathering together of the Irish societies in one parade was, in part, a reaction to the anti-Irish campaigns of the nativist movement. The amalgamated Irish parade, in the face of nativist concerns about the Irish presence, meant that the parade became 'an oppositional event meant to demonstrate not only the strength and unity of Irish Catholics, but also the determination of Irish Catholics to be accepted as American'.[31]

The increased organizational management of the New York parade during the 1850s, and its move from a localized and ad hoc event to central control by a committee, certainly raised the profile of the event annually. It was now, for better or worse, more of a stage-managed performance. The parade followed an understood format, making it familiar and accessible to those who watched. Because it was so recognizable it was also potentially powerful. The crowds expected the parade to impress and entertain them; in meeting these expectations the performers were also able to convey messages about their self-declared significance in a host society, and their proud connection with an Irish homeland. The New York parade, which included marchers from across the nation, became an annual performance and spectacle of the Irish presence in America. It offered the 'irresistible drama that only massed marchers could provide', and it 'employed that drama to underscore the celebration's major themes',[32] such as the strength of labour, the success of the Irish in America and the force of Irish nationalism.

St Patrick's Day parades were now appearing across America, involving a diverse cross-section of Irish-American society. In Jacksonville, for example, St Patrick's Day celebrations in the 1850s and 1860s were organized and staged by various Irish railroad and roadwork gangs. These groups were rarely in the same place because of their labour commitments, and so were often considered itinerant, but the Jacksonville Irish still managed to assemble on St Patrick's Day. The 17 March parade, held under the joint auspices of the Hibernian Temperance and Benevolent Society and the Catholic Men's Association, was the high point of the year for the local Irish. With its messages of charity and abstinence, the procession did much to boost the image of Irish Catholics among the prohibitionist Protestant community.[33]

OBSERVANCE OF ST PATRICK'S DAY IN CANADA: *c.*1845–60

A monument at Gross Isle, near Quebec City, was erected in 1909 to memorialize loss of life among Irish immigrants to Canada during the famine exodus.[34] Gross Isle was established as a quarantine station during a cholera epidemic in 1832; by the mid-1840s it was receiving thousands of starving and sick Irish families who disembarked from passenger ships to the necessary isolation afforded by Gross Isle wharf. During 1847–8, as the inscription on the Gross Isle monument explained sixty years later, 'thousands of Irish emigrants ... ended here their sorrowful pilgrimage'.[35] Those famine Irish who survived tended to live on the fringes of urban centres, as in Toronto's so-called 'Cabbagetown', where numerous poor Irish arrivals took up residence in shanty dwellings. There was a noticeable influx of Irish Catholics into the Toronto region during the 1840s and 1850s, so much so that by 1861 more than 25 per cent of the city's population was, according to census data, of Irish birth or descent and self-identified as Catholic. This represented something of an ethno-religious transformation: before the intake of famine immigrants to Toronto, the city was referred to widely as the 'Belfast of Canada'. The Irish had long been the largest English-speaking group in Toronto; historically, the vast bulk of that ethnic community had also been Protestant.[36] How, then, did such demographic changes affect the observance of St Patrick's Day in Toronto, and, for that matter, the other Canadian cities in our study, Montreal and Quebec?

In 1846, westward expansion of the United States brought war with the British colonies over the territory of Oregon. Irish Canadians had served the empire with distinction in previous conflicts; it was assumed they would do so again. Sir Richard Bonnycastle, a keen loyalist observer, was in no doubt, regardless of the rising proportion of Irish Catholics. His memoirs, published in 1849, suggested a common commitment to Canada among all the Irish:

> As a proof of the loyalty of the Canadians . . . the press is teeming with calls to the volunteers and militia to sustain Britain in the Oregon war . . . Whilst I am writing, the Hibernian Society, in an immense Roman Catholic procession, passes by. There are four banners. The first is St Patrick, the second Queen Victoria, the third Father Mathew, the fourth the glorious Union flag . . . it is the 17th of March, St Patrick's Day, and the band plays God save the Queen!.[37]

Just as significantly, Bonnycastle's impressions of Protestant–Catholic relations in Canada were generally favourable, and he referred to St Patrick's Day as evidence of this peaceful co-existence. He recalled:

> public demonstrations upon St Patrick's Day at Montreal, Kingston, and Toronto, where the two parties, Protestant and Catholic, exhibited no party emblems, no flags but loyal ones, and where the ancient enmity between the rival houses of Capulet and Montague, the Green and the Orange, appeared to have vanished.[38]

Bonnycastle's assessment overlooked the potential for sectarian enmity in Canada: the rising number of post-famine Irish Catholics was of concern to local Protestants – perhaps a third of Protestant adult males were members of the Orange Order by the mid-nineteenth century.[39] The Orangemen were particularly active in Toronto where the lodge's 'reputation was replete . . . with the lore of faction fights and sectarian skirmishes on either 12 July or 17 March'.[40] It was, however, hardly the case that one-third of Orangemen were openly fighting Catholic neighbours on these dates.[41] Large-scale violence was unusual; ritualized provocation and intimidation tended to be the work of organized, militant minorities, whether Protestant or Catholic. During the early 1850s there was, indeed, little sign of sectarian disturbances on St Patrick's Day in Toronto.

The saint's day had, however, became religiously partisan in that the Catholic Church had assumed organization control over key aspects of Toronto's Patrician festivities. The Irish national day was about to become a celebration of Catholicism in a Protestant-dominated city: the commemorations were 'led by Church-sponsored societies, processions to the Cathedral now became a regular feature and the clergy assumed a prominent role throughout'.[42] Michael Cotterell concludes that Toronto's St Patrick's Day was thus transformed 'into an essentially religious event, [so as] to establish Catholicism as the primary identity of Irish immigrants and thereby strengthen clerical authority'.[43] However, Cotterell also points out that this type of hierarchical control 'frustrated the desire for leadership and initiative among the Irish-Catholic laity'. Because of that, he argues, Irish nationalism became all the more important in Toronto because 'it provided one of the few rationales for lay initiative independent of the clergy'.[44] This soon had implications for the staging of St Patrick's Day: in 1855 the Catholic Young Men's St Patrick's Association was installed as principal organizer of Toronto's Patrician celebrations, and under its control 'the event changed dramatically'. As Cotterell explains:

> Parades, which had previously been merely a prelude to the mass, now increased in size and colour to become major public demonstrations. In 1857, over one thousand people, their faces animated by 'a sacred patriotic fire', marched behind four hundred members of the Young Men's St Patrick's Association. Religious hymns were replaced by popular tunes and secular emblems, such as shamrocks, harps and wolfhounds were now more prominent than Catholic icons ... Clerically-induced temperance gave way to alcoholic good cheer, and instead of expressions of loyalty and three cheers for the Queen, which had previously characterized the proceedings, mildly anglophobic speeches were now heard.[45]

Predictably, the Orange Order was mortified by this radicalization of 17 March as Irish nationalist. Angry verbal exchanges ensued in the following two years, but St Patrick's Day of 1858 was particularly acrimonious. Cotterell reports that 'Orange attempts to disrupt the parade resulted in widespread violence during which one Catholic was fatally stabbed with a pitchfork.'[46] With little confidence in the Toronto police or the rule of law, Irish-Catholic leaders, both clerical and lay, met in crisis talks. They concluded that the most prudent course of action would be to postpone the parade indefinitely. They had effectively caved in to the British-Protestant dominant order instead of reclaiming their right to parade on 17 March.[47] Yet, as we see in Chapter 3, this was not the end of the story; a group of Toronto's Irish Catholics were soon planning to take to the streets in a show of defiance.

St Patrick's Day celebrations in the largely Catholic and French-speaking cities of Montreal and Quebec were, by comparison, amicable. The Société Saint-Jean-Baptiste, which was formed in 1842, took part in Quebec's St Patrick's Day parade along with English and Scottish national societies. The Frenchmen often provided the marching band for a procession that was now well organized and striking as a spectacle. The *Quebec Mercury* reported that 'at least 2,500 persons were assembled and marched' in the 1848 parade.[48] The only hint of conflict arose within the Irish community itself: the Friendly Sons of St Patrick was formed in 1848 as a rival to the existing St Patrick's Society, so by 1849 the annual parade featured two national societies 'vying with each other' for precedence.[49] By chance 17 March 1850 fell on Passion Sunday: it was usual to delay St Patrick's festivities if they fell on a Sunday, but in this case 'it was decided to forego the procession and other festivities altogether in favour of a charitable donation'.[50] The famine years had encouraged benevolence on St Patrick's Day; in this case it was also politically expedient in that it avoided a repetition of factionalism on 17 March. The lacuna was beneficial: cool heads prevailed so that by 1852 the Friendly Sons had come to terms with the St Patrick's Society – even agreeing to join their fold. The result was an emphatic display of Irish unity in Quebec; and, more than that, a demonstration of Irish civic importance in a multi-ethnic society. The parade route was festooned with sprigs of greenery and the flags of the marching groups, each of whom processed through numerous 'arches of evergreen' to tunes played by the Société Saint-Jean-Baptiste band. The cavalcade paused at pre-arranged sites along the route to enable marchers to pay tribute to the diverse national groups that constituted the city. For example, at St Andrew's School the parade paused to salute the St Andrew's Society, with the band playing 'Auld Lang Syne'; further along another pause recognized the English and French societies; then the band played 'Vive le Canadienne' before the city's French-Canadian mayor. Somewhere in all of this was St Patrick. To give the Société Saint-Jean-Baptiste band its due, it performed several renditions of the popular air 'St Patrick's Day', as well as 'Exile of Erin' and 'The Boys of Kilkenny'.[51] Unlike Quebec's inaugural Patrician celebration of 1765 the French now had a place – even a voice – on St Patrick's Day in the mid-nineteenth century.

On St Patrick's Day, 1847, the St Patrick's Church of Montreal was officially opened.[52] It was now the epicentre of Christian worship for local Irish Catholics. With a Catholic church of their very own, Montreal's Irish experienced a greater sense of religious solidarity. Previously, they were Catholics among French, German and other national congregations. They were now demonstrably Irish Catholic. The construction of St Patrick's church happened to coincide with the famine intake of Irish to Montreal, many of whom were also Catholic. They arrived at a time when local Irish Catholics were fully establishing themselves as a distinctive community, the newly erected church being the most visible sign of that development. There was an increasingly assertive aspect to this collective sense of self; Irish Catholics were now emerging as a constituency that was either distant or removed from local Irish Protestants. Evidence for this transformation can be found in the organization and observance of the day that was meant to bring all the Irish together – St Patrick's Day.

In the mid-1840s there was little sign of ethno-religious separatism among Montreal's Irish. The *Gazette* reported that St Patrick's Day of 1845 'was duly commemorated by those of Irish origin resident in Montreal'.[53] As usual, the St Patrick's Society was key organizer, though on this occasion with support from the Catholic Total Abstinence Society. Eleven years later the St Patrick's Society was split along Catholic–Protestant lines, and the anniversary of the Irish patron saint was beset with sectarian tensions. Kevin James, in his study of the associational culture of the St Patrick's Society, concludes that the partition of the group was 'the result of a process of confessionalisation that became increasingly acute in the 1850s'.[54] By that time Montreal's Irish Catholics 'had their own parish, and with it, a locus for communal activities, their own meeting hall and annual bazaar, their own army regiments and fire companies, even their own banks'.[55] This development was of concern to the *Gazette*; it feared ethnic separatism in what was already a multi-ethnic city, and so spoke in favour of unity under the banner of Canadian nationalism:

It is as much to be desired here as in the United States, that in so far as possible, all races should become blended and fused so as to form one people – that we should all remember we are Canadians alike, and not set up our distinctive national origins as reasons for keeping us apart.[56]

The *Gazette* was hardly in a position to insist that the French, the English, or the Irish of Montreal abandon differences of language, history and culture. But it was concerned that social organizations like the fire department, banks and the militia corps were now being established along exclusively Irish-Catholic lines. To the *Gazette*, this risked pushing people apart rather than bringing them together.[57]

The move towards Catholic privatism in various spheres was also felt in the St Patrick's Society of Montreal itself. This association had long been open to all Irishmen, whatever their religion, although the largely Protestant leadership of the 1830s had the luxury of power by virtue of a greater number of members. The swelling of Catholic ranks in the early 1850s was a precursor to a changing balance of power in the St Patrick's Society, but it need not have been a rationale for sectarianism. However, in a political climate of Irish-Catholic wariness about militant Orangeism and the nativism of the Know Nothing movement, clerical assertiveness through privatism and separatism was an understandable, if socially destabilizing, strategy. In terms of the St Patrick's Society, Catholics set about reshaping the association to better represent their religious interests. For some members, denominational concerns had no place in what was a national rather than religious body. Protestants, predictably, were outraged, fearing a Catholic take-over of the association. In 1853, a member of the St Andrew's Society complained that his group's office bearers were placed in an 'embarrassed position' when attending the annual dinner of the St Patrick's Society. The issue, he explained to the Irish association, was that the assembly had been asked to drink the 'health of the Pope'. Implicit in this complaint was that the pontiff was a religious, rather than national figure, and the St Patrick's Society was supposed to be non-denominational. In reply, the president of the St Patrick's Society 'explained that the health of the Pope was proposed "after the Queen"'; implicit in this statement was that Queen Victoria, while a national figure, was de facto head of the Church of England. The president concluded with an unambiguous reference to the religious status of the St Patrick's Society: 'as a Catholic Society they drank the health of the Pope in a similar manner to what the St Andrew's Society drank that of the "Kirk [Church] of Scotland"'. This was an astute response, for the other English-speaking societies were all Protestant dominated – even if Catholics were not barred from membership – and Great Britain herself was a Protestant and largely anti-Catholic group of nations. However, the St Patrick's Society of Montreal was by now describing itself *explicitly* as a Catholic organization. This was a far cry from the assocation's early years when, although the membership was predominantly Protestant, the Roman Catholic Archbishop of Kingston was appointed an honorary member in 1839.[58]

The position of Protestants within the St Patrick's Society had become untenable. On 28 March 1856 they were, indeed, virtually obliged to leave when the Young Men's St Patrick's Association – a staunchly Catholic body – merged with the existing St Patrick's Society to form a 'new' organization under the same name of the former parent body. The local Catholic newspaper *True Witness* welcomed 'the progress of this truly Catholic and therefore – in the noblest sense of the word – truly National Society'.[59] The paper defended its position by emphasizing that 'St Patrick himself was a Catholic', and since he partook of bread and wine according to Roman Catholic custom, he was 'according to the teachings of Protestantism, an idolator'.[60] *True Witness* argued further that it was 'ridiculous on the part of Protestants to seek admission to a Saint Patrick's Society – a society designated by the name of a Popish Saint'. The paper concluded that: 'A "St Patrick's Society" is not only a national, but a religious, Society – or why the name of St Patrick?'; and, 'If Irish Protestants want to form themselves into a Society they are welcome to do so; but let it be under a proper designation ... Besides, have not the Irish Protestants Orange Societies already?'[61] The writing was on the wall, let alone in the paper, despite protests from Protestant members of the St Patrick's Society. As this Irish national association reconstituted itself under Catholic clerical patronage, the 'expelled' Protestant members formed their own sectional body, the Irish Protestant Benevolent Society. Since the early nineteenth century national societies in Montreal had dined annually at the table of their counterparts, thereby honouring another group's patron saint. The partition of the St Patrick's Society was, however, indicative of sectarian tensions starting to dominate associational culture. By 1864 this transformation seemed complete: the St Andrew's, St George's and Irish Protestant Benevolent Societies set about establishing a 'United Protestant Immigrants' Home'.[62]

ST PATRICK'S DAY IN AUSTRALIA: 1845–60

For colonists who sought to create a new Britannia in the Antipodes, the continuing flow of convicts to Australia made the evolution of a 'good' society problematic. After protracted debate between 1849 and 1851, the British government accepted local demands that transportation to eastern Australia be discontinued from 1852.[63] Subsequently, by the late 1850s, the colonies were granted responsible government under the auspices of empire.[64] The colonies also grew in stature because of the discovery of gold in eastern Australia in the early 1850s; this brought new wealth to the settlers, as well as a flurry of immigrant speculators, the vast majority of whom were Chinese.[65] The decade prior to this, of course, had seen famine in Ireland and the departure of hundreds of emigrant ships abroad. It is therefore commonly assumed that this was the era in which large-scale movement of Irish people to Australia began. But the vast majority of Irish passenger vessels made their way to North America during the 1840s, with just 2 per cent of all Irish emigrants (or a total of 23,000) making the much longer journey to Australia.[66] By comparison, during the 1850s gold rush decade, five times that many Irish people (or 8 per cent of the total volume of Irish emigrants during that period) travelled to Australia. In post-famine Ireland most emigrants received assisted passage to the Antipodes, yet a significant minority also came, as had other immigrant groups, as self-funded passengers in search of gold.[67] By the late 1850s, Irish-born settlers and locally-born descendants of Irish colonists constituted around 25–30 per cent of the population of New South Wales, and some 20–25 per cent of the population of Victoria.[68] Our interest, in what follows, is with St Patrick's Day commemorations in the capital cities of these colonies, Sydney and Melbourne, respectively.

The Irish were the second largest ethnic group in Australia after the dominant English, but they were not noticeably tribal either in location or vocation. O'Farrell accepts that there were pockets of major cities with a significant presence of Irish residents, but he argues that 'even in streets blazoning forth Irish allegiance – St Patrick's Lane, Shamrock Alley – there was no Irish monopoly, or endeavour to create one'.[69] Neighbours tended to be fellow workers – a mixed bag of English, Scots, Welsh, Irish and Australian-born. O'Farrell also emphasizes that compared with their Celtic counterparts in the United States, Australia's Irish were 'intensely mobile', often moving in search of seasonal employment opportunities. This told against the formation of Irish ghettos, while it also worked towards Irish interaction with other ethnic groups.[70] Tribalism was, nonetheless, apparent within the Irish community, and both 17 March and 12 July were key settings for its expression by the mid-1840s.

The formation of the St Patrick's Society in Sydney in 1841 prompted the rise of a sibling organization in Melbourne the following year – the St Patrick's Society of Australia Felix.[71] The first Patrician parade in Melbourne was staged in 1843: it involved both Catholics and Protestants, who not only marched but sang together. They separated once the procession paused at the church occupied by Melbourne's inaugural Catholic priest, Patrick Geoghegan. This 'rough little chapel' was nothing to boast about, but Geoghegan was thankful for the assistance of local Protestants when erecting the building. The experience confirmed his already liberal attitude towards devout non-Catholics. Edmund Campion explains that, 'Geoghegan consistently promoted religious toleration. He asserted that everyone had the right to worship according to his conscience: the state could not determine belief.'[72] By 1846, just three years after the ecumenical St Patrick's Day parade had begun, Geoghegan wrote despairingly to the Archbishop of Dublin, informing him of sectarian conflict in Melbourne. Even more worrying for Geoghegan was his personal safety: 'three distinct attempts were made lately on my life', he told the Archbishop.[73] What had taken place in the intervening years to bring about such violence and tension in Melbourne?

In 1843, two Irish societies were formed. The first, as we have seen, was the St Patrick's Society of Australia Felix. The second was the Orange Society, which proposed its own parade for 12 July 1844. However, as Campion writes, 'Catholics would not allow it. They organised a hurling match on the same day and the presence of so many burly men with hurling sticks in their hands cancelled the Orange march.'[74] The St Patrick's Day procession of 1845 went ahead, but again Catholics used the prospect of physical force to dissuade the Orangemen from parading. The 12th of July 1846 was no better for the Orange Society: intimidated against marching they commemorated the anniversary at a local public house, but this soon became a focus for political violence. Ken Inglis informs us that, 'shots were fired into a crowd protesting against Orange banners hung from the windows of a hotel in which the William-worshippers – as Catholics called them – were celebrating their anniversary'.[75] Colonial administrators were appalled: in response, the Legislative Council of NSW passed the 'Party Processions Bill' aimed at curtailing parades of a 'contentious' nature. The bill, which became operational in 1847, applied to both Melbourne and Sydney,[76] though the Irish in the harbour city could be forgiven for being miffed; they had to bear the effects of legislation that had been passed to bring order to the streets of Melbourne.

A St Patrick's Day parade actually went ahead in Sydney in 1847. This led to the intervention of the Attorney-General of NSW, John Plunkett, who wrote to the Secretary of the St Patrick's Society, the Reverend John

McEnroe, asking for an explanation. An exchange of letters followed, each of which was printed in full in the colonial press. Intriguingly, both of the correspondents were Catholic, so this was no simple case of protecting vested interests. Indeed, McEnroe conjured up an ingenious defence of the St Patrick's Day parade: he argued that the march was not religious, but instead a procession of Catholic and Protestant members of the St Patrick's Total Abstinence Society. This was a parade, in other words, in the cause of temperance and civic virtue, with no hint of sectarian or religious connotations. Plunkett was not persuaded: he pointed to the fact that the parade concluded in front of St Patrick's Church, where Catholics duly attended divine service.[77] He reminded McEnroe of the first section of the Party Processions Act:

> That any body of persons who shall meet and parade together, or join in procession for the purpose (among others) of demonstrating any religious or political distinction, or difference between any classes of her Majesty's, &c., shall be deemed guilty of a misdemeanour, and shall, upon conviction thereof, be liable to be punished accordingly.[78]

Plunkett informed McEnroe that he was obliged to exercise the law to the letter, and so he announced that all those who took part would be prosecuted. The St Patrick's Society, after holding an emergency meeting, duly apologized for having transgressed; but it never moved from its stance that the parade was non-religious, and a demonstration specifically in the cause of temperance. Plunkett stuck to his guns: he informed the Society that they had breached the law and were accountable for their actions.[79] Suffice to say that St Patrick's Day parades in both Sydney and Melbourne were now in recess. The 17 of March was, therefore, commemorated privately, at St Patrick's Society dinners and balls, and at special mass. This kept the infighting off of the streets, but as we see in Chapter 3, there was more of the same behind closed doors.

ST PATRICK'S DAY AND TEMPERANCE

During the first half of the nineteenth century, ideas about temperance or total abstinence from alcohol were debated with intensity in Britain and Ireland. This had much to do with discussions about the role of social welfare in societies where, increasingly, the able-bodied were considered solely responsible for their individual circumstances. Too much taxpayers' money had been spent, argued critics, on the 'undeserving' poor, among whom were people whose reliance on alcohol prevented them from earning a sufficient income; or, if they did hold down a job, their drinking habit resulted in wages spent on alcohol rather than food and lodgings. Alcoholism was, at this time, thought to be a social choice rather than a con-

[handwritten: ? No such thing as alcoholism]

dition demanding medical treatment. There was also a pervasive class dimension to such ideas: drinking was a 'problem' only among those who could least afford to drink it – the working class and peasantry. *[handwritten: // drinking was a problem among]*

In Ireland, various temperance organizations arose in the 1830s and 1840s, but it was the leadership of a Catholic priest, the reverend Father Mathew, that transformed anti-drink societies into an influential movement.[80] Mathew was renowned for staging public meetings and making speeches in the cause of temperance, not just in Ireland but in Britain and North America. A high point of the temperance calendar was St Patrick's Day: not only did it bring together Irish people at home and abroad, it was renowned as a break from the Lenten fast in which liberal indulgence of alcohol was customary. Temperance crusaders saw drink as *the cause* of family breakdown; anyone downing a pint in a bar was well on the way to abusive self-indulgence with awful consequences for those who depended on them. St Patrick's Day, in this view, was a danger to the family unit; only by taking the pledge of abstinence could adults aspire to be good citizens and role models on the saint's day. *[handwritten:)) St. Patrick's day : alcohol]*

Given long-standing drinking customs among the Irish at home and abroad, temperance was a difficult prospect. Traditions such as drinking to the health of Ireland and the patron saint, as well as the renowned 'wetting the shamrock' held considerable sway on St Patrick's Day. In light of temperance campaigns, moderation in drinking came to the forefront of Patrician festivities in the mid-nineteenth century, but for many celebrants total abstinence was anathema. That said, drunken indulgence was no longer publicly acceptable on St Patrick's Day; instead moderation or abstinence were signs of one's social virtue. *[handwritten: // not respected to indulge in alcohol]*

In 1842, mass temperance parades took place all over Ireland in honour of St Patrick. There had been concerns in the run-up to 17 March that the assemblies might be banned by the government because of an upsurge in riotous behaviour in Ireland.[81] It appeared that the supporters of temperance would be denied their St Patrick's Day parade because of the activities of fellow Irishmen elsewhere in the country. The concerns abated, however, and on 14 March Dublin Castle assured various temperance branches that their processions could go ahead.[82] The stamp of approval from Dublin Castle demonstrates the authorities' high regard for the crusade against alcohol.

This was, of course, part and parcel of a British desire to see the Irish sober and morally upstanding. As a result, St Patrick's Day became a regular focus of campaigns to change Irish drinking habits. The *Illustrated London News* led the way in 1847, publishing a full-page illustration for St Patrick's Day, thereby symbolizing two contrasting choices open to the Irish. One half of the image depicted the well-known story of St Patrick 'driving the snakes from Ireland', in this case watched by a dutiful crowd. Opposite the patron saint was the leader of the Temperance Movement, Father Mathew, again attended by a large crowd, all kneeling and taking the temperance pledge. Underneath were two smaller illustrations. The first, of a wealthy-looking family at dinner, suggested a group that had followed the line of piety and temperance. The second, a brawling mass, fighting and fornicating, pointed towards the result of a life spent with drink.[83] The 'drunken Paddy' was demonized as a despicable and destructive character whose 'inevitable' criminality was 'traceable from the flowing can, the beloved bottle, and the noggin'. Respectable alternatives included 'the innocent recreation of the dance ... the happy tea party', which were 'indicative of the regeneration of Ireland'.[84] For the *Illustrated London News*, then, temperance would lead to the creation of an Irish people who behaved soberly like the English. Once this had been achieved, the paper concluded, it would be possible for all those celebrating 17 March 'to honour our Empire on St Patrick's Day'.[85]

From newspaper reports of temperance parades in the decade leading to the famine years, it appears that it was those promoting a morally upright vision of St Patrick's Day observance who advanced the cause of the 'grand' St Patrick's Day parade in Ireland. A letter from 'a teetotaller, Charleville' to the *Cork Examiner* describes 'thousands marching behind the combined bands of Charleville and Kilmallock in a grand Temperance jubilee on St Patrick's Day'.[86] A report in the *Dublin Evening Post* tells how

> the third annual great moral display of our fellow countrymen who have abjured the use of all intoxicating liqueurs, an anniversary set apart for the wildest dissipation among all classes. As on former occasions, the greater portions of members of the Temperance societies who joined in the procession wore scarves of tabinet, or other material, and handsome rosettes. All carried white wands decorated with ribbons, shamrock &c.[87]

The development of a carnivalesque parade by the Temperance movement, with bands, decorations and large numbers of both marchers and spectators, was a new departure for St Patrick's Day in Ireland. While there had been marches across Ireland on St Patrick's Day in the years prior to the 1840s, they had not been on the same scale as those organized by the Temperance movement. The anti-drink parades were held on a national scale, co-ordinated by various Father Mathew associations.

Also, and potentially most important given the constant vigilance of the government concerning possible insurgency in Ireland, the Temperance parades, because they were seen as respectable, were given the support of authorities and were not interfered with by 'party procession' or 'public order' legislation of the time. The change in atmosphere brought about by a St Patrick's Day sponsored and organized by the Temperance movement marked a clear shift away from more spontaneous, chaotic and irreverent forms of celebration, a fact not lost on Dublin's *Freeman's Journal*:

> What a happy change did that scene [the St Patrick's Day procession] present when contrasted with similar anniversaries of the patron saint of Ireland! Here were thousands of persons congregated together peaceably and orderly, a considerable number of whom had on many former festivals of Saint Patrick deemed it an honour to celebrate it by the commission of the most odious and detestable properties – drunkenness, riot and disorder prevailed to an extent which was frightful to contemplate; but happily those exhibitions have passed away, never again we trust to be repeated, and the actors in those disgraceful transactions have become good citizens and good subjects, imparting peace and happiness in the domestic circle, which had previously been characterised by pictures of misery, despair and poverty.[88]

The ideas of the temperance movement soon crossed the Atlantic. By 1841, the Albany Catholic Total Abstinence Association was promoting the message to avoid drink at St Patrick's Day celebrations in the local area, while by 1843 the Pennsylvania Catholic Total Abstinence Society was using tunes written specially by James Gibbons to promote the twin causes of temperance and Irish national freedom.[89]

During the 1850s the Temperance movement, which had been so important to pre-famine St Patrick's Day parades in Ireland, attempted to win converts in America.[90] As in Ireland, the annual celebration of St Patrick's Day became a focus for anti-drink campaigners. In 1850, Father Mathew travelled from Ireland to America to promote his temperance campaign. As a way of marking his visit, but also in an attempt to utilize the St Patrick's Day parade to promote the cause of temperance, the Roman Catholic Total Abstinence and Benevolent Society joined the parade that year.[91] The arrival of Mathew in America, and the warm reception he received were important as it coincided with a large upswing in support for, and numbers marching in, St Patrick's Day parades. The spirit and respectability of temperance were echoed by the organizers of American parades at the time, such as the Irish Benefit Society. They wished to project an image of the Irish as respectable, temperate, industrious and law-abiding 'adopted citizens'.[92]

In addition to campaigning against the drunken excesses of St Patrick's Day, the supporters of temperance in America turned their attention to the ever-increasing paraphernalia, such as sashes, rosettes and costumes, that was becoming a common feature of American parades. In 1857, the *Irish News* implored its readers to remember St Patrick with 'gratitude and reverence' and to spend their money on a monument celebrating the work of the keystone in the temperance cause, Father Mathew. This would be better than spending the money, 'which might otherwise be thrown away on sashes, gew-gaws, military bands and other ostentatious expenses of the kind'.[93]

The focus of the *Irish News* on the possible excesses of St Patrick's Day was important. It revealed an increasing battle that would become central to the future of 17 March celebrations. The post-famine years are central in understanding the charitable and respectable themes that were so important to the Irish diaspora communities. The famine had cast the Irish across the globe, and they had been met, despite their hardships, by much opposition and discrimination. St Patrick's Day was an important forum for stressing their identity, for reminding the host population of the strength of the Irish, and also for offering proof, if such was needed, of the innate respectability and devout nature of the immigrant communities. The charitable nature of St Patrick's Day, so evidenced by collections specifically for famine relief, was continued throughout the period to 1860. In England, the Benevolent Society of St Patrick, founded in 1783, met annually for a dinner. In his speech at the 1854 gathering, the Chairman was able to inform the Society's members that 500 poor children were being educated as a result of their charitable work in the name of Ireland's patron saint. The children were all clothed and educated by the Society, and 'the girls were all instructed in needlework, and were thereby enabled to make up all the undergarments required in the schools'.[94] The work of the Benevolent Society of St Patrick was a clear illustration of the continuing charitable nature of 17 March, and therefore of the good work of the Irish. Such sentiments were to be challenged in the last decades of the nineteenth century, overtaken by an increasing focus on the force of Irish nationalism, and a growth of a St Patrick's Day that spoke of self-indulgence and self-congratulation.

self help

CHAPTER 3

VISUALIZING IRELAND

Nationalism and diaspora

— ℰℐℴ —

The grand old days when St Patrick dwelt upon our native soil –
The days when Irish homes enjoyed the fruits of Irish toil;
The relics of a glorious past, sublime amidst decay,
Show what we were and yet may be upon St Patrick's Day.[1]

REVIVING ST PATRICK'S DAY IN IRELAND

Dublin's Anglo-Irish elite, who had been little affected by the famine, soon re-established St Patrick's Day as a high profile social occasion. Dublin Castle was a focus for Patrician celebrations, and while this allowed traditions of sumptuous dinners and aristocratic balls to continue, there was now some effort to engage with the public at large. The most popular civic event at Dublin Castle on St Patrick's Day was the 'trooping of the guard' ceremony. In 1860 the *Freeman's Journal* reported that despite poor weather the performance was watched by 'a considerable crowd, composed principally of the humbler classes', among whom were a 'considerable number of females'.[2] Inside the confines of the Dublin Castle yard, members of the 76th regiment, the 1st Royals, and the 15th Hussars, relieved and trooped the 36th Foot and 3rd Light Dragoons. This ritual was accompanied by military bands playing national and popular airs. There was, according to the *Freeman's Journal*, much excitement generated by this music, to the extent that the 'humbler classes' indulged themselves in what a reporter described as 'a series of grotesque dances before the balcony'.[3] Although the newspaper's sense of decorum was offended by these actions, it was nonetheless pleased to report that the loudest cheers were for the Irish Lord Lieutenant who was attired 'as a private gentleman' and, in keeping with Patrician custom, 'wore a large bunch of shamrock in his hat'.[4] The ceremony at the Castle had, up to the 1860s, 'usually attracted a large crowd of onlookers, many of them poor, seeking entertainment'.[5]

Despite annual press reports about the Castle ritual being a high profile event on St Patrick's Day, this Dublin tradition was not representative of popular sentiment elsewhere in the country. The trooping of the colour ceremony remained, until its demise in the First World War, an event dominated and celebrated by the Anglo-Irish elite. Its lack of relevance to the larger population, even as early as 1860, can be judged by the fact that the event was trouble-free because, as the *Freeman's Journal* put it, 'the presence of police in considerable force deterred them [potential troublemakers] from carrying out their reckless and unpleasant amusements'.[6]

The pomp and circumstance of the Castle's trooping of the colour can be contrasted with less spectacular ways of commemorating St Patrick's Day. 'Ordinary' folk routinely attended mass on the patron saint's anniversary, but there were numerous opportunities for recreation and conviviality. The *Freeman's Journal* of March 1870 reported that St Patrick's Day had been celebrated in leisurely fashion

> by a harmless drive to the marine villas of Irishtown and Sandymount, and the day was concluded in the theatre. A few of the more favoured portion of the citizens made a small picnic in the country, and had a domestic and friendly 'drum' in the evening. But there were thousands who walked about the streets for hours and indulged in bibulous enjoyments and endured the usual results.[7]

The *Freeman's Journal* described scenes that were common to Patrician festivals across the world. Without a formal focus beyond the morning church service, St Patrick's Day, for those fortunate to be granted a day off work, was a time of self-indulgent leisure.

Throughout the 1860s, there was a growing belief among the leaders of trade guilds that there should be some form of organized focus for St Patrick's Day in Dublin. Increasing numbers of white-collar workers in the city were being granted the day as a holiday, and there was a desire amongst the organizers that amusements should be provided that would not be morally corrupting, but focus instead on the positive virtues of the Patrician traditions, such as faith and nation. In 1869 a National Anniversary Celebration Committee was formed to organize a grand celebration of St Patrick's Day in Dublin. The Committee, and the resultant celebration in 1870, were a product of the city's trades guilds, and all meetings to plan the event were held in the Mechanic's Institute. The Committee had a twofold objective: to encourage a decidedly 'Irish' form of festivity on St Patrick's Day, and to promote dignified behaviour among those who commemorated 17 March. The NACC strategy centred on a programme of traditional cultural performances – music and dance – to entice 'respectable' craftsmen, artisans and labourers to a family-oriented celebration of the national apostle in a spirit of temperance.[8]

The People's Festival, as the event became popularly known, was held at Dublin's Exhibition Palace on St Patrick's Day, 1870.[9] The price of admission to the festival was a modest 6d.: patrons were welcome to inspect Patrician displays in the galleries, partake of food and non-alcoholic drink at marquees, and listen to Dublin bands play 'national airs'. The day's programme also included Irish sporting events open to allcomers; and, in an era before amateurism dominated Irish sporting culture, cash prizes. The seemingly inimitable 'Professor Corteous' was of particular interest: in an 'extraordinary' half-hour performance he walked one mile, ran half a mile, picked up thirty eggs one yard apart, jumped 225 steeplechase hurdles, threw twenty 56-pound weights over his head, and completed his display with six flying somersaults. After the completion of the day's gallery and sporting exhibitions, an evening programme of music and literature awaited. For a shilling more than the basic entry fee patrons could stay for the evening's 'Promenades' and 'Monster Ball', although a further 2s. 6d. was required for entry to the prestigious 'Grand Ball'. The programme for the latter featured well-known Irish tunes such as 'The Shamrock', 'Come Back to Erin', and 'Ould Ireland you're my Darlin'', a selection of harp music and bell ringing, and 'Mrs Griffin' reading excerpts from a political biography – *Gerald Barry: A Story of '98*.[10] It had become, by now, a very full day out. The People's Festival also made St Patrick's Day more of a commercial opportunity. In the weeks before 17 March, newspapers were replete with advertisements for special St Patrick's Day green sashes, rosettes, scarves, ties, dresses and shirts.[11] It was therefore a day to 'be seen'. But it was not intended to be socially exclusive: offers of cheap rail excursions to the festival were made to attract working-class commuters.[12]

The People's Festival of 1870 was a great success: both the scale of events and the level of popular involvement were unprecedented for a St Patrick's Day in Dublin. The press reported that tens of thousands of people attended the event, large crowds mingled peacefully, and there was a notable absence of flagrant drunkenness. The *Freeman's Journal* noted wryly that 'the very fact that ... working men brought their wives and daughters to the festival argued a determination to be vigilant against temptation'.[13] Patrician observance, while convivial and celebratory, was also an opportunity for political messages to be conveyed publicly. This was most noticeable in trade-union banners hung in various rooms and galleries of the festival's Exhibition Hall, where the overriding theme was Irish nationalism. The Shop and Warehousemen's Porter Society banner featured the slogan 'Let Erin's Sons be Free', the ropemakers' banner called for the 'Unconditional Release of All Political Prisoners', while the chimney cleaners' flags, which featured portraits of O'Connell and Erin, carried the inscription, 'Ireland Remembers O'Connell'.[14] This type of symbolism was apparent also in the selection of music and ballads played on St Patrick's Day: tunes and songs were patriotic in the sense of celebrating Ireland, but they emphasized the centrality of Irish nationalism within that context. Despite public support of the People's Festival in 1870, together with its commercial and political significance, it was not a catalyst to further demonstrations of this magnitude in Dublin. It appears that while the Festival was successful in terms of total attendance, the financial outlay and the organizational input involved deterred the

Celebration Committee from such an undertaking again. Instead, St Patrick's Day reverted to a more traditional pattern of loosely organized spectacle, disparate events and localized custom.

Over the next three decades St Patrick's Day was never again established as a major public event in Ireland. It was unquestionably an important religious day, and for many had also become a day free from work, but Patrician observance did not become, as it had in North America and Australia, a day for street parades and ostentatious public celebration.[15] In 1874, even the usual Dublin Castle events were cancelled; neither the St Patrick's Day Ball nor the trooping of the colours took place. This coincided with a change of government at Westminster: the Liberal party of Gladstone, generally seen as favourable to Irish self-rule under the auspices of the British Empire, was now superseded by Disraeli's Conservative administration, which was hostile to Home Rule. Indeed, on St Patrick's Day, 1874, Dublin's *Freeman's Journal* feared that 'Mr Disraeli and his government would be very ready to denationalize us altogether'.[16]

The cancellation of Dublin Castle's St Patrick's Day events had other implications. Previously, Castle recognition of 17 March had given this anniversary public profile and official respectability. Now, in the absence of such civic leadership, social commentators worried that public celebrations were more likely to feature irresponsible public behaviour. Two perennial problems were highlighted by the *Freeman's Journal*. First, the newspaper feared that 17 March would again be a 'barbarous profanity of a commemoration' which would be 'marred by scenes of drunkenness and disorder' and, ultimately, public 'disgrace'.[17] The memory of St Patrick would be sullied by the endemic problem of insobriety and ensuing rowdy behaviour. The paper never said so, but intoxication and public disorder were almost exclusively associated with Irish males. Second, the *Freeman's Journal* worried that St Patrick's Day was more likely to be a forum for acrimonious exchanges between long-time political adversaries. Of particular concern was the observance of 17 March in the north-eastern counties of Ireland, where Protestants outnumbered Catholics, and where sectarian disputes about the denominational 'ownership' of St Patrick had emerged.

The Orangemen of Ulster had a long-standing tradition of parading to celebrate their links with Britain and, some would say, their underlying Protestantism (even though the Orange Society claimed to be non-sectarian). Their parading calendar did not include St Patrick's Day: 17 March had ecumenical origins and was touted as a day for all the Irish, whereas Orangeism lionized Britishness and, in many cases, denied Irishness. The political significance of St Patrick's Day to the Orange Order first emerged in the early nineteenth century when Orange marches were banned but St Patrick's Day parades allowed to continue. The former was considered by Dublin Castle to be a 'party procession', the latter a 'national anniversary'. The repeal of the Party Processions Act in 1872 gave new life to Orange parades;

this, unintentionally, also raised the political significance of 17 March. For Catholics and nationalists in Ulster, St Patrick's Day parades had a capacity to serve as counterpoints to the revived 12 July processions; and this was all the more likely if both the saint and the anniversary could be claimed as 'their own'. Orangemen, whose day of reckoning was 12 July, were not about to de-green 17 March. Their strategy, instead, was to disrupt what they took to be the nationalist triumphalism associated with Catholic-dominated St Patrick's Day parades in Ulster. In 1874, there was a violent clash in Lurgan between Catholics who had taken part in a peaceful St Patrick's Day parade, and a group of Orangemen who took exception to the proceedings. The severity of the violence meant that the Riot Act had to be read, with the streets forcibly cleared by troops.[18] This sort of disruption was not unexpected given that Protestant-controlled Belfast newspapers were prone to label St Patrick's Day marchers as closet Fenians. By the 1870s, then, there was a belief that St Patrick was being poorly honoured throughout Ireland. The Dublin's People's Festival had gone as quickly as it arrived; Dublin Castle had become aloof to its long-standing commemoration of 17 March; while St Patrick's Day was, more than ever, a source of sectarian tension in Ulster. Given these circumstances, the problematic commemoration of St Patrick's Day in Ireland was unlikely to change.[19] The diminishing interest in the Castle events, which had restarted in 1875, was plain to see. From 1880, the public were no longer allowed in the Castle Yard to witness the trooping of the colours. By 1885, the St Patrick's Day event was attended only by 'a body of detectives and some idlers who looked and listened through the gateway', while by 1890, the *Irish Times* reported that the 'attendance was small'.[20]

ST PATRICK'S DAY POLITICS: HOME AND ABROAD

Ireland: 1860–1914

Virtually any public holiday or act of commemoration was a concern for British authorities in Ireland during the second half of the nineteenth century. There was a widespread belief among those who directed Irish policy, both in London and Dublin Castle, that such public occasions were a source of trouble. It was felt that any public event could provide the Irish with a platform for protest, whether the issue was land ownership, nationalism, or a local grievance. Public holidays, party parades and religious processions were more complex and problematic within Ulster. The presence of two often antagonistic religious groupings, side by side and in great numbers, sometimes resulted in intercommunal violence.

Despite potential risks to public order, a decision had been made in 1872 to repeal the Party Processions Act, one of the pieces of legislation that was regularly used to proscribe marches and gatherings of a political nature. The Orange Order, which had been one of the chief targets of the legislation, especially its 12 of July parades, had made constant appeals to the government to bring about its repeal. One outcome of the removal of the legislation, which would have not been the aim of the Orange Order, was an upsurge in the popularity of St Patrick's Day parades in Ulster amongst Catholics. Previously, parades were either Protestant organized, such as that in Downpatrick, or else were localized Catholic observances constantly under threat of proscription.

The scale of Patrician observance amongst Catholics in Ulster, especially through parading in 1873, alarmed Dublin Castle authorities. A decision was taken in 1874 to supervise all St Patrick's Day parades in Ulster, and to monitor levels of political activity that were part of various processions. This monitoring was carried out by members of the Royal Irish Constabulary (RIC): the reports they compiled about sixty St Patrick's Day parades in 1874 provides the most complete official description of Patrician processions in nineteenth-century Ulster. The local officers of the RIC were sent a standard form by Dublin Castle to complete on the basis of their observations. The form listed nine questions, so that the extent of the parade and its political aspects could be identified. Informants were to provide details about the number of marchers, their social class, the type of musical accompaniment, whether any banners or flags were carried, the nature of any political slogans or songs and whether any violence took place.[21] Cumulatively, the reports estimated that a total of 60,680 marchers paraded on St Patrick's Day in Ulster, 1874.[22] The processions were predominantly peaceful, although there were reports of minor incidents in Lurgan (windows broken), Mountnugent (assault) and Banbridge (stone throwing), as well as small-scale riots in Bellaghy, Castledawson and Magherafelt.

The reports from each area vary, but there is significant common ground. All but three of the parades featured musical instruments, flags and banners, most of which featured what RIC officers took to be 'disloyal mottoes or designs'. Marchers were labelled as being 'of the lowest class',[23] though some RIC officers acknowledged the presence of 'a few tradesmen'.[24] The music accompanying the marchers 'appeared of a general kind, national airs, quick steps and marches – "St Patrick's Day" was frequently played'.[25] The music was performed by bands of various sizes in the different locations, but drum and fife dominated the proceedings. Many of the RIC officers recording the marches had great difficulty in identifying the tunes played, so noted only those they were able recognize, such as the well-known 'St Patrick's Day', 'Garryowne' and 'Whitecockade'. Yet the officers differed in opinion as to whether or not such tunes were disloyal or seditious. Some saw the tune 'St Patrick's Day' as unproblematic and part of a non-political celebration, while others identified its playing as a deliberately inflammatory act. Similar differences of interpretation emerged in respect of banners carried by the marchers. The large banners, details of which were diligently recorded by the RIC officers, featured many familiar slogans. In Fivemiletown, for example, there were nine flags, 'one 6 feet long by 6 feet wide, the others varied in size from 3 feet by 3 feet and 2 feet by 2 feet, all of green cashmere with wide borders'.[26] Other banners and flags across the country were made of silk, the largest of which were carried between two poles. The slogans on the banners included 'Our Own Again', 'God Save Ireland', 'Ireland as a Nation', 'Wolfe Tone and Amnesty', 'Erin Go Bragh', 'Emmet Come Back, God Save Ireland', and 'I know the strength of the cause I support'. Some phrases, such as those referring to Emmet or Tone, were clearly identified as disloyal; others were ruled by the RIC observers as disloyal, despite their apparent innocuous nature – such as those referring to heroes of Irish constitutionalism like Daniel O'Connell. On the final report, a written amendment records the decision that, 'the motto God Save Ireland has been dealt with as disloyal in this summary as it is always used in memory of the Manchester Martyrs'. In the same vein, 'the design, the harp without the crown has been treated as a disloyal emblem, as it intended as such'.[27] Each of the reports noted that the individual marchers, and many of those watching, wore green sashes, green ties, or scarves. The end of the parade was marked in some places by meetings of a political nature, usually relating to Home Rule or issues of land reform.

From the viewpoint of Castle authorities, the alarming image of thousands of Catholics gathering together across Ireland on St Patrick's Day to march, sing disloyal songs, carry seditious banners and flags, and then close the day with political meetings, could not go unchallenged. The assessment of the 1874 report by J.H. Burke, Under-Secretary at the Ulster Office of Dublin Castle, concluded that these 'green walks' were 'organised by the Fenians'. He noted that the flags and banners, made as they were of silk, and because of their uniform nature across the country, were the product of 'some general as well as local organisation that must be at work in directing and encouraging demonstration'.[28] Despite Burke's concern that St Patrick's Day parades were a cover for Fenian activity, no decision was taken to reinforce the Party Processions Act, or to ban future observances. It appears that wholesale banning of St Patrick's Day parades was seen as logistically impossible, and an action that would create a political backlash. It was easier to allow parades to continue but under surveillance; so long, as was the case in 1874, incidences of lawlessness were kept to a minimum.

Nonetheless, the practice of celebrating St Patrick's Day across Ireland, and the use of parades to publicly express political messages, were an ongoing concern to authorities. In 1878 the Chief Secretary of Dublin Castle's Ulster Office argued that continued toleration of St Patrick's Day parades by Catholics in Ulster had become, 'to a certain extent, a protection; namely they are supposed to have now a quasi-prescriptive right to march in procession, even when displaying disloyal banners calculated to offend the feelings of loyal subjects'.[29] In the same year, the MP Charles Lewis, in the face of growing concerns, especially in Ulster over the size, scale and purpose of St Patrick's Day parades, argued that, 'it is highly undesirable that more than 3 or 4 persons be allowed to walk together at any time in Ireland, especially on saints' days'.[30] Lewis's argument, though understood by many in Westminster, was nonetheless perceived as draconian, and in the context of the growing demands for Irish Home Rule, a politically inflammatory proposal.

St Patrick's Day parades were not always a cause for alarm; much depended on the political situation in any given year. By contrast to the 1870s, the celebrations of 1880 were low key – which reflected poor economic conditions in Ireland at that time. Dublin's *Freeman's Journal*, reporting on woeful conditions across the country, including famine in rural areas and unemployment in cities, concluded:

> St Patrick's Day 1880, has come and gone. The circumstances under which Ireland celebrated it this year were not calculated to make her National Festival one of remarkable rejoicing. While starvation and misery are abroad in the land . . . people are not much inclined towards feelings of satisfaction or hilarity.[31]

Two years later, though, economic and political circumstances had improved to the extent that 17 March was again a focus for celebration and religious devotion. The *Freeman's Journal* of 18 March 1882 reported:

> Yesterday's St Patrick's Day was observed in the city [Dublin] with the customary manifestations of devotion to the memory of Ireland's patron saint. Though business was in no wise suspended, the streets showed unusual crowds all day, and needless to add, the national emblem (the shamrock) was prominently worn by young and old, male and female. Even the police constables, on and off duty, braved the peril of 'reasonable suspicion' by sporting a morsel of green leaf in their unspiked helmets. The day being a holiday of obligation, the Masses celebrated in Catholic churches were thronged from early morning till noon.[32]

There were, in addition, St Patrick's Day temperance dinners across Dublin in 1882, and the Castle revived its trooping of the colour ceremony and grand ball. The single event of concern to authorities was a concert for the Political Prisoner's Aid Society held in the Round Room of Dublin's Rotunda. Newspaper reports from towns and cities elsewhere in Ireland detail countless parades, church services, temperance meetings and various forms of popular entertainment. According to the *Freeman's Journal*, the only violence was in Dunmanway in Cork city, where a riot ensued after police attempted to clear the streets with rifles after stones had been thrown in their direction.[33]

In the absence of extreme economic conditions and political opportunism, the observance of St Patrick's Day in Ireland had settled into an annual pattern. The day was granted to many employees as a holiday, depending on a person's trade or profession. Church services were still the cornerstone of the day, while the wearing of shamrock or green ribbon was essential. Even by the 1880s the Irish had not, with the exception of parades from town and village centres to and from church for Mass, developed a custom of staging grand St Patrick's Day parades in the American mould. The day was viewed, from the perspective of society's moral custodians at least, as one of religious devotion and avoidance of improper temptation – most notably consumption of alcohol. Yet although abstinence and temperance had influential supporters, St Patrick's Day was still marked by excessive indulgence in drink. This had much to do with ideas about masculinity within Irish working-class culture: St Patrick's Day parades demonstrated 'the stamina and the pride of Irish men. Drinking, dining and symbolic expressions of Irish presence were as much a part of the parade as St Patrick was.'[34] That said, there was an overarching awareness that St Patrick's Day was a moment for Irish people to reflect upon their sense of self, about where they 'belonged'. Their community had become increasingly Anglicized in terms of language and education, while their hopes of political autonomy rested with politicians in London. On that basis it does not seem surprising that the romance of ancient Ireland and a nationalist vision for the future were prominent parts of St Patrick's Day. Across the diaspora, the period from the 1860s to the outbreak of the First World War was one of general transition. While St Patrick's Day often performed the function of declaring, almost belligerently, the presence of the Irish amidst their host community, anti-Irishness remained a feature of life in America, Australia, Britain and Canada. Despite such confrontations, the period witnessed the successful assimilation of many Irish into the society of their new location. Both Kirby Miller and Alan O'Day, with reference to America and Britain respectively, have argued that by the later years of the nineteenth century, the Irish had largely travelled beyond the poverty that had driven them overseas. They demonstrated that levels of anti-Irishness had reduced and, while still often retaining a sense of their origins, many Irish had assimilated into their new culture.[35] In a period where the Irish emigrant communities were undergoing a change in their social status and when their relationships with those around them were improving, what, then, was the place of St Patrick's Day? While it had origins that can be understood, as Miller has contended, as 'simply a product of Irish alienation or self-assertion in the New World',[36] surely the increased levels of assimilation through this period had reduced the need for such public display. It is clear, however, that while St Patrick's Day, throughout the diaspora, underwent many changes in the period to the First World

War, including the development of an increased respectability and gentility, it remained a centrally important day in the Irish calendar. Increasingly it demonstrated symbols and 'indications of compatible loyalties or eventual amalgamation'[37] rather than hostility and challenges to the existing power structures.

Britain: 1860–1914

By the last decades of the nineteenth century the political situation with respect of Ireland was relatively quiet. The Parnell controversy, which had seen Charles Stewart Parnell, the leader of the Irish Home Rule party in the divorce courts as a result of his affair with a married woman, had split his supporters. Although the split caused serious divisions within the Home Rule movement and led, in part, to a weakening of Gladstone's support for the Irish cause, the renewed dominance of the Conservatives in parliament made such divisions less relevant. The Conservative government had tentatively begun land reforms in Ireland, and the country, while not in a state of tranquillity, was not in open rebellion. This relative sense of calm was felt also among the diaspora. In Britain, the crude anti-Irishness of the immediate post-famine decades had receded, and although still greeted with deep suspicion in some quarters, the Irish were steadily becoming an accepted part of British life. An important, ongoing aspect of the Irish calendar in Britain was St Patrick's Day. Whereas newspapers in mid-nineteenth-century Britain had tainted St Patrick's Day festivities as a front for Fenian activity, a licence for drunkenness and as a catalyst to violent disorder, the day was greeted with comparatively little anxiety by British newspapers four decades on.

Part of the reason behind the respectability of St Patrick's Day in the last decades of the nineteenth century was its move off the streets and the concentration on indoor events. It was the parades that had always been a point of political contention. The public flexing of the Irish presence in various cities, and concomitant reactions from opponents such as the Orange Order, had led St Patrick's Day to be viewed as a flashpoint for disorder. By the 1860s, however, many St Patrick's Day events became comparatively genteel and respectable. These activities included the annual dinners of the National Brotherhood of St Patrick in London and other provincial English cities, the annual grand national soirée at Liverpool's concert hall, and meetings held by the Catholic Young Men's Societies.[38] As perhaps the ultimate mark of Victorian respectability, St Patrick's Day was even celebrated by those twenty-four Irish 'noblemen and gentlemen' studying at Eton school who gathered together for a grand breakfast with the school's headmaster to mark 17 March.[39] One of the most respectable organizations that promoted St Patrick's Day in Britain was the National Brotherhood of St Patrick. Founded in 1861 in Dublin, the Brotherhood's aims were 'the arrangement

✳of nationalist functions, the co-ordination of the efforts of all who advocated nationalist policies, and the celebration of the national feast of St Patrick's Day'.[40] The National Brotherhood's St Patrick's Day celebrations aimed at creating unity among the Irish population, and to rescue the day from 'personages who are truly English in birth and principle, and who condescend to take the chair on such occasions, to treat the Irish to a little speechifying'.[41] The St Patrick's Day celebrations utilized all the iconography and liturgy of Irish nationalism: tricolours, green flags and the portraits and images of St Patrick and famous Irish leaders were openly displayed. Tea parties and banquets were held, Irish music played and patriotic speeches made. Although 17 March was the centrepiece of the Brotherhood's year, its other activities, including reading rooms, clubs and outings, mark out the organization as a source of rational recreation and civic order.

This growing respectability and reduced contentiousness of St Patrick's Day, even at the parading level, were evident by the end of the century in England. The *Liverpool Mercury* gave only cursory reports of St Patrick's Day in 1895. It detailed the march at Everton-brow by the 54th Irish, reporting that the streets were 'crowded with men and women, boys and girls, all of whom were decorated with the shamrock or the more easily obtained green ribbon of the draper's shop'.[42] In other parts of the city there were church services to commemorate Ireland's patron saint, and on St Patrick's eve a concert featuring Irish music was staged at the city's Hope Hall. A further sign of the growing acceptability of the Irish population in Liverpool was the cancellation of a proposed procession on St Patrick's Day by the Orange Order; the society postponed its parade until the end of the month 'in order that no offence might be given' to the local Irish community.[43] The only reported disorder was a minor skirmish late in the night when 'four persons were locked up'.[44] In a city with such historic sectarian enmity, this was a mark of how far Patrician observances had now become accepted. Ten years on, in 1905, St Patrick's Day had, if anything, grown in Liverpool. There was the customary St Patrick's eve concert of Irish music at the Picton Lecture Hall, services at Catholic churches across the city, dinners and drinks at Irish pubs and an impressive parade. Throughout the festivities, reported the *Liverpool Mercury*, 'basket women ... did a roaring trade in the dear little plant which grows in our isle'.[45] The paper was incredulous at the business in shamrock; its wholesale price had soared to an unheard of 2s. per pound in the week leading up to St Patrick's Day. Perhaps the most important mark of civic recognition of St Patrick's Day in Liverpool was the decision by the city's Lord Mayor to hoist 'the national emblem over the Town Hall in the highest position of honour the municipality possesses'.[46] For many years the *Liverpool Mercury* had focused on public violence and details of arrests on St Patrick's Day; now the paper argued that the Lord Mayor's gesture would enable 'all Irishmen, of whatever section, to unite and delight in honouring St Patrick's Day'.[47]✳

The 'respectability' of St Patrick's Day in Britain was all the more likely if it was declared a public holiday in Ireland. As explained later, 17 March was eventually recognized as a Bank Holiday in Ireland from 1903. Our interest here is with one of the driving forces behind the holiday campaign – the Gaelic League. This Irish association was formed in 1893 with the purpose of reviving Irish-Gaelic as a spoken and written language. Its founders were anxious about the Anglicization of Irish culture; one way of challenging what they saw as cultural imperialism was to encourage expression in the native tongue. An obvious problem, however, was that English was the official language in Ireland and had been taught as such in schools for many years. A result of this was that most Catholic church services were conducted in English; there were too few fluent Irish speakers for it to be otherwise. The Gaelic League – Connradh na Gaeilge – began as a movement promoting cultural nationalism, so it attracted supporters from across the religious and political spectrum. By 1915, however, the League had been infiltrated by the Irish Republican Brotherhood; this meant that the Irish language was now linked inextricably to political nationalism.[48] Indeed, in 1919, in the wake of British reprisals against republican activism, the Gaelic League was declared an 'illegal' organization. During the twenty years before the First World War, however, the cultural aspirations of the League were well known and received much sympathy in Britain; branches of the movement were even established in London. The main thrust of League activities was the promotion of 'authentic' Irish culture, which included Irish language, literature and music. This quest for authenticity had also been apparent in the rise of the Gaelic Athletic Association in 1884; its members were committed to playing only those sports that were 'genuinely' Irish and local in origin – namely, Gaelic football and hurling. The high point of the League's social calendar was its national festival, An tOireachtas, a music and folk celebration similar to that of the Welsh Eisteddfod.[49]

The Gaelic League was also active on St Patrick's Day. Eoin MacNeill, one of the group's founders, had a strong interest in the historical St Patrick. He saw in the national apostle a welcome symbolic link between the ancient Celts and the influx of Christians in Ireland. As MacNeill saw it, here was a 'noble race' of people who, until invasions by Normans and Anglo-Saxons, had flourished 'independently' with their own language, religion and distinct cultural practices. The 'revival' of Gaelic was, therefore, as much about culture as language.[50] St Patrick's Day, in this regard, appears to have been an ideal time for the Gaelic League to promote its revivalist message. The connection was not lost on the Irish nationalist press. On St Patrick's Day 1916 the *Gael* urged its readers:

> You must meet the encroachment of vile anglicisation . . . and hurl it back into the sea, as Patrick hurled the snakes, from our land . . . Surely you, who cannot speak Patrick's language cannot expect to number

among the many he will have on his right hand, whom he will style in presenting them to God, 'My Celtic children, whom I have preserved for your Kingdom'. Ah! No. Here you are not under the banner of St Patrick, for you are either ashamed to speak his language or to[o] idle to learn it ... and we are Catholics! Ah! Many the tear St Patrick must shed for us in heaven ... and great must be his humiliation.[51]

The Gaelic League had lobbied for 17 March as a holiday, so it was no surprise that it used the national anniversary for purposes of self-promotion. There were annual examples of an explicit connection between the League and St Patrick's Day. According to *Saoirse na hÉireann* (*Irish Freedom*) the 'great feature' of St Patrick's Day in Dublin in 1913 was the 'Language procession'. Although this nationalist paper expressed reservations about the practicality of reviving Gaelic as the native tongue, it was nonetheless impressed by the associated patriotic sentiments. It concluded that 'the Language procession was a fine turn out and worthy of the Gaelic League'.[52] St Patrick's Day was also a prime opportunity for the League to raise funds for its work in promoting the Irish language. *New Ireland* of March 1917 noted that 'elaborate arrangements' had been made for the 'Language Flag Day' on St Patrick's Day in Dublin. The paper explained that the entire city had been mapped out into districts for the purposes of collecting money, and 'upwards of 1,000 cailíní [girls] will see to it that everybody is afforded an opportunity of contributing towards the Language movement on the Festival of the Patron Saint'. This was of great importance to the cause, argued *New Ireland*: it was expected that 'a large sum will accrue as a result of the Flag Day, especially considering that the money is intended for the Gaeltacht', where 'successful local teaching schemes are at present in progress'.[53]

The Gaelic League was also an active participant in the festive celebration of St Patrick's Day. In 1917, for example, the 'St Patrick's Week Ceilidhe of the Dublin Gaelic League' was held at the Mansion House.[54] The language movement was also involved in various Feisanna and formal concerts. Again, though, these events were also opportunities for fundraising. In 1916, proceeds from the St Patrick's Night Concert at the Rotunda Rink were to be allocated to the 'Irish Language Fund', the 'Irish Volunteer Fund', and the Rooney Memorial Hall.[55] The Gaelic League was also credited with restoring order and sobriety to St Patrick's Day in Ireland. In March 1912, *Saoirse na hÉireann* concluded that the League had performed 'notable work' in the cause of temperance, not only during the Patrician festival but at other public occasions as well. Before the advent of the League 'it would have been almost impossible to hold such large gatherings ... without occasioning much drunkenness and disorder'.[56]

In London, too, the Gaelic League was active on St Patrick's Day, organizing various literary and musical events in partnership with other Irish groups. In 1901, the *United Irishman* reflected favourably on Patrician cele-brations at Holborn Town Hall, where 'the language advocates joined hands with the devotees of Gaelic pastimes, and professional men of high standing seemed to have no concern but to rival the pupils of Professor O'Brien's step-dancing class in the execution of hornpipe, jig and reel'.[57] London had rarely seen Irish parades on St Patrick's Day, but the League now promoted language processions which, even if modest in scale, raised awareness among Irish emigrants about the 'native tongue'.[58] Also in London, some Catholic church services and hymns were observed in Irish Gaelic: these were organ-ized especially for St Patrick's Day and supported the efforts of the language movement.[59] The role of the Gaelic League in London on the Irish national anniversary was, according to the *United Irishman*, all the more important because of a local tendency towards 'sham patriotism'. The paper lauded the 'authenticity' of the Gaelic League and the Gaelic Athletic Association as both cultural and national movements. It warned against 'other Irish socie-ties, unquestionably misnamed, advertising "Grand Irish Nights"' on St Patrick's Day. These should not be supported, argued the *United Irishman*, 'as they tend more to denationalise and demoralise our people than provide healthy amusement'. The paper concluded: 'It is not our intention to dispar-age ... the work of any Irish body in London, but when we see so-called Irish societies more English than the English, we feel it imperative to warn Irishmen and women of these traps.'[60] St Patrick's Day was, in that sense, something of a litmus test for the 'authenticity' of the London-based Irish.

(handwritten margin note: critizied for not being irish enough)

(handwritten margin note: are the societies irish enough?)

United States: 1860–1914

The huge increase in the numbers of Irish who emigrated from Ireland to North America in the wake of the famine had a powerful impact in the United States. Not only did the Irish population grow in the cities of the eastern seaboard, thereby increasing the importance and profile of events such as the New York City St Patrick's Day parade, but they spread across the nation.[61] By 1860, the *Boston Pilot* reported St Patrick's Day celebrations in fourteen states and three Canadian provinces, including Parkersburg, Vir-ginia, Covington, Kentucky, New Albany, Indiana, Adrian, Michigan and Guelph, Ontario.[62] The steady growth of the Irish population right across America, and their concentration in specific cities and ghettos, meant that they were easily organized into groups, clubs and associations – a process that was furthered by the large number of Irish-American newspapers. These societies, especially those that managed St Patrick's Day celebrations, 'allowed immigrants to express their nationality freely', a chance they took full advantage of with 'monster parades' on 17 March.[63] The continued growth of the local Irish population, together with the increased number of Irish organizations, raised the profile of St Patrick's Day across the country.[64] But what did the increase in Patrician observance signal and represent in this period? First, it appears that St Patrick's Day was used by Irish Americans as a way of focusing attention on the position of the Irish back home, and for Irish nationalists the ongoing political battle against the British presence in Ireland. Second, St Patrick's Day turned the spotlight on the position of the diaspora within their host society. In having these twin functions, St Patrick's Day became a key time for Irish-American public expression: this was no more important than in New York which developed, during the second half of the nineteenth century, as 'the international headquarters of Irish nationalist agitation'.[65] All radical groups, such as the Fenians, Clan na Gael and the Land League found support and funds in New York, and the enthusiasm in the city for such causes, and for the Irish generally, made St Patrick's Day all the more important.

The political struggle for Irish self-government had won the support of many Irish migrants and expatriates in the United States. Home Rule was a basic expectation, so this campaign was followed closely by the Irish-American press. Additionally, though, a more virulent form of nationalism had emerged in the wake of the Fenian uprising in Ireland in 1848. Not content with self-government under the auspices of Britain, Fenians championed a republican and separatist future for Ireland, and they were prepared to use military force to achieve their goals. The 'Young Ireland rebellion' of 1848 was, however, a failure. In the midst of reprisals many Fenians fled abroad, the majority finding sanctuary in the United States – a republic that had already severed ties with Britain after military conflict. This is not to suggest that Young Irelanders found a welcoming sanctuary; American authorities closely monitored their activities, particularly as local membership of the Fenian organization had grown over the previous decade. Yet local support for Irish republicans – for separatist politics rather than the reformist Home Rule campaign – was stronger in the United States than anywhere else outside of Ireland. Exiled Fenians lobbied Irish Americans for support and attempted, wherever possible, to raise money from them for those campaigning and fighting against the British in Ireland.

This presence of exiled Irish political activists in America was readily visible on St Patrick's Day. In 1861, Thomas Meagher, one of the leaders of the 1848 rebellion, observed the New York parade from the review stand, while a military contingent of Fenians marched in the procession under the pseudonym of the 'Phoenix Zouvers'. In allowing this, the St Patrick's Day parade organizers were effectively sanctioning the use of physical force in the campaign for independence in Ireland.[66] Indeed, a Fenian presence in the march posed problems for both parade organizers and New York authorities. Such a public embrace of an armed, secretive organization that represented militant separatism, particularly angered New York's Orange Order. This group was already perturbed by the growing number of Catholics in America, their rise to prominence in politics and the labour movement and working-class Catholic support for Irish nationalism. The AOH clearly endorsed Irish separatist politics, but it was nonetheless wary about local reactions to its connection with Fenianism. Indeed, rumours of imminent violence were common in the weeks leading up to St Patrick's Day parades. In 1866, for instance, Orangemen spread rumours that 20,000 Fenians would join the 17 March procession. If the claim had substance, there were crowd management and public order issues to be dealt with in advance by New York police. The authorities took no risks, and despite the subsequent non-appearance of thousands of Fenians, the parade was supervised and escorted by six militia units.

One year later, the Fenian uprising in Ireland became something of a political cause to many Irish Americans with nationalist sympathies. The 1867 rising had emotional appeal: to them it was an understandable reaction to British culpability for the devastation of the famine, while the cause of separation from Britain, so dear to American patriots in their own history, had a new and romantic focus in the Irish struggle for liberation. Organizers of St Patrick's Day events in America in 1867 debated whether to use their celebrations to publicly promote the cause of the Fenians, or whether to suspend observance of 17 March and send money normally spent on the day direct to Ireland to support the nationalist cause. The influential and respectable temperance group, the Father Mathew society, chose to suspend all normal St Patrick's Day activity, instead donating money that would usually be spent on 17 March to 'the men in the gap, fighting for the libera-tion of Ireland', a decision that was applauded by America's *Irish People* newspaper.[67] Such debates about the utility of St Patrick's Day and Fenian-ism were similar to those discussed previously regarding recognition of tem-perance and famine on 17 March. While Ireland struggled with poverty, hunger and British government oppression, should Irish Americans be squandering large sums of money on rather self-indulgent celebratory parades and dinners? In 1867 the *Irish People* stressed that traditional St Patrick's Day celebrations were, in the context of political crisis, inappropri-ate. The newspaper, by lauding the choice of the Father Mathew society to suspend all celebrations, argued:

> Irishmen throughout America could serve their land well and nobly by taking example from these men. All demonstrations, banquets, etc., should be avoided, and every assistance given to redeem our country from its thraldom. If we do our duty at this crisis, on next St Patrick's Day we will be proud of our land and our race. No demonstrations at this time, but work like men for Ireland.[68]

Tellingly, though, the pleadings of the *Irish People* went largely ignored, for St Patrick's Day was celebrated in 1867 in a typically extroverted American style. It seems, therefore, that Irish Americans paid lip-service to the idea of rebellion in Ireland, and were broadly supportive of military action to expel the British from their homeland, but St Patrick's Day was too important in the domestic social and political context to be passed over in full favour of Ireland. Patrician parades, banquets and other celebrations performed many local functions for Irish Americans. Support for Ireland and its struggle for independence were worthy causes, but they were overshadowed by Irish-American concerns about their position and future in the United States. St Patrick's Day was, in that respect, a local demonstration of Irish-American numerical strength, political power and cultural influence. The *Irish People*, however, was concerned solely with the nationalist position in Ireland; it condemned Irish Americans for observing St Patrick's Day in the usual manner, dismissing the celebrations of 1867 as a day of irrelevant 'processions and feasting ... drinking and noisy speech making and music and holiday soldiering'.[69] The *Irish People* argued that these recreational events made a mockery of the struggle of the Fenians abroad, who were fighting a 'true battle'. Those who chose to parade and dine on St Patrick's Day were therefore both self-indulgent and traitors to the cause of Ireland. The *Irish People* concluded:

> the immortal green flag has been lifted there [Ireland], but for every hour it floats in the breeze, a brother's life blood pays the penalty. The arms that support it are not the leadless rifles and edgeless swords of procession marshals, but the ready revolver, and the farmer's scythe, and the blacksmith's hammer and the butcher's knife. The men who guard it do not parade at a safe distance, to be honoured by the stare of grinning mayors and sneering officials – they do not search the street windows for ladies' smiles – they do not retire after the day's march to festive halls and champagne suppers; but with a grim desperation unheard of since the world began, they surround the old banner that there, once more, represents hardship and death, or freedom and life.[70]

Tension between openly supporting the cause of Irish political independence on 17 March and celebrating St Patrick's Day in its American context recurred annually. Many Irish-American societies and newspapers were committed to the nationalist cause; hence publicity about an impending St Patrick's Day, as well as reports subsequently of its commemoration, almost always included references to the political situation in Ireland. Most Irish Americans, though, took exception to the posturing of the *Irish People*, instead voting with their feet that St Patrick's Day should not be impeded by troubles in Ireland. Hence, tales of hardship and bravery by republican activists in Ireland, as important as they were to St Patrick's Day in the United States, were not to interfere with long-established traditions of parading and sumptuous dining.

The balance between acknowledging the situation in Ireland while celebrating the patron saint of Ireland in the proper American fashion was apparent in reports of the *Irish Citizen* in 1868. This newspaper supported the traditional American St Patrick's Day, but reminded readers that the political liberties enjoyed by the Irish in the United States were not shared in Ireland. In New York, political banners and flags could be openly and proudly waved on St Patrick's Day, and the colour green displayed proudly without fear of arrest. In Ireland, by contrast, if such 'banners, sentiments and devices' were displayed, 'the ringleaders would assuredly be transported (by well packed juries) to the penal colonies'. Equally, the actual procession-ists were likely to be 'swept with her majesties [*sic*] grape shot and ridden down by her dragoons'.[71] The *Irish Citizen*, therefore, reminded Irish Ameri-cans that their freedom to observe St Patrick's Day was a product of liberties they enjoyed in an independent nation: to embrace 17 March and to parade openly and liberally were to acknowledge the resonance of the American experience. In this, the *Irish Citizen* was underlining a powerful aspect of patriotism and belonging among the Irish – and indeed other immigrant ethnic minorities – in the United States. While American authorities broadly understood and accepted the needs of ethnic groups to celebrate their collective identity, such observances had to be underpinned by an over-riding, unquestioning belief in the virtues of living in, and belonging to, America. This implied accommodation to a dominant order – though Irish Catholics assumed a minority position in a society dominated by Protestants of British and Irish descent. But St Patrick's Day was not simply about acquiescence; it was as much about assertion. For Irish Catholics, 17 March allowed triumphal displays of clerical leadership and lay support; for Irish nationalists it provided a forum in which to express aspirations of political autonomy, even independence, for the homeland.

According to the Irish-American press, St Patrick's Day parades were 'innocent and peaceful commemorations which could not possibly have offended Protestant sensibility'.[72] However, in New York, Boston and Chicago, the organization of parades was now the responsibility of the AOH, which was a staunchly Catholic and nationalist lobby group. This meant that St Patrick's Day incorporated religious symbols and political messages that either distanced or alienated Anglo- and Irish Protestants, particularly those with links to the Orange Order. The increased size of Catholic-dominated St Patrick's Day parades was a reflection of the rise to demographic prominence of this ethno-religious group within Irish America. The heightened profile of the parades seemed to mirror the rising influence of Irish Catholics in municipal politics, the police force and small business. For non-Catholic observers, the St Patrick's Day parade symbolized Irish-Catholic dominance of streets that were ordinarily public space. It was a show of ethno-religious power in which Americans from Irish-Protestant backgrounds played a comparatively minor part.[73] Sallie Ann Marston has argued that parades from the 1850s, when the nativist Know Nothing party espoused its anti-Irish message, became conduits for 'a symbolic challenge to the monopolisation of community power by the Yankees'.[74] In this light parades can be understood as annual challenges to the anti-Irish population, and thus a move beyond a basic embrace of the Irish experience in America. Such open challenges to their opponents meant that the parading Irish transformed 17 March into an annual show of strength, which reflected their growing power and influence within their host community.

The influence of Irish Americans was most evident in New York; Irish-dominated inner city areas and Irish-controlled municipal government were two key ways in which this ethnic group asserted its demographic presence and political clout. Irish Protestants were not excluded from this process, but Irish Catholics typically led the way, dominating fraternal societies and labour organizations that underpinned Irish political culture in New York. Indeed, America's Irish Catholics tended to act as an ethno-religious enclave in which Irish Protestants – almost always seen as anti-Catholic and pro-British – had little in common except ancestry. In 1861, a correspondent of the *London Times* found the spreading civic presence of the New York Irish impressive. He noted that there was scarcely 'a situation of honour or distinction, from the chief magistrate down to the police' that was not filled by an Irishman. He watched that year's St Patrick's Day parade, and was impressed by the 'decently dressed and comfortable participants . . . proud of the privilege of interrupting all the trade of the principal streets in which the Yankees most do congregate'.[75]

The political and cultural embraces of the Irish-Catholic population by Tammany Hall mayors and councillors were particularly visible on St Patrick's Day, though this was offensive to many Protestants – especially given the raised public profile of Irish Catholics in a mass display that was growing annually. In 1867, forty-four bands of music, fifty-two banners, seventeen carriages of officers, and 20,000 marching men made up New York's St Patrick's Day parade.[76] Such a display had a powerful symbolic impact, for it demonstrated the potential political strength of the Irish within the city. The right to celebrate St Patrick's Day was a cause that tended to unite the Irish, prompting them to defend their annual observance in the face of attacks from hostile groupings. A Patrician consensus among Irish Americans – Catholic and Protestant – meant that various politicians allied themselves openly with the celebrations on St Patrick's Day. That said, the civic leader most ready to embrace Irish Catholics, and thereby offend the Protestant population, was Abraham Oakley Hall. During his time as Mayor of New York, Hall reviewed the St Patrick's Day parade in full Irish regalia. He attended Patrician balls dressed in bottle green flytail coats and emerald silk shirts, jocularly claiming that the initials to his name really stood for 'Ancient Order of Hibernians'.[77] Such symbolic acts were underpinned, in Protestant eyes, in the sphere of policy: between 1869 and 1871 a cumulative total of US$1.5 million was granted by the state and city of New York to Catholic parochial schools and private Catholic charities.

One nativist newspaper, the *Tribune*, opined that the Irish 'had taken posses-sion of the city and the state'.[78] Such claims were rejected by the Irish-American press and editors such as James McMaster and John McClenahan who constantly focused on the good order and solemnity of St Patrick's Day parades and processions.[79] Despite continued nativist objections to the polit-ical messages aired on St Patrick's Day, the Irish-American press argued as early as the end of the 1860s that the day 'was a secular holiday replete with processions, dinners and balls'.[80] This was seen by many newspapers, most notably the *Irish Miscellaney*, as an unfortunate development. It argued that the day should be a celebration of *Catholic* faith, and that a religious festival should not be so readily subsumed by a solely festive procession representat-ive of Irish nationality.[81]

The single issue that brought many of these matters to a head was the banning, in 1871, of the annual New York Orange Order parade by Police Superintendent Kelso. This act was seen by Orangemen as blatantly dis-criminatory, particularly given that St Patrick's Day was still supported by civic authorities. The 12 July march went ahead in spite of the ban: wide-spread rioting ensued, culminating in the death of more than sixty civilians. In response to the chaos that surrounded the Orange parade, 'the tide of public opinion once again began to turn increasingly against the Irish and their St Patrick's Day parade'.[82] Criticism of the 17 March parade focused principally on the supposed threat the celebrations posed to public order. In 1872, the *New York Times* commented that the 'Irishman never looks more grotesque than when he is rigged out in a long black coat and silk hat, and yesterday some thousands of such caricatures of the ordinary human being paraded through the streets'. This depiction of an Irishman as a shadowy, if not ridiculous figure was followed by a clear message. The *New York Times* argued that the celebration of St Patrick's Day was being 'perverted to the apparent purpose of [the Irishman] displaying his numerical strength, and to manifesting his consciousness of his own power'.[83] St Patrick's Day, it appeared, was not solely a celebration of the Irish presence in the city, but was a direct challenge to both the non-Irish and non-Catholic. Even where there were no parades, any honouring of St Patrick was a statement made by the Irish need 'to symbolically proclaim to outsiders and insiders the vigour and power of the ethnic community'.[84] Assertions of Catholicism on 17 March were not peculiar to New York. According to Cardinal O'Connell, St Patrick's Day parades during the 1860s and 1870s in Lowell, Massachusetts, 'helped demonstrate the growing strength of the Catholic population in the city'.[85]

The parades of the 1870s in America were the most successful and numerous of the nineteenth century. The best guide to the marches and other events that took place across the country, as well as overriding politi-cal statements attached to 17 March in America, was the *Irish World*. In 1874 this newspaper made three claims for the Irish:

That there is no other nation as a whole, truer to principle than they.
That there is no other nation that has fought so long and so bravely for
Religion and Liberty as they.
That there is no other nation better fitted, by nature, for a high and
pure order of civilisation as they.[86]

Such assertions were common to many editorials in Irish newspapers around
the world in the second half of the nineteenth century. They symbolized a
belief in the Irish right to self-determination within their own country, and
to success and respect wherever they emigrated. The lofty principles
enshrined within the Irish people were a direct product, it was claimed, of
their existence as a separate 'race' that continued to suffer hardship, yet survived as a proud, civilized and religiously devout people. To understand the
presentation of such an image of civic respectability, especially in the
context of late nineteenth-century America, was to position the Irish as
'good' and Christian people. St Patrick's Day, for all its meanings, was,
according to the *Irish World* at least, the celebration of an Irish race which
was making a successful and worthy contribution to the progress of
America. The newspaper regularly described St Patrick's Day parades across
the country as virtuous moral undertakings, and was careful to always locate
the celebration of the Irish saint within the broader context of respect for
liberties offered by the American nation. In 1874 the newspaper depicted
the President of America and his cabinet reviewing the St Patrick's Day
parade in Washington. This picture of the event was draped with the
American flag as well as an Irish flag featuring harp and sunbursts. The
related text acknowledged that the importance of President Grant's observance of the parade was its 'complete and sufficient refutation of the
calumny which says that it is "a parade of foreigners"'.[87] Reports from elsewhere in the country reflected the same obsessions: the orderliness of the
marchers, their embrace by national or state officials, the involvement of
members of the military and links between the Irish role in the success of
the American nation and the future self-government of Ireland. The parades
that were reported on spread from San Francisco in the west to New York in
the east, Savannah in the south, and Wisconsin to the north, and included
over 120 parades in America and nine in Canada.[88]

The growth of St Patrick's Day in the second half of the nineteenth
century, despite the growing presence and power of the Irish in America,
was not problem-free. Although the AOH was the single most important
body within the organization of the parade in New York, St Patrick's Day
did not belong to it. The organization of the day's events was a collaboration
between the AOH and the Convention of Irish Societies. Between 1876 and
into the 1880s there was constant infighting between the two bodies, which
related to who controlled the parade, the order of different groups who
marched, and a host of other issues. The arguments had a devastating effect

on the procession itself, with support for it collapsing. In the absence of a single organizing body, or a central focus for potential marchers, people stayed away. In 1880, the number of marchers in the parade had dropped from the 1867 high of 20,000 to a mere 980. The problems continued, and although a steady recovery began in the 1880s, by 1884 only 3,000 joined the parade. Such a continued struggle to attract marchers and to provide a coherent structure for St Patrick's Day observance was now seen by some commentators as a mark of the day's irrelevance. Perhaps St Patrick's Day had, by the mid-1880s, served its purpose in America? The Irish were settled in the country, their rate of assimilation was high, and many had assumed positions of power and influence in American society. In the wake of the 1884 parade, the *New York Times* suggested that 'yesterday gave fresh evidence of the fact that in this city, at least, the glory of St Patrick's Day is fast departing'.[89] Rumours of the death of St Patrick's Day were, however, premature. As a result of public debate about the future of the parade and because of continued low turnouts, the AOH and the Convention of Irish Societies settled their differences and began building St Patrick's Day anew. By 1886, with divisions and arguments rapidly receding into memory, 10,000 marched. New technology, the refrigerated ship, also allowed the import of fresh shamrock direct from Ireland. This was worn by many of the marchers, and most notably by Mayor Grace on the reviewing stand.[90] A further mark of the steady recovery of St Patrick's Day in New York and its central place, both within the calendar of the city and of the Irish diaspora elsewhere in the country, took place at the start of the twentieth century. Ever since 1881, the St Patrick's Day marchers had paraded past the city's St Patrick's Cathedral. Catholicism was a key part of the Irish-American experience, and central to the ethos and belief of the AOH. The centrality of the church to Irish Americans, and hence to St Patrick's Day, was signalled in 1901 when Archbishop Corrigan became the first head of the Roman Catholic Diocese of New York to review the parade.

The fluctuating fortunes of the parade in New York were part of a national pattern. During the last two decades of the nineteenth century, and in the context of a growth in anti-Catholicism, many parades across the country suffered a downturn in support. In addition to external political issues that impacted on the popularity of parades during this period, there were also a series of changes within the Irish-American community itself. It appears that the late nineteenth century witnessed a serious questioning of the value of parades. The efforts of the temperance movement worked against these mass displays, as they were often seen as precursors to drunken indulgence. The growing cost of the parades and their increasingly elaborate nature also turned many away from participation. There was a belief that money earmarked for the annual cavalcade could be better spent on charity either in Ireland or at home in America. Throughout the 1880s and 1890s, then, the number of groups marching in parades across the country reduced as they chose to donate their money to worthy causes, and sometimes to the political struggle in Ireland. The effects of these changes can be seen most dramatically in the failure to stage a Boston parade between 1881 and 1885, and the complete abandonment of parades in Philadelphia, Lawrence, MA, and Wilmington, DE. The *Boston Pilot* reported that 'the customary processions, banquets and other festivities were generally dispensed with ... the proceeds to be diverted to the alleviation of the sufferers by the famine in Ireland'.[91] The official parade in New York was also dispensed with for the same reason, though an informal procession from Broadway to Fifty-Seventh Street did take place.[92] A final shift in the Irish-American community that damaged late nineteenth-century celebrations was the cult of self-improvement. St Patrick's Day had traditionally been a celebration, most notably in terms of parades, dominated by men. In the later decades of the nineteenth century, movements for rational recreation and broad-based education took hold across a whole range of men's organizations, including those devoted to the interests of Irish Americans. Parading was increasingly viewed as frivolous; hence many 'self-improving' Irishmen turned away from the bands, fancy dress and paraphernalia of 17 March, instead joining mechanics' institutes, literary groups and sporting organizations.[93]

The division between the Irish and those of a nativist position remained, particularly so in New York, and they were demonstrated forcefully in 1886. The city election that year was won by Abram Hewitt, a nativist politician with a clear-cut agenda to support an 'authentic', Anglo-Saxon American, rather than an 'uncohesive', ethnic-American society. He demanded that all immigrants face a literacy test, and that the naturalization period for immigrants be increased to twenty-one years. Such anti-ethnic thinking soon affected St Patrick's Day, with Hewitt the first New York mayor in thirty-seven years to refuse to review the annual parade. He also failed to sanction the usual flying of the shamrock flag on city hall. Hewitt, in one of his more outspoken moments, suggested to his predominantly Irish-American Board of Aldermen that those in America who preferred any other national flag should go back where they came from. Perhaps, unsurprisingly, given his political opinions and the strength of the Irish and other ethnic groups within New York politics, Hewitt was not re-elected.[94] The following year, the new mayor, Hugh Grant, reinstated Irish flags over City Hall and reviewed the parade. Despite the return to what might be considered normality under Mayor Grant, the nativist position still had much support. In 1894, the American Protective Association mounted a campaign objecting to any foreign flag flown over state buildings. The campaign was successful, and in 1895 the Flag Bill prohibited the display of foreign flags on public buildings; this legislation included the flying of any Irish flags on St Patrick's Day.

During the 1890s St Patrick's Day celebrations slowly regained their popularity, becoming a permanent fixture on the American social calendar.

In 1890, Boston's Charitable Irish Society enjoyed its traditional sumptuous banquet, 5,000 members of the AOH marched through New York in front of a large crowd, the Friendly Sons of St Patrick dined at Delmonico's Restaurant in New York, and the Hibernian Hall Division of the AOH marched in Brooklyn.[95] Elsewhere in America branches of the AOH organized local parades and dinners, as did a host of other Irish-American organizations. The AOH tightly controlled its members, so that a positive image of the organization and of Irishness was projected. The AOH in Butte was one of many Irish-American groups that would expel members who celebrated St Patrick's Day too 'enthusiastically'.[96] The steady growth of Patrician events meant that in Massachusetts alone, over twenty large-scale events in towns and cities across the state were reported in local newspapers.[97] Despite these obvious signs that St Patrick's Day was alive and well in the hearts of Irish Americans, there were complaints that the celebrations were becoming increasingly 'Americanized'. While it was expected that a degree of assimilation would have taken place by the end of the nineteenth century, many older immigrants bemoaned the fact that the new generation were overseeing a process whereby,

> old Irish folk songs were giving way to tin pan alley tunes, gigs to the 'turkey trot' and the hurley stick to the baseball. 'I'm makin for Macon Georgia' even crept onto the concert bill of one St Patrick's Day programme of 1915.[98]

In addition to popular parades were the celebrations of the Irish-American elite on St Patrick's Day. Organizations such as the Knights of St Patrick and the Irish American Society in St Louis, founded in 1870 and 1900 respectively, 'served as highly selective and prestige giving links to the Irish community'. These bodies, though, only had one function: 'elaborate and impressive St Patrick's Day banquets at the city's leading hotels'.[99] The elite nature of these groups, which contrasts with the social background of the majority of Irish immigrants, was evidenced by the fact that 96 per cent of officers and committee chairmen in the first two decades of the twentieth century were business owners or professional men.[100] That other elite body of Irish Americans, the Friendly Sons of St Patrick, changed its annual observance little in the decades following the famine. The group met annually for dinner at one of New York's best restaurants, and was addressed by one of its number, or else a politician or businessman with Irish connections. Initially, there is little in recorded images of these events that suggests nationalism as an ideological force behind the society's St Patrick's Day meetings. Pictures on the St Patrick's programme show large dining rooms full of affluent men in dinner jackets. The dining rooms were heavily decorated, but the red, white and blue colours of America always appeared to dominate the green of Ireland.[101] The dinners were, however, an important and power-

ful focus for discussions about nationalism. Each year a high-quality programme of events was produced for all the diners. The front covers of the
different programmes depict scenes from Irish historic or contemporary life,
the majority of which openly embraced themes of separatist nationalism.
Indeed, for the 1898 St Patrick's Day dinner, the Friendly Sons of St Patrick
programme celebrated the centenary of the United Irishmen's failed rebellion. The cover has at its heart a picture of Wolfe Tone and Robert Emmet.
To their left stands a man with a pike, ready to defend his wife and child
who are sheltering in front of their cottage. To the right of Tone and Emmet
is St Patrick, holding a harp and teaching a young Irish woman. The top of
the programme cover depicts a famine ship and the American flag. The
whole image seeks to firmly locate Irish revolutionary activity within the
teachings of St Patrick, and in the context of the hasty but ultimately successful emigration of the Irish to America.[102] In 1895, the central role of
America in the future freedom of Ireland was illustrated on the St Patrick's
night dinner programme. In the distance stands the Statue of Liberty surrounded by sunbursts. In the foreground a woman, Hibernia, used to depict
Ireland, is kneeling in a field of shamrock with arms outstretched. Behind
her is a partially destroyed round tower. She appears to be pleading with a
woman across a small stretch of water – Liberty, symbol of America, who
stands tall and erect and is offering Hibernia an olive branch. The programme cover illustrates a commonly held belief among Irish Americans
that their new home was the arbiter of freedom and liberty, whereas Ireland
lay broken under the yoke of British rule.[103] The function of America to the
emigrants was therefore twofold: to provide a home to those Irish who
wished to leave their homeland, and to facilitate the eventual freedom of
Ireland. Such imagery was common to Irish Americans, especially on St
Patrick's Day at the turn of the century, and portrayed a series of ideals that
did much to motivate nationalist leaders, such as de Valera, to travel to
America to find support for political freedom during the Irish War of
Independence.

The speakers on St Patrick's night echoed themes that were evident on the
dinner programme covers. In 1889, the campaign for Home Rule was openly
touted and supported by John S. Wise of Virginia, who spoke in response to
the toast 'Ireland'. Wise explained that it was impossible for Americans to
understand the minutiae of Irish politics, but argued that it was straightforward for all to acknowledge and support the plea for Home Rule. Wise's
speech is important in that it demonstrates how changes in tactic within the
nationalist movement in Ireland were embraced by Irish-American sympathizers, especially when they considered Irish politics on St Patrick's Day. At
times, Irish Americans had been, and would continue to be, supportive of
campaigns of violence against British rule in Ireland. Throughout the last
three decades of the nineteenth century, however, the Friendly Sons, as with
most Irish Americans, were fully supportive of constitutional attempts to win

Home Rule. The most important focus at the time of Wise's speech was the campaign of Parnell. Wise explained to his audience:

> we behold the efforts of Ireland controlled and directed in lawful con-
> stitutional methods ... we believe that Irishmen are right in the spirit
> of manhood which prompts them. And we believe the hour is near at
> hand when the long struggle of your great nation will be ended glori-
> ously and culminate, not in revolutionary bloodshed, but in constitu-
> tional liberty sought and obtained by lawful methods.[104]

The tenor of the speeches on St Patrick's night were supported by cable-grams the Friendly Sons sent on this occasion, and which were read out to the assembled guests. The messages to British Prime Minister Gladstone and Irish leader Parnell both closed with the plea, 'Success to Parnellism and patriotism, defeat to Toryism and crime'.[105] The speeches, as with the pro-gramme covers, constantly reiterated the apparent success of the Irish Home Rule movement in campaigning for Irish national freedom and the key role of Irish Americans in supporting this. In the closing remarks at the 1898 dinner, the Friendly Sons' President, Joseph J. O'Donohue, acknowledged how promising the future of Ireland looked, paid thanks to the American people and the American press, and concluded that 'only a free man can truly appreciate the blessing of freedom'.[106] A similar connection between Ireland's fortunes and America's liberating role had been evident a decade earlier in a speech made by Mr Richardson. He informed the gathering of the Friendly Sons of St Patrick that 'Ireland today speaks through America more than it speaks through the mother country', and that any preparation for political activity in Ireland had to take place in America, as it was 'here that there is an opportunity to develop the capacities of the Irish race, such as cannot be obtained even in Ireland itself'.[107]

The Friendly Sons of St Patrick's annual Patrician dinners, while serving charitable, fraternal and business purposes for elite Irish Americans, were also venues for expressions of Irish nationalism. They linked the ongoing campaign for Irish home rule with the successful Irish American diaspora, and made 17 March a key date in the promotion of the Irish cause. Outside the dinners, the public celebration of St Patrick's Day during this period was heightened by the arrival from Ireland of shamrock in letters and parcels. For fresh shamrock New Yorkers could turn to Charles Hunt's Sons on Staten Island, who grew the plant in greenhouses from 1882.[108] What-ever the social, commercial and dining opportunities afforded by 17 March, it is clear that St Patrick's Day celebrations in America, in the decades following the famine, helped redefine Irish Americans. While the various events held on 17 March embraced Irish nationalism, they also served to push the Irish closer towards their American context and to redefine them-selves as Americans.

Canada: 1860–1914

In 1871, when Canada had its first full census, residents who claimed an Irish heritage comprised 24.3 per cent of the population, outnumbering other English-speaking groups (English 20.3 per cent and Scottish 15.8 per cent), though falling short of the French (31.1 per cent).[109] The famine exodus had also increased the proportion of the Irish among Catholics in Canada. Toronto's Catholic population, for instance, was 95 per cent Irish in 1880, and still 80 per cent Irish by 1890. At the same time, though, the overall proportion of Catholics in Toronto was in decline – from a high point of 27 per cent in 1861 to only 15 per cent in 1891.[110] The wider points from this and related census information is that the Irish in Canada were a significant ethnic group for the remainder of the nineteenth century, both as Protestants and Catholics; and, despite fears among the Orange Order, the volume of Irish Catholics had not grown exponentially. Yet perception is so often more persuasive than fact. During this time many Irish Protestants felt threatened by Irish Catholics in their midst, particularly in English-speaking parts of Canada, such as Toronto. With Irish Catholics asserting their legitimate place in the society and Irish Protestants feeling a threat to their ascendancy, sectarian tensions – though not inevitable – smouldered away. There were, indeed, plenty of sparks being thrown into the kindling by non-Irish Protestants, as indicated by the following excerpt from a Presbyterian sermon in Toronto:

> O Lord we approach thee this morning in an attitude of prayer and like-wise of complaint. When we came to Canada we expected to find a land flowing with milk and honey, but instead we find a land peopled by the ungodly Irish. O Lord, in thy mercy drive them to the uttermost parts of Canada … If ye have any favours to bestow, or any good land to give away, give it to thine own peculiar people, the Scots … for the ungodly Irish, take them by the heels and shake them over the pit of hell.[111]

By the late 1850s, Toronto's Irish Catholics were split over whether to challenge or ignore various forms of victimization. Priests and churches had been set upon by militant Orangemen, in defiance of that organization's regulations forbidding violence. Catholics also faced discrimination: there were hardly any Catholics in Toronto's civic administration, while efforts to establish Catholic schools faced concerted opposition from Protestant critics who decried the 'Romanizing' of Canadian children. Catholics who favoured an assertive response formed the Hibernian Benevolent Society in 1858; this association emerged in the wake of violence and murder on St Patrick's Day earlier in that year, so it was expected to 'protect Catholics from Orange aggression'.[112] But the group's focus was hardly St Patrick's Day itself: the Irish-Catholic elite, which favoured accommodation to the existing order, had already cancelled the annual parade.[113] Instead the Hibernians concentrated initially on making Toronto a safer place for Catholics – their usual response was systematic reprisals against aggressors. Just as importantly, the Hibernian Benevolent Society offered insurance for Catholic workers in the forms of sickness and funeral benefits. Most significantly, from our point of view, the Hibernians soon became very influential in the social life of many male, mostly working-class, Catholics. The association was determined, as Michael Cotterell has put it, 'to inject a more nationalist spirit into the Irish community, to engender pride and self-confidence', thereby bolstering their wider 'demand for recognition and respect' for Irish Catholics in Toronto. Indeed, one of the most powerful initiatives of the Hibernians was to 'reassert the Irish-Catholic right to the streets of the city by resuming parades on St Patrick's Day'.[114]

From the beginning, the Hibernians consulted with the Catholic Church over its plans for St Patrick's Day, thereafter receiving the support of Toronto's newly appointed Bishop, John Joseph Lynch. The decision provoked much criticism from the local Irish-Catholic elite; they feared that such a mass display would antagonize the Protestant population. Lynch, however, was unmoved. He even addressed the revived parade of 1862 from the steps of the cathedral, congratulating the organizers for their 'noble efforts on behalf of faith and fatherland'.[115] Behind the scenes, however, the bishop may not have known that the Hibernian president, Michael Murphy, had been secretly collaborating with the Fenian Brotherhood in the United States, and that he was leader of that movement's Toronto chapter. The St Patrick's Day parade of 1862 had been staged by the Hibernians with little hint of rancour; indeed, Lynch's public sanction provided the event with much needed respectability. But it was merely a dress rehearsal for a much more politically assertive St Patrick's Day in the years to follow. The parades of 1863 and 1864 were unprecedented in scale, though the greatest causes for excitement were the style of the cavalcade and the messages conveyed. Martial tunes, such as 'The Croppy Boy' and 'God Save Ireland' were introduced, and the route was lengthened – thereby taking the marchers past several of the Orange Lodges, which was doubtless intended as provocation. Among the crowds, too, there was evidence of political militancy: the press reported a 'proliferation of Fenian sunburst banners' and, at the conclusion of the parade, 'open expressions of support for Fenianism'.[116] Michael Murphy addressed supporters from a podium, from where he launched scathing verbal attacks on those who suppressed Irish Catholics. The speeches, which advocated militancy on the part of Irish Canadians, were tantamount to treason. The fact that Bishop Lynch stood alongside Murphy during his speeches – both in 1863 and 1864 – was of great concern to the Catholic Church, for its spiritual leader in Toronto seemed to be sanctioning Fenian sentiments. Under pressure from fellow clergy, as well as moderates within the Irish-Catholic laity, Lynch eventually appealed to Catholics to distance themselves from the Hibernians who, in the bishop's words, had 'fallen away from Catholic principles'. There was also some compromise by the Hibernians: after a request from Bishop Lynch they agreed not to stage the St Patrick's Day parade of 1865. Political moderation had, it seemed, triumphed over assertiveness.[117]

Yet controversy loomed again the following year in Toronto. There were powerful rumours that a Fenian invasion of Canada was being planned from the United States, where Irish militants planned to 'liberate' the provinces from British rule. A military invasion from the Fenians, while it had long been anticipated as a possibility, was now said to be 'timed to coincide with a huge St Patrick's Day parade organised by the Hibernians'.[118] Politically moderate Irish Catholics were alarmed at the prospect of being seen by local Protestants as disloyal to Canada. Hence they were openly critical of the Hibernian Benevolent Society, which was considered a haven for Fenian sympathizers, and they declared their opposition to Fenian forces should they intervene militarily in Canada. Bishop Lynch was under extreme pressure to ban the St Patrick's Day parade of 1866, which he did in principle 'by advising all Catholics to spend the day either in Church or at home'.[119] But in practice he was unable to either persuade nor prevent the Hibernians from marching along the streets of Toronto on the very day that American Fenians were 'expected' to invade Canada. There was, however, no Fenian rising on St Patrick's Day, and 'only the die-hard Hibernians turned out to march in the smallest parade in years'.[120]

Fears of a looming Fenian invasion were nonetheless realized just three months later, with further uprisings during the second half of 1866. The raids were quelled by loyalist forces, so were abortive in the long term. But there was a lingering political impact for Toronto's Irish, though more so for Catholics than Protestants. The local Orange Order had long demonstrated its loyalty to British rule in Canada; its members swore allegiance to the monarchy and supported the Protestant ascendancy in the English-speaking provinces. The local Hibernians, on the other hand, had demonstrated sympathy for Fenian ideals. They were a Catholic organization with largely working-class lay support, yet as far as many British-Canadian patriots were concerned, all of Toronto's Irish Catholics were guilty of either disloyalty or sedition. They had been tarred black, it seemed, by the broad brush of treason. The strategy of leading Catholic moderates, including the clergy, was twofold: to distance themselves from the Hibernians and to promote a virtuous sense of Irish-Catholic 'place' in what was more than ever a British-Protestant-dominated Toronto. In this regard, Catholic leaders opted for a low profile for both church and laity; this included the commemoration of St Patrick's Day, which in 1867 was observed 'in-house' without the spectacle of a public parade.[121] Yet as far as loyalists were concerned, there was plenty to celebrate openly in March 1867: a bill to secure the Confederation of Canada was passed that month in Westminster, and, just four months later, the self-governing British Dominion of Canada was inaugurated on 1 July.[122]

The Hibernian spirit in Toronto was restrained but not silenced. Bishop Lynch allowed the St Patrick's Day parade to resume in 1868, and four hundred Hibernians led the march. However, the attendance was low compared to the crowds of the early 1860s, and 'a subdued atmosphere pervaded the celebrations'.[123] For Irish-Catholic radicals there was, indeed, nothing to chortle about. Frank Boyle, editor of the Irish nationalist newspaper the *Irish Canadian*, gave the St Patrick's Day oration in which he bemoaned the 'plight of Fenian prisoners in Canadian jails'.[124] The St Patrick's Day keynote speech of 1869 was, however, pragmatic about Irish-Catholic priorities in the newly established nation–state. The speaker, John O'Donohoe, a former member of the corporation of Toronto, focused on the need for Irish Catholics to establish themselves more fully within the body politic. One year later the Catholic League was formed, a lobby group intended to further the socio-political interests of Ontario's Catholics, and to support Irish-Catholic candidates who stood for election to the province's government. The emphasis now, more than ever, was for Toronto's Irish Catholics to immerse themselves in the political system and represent their ethno-religious constituency. During the early 1870s, St Patrick's Day parades and speeches reflected this sense of civic engagement, for they represented something of a 'respectable' collective face to the public of Toronto. Hibernian radicals had an innocuous presence in the parade, whereas the socially 'virtuous' Father Mathew Temperance Society and the politically 'moderate' Emerald Benevolent Association were now more noticeable. This strategy of appeasement on St Patrick's Day reflected a greater consensus within Toronto's Irish-Catholic community. Yet in 1877 the city's annual St Patrick's Day parade was cancelled, and it stayed that way for the next one hundred years.[125] How might this rapid shift from rapprochement to banishment be explained?

Michael Cotterell contends that St Patrick's Day parades were now seen by organizers as unhelpful in that they perpetuated the Irish-Catholic sense of distance and difference from other groups in Toronto. At a time when they were growing in confidence politically, it was no longer necessary for Irish Catholics to parade down city streets to affirm ethno-religious solidarity, particularly as many local descendants of Irish parents saw themselves foremost as Canadian Catholic.[126] While Cotterell focuses on 'internal' factors leading to the change of observance on St Patrick's Day, 'external' forces fundamentally influenced the abandonment of the parade. Of particular note here was the Jubilee riots of 1875, which Gregory Kealey describes as 'undoubtedly the bloodiest sectarian struggles in Toronto's history'.[127] The Pope had declared 1875 to be a 'Jubilee year' of the Catholic Church; hence Toronto's faithful prepared for 'a procession to be held for Catholic bishops visiting the city', and they also 'planned to march on church visitations to gain indulgences' connected with the anniversary.[128] There was, indeed, much excitement among the Catholic clergy and laity; it was therefore understandable that they wished to venerate the Jubilee publicly. But context is everything. In August, a month before the Jubilee procession, Irish Catholics staged an 'unprecedented' public celebration of the life of the legendary Irish leader, Daniel O'Connell. Kealey reckons this was 'probably the largest Catholic demonstration ever held in Toronto'; it was also organized by the Hibernians.[129] The Orange Order was agitated by this development – even more so given that the planned Jubilee procession was to follow in just six weeks.

Protestant appeals to Bishop Lynch to cancel the celebrations were met with stony silence. Catholics were still scheduled to meet in procession on Sunday 26 September and Sunday 2 October. On the first occasion they were met by angry parading Orangemen and minor scuffles ensued. In a shrewd move, the Orange Order then argued that 'both sides refrain from marching on the coming Sunday'.[130] This made it seem as if Protestants were offering a concession of their own, although the effect of the strategy was to deny Catholics the right to public assembly during their Jubilee celebrations. A furious Bishop Lynch confronted Toronto's Orange mayor, Frances Medcalf, demanding protection for marchers who were determined to continue despite Protestant threats of intimidation. The mayor relented, agreeing to guarantee right of passage for the Catholics in their procession. This decision did not prevent a riot involving some 8,000 marchers and their opponents, but property damage was not extensive and the protagonists incurred relatively minor injuries. This might be attributed to a heavy police presence: Toronto's law enforcers were overwhelmingly Protestant, but they had a collective responsibility to keep the peace.[131] Was the response of the mayor and the police indicative of a softening of the anti-Catholic stance of Orange-dominated institutions? To ascertain that we need to look at Catholic processions beyond the Jubilee year, when St Patrick's Day returned as the key moment of the Irish-Catholic calendar in Toronto.[132]

St Patrick's Day parades and green paraphernalia 'were acceptable' to the Orange Order in the mid-1870s.[133] The express Protestant concern of 1875 was the Jubilee procession, which the Order took to be excessively triumphal and ultramontane. Yet, Toronto's St Patrick's Day parade of 1876 suffered 'an extremely poor turnout' which led, in the following year, to its abandonment. Hence, the demise of the march seems to have been a consequence of 'internal' pressures. There was no ban on parading on 17 March, and the Orange Order had been rebuked for disrupting Catholic processions in 1875. Yet the spectre of public confrontation remained, as the Hibernian Patrick Boyle admitted in the *Irish Canadian*:

As a duty to the concord of society, to peace and order, to industry and steadiness, to the perfect unity which proves strength to the State, those processions which are instances of bad citizenship in this country . . . ought to be abandoned.[134]

Boyle hints at 'external' pressures having forced the hand of Irish Catholics. St Patrick's Day of 1866 did not receive much of a turnout, but given the Jubilee riots just six months earlier it is reasonable to assume that some of the usual marchers were reluctant to take part in another procession – albeit a more traditional fair – out of fear for their own safety. There were indeed precedents for violence on St Patrick's Day, such as in 1871 when 'an Orange carter drove his horse through a Catholic procession'.[135] There was also the affronting spectacle, on 17 March 1872, of Orange bands parading through Catholic neighbourhoods 'playing their favourite party tunes'.[136]

There is a further factor to consider. In 1877 Hibernians may well have conceded that their Patrician parade was either antiquated as a form of ethnic solidarity, too problematic to stage, or a combination of the two, but a quick glance at St Patrick's Day, of 1878 suggests that Irish Catholics – particularly those with Irish nationalist sympathies – were not about to abandon 17 March as a time for self-reflection. The absence of a parade meant that the fanfare of St Patrick's Day, 1878 was diminished, but Hibernians organized an alternative attraction – a public speech by the legendary Fenian leader Jeremiah O'Donovan Rossa. Large crowds assembled to hear O'Donovan Rossa's address, but the event was soon marred by violence on the part of agitated Orangemen, as well as the intervention of police to 'restore order'. Rossa, however, received little protection from the authorities; indeed, the police themselves 'took a severe beating' from the Catholic multitude.[137] Hence, while Cotterell sees the demise of the St Patrick's Day parade as reluctance on the part of Irish Catholics to appear separate from the Toronto community, as well as their desire to be respected as acculturated Canadian citizens, there were also sectarian pressures that brought an end to the 17th of March procession. Concurrently, the Orange Order itself seems to have placed less emphasis on the 12th of July parades after the violence of the 1870s. Kealey's study of Protestant–Catholic relations suggests an ameloriation of overt sectarian tensions in Toronto: there were only four sectarian riots between 1879 and 1892, whereas there had been twenty-two such incidents between 1867 and 1878.[138] By the late nineteenth century Irish Catholics played a more active role in the labour movement and, to a lesser degree, in civic administration. Mark McGowan argues that they were generally no longer seen as separate from the rest of Toronto's English-speaking community, and by the turn of the century had 'considerable confidence, both in their faith and in their status as citizens of Canada'.[139] However, 'co-existence did not necessarily imply social acceptance'.[140]

In French-speaking Canada there was, as might be expected, less controversy about staging St Patrick's Day celebrations. As we pointed out previously, the resident Irish were principally Catholic, as were the numerically dominant French. Notwithstanding the demise of Toronto's St Patrick's Day parade in 1877, annual Patrician marches continued in Montreal and Quebec City. It should be noted, however, that 17 March was but one of several 'national' days in the social calendar of these cities, which included French observance of Saint Jean-Baptiste's Day and Bastille Day. From the late nineteenth century labour organizations also celebrated a collective sense of self, with parades of workers on May Day. The wider point of this is that street parades were not solely a component of St Patrick's Day; they were part and parcel of other festivals and ceremonies in Canada as well. Indeed, in 1872 the largest crowd ever assembled at a public event in Montreal witnessed the funeral procession of the high profile Irish-Catholic figure, Thomas D'Arcy McGee.[141]

There were odd moments of intrigue on St Patrick's Day in the Quebec region from 1860 to the early 1900s. Predictably, there was concern about an anticipated Fenian rising on St Patrick's Day, 1866, although this produced contrasting responses. Montreal went ahead with a parade which, unlike that of Toronto, was well attended. In Quebec City, meanwhile, the usual procession was cancelled: the Irish Protestant Benevolent Society withdrew because of the 'prevailing excitement in the city', while Catholic clergy also deemed it unwise to proceed under the circumstances.[142] One year later the Quebec parade was back in full swing. However, in keeping with local tradition, because St Patrick's Day fell on a Sunday, the Patrician mass, parade and evening concert were each held over to the Monday.[143] In subsequent years the celebrations continued in their usual form, except when poor weather intervened or Sabbatarian considerations demanded postponement to an alternative day. Triumphal arches were a feature of the Quebec parades: the *Morning Chronicle* in March 1876 wrote, admiringly, of a 'pretty and tasteful ... triumphal arch' being put together by young ladies who were 'in spite of the gale that howled around them, putting the finishing touches, in the shape of flowers, golden hearts, crosses, anchors, and several other religious symbols upon the evergreens'. There were even alcoves in the arches so that 'appropriately dressed children' could occupy them for further aesthetic effect.[144] Hereafter Quebec's St Patrick's Day festivities were cancelled only twice – in 1880 and 1881. Curiously, although Patrician parades were staged during the famine, there was now concern that this type of celebration was inappropriate at a time of recession that had brought 'national distress in the motherland'. Under these circumstances, argued the *Morning Chronicle*, a St Patrick's Day procession would be tantamount to 'dancing at a wake'.[145] By the mid-1880s, however, the city's Patrician festivities were back in full swing, continuing unabated until the crisis of the First World War.

For parade-goers in Montreal, the weather on 17 March was almost always of concern. On St Patrick's Day, 1865, for instance, the *Gazette* reported that 'heavy foggy weather prevailed all day and the roads were almost impregnable owing to the thaw'.[146] The march nonetheless continued, prompting Mr Coyle, President of the Catholic Young Men's Society, to remark that 'every Irishman who had witnessed the procession

that day must feel proud'.[147] Compared to Montreal's ecumenical St
Patrick's Day festivities before the 1850s, this was a more Irish nationalist
and Catholic affair. The order of parade was printed in the *Gazette*: there was
no mention of representatives of other national groups, such as the St
George's or St Andrew's societies; and the procession was dominated by
Catholic school groups, Catholic religious sodalities, Catholic Total Abstinence societies, members of the St Patrick's Society (which had become
exclusively Catholic in 1856), and the congregation of St Patrick's Catholic
church. At the subsequent St Patrick's Day dinner, a key theme was political
and religious 'liberation' of the homeland. As Thomas McKenna, Vice-
President of the St Patrick's Society put it: 'we proclaim that Ireland must
and shall triumph in the cause of justice and of right, and that the demon of
discord, denominational supremacy, will, ere long, be banished forever from
the land (Cheers)'.[148]

Irish-Protestant observance of St Patrick's Day in Montreal is difficult to
discern; there does not appear to have been societies or associations in the
parade representing the non-Catholic Irish community. It would seem,
therefore, that many Irish Protestants who observed St Patrick's Day did so
privately and separately from Irish Catholics in Montreal. Newspaper
records offer rare references to Protestant participation; this tended to be in
the form of a special invitation to leading Irish Protestants with a 'liberal'
political disposition. In 1865, for example, the Reverend Mr Cordner was a
guest at the Patrician dinner organized by the St Patrick's Society. Introduc-
ing Cordner, the Society's president, Bernard Devlin, emphasized that their
guest 'had come on this occasion to join in the celebration of the patron
Saint', and 'he trusted he would leave ... with a warm sense of welcome'.
Devlin explained that Cordner, while 'a Protestant minister ... had
extended the hand of friendship to the Irish Roman Catholic. They had one
common object and met under one roof, to celebrate the glorious memories
of Ireland.' Cordner, predictably, was judicious in reply. He spoke glowingly
of Irish boyhood memories of Daniel O'Connell, whose life had inspired in
him a message: 'to deprive a man of his political privileges on account of his
religion, was ... one of the most serious offences any government could be
guilty of'. Cordner stressed that Irishmen of all backgrounds were able to
prosper in North America: here all of the Irish people 'had free scope to
make headway, without being hampered as they were at home'. Devlin,
when speaking before Cordner, had already established the political tenor of
his guest's speech: it is 'beyond the power of any government', he thundered, to deprive Irish people of 'the right of governing themselves as they
did in Canada'. The Protestant minister, following on, was under no illu-
sions about what the Society expected to hear from him.[149]

By the 1870s there was, indeed, an expectation among many of Montreal's Irish – Catholic or Protestant – that Home Rule for Ireland was desirable along similar lines to that which had been granted to Canada. Symbolic

support for this view was clear on St Patrick's Day, 1875. The *Gazette*, describing the splendour of decorations along the parade route, was particularly taken with ceremonial arches, among which was an evergreen-covered structure displaying the mottoes 'Home Rule for the land of our forefathers' and 'Ireland and France are true friends'. Canada was, of course, a Dominion of Britain, so the arrangement of other St Patrick's Day arches and emblems also emphasized loyalty to the Empire, albeit with a concurrent desire for Ireland to be accepted into the fold as a self-governing nation. Among the symbols was an ornate display of flags, the centrepiece of which was the British ensign; to either side hung the Irish, French and American flags. Irish-Canadian loyalty to Britain and local confidence in the evolution of Irish self-determination under the auspices of Empire were embodied in the symbol perched atop St Patrick's Hall. There, as parade marchers paced by, was a *single* flag – the British ensign swaying 'proudly to the breeze'.[150] This very visible demonstration of Irish loyalty to Britain was, of course, a counterpoint to accusations in the mid-1860s of Irish – particularly Irish-Catholic – support for a Fenian overthrow of Canada.

Symbols are, however, only emblematic; they may disguise as much as they reveal. In 1877, just two years after the Union flag was flown above St Patrick's Hall on 17 March, an Orange parade in Montreal was cancelled owing to hostility on the part of Irish Catholics. Tensions led to a brawl among angry groups of Protestants and Catholics, with one man shot and killed in Victoria Square.[151] On the one hand, support for the principle of Irish Home Rule was widely established; on the other hand, ideas about the balance of political and religious liberties within a self-governing Irish nation were very contentious.

Such bipolarization of allegiances and instability of intergroup relationships were evident, yet again, on St Patrick's Day, 1881. In a letter to the St Patrick's Society of Montreal, the Irish Protestant Benevolent Association asked that 'officers of both societies walk together in the procession' of 17 March – a request that received 'unanimous agreement'.[152] By contrast, nine years later the official Montreal St Patrick's Day programme, which included details of the order of parade, made no reference to Protestant participation. Instead, the souvenir document stressed the partisan religious nature of the 1890 celebration:

> Our Sainted Apostle . . . was the quintessence of a Catholic, and would not for a thousand worlds pass for anything else. What upright man should not burn with indignation at the persistent efforts that have been made to classify him amongst the Episcopalians and Presbyterians? . . . Our national Saint was a votary of the Papacy . . . He was proud in being a subject of the Sovereign Pontiff . . . He was a Roman of the Romans. His mission was from Rome and all his teaching were from Rome . . . he was called by God to be the apostle of the Irish, yet

he would not answer His call until he had been authorized by His sacred Viceregent ... He turned his steps towards the city of the Popes and solicited an audience from the reigning Pontiff ... Patrick, having come to Rome was honorably received by the holy Pope Celestine, and he was sent to Ireland by the same Pope ... All that our Saint taught in the land of his adoption was identical in every respect with what prevailed in the Pontifical city. Had he taught anything different, the Roman Breviary would take good care not to honor his memory, and the Catholic Church would never think of invoking his intercession.[153]

The 1890 souvenir programme contained an intriguing mix of zealous Catholicism and reformist Irish nationalism. The Irish who observed St Patrick's Day in Montreal were assumed to be from one religious tradition. J.J. Curran, whose St Patrick's Day oration was recorded in the souvenir document, stressed: 'Annually you solemnize the 17th of March ... it chiefly reminds you of the Christian inheritance which you enjoy ... you have vowed, and everlastingly, allegiance to Rome and Ireland.'[154] This claim of Catholic proprietorship of St Patrick's Day, together with loyalty to Rome before all else, was the type of religious 'bravado' that incensed Irish Protestants. The speaker seemed, however, oblivious to Irish intergroup sensibilities, instead affirming Irish-Catholic expectations of Home Rule. He asked:

some people claimed that home rule meant separation. Did home rule in Canada mean separation? Were not the English, Scotch and French in Canada loyal? And ... was there a more loyal body of men in this Dominion than the Irish Catholics?[155]

The answer to that question depended very much on who was making the reply. Mr Curran's speech was made before an enthusiastic Irish-Catholic audience. His query was therefore met, not surprisingly, with 'loud cheers' and 'elicited deafening applause'.[156] Many Irish Canadians anticipated Home Rule for Ireland under the auspices of Empire. There was, however, considerable disagreement as to the form it should take, as well as the communities that would be represented most equitably under a system of self-government.

By 1893, Montreal's Patrician festivities had grown to such an extent that a demand for specialized event management emerged. The newly formed Irish-Catholic Committee, which included a delegate from the St Patrick's Society, seems to have been established for the sole purpose of organizing the annual 17th of March parade. Peggy Regan, after obtaining archival access to the minutes of meetings for both the St Patrick's Society of Montreal and the Irish-Catholic Committee, concludes that 'the change, though abrupt, seems to have been instituted harmoniously, with the St Patrick's Society retaining its position at the end of the parade, accompanying the mayor and invited guests'.[157] Regan notes that by 1899 some twenty Irish associations or church congregations featured in the St Patrick's Day parade; among them was an impressive assembly of Hibernian Knights and representatives of the Ancient Order of Hibernians. The *Gazette* was struck by the pageantry of the presence of an estimate 1,500 Hibernians:

> their smart costumes and soldierly bearing brought frequent applause along the line ... The A.O.H. looked remarkably well in the procession. The men were of a uniform stature, dressed in black, and all wore silk hats, which gave them a striking appearance as they marched past.[158]

Whereas the St Patrick's Society had once assumed sole responsibility for staging St Patrick's Day celebrations in Montreal, the emergence of a dedicated organizational committee with delegates from various Irish associations meant that the festival was now open to new influences. Key among them was the AOH: this American-dominated Hibernian society had Canadian chapters by the late nineteenth century and, by 1908, an estimated 6,000 members.[159] It was also an officially recognized body: in 1903 the AOH received its charter from a Canadian government which, at the time, was unaware of the group's republican sympathies.[160] As we discuss in Chapters 4 and 5, the AOH eventually assumed control of St Patrick's Day in Montreal, dominating its observance between 1919 and 1929. The decade prior to that offers hints that the AOH, while adhering to the democratic and representative structure of the Irish-Catholic Committee, was anxious to assert itself within the group.

The main issue that separated the AOH from other Irish national associations in the early 1900s was that of republicanism. This was, as we have seen, a time when most locals anticipated Home Rule along similar lines to that of Canada; given that expectation, separatist politics lacked broad-based support, except within the AOH and among remnants of the Fenian movement. Two Patrician dinners provide insights along these lines. The St Patrick's Society's annual dinner for 1900 was an intercommunity affair; among the guests were the St Jean-Baptiste Society, the Caledonian and St Andrew's Societies, the Consul-General of the United States, the Archbishop of Montreal and the President of the Irish Protestant Society.[161] The AOH's St Patrick's Day dinner in Montreal was more of a private event for its members: this included men who were Irish, whether by birth or descent, and who were practising Catholics. Active membership was restricted to men of between eighteen and forty-five years of age in sound physical health; Hibernians who did not fit this criteria were eligible for honorary membership. This emphasis on active compared to passive members reflected the AOH's martial ethos; within the movement were fledgling military groups, such as the Hibernian Knights and the Hibernian Rifles, who were prepared

– literally – to defend Ireland's right to self-government. At the AOH dinner, the keynote address was delivered by Edward O'Brien Kennedy: he was introduced as an Irish patriot 'who had spent sixteen years in English prisons'. His speech therefore focused on British incarceration of Irish prisoners. Embittered by these experiences, Kennedy's speech concluded with an emphatic declaration of his 'unfaltering hatred' for the British. According to the *Gazette*, the audience was not unanimous in its support for this view.[162] Moreover, it was possible for a member of the AOH also to be part of the St Patrick's Society, and vice versa. By and large, though, zealous Republicans were more likely to be found among the AOH, while steadfast advocates of Home Rule were more prominent among the St Patrick's Society.

In the decade prior to the First World War, the AOH exerted some influence over the nature of the St Patrick's Day parade in Montreal. The Hibernians were, of course, given a prominent place in the cavalcade, but so were other Irish societies. More significant was the fact that, as Peggy Regan has put it, 'the A.O.H. was now indispensable to the event'.[163] Evidence for this emerges from the postponement of Montreal's 1907 parade until Monday 18 March. On St Patrick's Day, 1907 the Montreal chapter of the AOH marched instead in Quebec City's annual procession. The minutes of the Irish-Catholic Committee indicate that the AOH was already trying to change some of the traditions of the Montreal parade. Among these was a Hibernian objection to 'ragtime' music, which by 1907 was deemed inappropriate to a festival in which only Irish music ought to be played. Seven years on the AOH was concerned about the scope and direction of the parade route. It argued against the traditional cavalcade along the lower parts of the city, where an Irish community had first grown, to a 'route of the parade [that] would spread itself to advantage and where people from the remotest sections of Montreal would be most apt to congregate to witness the display'. The AOH reminded the organizing committee that 'The Irish were not parading for their own but rather to advertise their members and influence and strengths to the other members of the Community.'[164] In this instance the traditionalists prevailed, but as we see in Chapter 4, the AOH was hardly about to abandon its reformist agenda.

ST PATRICK'S DAY IN AUSTRALIA: 1860–1914

No clear picture of St Patrick's Day in Sydney and Melbourne emerges during the second half of the nineteenth century. There is evidence for integration and sectionalism in the manner of its celebration. During the 1860s St Patrick's Day was generally accepted as a holiday in both cities; it was customary for banks and businesses to close for the day, with people from various backgrounds joining in the festivities. But colonial premiers were responsible for declaring St Patrick's Day a public holiday, and they had different attitudes towards the celebrations. In Melbourne, 17 March was a holiday under a Catholic premier in 1863, but not the following year under the leadership of a Presbyterian premier. This implies sectarian differences regarding government sanction of St Patrick's Day as a holiday. But other data complicate such a conclusion. In Sydney, an Anglican premier declared 17 March 1865 to be a holiday, and a 'lapsed' Catholic premier concurred the following year.[165] This ambiguity about the status of St Patrick's Day was compounded by a lack of uniformity in the annual celebrations themselves. Legislation had ended the parade by 1847, and nothing had emerged during the 1850s to make St Patrick's Day particularly special. This was, of course, the gold rush decade, so on 17 March Irish Australians were just as likely to be at the diggings in rural Ballarat or Bendigo chasing their very own pot of gold. By the early 1860s much of that gilt-edged excitement was over, so a return to 'normality' was imminent. But would St Patrick's Day resume its status as *the* day for Irish colonists?

In February 1860, a meeting of Melbourne's St Patrick's Society was uncertain 'as to the most suitable manner of celebrating St Patrick's Day'.[166] So they relied on the old chestnuts of a dance and supper in St Patrick's Hall. According to the *Argus*, the organizing committee did very well every year as caterers and entertainers. The paper described the 1864 festivities as being 'as enjoyable and attractive as any preceding it'; it then made a point of reporting loyal toasts to 'Her Majesty and the Royal Family', 'Our Native Land', and 'Victoria, our adopted country'.[167] This pattern of observance was repeated annually, with only subtle variations in food, music and decorations. The highlight of the 1865 ball and supper, for example, was 'a handsome harp of Erin flared in gas-jets over the front entrance' of St Patrick's Hall.[168] This embellishment was, for its time, rather 'high-tech'. The St Patrick's Society was, after all, financially well endowed, so it did not need to skimp on decorations. Indeed, an August 1860 meeting had puzzled over how much of the Society's £3,000 reserve fund ought to be spent on busts and paintings of great Irish historical figures.[169] By the following year, though, the association discovered that it had a social role. In response to a large number of passenger ships arriving in Victoria, the St Patrick's Society announced that it would investigate 'what steps should be taken to render assistance to the newly-arrived Irish immigrants'.[170] A major initiative was the establishment of a 'benefit fund' offering sickness and accident cover for Irish workers. Ironically, it exposed plenty of ill-will within the organization itself, including wrangling over payments. This led, throughout the 1860s, to what the *Argus* described as 'disgraceful disorder' at St Patrick's Society meetings.[171] It was not an atmosphere conducive to raising the profile of St Patrick's Day festivities in Melbourne.

In addition to in-fighting among the organizers of St Patrick's Day, sectarianism raised its ugly head to muddy the waters on 17 March. This arose in the wake of the first royal tour of Australia. In Sydney, on the specially declared 'royal holiday' of 12 March 1868, an attempt was made to assassinate the visiting Prince Alfred, Duke of Edinburgh. The gunman, Henry James O'Farrell, was of Irish descent and, according to his own confession, had once been connected with the Fenian movement. This led the anti-Catholic Henry Parkes, Colonial Secretary of New South Wales, to allege that this action was part of an organized Fenian plot. O'Farrell, meanwhile, insisted that he had acted alone.[172] A diary found in his room confirmed his Irish republican sympathies, but was silent on any local Fenian connection. Subsequently, though, warders at Darlinghurst Gaol claimed that O'Farrell had told them otherwise. As Inglis summarizes:

> Ten members of a fenian organisation, according to the warders' version, had determined to kill both the prince and Earl of Belmore; but when the governor announced his patronage of St Patrick's Day the ten decided that he should not die. (If that were true, it might be said that St Patrick had saved Lord Belmore's life.) The assassin of the prince was then chosen by lot and the task fell to O'Farrell.[173]

Bitter exchanges between the Catholic press and leading daily newspapers ensued. The Irish, it seemed, were somehow 'collectively responsible' for the near tragedy of the shooting. St Patrick's Day in Sydney, just five days after the shooting, was thus 'a grim occasion'.[174] The St Patrick's Society observed the anniversary as usual, but was at pains to express its 'outrage' at the crime, and its wish for 'the speedy recovery, health, and happiness of Prince Alfred'.[175]

The sectarian climate prompted the English-born Catholic Archbishop of Sydney, John Polding, to reiterate his long-standing edict that 'attachment to Ireland' should be 'discarded as quickly as possible' in Australia.[176] But the predominantly Irish-Catholic clergy in the colonies did not forget their homeland, which had always been an inextricable part of their faith. Hence 17 March would remain an occasion in which Irish-Australian orators 'dwelt on Ireland's modern wrongs as well as her ancient pains and glories'.[177] Admittedly, the day did not take on obvious political overtones until the 1880s, for it was in this decade, argues McConville, that 'Home Rule politics ousted the frivolity' of the St Patrick's Day celebrations.[178]

Of particular importance was the visit of the Irish brothers Redmond to Australia in 1883. They promoted the cause of Home Rule to Irish Australians, arguing that it would be similar to the form of responsible democratic government in the colonies. The subsequent St Patrick's Day celebrations in Sydney and Melbourne drew many more followers than was usual, with supporters of the Redmonds taking up collections to support the Irish Parliamentary Party.[179] But the presence of the Redmonds also inspired meetings of thousands of angry empire loyalists, who associated the Irish political activists with sedition.[180] Further complicating matters, the Sydney Hibernian Society split in the mid-1880s over whether the festivities 'were to be non-political or a celebration of the Home Rule cause'.[181] In short: should St Patrick's Day be a time for religious devotion and sentimental reminiscing about the old country, or could it also involve expressions of hope for Irish self-government?

The adoption of the policy of Home Rule for Ireland by British Prime Minister Gladstone in 1886 meant that this was now a 'respectable' position in Australia. It could no longer be easily portrayed by its opponents in the colonies as a threat to the unity of the British Empire.[182] This also helped settle the question of whether references to Home Rule were a legitimate part of St Patrick's Day banners and speeches. MacDonagh remarks that the Sydney celebrations of 1888 were 'like an annual report for 1887 on the Irish struggle', but there was little in the way of hostility towards Britain, for Home Rule was no longer inimical to Empire. The Melbourne celebrations had an even more conjunctive tone, with leading speakers emphasizing 'Home Rule as imperial strength'.[183]

But overseas events again changed the political atmosphere in which the day was celebrated. There was a damaging split in the Home Rule Party in 1891, and the second Home Rule Bill was defeated in 1893. Concurrently, sectarian differences were heightened in Ireland as Ulster Protestants employed the slogan 'Home Rule meant Rome Rule', suggesting their fear of 'becoming a minority in a Catholic-dominated Home Rule Ireland'.[184] Their Victorian brethren followed this lead: on 12 July 1895 Orangemen marched down the streets of Melbourne in full orange and purple regalia to celebrate the two hundredth anniversary of the Battle of the Boyne. But the procession was stopped by men with green badges who ripped at their sashes, forcing the Orangemen to take refuge in a Wesleyan Chapel. The Orange Lodges again attempted to march on 12 July 1897, but were met by thousands of green-ribboned Catholics who, despite a strong presence of police as peacekeepers, effectively persuaded the Ulster Protestants that future displays would not be tolerated.[185]

St Patrick's Day marches returned to Melbourne in the 1880s. New regulations superseded the Party Processions legislation of 1847: from 1879 'permission for processions to be held in Melbourne's streets were regularly granted at the discretion of the mayor'.[186] A consequence of this change was a rise in the number and range of processions in the city from hereon.[187] St Patrick's Day was among these; during the 1880s it emerged as a key moment to express Catholic faith, as well as any sentiment towards Ireland. Irish-born Archbishop Carr took part in the annual procession organized by the St Patrick's Society. He encouraged Melbourne's Catholics to involve themselves in the celebration as a visible sign of their important place in Australian society. The politically moderate Carr was optimistic that the Protestant majority would better accept Catholics if they used 17 March to remember Ireland, yet demonstrate loyalty to Australia and Empire. In this view, St Patrick's Day was not sectional, but a demonstration of ethnic and religious diversity within a wider community. These sentiments were not complicated by references to Home Rule on St Patrick's Day because by the early 1900s the policy had once again become 'respectable' in British politics and, by association, in Australia.[188]

By comparison, Sydney's first Irish-born Catholic leader, Cardinal Moran, had moved to minimize any political significance arising from St Patrick's Day. Moran, like Carr, was a moderate on the subject of Irish nationalism but, unlike the Victorian archbishop, he took personal leadership of Sydney's St Patrick's Day celebrations from 1896. He emphasized that 17 March was essentially a religious day and, in keeping with this view, he ordered that funds raised on the day would be donated to Catholic charities and not to the Irish Home Rule party. He also put a stop to the annual procession which, over the past ten years, 'had a strong tendency to disperse into hotels for the remainder of the day'.[189] As a consequence, Sydney's St Patrick's Day became 'a mass demonstration of Catholicity', and a family-based sports day was substituted for the former procession.[190] Like Polding before him, Moran emphasized that Catholics were Australians first. He was not unsympathetic to Home Rule for Ireland, but he refused to support any Irish faction and did not consider a saint's day an appropriate time for the expression of politics.[191] However, there were generally poor attendances at St Patrick's Day sports carnivals, and three years after Moran's death in 1911 'only 4685 of Sydney's 185,000 Catholics attended the "monster" sports meeting'.[192] So despite the archbishop's leadership of St Patrick's Day, its feature spectacle does not seem to have been particularly captivating. It was mainly attended by schoolchildren organized to put on gymnastic displays, and parents who went along to cheer them. But it was hardly an imposing demonstration of Catholic pride or community.

The contrast with Melbourne in the early 1900s is startling. O'Farrell has suggested that St Patrick's Day celebrations were generally poorly attended around this time, but by 1908 the parades were 'well into the phase of a revival'. In that year the St Patrick's Day sports carnival attracted around 17,000 patrons and the 'procession was the longest ever witnessed in Melbourne, watched by 100,000 in the streets'.[193] In 1909 the crowds were even bigger,[194] and the success of the St Patrick's Day spectacles continued in the next decade. For example, the *Age* reported that before the 1913 procession had begun 'the streets along the line of the march to the Exhibition were packed with people anxious to see . . . this annual display'.[195]

In part, this enthusiasm for Melbourne's St Patrick's Day related to the popularity of the procession as a form of entertainment, for the marchers, floats and music were an attraction in themselves. Moreover, by comparison with the depression years of the 1890s, more money could be committed to the presentation of the spectacle. While Irish traditions and legends were depicted in floats and banners, the contribution of the Irish people to Australia was also emphasized, thereby making the celebration seem unifying, not merely sectional. The presence of civic leaders as invited guests also gave the occasion an impression of respectability. Moreover, by comparison with Sydney, there was a much stronger membership of Irish groups committed to Home Rule, such as the Shamrock and Celtic clubs. They generally expected that responsible government for Ireland would be granted by the British Parliament and, for them, St Patrick's Day and its procession were moments to celebrate old Irish traditions and imminent self-determination.[196] But the political significance of St Patrick's Day should not be exaggerated. Much of the enthusiasm for the saint's day can be attributed to an increased involvement by Catholic sodalities, such as the League of the Cross, which had become highly active after the debilitating 1890s depression.[197]

As mentioned earlier, under Moran's stewardship in Sydney, discussion of Home Rule politics was eschewed on St Patrick's Day, and the annual procession was ended in 1895.[198] The absence of these features, so central to the Victorian celebration, can help to explain why Sydney's festivities paled in comparison with those in Melbourne. But what was common about St Patrick's Day in both cities was that much of their former non-denominational characteristics had been eroded. This had mainly arisen because of increased clerical control of the Irish day as a *Catholic* celebration.[199] However, non-Catholic Irish Australians were not, as a consequence, excluded. The St Patrick's Society, a long-time organizer of the procession, was an Irish national, rather than denominational group; and the Irish National Foresters, a non-sectarian Irish friendly society, was an active participant in St Patrick's Day celebrations. Nevertheless, Catholics were a prominent part of the annual procession, including marchers representing the Hibernian Australasian Catholic Benefit Society, and Catholic schools. The clerical leaders wanted St Patrick's Day to be an advertisement for the wider acceptance of Catholics in Australian society, yet the annual celebrations were becoming increasingly denominational.

However, this increasingly Catholic flavour of St Patrick's Day was not a contentious development. It reflected a long-standing demographic majority of Catholics among Irish Australians and their descendants, which gave the appearance of a symbiotic Irish-Catholic relationship. Moreover, Catholic newspapers such as the *Advocate*, the *Freeman's Journal* and the *Catholic Press* had a strongly Irish flavour, providing regular news about the church in Ireland, as well as discussions of Irish politics.[200] For the vast majority of Irish Catholics, loyalty to faith and homeland were not incompatible with allegiance to Australia and Empire. That said, imminent wartime crises in both Australia and Ireland were catalysts for the emergence of new divisions between Catholic and Protestant, Irish and British, as well as the hardening of old sectarian and political hostilities. A key battleground for this, as we see in Chapter 4, was Melbourne's St Patrick's Day procession.

THE YEARS UP TO THE FIRST WORLD WAR

In 1900, John Redmond took the leadership of the Irish Home Parliamentary Party, and dedicated the remainder of his life to the cause of winning Irish Home Rule through constitutional means. In his campaign, which was broadly supported across Ireland, Redmond was backed by various bodies that had emerged during the Irish cultural revolution of the 1880s and 1890s, notably the Gaelic Athletic Association and the Gaelic League. His major opponents were the advanced nationalists of Sinn Féin and the Irish Republican Brotherhood. Even these organizations were prepared to stand back and wait to see if Redmond could achieve his goal. As a result of the close election result in the 1910 general election, Redmond was left holding the balance of power. He traded his support for the Liberal government in return for Home Rule for Ireland. The Home Rule Act was passed in 1912, and after temporary defeat in the House of Lords, was due to become law in 1914. As the most successful exponent of Irish nationalist aspirations, Redmond and his constitutional cause received support, not only in Ireland, but across the diaspora. Such constitutional means, born of political sophistication, but also a mark of late Victorian respectability and democracy, were to shape many St Patrick's Day celebrations through to the First World War.

At the start of the new century, links between St Patrick's Day parades in the diaspora and the politics of Ireland were extended. At a basic level, there were explicit connections between expatriate organizations and counties in Ireland, with civic representatives from the homeland playing a more visible role as guests in American commemorations of 17 March. In 1901, for instance, John Daly, the mayor of Limerick, travelled to New York to take a prominent place in the parade. At a more complex level, political struggles in Ireland were given profile by the appearance of militant Irish nationalists in St Patrick's Day marches. In 1904, for example, O'Donovan Rossa, the legendary Fenian leader, was guest of the AOH in New York.[201] Many Irish-American groups took an avid – even if romantic – interest in Fenian ideals and a republican vision for Ireland's future, so they lauded expatriate Irish radicals. St Patrick's Day, in that sense, allowed these groups to demonstrate an explicit connection with the 'Irish cause' by placing prominent political dissidents on parade. But such sanction for a militant overthrow of British rule in Ireland was countered, increasingly, by a realization in America that reformist politics had moved into the ascendancy. Indeed, the level of support was so unequivocal and formalized that Clan na Gael refused to march in the New York parade from 1909. They argued that the politics of the New York celebration were too overtly pro-Redmondite Home Rule.[202]

New York's Friendly Sons of St Patrick vociferously backed the Home Rule campaign by Redmond, using the St Patrick's night dinner to demonstrate its support via a series of speeches from officials of the organization and other invited dignitaries. Such open sanction of Irish political aspirations was often legitimized by references to the life, work and mission of St Patrick. In 1910, for instance, the president of the FSSP reminded his audience that the Irish in America

> have not, amid the multitudinous distractions of their lives as American citizens, forgotten the wholesome lessons of life which they or their fathers or their father's fathers learned in holy Ireland. Standards and ideals of which the Saintly Patrick has for centuries been recognised by all the world as the great exemplar among men.[203]

In response to the president's address, the guest speaker of the evening, the Hon. Luke Stapleton, spoke about the need for Irishmen at home and abroad to take political action in the name of Irish freedom. He signalled Redmond as a worthy successor of Charles Stewart Parnell, and presumed that Home Rule was imminent. He warned, however, that Irish Americans had to carefully focus their attention on the 'real' issue of Irish freedom, and not, as many of them had done, seek self-aggrandisement via this cause. He pleaded:

> let Irishmen be a single army, invincible in unanimity, undistracted in purpose, gathering glory from the triumph of the cause, subordinating and achieving victory. Ireland's aspiration is human. Her plea is for restored government. Her rebellion is against aliens in country and race. Her claim is for the rights of life, liberty and the pursuit of happiness under Irish auspices. Her complaint is against an invader. Her demand is to remedy breaches of faith. Her struggle and her hope are for absolute and unconditional independence.[204]

Stapleton, like other speakers at the dinner, implored his audience to appreciate the political significance of Home Rule for Ireland. St Patrick's Day was, in that sense, used consistently as a time to refocus American minds on key political developments in Ireland.

In Ireland, and away from Home Rule politics, was the steady acceptance, albeit without formal legal approval, of St Patrick's Day as a public holiday. This was reflected in newspaper articles of the time. In 1902, the *Irish Times* reported that 'St Patrick's Day was generally regarded as a holiday in Dublin. Many of the leading factories were closed and, as far as possible, the working classes were afforded the opportunity to enjoy a country excursion.'[205]

St Patrick's Day was, of course, not only a time for political manoeuvring. In Ireland, particularly since the disaster of the famine, 17 March had been an important day for religious observance and a non-official break from the routine of work. There was consensus among many workers and employers that it ought to be a bona fide holiday, yet 17 March was not part of the debate that gave legislative sanction to various official public holidays in Britain during the late 1860s and early 1870s.[206] However, by the early 1900s John Redmond and his colleagues in the Irish Parliamentary Party, accompanied and supported by the Gaelic League, began campaigning for the legal declaration of St Patrick's Day as a public holiday in Ireland.[207] They were eventually successful when on 27 March 1903 the Bank Holiday (Ireland) Act came into force. The bill for a St Patrick's Day holiday in Ireland had been proposed in Parliament by John Redmond, William O'Brien, John Dillon, and T.W. Russell. It was passed unopposed and its progress through the legislative process elicited little negative debate.[208]

With the advent of 17 March as an official and legally approved public holiday, the accompanying large number of cheap packages offered by railway companies at the turn of the century made trips either into or out of the big cities easier. In 1905, for example, the Dublin United Tramways Company offered more frequent services, while the Dublin and Blessington Steam Tram Company announced a special excursion to Poulaphouca.[209] By 1905, the observance of the public holiday, and thus of St Patrick's Day in Ireland was noteworthy. The *Liverpool Mercury*, for instance, reported that 'in Dublin yesterday, business was almost entirely suspended, and the law courts, banks and other public offices were closed'.[210] With all business, apart from those that serviced the holiday, halted, and the religious significance of St Patrick's Day limited, for many people, to the morning Church service, the day then became one of self-indulgent leisure. In that respect St Patrick's Day was becoming more of a secular holiday rather than a devotional commemoration of the life of Ireland's patron saint.

Whereas in Ireland St Patrick's Day was a public holiday by the early 1900s, the situation in America was more complex. In the absence of nationwide legislation, the granting of a day off work relied on local agreements. In Lowell, Massachusetts, the city's Irish mill labourers declared 17 March a holiday, but did not attain the sanction of factory owners. Yet their unilateral declaration of a day off work was accepted, if grudgingly, by their employers. As Cardinal O'Connell, who ministered in this region, recalled: 'to the chagrin of the mill-owners and managers, the workers made the seventeenth of March a great holiday, and to their wonder, and one might say their anxiety as well, the machinery had to be stopped and the mill gates closed'.[211] Considering that the mills did not even close for Christmas, the self-declared St Patrick's Day holiday illustrates the political influence of Irish leaders of working-class labour. In Butte, by contrast, mine workers had to rely on their employers being willing to close down for the day. The eventual sanction of 17 March as a holiday was the product of spirited debate between mine owners, the AOH, and the Robert Emmet Literary Association. In large part, St Patrick's Day was recognized as special in Butte because the Irish dominated the workforce. By 1913, however, the

Irish were challenged for jobs in the mines by immigrant Austrians and Germans. Mine owners now felt it was unnecessary to declare 17 March a holiday for their work force.[212] These *ad hoc* holiday declarations for St Patrick's Day were typical in the United States.

The advent of a public holiday to mark St Patrick's Day in Ireland gave entrepreneurs added opportunities to retail merchandise for the occasion. There was, of course, a long tradition of selling shamrock and green ribbons to adorn clothing on St Patrick's Day. But the new status of 17 March as a public holiday prompted the manufacture and marketing of products related to the life and legend of the country's patron saint. St Patrick, it seemed, was entering the heady world of commercialization and personal endorsements. In 1912, the soft drinks manufacturer Cantrell & Cochrane Ltd., advertised its brand of Ginger Ale:

> In the olden times it was the custom to drink from St Patrick's Well on St Patrick's Day. The clear fresh water from this famous old well is used to-day in the manufacture of Cantrell & Cochrane's Ginger Ale. Celebrate St Patrick's Day by drinking a bottle of this delicious Irish Ginger Ale.[213]

There was plenty of blarney about this claim, but the wider point is that in the wake of legislation enacting 17 March as a public holiday, entrepreneurs in Ireland were attempting more than ever to connect themselves with St Patrick; there was an assumption that their 'designer' products would be attractive to consumers during Patrician festivities.

The shamrock had a long pedigree in the Irish celebration of St Patrick's Day: it was a physical metaphor for the patron saint's explanation of the Holy Trinity. Intriguingly, though, for much of the nineteenth century it was seen by some in Ireland and Britain as a symbol of dissent, and thus a marker of disloyalty. In the decades following the famine, the shamrock had been popular among the Irish as an icon promoting separatist Irish nationalism, and thus the public rejection, for one day at least, of British rule in Ireland. Certainly in Britain there was concern about political allegiances expressed via the shamrock symbol: Queen Victoria had prohibited her Irish troops from having the shamrock as part of their regimental emblem. By the turn of the century, however, the shamrock ceased to be seen in Britain as a symbol of an aggressive or potentially dangerous Ireland, becoming instead a politically innocuous emblem of Irishness that was accepted as a routine part of St Patrick's Day.

A variety of different issues explain this shift: the ascendancy of Redmond's constitutional Home Rule movement, the relative lack of political agitation within Ireland, and the apparent demise of the Fenian threat. Cumulatively, this meant that the Irish were no longer seen so readily in Britain as a 'danger'. The Irish community in Britain had also become less threatening as a result of wider social and cultural changes. Post-famine emigration from Ireland to Britain had not caused the chaos that had first been imagined by the host society. Indeed, the Irish had integrated with considerable success: many of them were doing far better economically than those they had left behind in the homeland. Back in the 1860s the Irish had been portrayed pejoratively in the British press as a seditious and violent people. The 'Pat' character so popular with cartoonists was a British-hating Fenian with simian features. By the turn of the century, the depiction of the Irish, though still deeply racist by today's standards, had been transformed into a comic figure – the stage Irishman dressed in green, carrying a shille-lagh, and decorated with a shamrock. As offensive as the stage Irishman may have been to the Irish themselves, this popularization reflected a benign shift in British perspectives of the Irish generally. This also had implications for the observance of St Patrick's Day. Whereas the robust celebrations of 17 March had previously worried British authorities, the widespread acceptance of the stage Irishman – a figure still immortalized on St Patrick's Day greet-ings cards and on T-shirts today – helped to transform St Patrick's Day into a more amusing, and thus less threatening, celebration.

A major change of policy on the shamrock came from the British royal family. Whereas Queen Victoria had previously banned the shamrock as an emblem for Irish troops in the British army, she reinvented it as a benign symbol of Anglo-Irishness by presenting sprigs of the plant to her Irish regi-ments as a mark of their loyal service to the empire in the Boer War. This caused a stir in Ireland, where ardent nationalists decried British appropria-tion of the shamrock as a symbol of loyalty to the sovereign, and they deplored the use of the plant as recognizing Irish military service in South Africa. The *United Irishman* considered it to be an 'absurdity', because 'an Irishman wearing the livery of England was unworthy to wear the distinc-tive token of Irish nationality'.[214] The Reverend H.M. Kennedy, Vicar of Plumpton, Cumberland, even announced his own protest against this use of the shamrock:

> I intend, if I wear one at all this year, to do so in mourning on my left sleeve. The shamrock is green and not the emblem of murder. An order to wear it because the green of the veldt has been dyed red by the blood of the slain Irish, where Irish ought not to be, is a pitiful concern.[215]

Such was the depth of Irish nationalist feeling during the Boer War that St Patrick's Day became a time for protest against British militarism in South Africa and the involvement of Irish troops on the side of Britain. This was also an opportunity for critics to lend symbolic support to the Boers, as well as the Irish Brigade that was fighting alongside them against the British. For example, on St Patrick's Day in Cork 'a procession marched through the city headed by the Transvaal and Irish flags', and at a subsequent meeting of the Cork Nationalists the following resolution was read: 'we express our deep sympathy with the Boers in their gallant struggle against the tyranny sought to be imposed upon them by England; a tyranny similar to that which has had baneful results in our own country'.[216]

Subsequent shifts in attitudes towards the shamrock specifically, and to St Patrick's Day generally, were noted by the *Irish Times*. In 1902 the paper discussed the readiness with which non-Irish people in England, Scotland and Wales wore the shamrock on 17 March. It claimed that the shamrock had been transformed from a symbol of difference and sedition into one of commonality and friendship. This was a favourable development, argued the *Irish Times*: 'we read in telegrams from across the Channel that the shamrock was yesterday universally worn and the Irish flag honoured. Why should it not be so?'[217] The British embrace of the shamrock was, nonetheless, read by many Irish nationalists as in keeping with the innocuous celebration of St Patrick's Day as a civic festival, and its appropriation by non-Irish locals as a comical annual diversion. The change had no relevance, they argued, to any considered reassessment of British policy towards Ireland. It was icing with no cake.

In the United States, St Patrick's Day celebrations prior to the First World War reflected the self-confidence of Irish Americans within their own nation. In 1910, the United States President, William Taft, addressed a St Patrick's night banquet in Chicago. The decision, by a serving President, to mark 17 March in such a way demonstrated that the anniversary had become very important for Irish Americans, but the day also provided opportunities for elected officials to court the Irish-American electorate. In this case, Chicago's AOH had gone to great trouble to plant a grassroots link between the American presidency and the Irish homeland. Organizers had imported 'a piece of the ould sod' from Ireland for Taft to stand on while he made his address. This ceremony involving the 'real soil of the Emerald Isle' was much anticipated, for in the days before the banquet the 'ould sod' had been on public display, with many Irish expatriates 'crying at the sight of it'. However, such was the excitement for some viewers that they could not resist carrying the soil away with them, so President Taft was left with no soil to stand on![218] Nonetheless, the presence of the US president at a St Patrick's Day dinner was a clear measure of the importance of the anniversary in the American calendar, and the political significance of the Irish within American society.

The civic significance of St Patrick's Day in the United States was apparent in other ways. In 1912, some 15,000 men took part in New York's parade. They were watched from the steps of St Patrick's Cathedral by Cardinal Farley and Mayor Gaynor. One of the AOH bands injected some humour into the proceedings by playing 'Where did you get that hat?' as they passed the Cardinal in his full ceremonial outfit.[219] The parade demonstrated once again the power of the Irish-American community within the city, as both the church hierarchy and city officials paid homage to the parade. At the Friendly Sons of St Patrick dinner in 1912, Dr James Guerin, former mayor of Montreal, and one of the key after-dinner speakers, focused on the importance to the Irish-American community of self-determination for the Irish homeland. Guerin firmly expected that Ireland would be granted Home Rule before the Friendly Sons met in 1913; such a status, he concluded, was vital to the political integrity and social happiness of Ireland.[220] Despite the overarching support for the constitutional Home Rule movement, the AOH was always ready to remind its members of the physical force legacy of Ireland's past. The AOH's 'St Patrick's Day Souvenir 1905' from Savannah, GA, reminded its readers that while the order was 'dedicated to St Patrick' and that 17 March was to 'show our respect for his memory', it was a day 'bedewed with the tears of national sufferings for centuries, and red with the blood of countless martyrs'.[221]

During the early years of the twentieth century, St Patrick's Day in Ireland became increasingly allied with the forces of nationalism. Despite this transition, Dublin Castle continued to celebrate 17 March, but it was no longer a key date in its social calendar. The grand ball had ceased to be an important feature of St Patrick's Day celebrations by the early years of the twentieth century.[222] Attendance had become politically problematic for many Unionists, and the vulgarity of the evening kept many staunch nationalists away. In 1907, however, Countess Markievicz, a future rebel of Easter 1916, danced at the grand ball.[223] The main focus for Dublin Castle observance of 17 March was the ceremonial trooping of the colour. The event had been held since the late nineteenth century, primarily because of its role as a form of military exercise, but also as a counterpoint to what the Castle took to be more frivolous and extravagant forms of Patrician observance. The trooping of the colour on St Patrick's Day in the early 1900s was an unchanging ritual. The ceremonial etiquette was identical each year, as was the music played, and so was the order of sections within the march. Despite this annual observance, the trooping of the colour provided a measure of the comparative unpopularity of the British presence in Ireland, especially its military, in the early twentieth century. The event, rather than taking the form of a public procession through the streets of Dublin, was carried out entirely within the walls of Dublin Castle (a marked difference to the public procession later instigated by the Irish Free State upon its formation). Those in attendance were drawn from the ranks of Dublin Castle staff, military personnel and the elite of Dublin's Anglo-Irish community. Those members of the public who attended were obliged to gather in the lower yard of the Castle.

The trooping of the colour appears as a peculiar footnote in the late history of the British presence at Dublin Castle; here was an elite group, often unsure about its function, celebrating the Irish patron saint with full British military honours. The last trooping of the colour took place in 1914, and was notable only for the participation of the 1st City of Dublin Cadets. The Cadets, a youth organization formed in 1911 by Captain Bernard Cunningham, aimed to train boys to 'defend their homes and country if ever the necessity should arise'.[224] It was the boys who received most of the press attention, but even they provoked little public interest from spectators. According to the *Irish Times*, 17 March, a public holiday, 'was availed of [by the people] as they eagerly seize upon every holiday'.[225] The main group watching the events in Dublin Castle were those invited by the Lord Lieutenant and Countess of Aberdeen, who, according to the *Irish Times*, 'viewed the spectacle from the state apartments, which were crowded'.[226] In 1915, the first St Patrick's Day of the First World War, the trooping of the colour procession was dispensed with. A Dublin Castle memo informed that 'the GOC thinks it would be undesirable to have this ceremonial during the war. The New Armies are not trained in ceremonial parades, and such training would interfere with their preparation for war.'[227]

While the war marked the end of St Patrick's Day observances by the British administration of Dublin Castle, the cancelled 1915 event did offer a preliminary insight into technological changes that took visual footage of parades into newsreels and cinemas. As the Dublin Castle trooping of the colour was virtually a closed event, Norman Witter of the General Film Supply Company asked permission to 'take a cinematograph film of Trooping of Colours on March 17'. This technology had already been applied to St Patrick's Day parades in the United States and Australia, with the effect that the local Irish were given an annual profile via public screenings in the wider community.[228]

By the outbreak of the First World War, St Patrick's Day was closely linked with the cause of Irish independence. John Redmond, from the time of his ascendancy to leader of the IPP, consistently used 17 March as an occasion for making high profile political speeches. Such pieces of oratory often took place in Irish towns, but were more regularly staged in Britain to garner support from the Irish diaspora there. In 1907, for instance, John Redmond spoke at a St Patrick's eve meeting in Liverpool and a St Patrick's Day celebration in Bradford, while his deputy John Dillon addressed a similar gathering in Wolverhampton. The speeches all revolved around the imminent prospects of Home Rule, and the role that the Irish diaspora in Britain could play in the campaign leading to self-government. While the content or nature of the speeches was not radically different from that which Redmond and Dillon made at any other time of the year, the application of such oratory on St Patrick's Day gave the message extra impact. As 17 March was Ireland's national day, the emotional poignancy of Redmond's pleas increased as the thoughts of his audience undoubtedly turned to home. Just as important was that St Patrick's Day was news in itself: this meant that the press, especially in England, would give attention to speeches relating to Ireland.

In 1914 Ireland stood on the brink of achieving Home Rule. Its diaspora, although still sometimes suffering hardships and discrimination, had rapidly assimilated into its respective host societies. St Patrick's Day, an event that had been so important in sustaining and displaying both Irish nationalism and the diaspora, could have become, had Home Rule been enacted, a day of global celebration for the new constitutional Irish state. In the event, Ireland had to win its independence through a bitter campaign of insurgency. In the rapidly changing circumstances of the period 1914–23, one of world war, insurrection, revolution and civil war, St Patrick's Day was about to take on new guises, once more reflecting the changing circumstances of the Irish people and its diaspora.

CHAPTER 4

CONTESTING IRELAND

Republicanism and militarism

—— ⊘⊙ ——

[On 17 March 1921] the enemy was hammering us his hardest and the hangman was so busy that few of us expected to see another St Patrick's day ... no one would have expected to see our friends, the auxiliaries, Black and Tans, and British soldiers sailing away and civilians or semi-civilians occupants of Dublin Castle.[1]

THE FIRST WORLD WAR

The period from 1914 until the ending of the Civil War in 1923 was one of great upheaval and uncertainty in Ireland. The events in Ireland were felt across the diaspora, and had a profound effect on how St Patrick's Day was celebrated. As will be shown later, the most politicized St Patrick's Day parades during this period, where events such as the First World War and the Easter Rising had greatest impact, was Australia. How, though, did people celebrate St Patrick's Day in Ireland during this momentous period of transition? During the First World War the majority of Irish people continued to support Redmond's stance of Irish military participation in the conflict. St Patrick's Day celebrations were, understandably, muted: in 1915, few public or civic events took place in Ireland on 17 March. There was a common belief that the participation of many thousands of Irish troops in the war meant that, as the *Irish Independent* put it, 'in these melancholy circumstances it would have been unseemly to have indulged in the festivities which are customarily associated with the celebration of St Patrick's Day'.[2]

Despite widespread support for Redmond's decision to take Ireland into the war, it appears that many Irish Americans were unhappy with the blatantly imperialist and pro-British nature of the war, and while they could rationalize the reasons behind Irish involvement, were less than happy to embrace the jingoism that was a feature of wartime Britain. The 1915 St Patrick's Day parade in New York illustrated this dichotomy. While the parade as a whole was supportive of the Redmondite involvement in the war, the Chair of the Arrangements Committee, Roderick Kennedy, banned the playing of the popular wartime tune 'It's a Long Way to Tipperary', because of its British overtones. In the event only one band, the Eccentric Fishermen, played the tune, and, as a result, the members of the reviewing stand were duly entertained by the sight of Roderick Kennedy jumping from his seat in the stand to stop the band playing. He threatened them with instant expulsion if they did not refrain from playing this music. The band acquiesced, so Kennedy was able to resume his place in the stand.[3] The playing of the tune did, despite Kennedy's objections, draw a smile of support from Cardinal Farley, who claimed it as one of his favourites.[4]

The 1916 parade in New York was an abject failure because of infighting over whether or not Redmond warranted the support of Irish America. The organizer of the parade was P.J. McNulty, described by the *Gaelic American* as 'a pro-Britisher who supports Redmond in his treason to Ireland and a political schemer'.[5] The parade attracted only 1,700 marchers, and a comparably small presence of spectators. The traditional stalwarts of the parade, including the bulk of the AOH, the 69th regiment and Cardinal Farley all refused to take part as a result of McNulty's open support for Redmond. The *Gaelic American* concluded that the low turnout was a direct result of the divisiveness of McNulty's stance, and that the message from New York to London was that there was no approval for 'John Redmond's sale of Ireland', nor were they 'in favour of England in the war'.[6] In contrast to the failure of a blatantly pro-Redmondite parade, the most popular events in New York on St Patrick's Day 1916 were a parade of Irish Volunteers in full dress uniform in Manhattan, and the annual dinner of the Veterans of the Fenian Movement. The success of these events, and the boycott of the main parade demonstrate that Irish-American opinion had, by 1916, been transformed from one that supported the goal of Redmondite Home Rule and participation in the war, to one which looked for more radical alternatives. The significance of St Patrick's Day as a marker of Irish collective sentiment in the calendar, was that it was a barometer for the political thinking of influential Irish Americans.

THE EASTER RISING: 1916

Prior to the Easter Rising in Dublin, St Patrick's Day was enthusiastically celebrated by the Irish Volunteers and other nationalist organizations. As with the 1874 parades, which were so closely observed by the British authorities, so the situation was the same in 1916. The observations made by the Royal Irish Constabulary in 1916 were not as detailed as those made in 1874. It is clear, however, that in the heady political atmosphere of the second year of world war, the activities of nationalists who refused to support the war effort were of great interest to the authorities. The Irish Volunteers' choice of St Patrick's Day to parade, a date in the calendar that had become increasingly allied to nationalist politics in the late nineteenth and early twentieth centuries, provided the authorities with a conundrum. Although many of the parades were seen as a potential risk to public order, and were certainly read as disloyal in many quarters, the majority of the assemblies were based on marches to and from local churches, with a focus on the observance of the

Irish patron saint at a special mass. The RIC records list thirty-eight parades across the country: they involved 5,995 marchers, 2,637 of whom were said to be armed. Although the parades were not a large-scale undertaking, and reflect the strength of the Irish Volunteers at the time, the celebration of the nation's patron saint by armed men probably did little to endear St Patrick to British authorities in Ireland. The parades themselves ranged from the largest in Cork City, which included 560 armed and 520 unarmed participants and a crowd estimated at 2,000 persons, to the smallest in Tyrellspass, Co. West-meath which attracted only 15 unarmed marchers and no recorded spectators. As mentioned previously, the majority of the parades culminated with a church service, but many others had a different focus. The procession at Coal-island, Co. Tyrone and Enniscorthy, Co. Wexford, were based on route marches; the parade at Mullenabreena, Co. Sligo, climaxed with participation of the local Volunteers at a sports day; the marchers at Ardpatrick, Co. Lim-erick congregated at a Gaelic League meeting; while in Limerick town the whole parade functioned as a political demonstration.[7]

It is difficult to know what motivated the men and women who took part in the Easter Rising, but many of those involved, such as Michael Collins and Cathal Brugha, were returned emigrants. It is clear that the Irish dia-spora promoted and sustained a love of Ireland, and various organizations in far-flung cities across the globe supported the growth and development of the Irish nationalist cause. Although it is impossible to create a direct link between participation in St Patrick's Day celebrations and active involve-ment in the struggle for Irish freedom, such events undoubtedly concen-trated the mind of the emigrant on the situation at home. Batt O'Connor, who returned to Ireland from America to take part in the 1916 Rising, wrote after taking part in a New York St Patrick's Day parade, 'I walked in that procession and in the emotion I felt, walking as one of that vast crowd of Irish immigrants celebrating our national festival, I woke to the full con-sciousness of my love for my country.'[8]

Alongside the involvement of returned emigrants like O'Connor in Patri-cian events in Ireland, the rapidly changing political landscape exerted a powerful pull on American St Patrick's Day celebrations. Many of them were spurred on by a feeling that Ireland had been betrayed, not solely by the executions of the leading rebels of 1916, but by the general arrogance of the British attitude towards the political situation in Ireland. A speech one year after the Rising illustrates that point: Justice John W. Goff of the New York Supreme Court, addressing a St Patrick's night dinner in Buffalo, argued that the recognition of the shamrock was part of

a tendency to recognise a very mild type of Irish national pride, for only a year ago, almost within sound of the bell that tolled as Roger Casement[9] ascended the steps of the scaffold, titled ladies sold sprigs of shamrock in Regent Street, London, for the Army Hospital Fund.[10]

The 1918 parade in New York reflected seismic shifts taking place in Irish politics. In the wake of the Easter Rising, and as a result of the huge loss of life on the western front, Redmond's policy of involvement in the war was now bankrupt. The Irish Parliamentary Party was in retreat and Sinn Féin had begun its meteoric political rise. The 1918 New York parade had to juggle competing issues. It had to come to terms with recent political changes in Ireland and the immediate legacy of the 1916 Rising. Second, it had to balance rejection of involvement in the First World War by Irish Republicans, with the active participation, since 1917, of the America they swore allegiance to, in that very conflict. In the event, the parade was supportive, and proud, of those Irish who were fighting with the Americans in the war, and also included a new strand of marchers. The first distinct women's society, Cumann na mBan, took its place in the parade, while the nationalist group Friends of Irish Freedom also marched for the first time. Clan na Gael rejoined the parade, thereby ending their boycott which had begun in 1909. The involvement of these three bodies in the parade marked a new radicalism within St Patrick's Day celebrations, which increasingly allied Irish America with the cause of Irish Republicanism.

The end of the First World War and the rise of Sinn Féin, culminating in its victory in the 1918 Irish election, altered perspectives of Irish politics both in Ireland and beyond. In New York, many Irish Americans, attracted by the republicanism of Sinn Féin and the links of many of its leaders with the 1916 Rising, supported the party. On St Patrick's Day in 1919 members of the St Columcille branch of the Friends of Irish Freedom had marched in the parade. This group consisted entirely of women, and their appearance in the parade came only one year after the official admittance of women into the march. The Friends of Irish Freedom, which had its headquarters in New York and claimed some 275,000 members – male and female – by 1919, backed Sinn Féin fully.[11]

The ever closer links between Irish America, Sinn Féin and the cause of Irish Republicanism were embodied in 1920 by the appearance of the leader of Sinn Féin, Eamon de Valera, on the parade review stand in New York. The liturgy of the new Ireland that was being fought for at that time in the Irish War of Independence was now clear for all to see. For the first time in the history of New York's parade, the orange, green and white Irish tricolour completely replaced the all-green flags that had once represented Ireland. In the march itself, Sinn Féin-related banners superceded the majority of those that had been used in the past, the symbolism of the harp and the colour green completely overshadowed by the livery of Irish Republicans. With new colours followed changing styles of performance. The most bizarre of these was a county association that featured a group of marchers dressed as Hindus, sporting turbans of orange, green and white.[12]

IRISH WAR OF INDEPENDENCE: 1919–21

The rise of Sinn Féin in 1917 and 1918, culminating in its overwhelming victory in Ireland in the first post-war election, signalled the demise of Redmondite nationalism in Ireland. By 1918, the insurgents of the Easter Rising were venerated in many quarters as heroes, and a more belligerent nationalism was in the ascendancy. Irish freedom from Britain was to be won, argued many leading Irish nationalists, by force of arms, not through peaceful constitutional agreement. The nationalism of Sinn Féin, which dominated Irish politics by the end of the First World War, embraced the long history of Ireland's myths and legends. It located itself as much in the contemporary world as it did within the ancient Celtic or Gaelic past of Ireland. Within such thinking St Patrick grew in importance; he was an unsullied symbol and hero of a strong and independent Ireland. St Patrick, it was argued in 1918, stood above Church and State. His position as a role model for the Irish was unquestioned. According to a commentator in Cork he was 'the patron of the religion and idealism of the people ... uniting in himself the highest qualities of patriotism and religion'.[13]

Through the revolutionary war, however, the observance of St Patrick's Day understandably slipped from the diary. The violent progress of the conflict through many parts of Ireland, particularly in the wake of the introduction of the Black and Tans and the escalation of reprisal attacks on both sides, meant that large-scale and spontaneous public observances on 17 March were impractical. St Patrick's Day in 1920 was, nonetheless, a time for symbolic resistance against the British presence in Ireland. Large crowds travelled to Glasnevin cemetery to visit the graves of Ireland's nationalist dead, and across the country people attended staid church services. The *Irish Independent* noted that 'Irish sermons were a conspicuous feature in the solemnities in connection with the national festival throughout the country.'[14] Services such as these were by now conducted partly in Irish, a fact which flew in the face of British legislation that banned the official use of the native language. The paper's editorial argued that such Irish services 'served to show that the Castle ban on the teaching of the language is doomed to fail'.[15] In Waterford, the most blatant political act of the day took place when the local St Patrick's Day parade featured Sinn Féin councillors of the city corporation, the Gaelic League, and uniformed members of the Irish Volunteers. The editor of the *Irish Independent* concluded that, despite such displays, it was surprising that the British did not elect for a more ferocious show of force on St Patrick's Day:

Apart from the usual military raids in the early hours of the morning, the National Festival was allowed to pass without any spectacular display of armed force by the ruling powers. This was more than the average person expected. There was a general belief that the occasion would be availed for some awe inspiring demonstration calculated to show that the policy of coercion had lost none of its vigour.[16]

Within the mindset of the IRA machine conducting the war, St Patrick may have been one of many important Irish heroes who inspired them in their fight, but there was no specific reference to him during the period of the war. *An tOglác*, the official organ of the Irish Volunteers through the War of Independence, makes no mention of St Patrick or of 17 March observances between 1919 and 1922.[17]

On a more self-indulgent level, the *Irish Independent* of March 1920 reported a large number of visitors to Dublin for the national festival, as well as other sites around Ireland. The main social events included the annual St Patrick's Day meeting at Baldoyle races, an unveiling by the Gaelic Athletic Association of a statue dedicated to their founder, Michael Cusack, in Thurles; and, because the weather was favourable, trips to the coast.[18]

Although a muted celebration, as one would expect in a time of war, St Patrick's Day was still an important focus for the expression of Irishness in the face of British coercion. The observance of St Patrick's Day, whether through social events that stressed a sense of normality, or through church services that included an element of political defiance, was part of the ideological battle against the British. As well as being a general celebration of Irishness across the world, St Patrick's Day observances had, throughout the second half of the nineteenth and into the early twentieth century, embraced the cause of Irish nationalism.

TREATY AND CIVIL WAR

The debates that swirled around the end of the War of Independence and the terms on which the Irish should settle their dispute with Britain exerted a powerful effect on both the Irish and their diaspora. The Anglo-Irish Treaty signed in December 1921, and ratified by Dáil Éireann in January 1922 bitterly divided opinion, and was the catalyst that led to civil war in Ireland, which would last until 1923.

In Ireland, St Patrick's Day in 1922 was understandably muted. Patrician observance in 1921 had centred on attendance at church services and the pursuit of political goals, and 1922 was little different. There were no official St Patrick's Day events that involved a partnership of state and people, and thus the majority celebrated the day by attending Mass. The war of words that circled the decision to sign the treaty was played out across the country; as St Patrick's Day was a public holiday, politicians hoped that public meetings would attract large crowds. The anti-treatyites gathered together across the country. At Harold's Cross in Dublin a meeting was addressed by Countess Markievicz and Erskine Childers, and de Valera spoke in Waterford. In the context of 1922, political meetings were far from unusual. St Patrick's Day, because of its place as the national day, was deliberately targeted for the staging of the biggest meetings. In that, Collins, de Valera and others were no different from Redmond, Parnell, O'Connell and those that had gone before. Despite the concentration on politics, and the lack of a state observance of St Patrick's Day, 17 March was still embraced as special by the Irish population. Those who attended church could listen to services delivered in Irish without fear of prosecution, while those who travelled the country to attend sporting and other cultural events could do so without being delayed by the British army checking their papers. Although there were no special excursions laid on by the railway companies because of the political situation, the perennial St Patrick's Day race meeting at Baldoyle did take place. As the *Irish Times* stressed, 'notwithstanding the political distractions of the moment, there is no reason to think that the majority of Irishmen will not light-heartedly celebrate the national festival today'.[19]

The divisions that the treaty caused were reflected in America. There was a belief that the agreement, which allowed for the partition of Ireland and the creation of the Irish Free State, had failed to deliver on the substantive goal that had long united Irish America – the creation of a unified Irish Republic. The question for Irish America was whether the signing of the Treaty was merely a staging post on the road to a republic, as Michael Collins and other supporters argued, or was it a copper-fastened agreement that permanently divided Ireland? In 1922, the Grand Marshal of the New York parade, Edward J. Gavegan, sent a telegram to Michael Collins on St Patrick's Day that demonstrated the Irish-American difficulty with the Treaty. He wrote:

Fifty thousand Americans of Irish blood in New York city marching in honour of St Patrick, with half a million others on the side lines, presented an example of faith and hope which we are sure will not be lost on compatriots. We believe and resolve with them, that if the Treaty is accepted as a payment on account, the balance in full shall be collected in due course.[20]

The telegram was clear in its argument, marking Irish America generally and the New York St Patrick's Day parade specifically, as holding a broad anti-Treaty position. The Treaty, it was hoped, was a strategy on the road to the republic. For those involved in the St Patrick's Day parade of 1922, the sentiments of Gavegan's telegram, underpinned by the banner under which Cumann na mBan marched – 'Trust in God and Keep Your Powder Dry' – summed up their perspective on the Irish situation. The evidence of the anti-Treaty position held by a majority of marchers was apparent in the 1923 New York St Patrick's Day parade. Whereas 50,000 people had marched in 1922, a mere 5,000 did so one year later. Irish America had turned its back on the Ireland that the Treaty had created and the bitterness that the civil war produced. The splits that occurred within the diaspora were an obvious concern for all sides involved in the civil war. Both used St Patrick's Day to promote and justify their decisions to pursue either the pro- or anti-Treaty line.

In 1922, Michael Collins, the head of the Irish Provincial government, sent an open message to the American people, which was printed in a wide range of newspapers. Collins argued that with the signing of the Treaty, the Irish people were taking control of their destiny. In sending St Patrick's Day greetings to the American people, he also sought to convey 'the Irish Nation's gratitude for the generous support given by America through the long years of its struggle for freedom'.[21] Although in government, Collins and the pro-treatyites did not have sole access to the American media. De Valera, as head of the anti-treatyites, and because of his long-standing personal relationship with Irish America, was also given wide coverage in the press. Whereas Collins had appealed to Irish America to accept the terms of the Treaty as it allowed for the creation of an Irish nation, de Valera urged rejection. He argued that 'if the treaty is accepted, the Irish, instead of fighting foreign soldiers, will have to fight Irish soldiers belonging to an Irish government'.[22] Both Collins and de Valera were using their St Patrick's Day messages to win Irish Americans over to their respective causes. The centrality of 17 March in the Irish calendar, and the importance of Irish America to the politicians of Ireland, meant that the reasoning behind the pro- and anti-treaty positions was played out in America in 1922. The verbal jousting of St Patrick's Day was soon transformed into the bitterness of the civil war. While the firing line in this conflict did not extend to America, the battle lines were drawn across the Irish-American community, and they featured in the symbolism of St Patrick's Day.

ST PATRICK'S DAY IN CANADA, 1914–22

The First World War had a varied impact on the observance of St Patrick's Day in Canada. Quebec City organizers dispensed with the annual parade in 1916: the reason they gave was that many of the usual military and civilian marchers were now engaged in the war effort. But as late as 1920 the parade had still not resumed; this was some two years after the end of the conflict in Europe.[23] In Montreal, by contrast, St Patrick's Day was commemorated with a parade in 1916 and 1917 despite the absence of many Irish-Canadian servicemen. The anniversary was a time in which Montreal's Irish community gave voice to their desire for Home Rule, and this cause had gathered considerable momentum in the years leading up to the war. In March 1913, an estimated 6,000 participants took part in the largest St Patrick's Day parade in Montreal's history; the contingent now included the United Irish League, which carried a banner bearing the emblem of John Redmond.[24]

The following parade of 1914 was described by the *Gazette* as 'a decidedly imposing demonstration of the solidarity of the Irish people of Montreal'. The newspaper was impressed by the spectacle of the parade, particularly the Young Irelanders 'with each member of the order in silk hat festooned with shamrock, and wearing buttonholes of green carnations'. But the *Gazette* also acknowledged that this was a demonstration in hope of a cause – Home Rule for the Irish homeland. Excerpts from St Patrick's Day speeches were reproduced in the paper, such as the view of Father Heffernan, who had 'a fervent hope that the national flag would soon wave over College Green'.[25] The subsequent wartime suspension of Home Rule legislation suspended this dream and, for some Irish Canadians, altered their perception of what would be required to achieve self-government. Reformists were alarmed by the republican violence of the Easter Rising, but they were also very concerned by a policy change of the British Government just one month later. In May 1916, Westminster tried to introduce an amended Government of Ireland Act; this revised measure would allow the six predominantly Protestant counties of Ulster to withdraw from Home Rule provisions. Radical nationalists saw the spectre of partition as confirmation of their view that the British Government was never going to play the Home Rule game with a straight bat. In July 1916, the AOH of Montreal abandoned its support for Redmond's policy of parliamentary reform. The Society had, for some years, been arguing for a more assertive approach to Irish politics; now it openly preached militant republicanism.[26] These political pressures were, as we now explain, about to shape the wartime observance of St Patrick's Day in Montreal.

In January 1916, a committee of well-respected, politically moderate Irish leaders assembled in Montreal to establish an Irish regiment to serve in the Canadian militia. The Irish Canadian Rangers were duly authorized for service two months later, its members fitted out with 'a shamrock on the cap and a harp on the collar'.[27] By the following St Patrick's Day, the Rangers were actively recruiting; they also used the anniversary to raise operational funds. A Patrician concert was staged jointly by the St Patrick's Society and the Irish Protestant Benevolent Society, with profits going to the Rangers. This was a significant initiative, for it was 'the first time in sixty years that both societies had met together'.[28] St Patrick's Day, 1916 henceforth became a demonstration of the 'unity' of the Irish-Canadian community of Montreal, and its unfailing 'loyalty' to Britain at a time of crisis. This was exemplified during the St Patrick's Day parade by the re-inclusion of the Union flag in the colour party. As the *Gazette* noted, 'in past years' this British symbol had been 'conspicuous by its absence'.[29] At this point, of course, reformists were still optimistic about the prospect of Dominion-style status for Ireland. After all, tens of thousands of Irishmen had already volunteered to serve the Imperial Force. However, the Rising of 1916 and British Government fudging of the Home Rule Act stifled confidence about reform among Irish

Canadians. This helps, in part, to explain the rising influence of the AOH in Montreal, as well as its eventual control over the staging of the St Patrick's Day parade.

The AOH, while an influential part of the Irish-Catholic Committee, had been outvoted on several issues pertaining to the parade. For example, the AOH constitution stipulated that the procession must take place on 17 March; this position was countered by the Catholic Church, which argued for a march on the Sunday nearest St Patrick's Day. The Church, which held sway in the Committee, got its way. More controversial, and politically telling, was a formal objection in 1917 by the AOH about 'the presence of soldiers in uniform in the parade'.[30] This was a direct challenge to the propriety of the Irish Rangers at a time when, from an AOH perspective, the British Government had denied the Irish their right to self-government. The St Patrick's Society, meanwhile, continued to argue for Home Rule reforms 'constitutionally, moderately, and keeping always with the law of the realm'.[31] This remained the dominant sentiment among most of the Irish community of Montreal, but they were now very vocal, even agitated, about lack of progress towards parliamentary autonomy in the homeland. A mass meeting in St Ann's Hall on the eve of St Patrick's Day, 1917 resulted in a resolution to the Premier of Canada that 'in the interest of peace, the statute providing self-government for Ireland should be put into immediate operation'.[32] This tension was heightened by local responses to the Canadian Government's proposed referendum on wartime conscription. Montreal's St Patrick's Day march was held on Sunday 18 March: this 'large parade', replete with 'Irish jaunting car', was followed by a mass meeting at the St Louis Town Hall, where a vocal crowd passed a resolution against enforced military service, and in support of the present voluntary system of recruitment.[33] Somewhere in all of this the tradition of raising money for charity on St Patrick's Day continued. On 17 March 1917, some 800 'colleens' traversed the city, working all day until 8 p.m., to collect donations in aid of the St Patrick's Orphanage of Montreal.[34]

As the political climate in both Montreal and Ireland remained tense, St Patrick's Day of 1918 promised to be a testing time for the organizer of the parade, the Irish-Catholic Committee (ICC). There were two meetings to discuss 'a possible suspension of the parade'. In the first of these meetings, a motion to support that proposition was tabled, but it was 'defeated by an AOH-led opposition'. A second meeting was called in response to the untimely death of John Redmond in 1918. The AOH argued that the parade should still go ahead; this time, though, it was defeated. The ICC offered a list of reasons, but no coherent explanation: 'the war ... the absence of young men ... extraordinary conditions'.[35] The Conscription Act of 1917 was now in force: it was unpopular among many of the Irish community, and there was a fear 'that conscription officers would disrupt the official parade in its route along main streets'.[36] The implication was that if men could march on St Patrick's Day they were fit enough to serve as soldiers.

The St Patrick's Day parade was revived in 1919. By this time the AOH dominated meetings of the ICC, so the resumption of the march was no surprise. That said, the AOH did not have control over proceedings: it was still unable to convince the committee to stage the parade on 17 March, which in this year was a Monday. The Sunday procession remained. Yet there were hints during the parade itself that support for the AOH was on the rise. The *Gazette* noticed green, white and orange republican flags among the marchers: this was, the paper noted, 'the first occasion on which this emblem has been carried in a St Patrick's Day parade in Montreal'.[37] In 1920 the AOH took over the management of the St Patrick's Day march and the ICC was made redundant. The story here becomes hazy, largely because the AOH of Montreal today claims that its forebears kept no record of its administration of the parade; and, in any case, the Order does not allow public access to what its gatekeepers describe as 'private files'.[38] What little we know, then, comes from the contemporary press. The main issue of contention, which we elaborate upon in Chapter 5, was an ongoing dispute between the AOH and the Catholic Church over the route of the parade, the day on which it would be staged, and the venue for St Patrick's Day mass.

ST PATRICK'S DAY IN AUSTRALIA: 1914–22

In March 1914 Archbishop Carr remarked that people who had marched in Melbourne's St Patrick's Day procession 'could tell their children that they took part ... in the year that Ireland obtained Home Rule'. His colleague, coadjutor Archbishop Mannix, considered that with Home Rule imminent 'they were celebrating a new era of their old land'.[39] A week later, however, the *Age* reported that British troops had been ordered into Ulster and there were fears that a civil war might develop.[40] This was averted for the time being, but the onset of the First World War in August 1914 stalled the progress of Home Rule. Many Irish Australians were still confident that the policy would still be implemented. This was particularly so, it was felt, because so many Irishmen – both at home and abroad – had enlisted to defend the empire.[41]

The 1916 St Patrick's Day procession was performed before 'throngs of spectators'.[42] At some points the crowd spilled onto the roadway and floats had difficulty moving on. Support for the war effort was noticeable. The *Age* reported 'a liberal sprinkling of khaki amongst the spectators'; 500 soldiers of the Australian Expeditionary Force also took part in the procession.[43] At the St Patrick's Night concert, Archbishop Carr emphasized that although the war was 'vile and ruinous ... it had brought about a union of the Irish and British nation such as the most loyal never expected to witness to our day'.[44] But this rhetoric of commonality was shattered a month later by the Easter Rising in Dublin.

In Australia there was astonishment at this development. A meeting of the St Patrick's Society of Melbourne viewed the rebellion with 'surprise and indignation', declaring: 'We strongly adhere to the constitutional methods of the National Party in Ireland ... for finally consummating Home Rule.'[45] Subsequently, several Irish nationalist groups in Australia cabled messages to Redmond and British Prime Minister Asquith, pledging loyalty to empire and faith in Home Rule.[46] By contrast, Sydney's militant republican group, the Irish National Association, offered the rebels its support.[47] In this early phase, though, Irish Australians were generally not associated with support for Sinn Féin, nor with positions of 'disloyalty' to empire. Indeed, the staunchly pro-British daily, the *Argus*, stressed that 'the great mass of Irish people were as loyal as any in the Empire, and as eager to see the perpetrators punished'.[48]

Catholic leaders in Australia also responded to the crisis. Carr described the revolt as 'an outburst of madness, an anachronism, and a crime'.[49] Mannix's first reaction was that the uprising was 'truly deplorable', and its leaders 'misguided'.[50] By May 1916, however, British government reprisals under martial law, including the arrest and deportation to Wales of some 2,000 suspected Sinn Féin supporters, turned around the opinions of many in the Catholic hierarchy. The most outspoken and strident Catholic critic was Mannix who, while not exonerating the rebels, stressed that the British Government was also culpable in the tragic affair. In his time as president of Maynooth College in Ireland from 1903–13, Mannix's loyalty to empire and Crown had never been in question.[51] But on 30 April 1916, before the first executions of the rebels took place, he declared that 'the British Government, by its failure to deal with the treason of the Carsonites, and by its shifty policy on Home Rule has, unwittingly I suppose, led to the result which we must all deplore'.[52] Catholic newspapers in Australia also questioned the British reaction; and, while most Irish nationalist groups initially criticized the rebels' actions, they now tended to be more hostile to the extent of British reprisals.[53] There was now an onus on the British Government, argued the *Catholic Press* in May 1916, to establish Ireland's place in the empire by immediately declaring Home Rule.[54] But the Bill remained dormant.

Meanwhile, the Loyal Orange Lodges and various Protestant leaders in Australia voiced their approval of the British actions, with leading newspapers, notably Melbourne's *Argus*, joining them. They each tended to view Irish-Australian criticism of Britain's response to the crisis as evidence that the Irish were 'an essentially rebellious and untrustworthy race',[55] and they branded local Catholics as supporters of Sinn Féin.[56] Indeed, the annual 12th of July Loyal Orange Lodge demonstration in Melbourne Town Hall denounced Irish Catholics as 'traitors to empire', with Mannix their 'ringleader'.[57] On this occasion, with others to follow, there were calls for the Archbishop to be deported and sent back to Ireland.[58]

A 'test' of patriotic loyalties in Australia was imminent. On 30 August 1916, Prime Minister Billy Hughes announced that a referendum would be held to decide whether men would be conscripted to serve in the Australian Imperial Force, whose number of recruits had fallen considerably.[59] Hughes portrayed opponents of a 'yes' vote as disloyal to Australia and empire. The campaigns for and against were divisive; the key point here is that the defeat of the poll was, in large part, ascribed to the 'disloyalty' of Irish Catholics.[60] Indeed, Hughes considered that an 'overwhelming majority' of Irish Catholics had been influenced to vote 'no' by Sinn Féin and Archbishop Mannix.[61] This overlooked the dominant role of the trade union movement in the campaign for a 'no' vote.[62] Furthermore, most of the Catholic bishops, with Mannix a notable exception, had publicly favoured conscription in 1916, despite their discomfort at British reprisals to the Easter rebellion. Finally, a majority of voters in Mannix's home state of Victoria actually supported the referendum; and in New South Wales, where Archbishop Kelly favoured conscription, the referendum failed to pass.[63]

Despite sectarian tensions, Melbourne's St Patrick's Day procession of March 1917 was not contentious. Both the *Catholic Press* and the *Argus* declared that the pageant was 'one of the most successful yet witnessed in Melbourne'; the crowd lining the parade route was thought to comprise some 50,000 spectators.[64] The *Argus* emphasized: 'everywhere great enthusiasm was shown, not only by spectators of Irish extraction, but also by thousands of others'.[65] Archbishops Carr and Mannix were carried by motor transport in the cavalcade, followed by marching children from Catholic schools, as well as members of Irish societies with banners before them.[66] The most striking tableau read 'Erin weeps', a contrast to that of the previous year, 'Erin's hope'.[67] But the *Argus* found nothing in the parade to offend its sense of empire loyalty or its militantly pro-conscription stance. The marchers were headed by the Irish Pipers' Band and immediately after, in pride of place, marched 'a number of Australian soldiers who had been wounded in Gallipoli or France'.[68] The patriotism of the occasion was reiterated as the band stopped at the steps of Federal Parliament to play 'God Save the King'.[69] Two months later Archbishop Carr died, and Mannix assumed leadership of the Catholic Church in Melbourne. This ascendancy of the outspoken Mannix, combined with a second conscription referendum to follow, set the stage for a more dramatic St Patrick's Day in 1918.

In October 1916 Hughes had portrayed anti-conscriptionists as disloyal; by November 1917 he had labelled them as seditious.[70] It was alleged that Irish Catholics under the influence of Sinn Féin were leaders of the anti-conscription lobby. This was a misleading claim, for the trade union movement and the Labor Party were the principal organizers of the 'no' campaign in 1917.[71] But the accusation seemed to have substance in the high profile involvement of Mannix in anti-conscription rallies, and because he now spoke publicly of his sympathy for the ideals of Sinn Féin.[72] The failure of the second conscription referendum of 20 December 1917 raised sectarian tensions further, and Melbourne's St Patrick's parade became a key site for their expression.

On 6 December 1917 the St Patrick's Day Committee applied for permission from the Lord Mayor of Melbourne to conduct its annual procession on the Saturday closest to 17 March of the following year.[73] This was the usual method of application, and approval had long been a formality. But the request was put in the midst of a divisive conscription campaign, so Lord Mayor Frank Stapley did not welcome the timing of the application. He replied that 'in view of the present disturbed state of affairs, he is allowing no processions to be held in city streets'.[74] He did, however, consider an application early in the new year, and accepted that the procession could proceed.[75] After all, the St Patrick's Day parade of 1917 had not caused the council any concern. Why should 1918 be any different?

Santamaria claims that because of the failure of the second conscription referendum, the St Patrick's Day procession of March 1918 was sure to be 'something of a victory march'.[76] There is some merit in this view. After the poll result, the Victorian Catholic Federation organized a series of country picnics where tens of thousands of Catholics rallied together to celebrate. Then, in the lead up to St Patrick's Day, Mannix made 'a personal appeal to all Catholics to join in the procession'.[77] He urged: 'Those who do not belong to any of the Catholic or national societies taking part might enrol for the day under the banner of one or more of the local societies.'[78] Catholic clergy from the archdiocese of Melbourne took part in the parade 'for the first time', joining the cavalcade in motor cars. Marching behind them were 5,000 boys dressed in green and white, representing various Catholic schools and branches of the Hibernian society.[79] The *Catholic Press* concluded that Mannix's plea for support had 'made the line of marching men and boys longer than last year'.[80] The procession took over 45 minutes to pass a given point, with perhaps as many as 60,000 witnesses.[81] The St Patrick's Society carried a banner depicting a Queen of Erin, and Hibernian women were driven on floats – the lead one reading 'Long Live His Grace'.[82] Nothing controversial to speak of here.

But the procession also included 100 members of the Irish National Association (INA) who marched behind a Sinn Féin banner, each one of them carrying a Sinn Féin flag. This group had formed in Melbourne only three months earlier, and was thought to involve some 250 members.[83] The participation of the INA helps to explain a new republican flavour in the procession, although other groups also took up Sinn Féin colours and flags, such as the Robert Emmet branch of the Irish National Foresters. Least expected was the carrying of Sinn Féin colours and flags by Catholic Church groups. Those named in the press included 'the parishioners of St. John the

Baptist, Clifton Hill ... St. Joseph's West Brunswick, and the Sisters of the Good Samaritan'.[84] The Sinn Féin flag carried by the last group was made conspicuous by being 'bordered in black, as mourning for the dead rebels of Ireland'.[85] The Young Ireland Society also pursued this theme: its tableau featured 'a celtic cross and a grave, at the head of which was a scroll' listing the names of those executed after the Easter Rising.[86] As the procession paused for the playing of 'God Save the King' in front of parliament house, Mannix did not uncover his head as the usual sign of respect, although his colleagues Cattaneo and Foley did so. Mannix was criticized for this inaction, particularly as he 'uncovered his head in lowly reverence to the banner with the inscription, "To the Martyrs of Easter Week" '.[87]

Predictably, empire loyalists were horrified. The (non-Catholic) Council of Churches argued that the parade was 'aggressively disloyal and ... flagrantly contemptuous of British criminal law'. It was a 'treasonable pageant'.[88] A letter to the *Argus* talked of 'enemy flags' being flown as if Australia was at war with Ireland, not Germany.[89] A very different letter argued that charges of treason could not be laid because 'neither by statute or by proclamation ... has the British Government outlawed Sinn Féin or its flag'.[90] The former view was held widely by Australians of British-Protestant background. Dr Alex Leeper, former warden of Trinity College at the University of Melbourne, and Herbert Brookes, close confidant of Prime Minister Hughes, headed a deputation of some 3,000 angry citizens at the Melbourne town hall. To them, Sinn Féin was an 'enemy organization' and Mannix an 'arch-traitor'.[91] Further such meetings followed: a result was the formation of groups such as the Citizens' Loyalist Committee (later the Loyalist League) and the Victorian Protestant Federation, as bulwarks against 'disloyalism'.[92]

Mayor Frank Stapley announced that if he had known there would be 'objectionable features' in the Melbourne parade he would not have agreed to it. He was not made aware of 'disloyal elements' until he received a phone call soon after the parade started. By this time, he argued, little could be done by the police to prevent the progress of the procession without risking 'a riot, with possibly serious consequences'.[93] But police later admitted that they did not know the Sinn Féin flag or its colours, and they had no understanding of the tableaux on display. Their job, as they saw it, was simply to manage the crowd.[94]

There were now calls for Melbourne's St Patrick's Day march to be regulated or even banned so that 'disloyal' elements would not reappear.[95] Hence there were discussions about what laws could be applied to regulate the parade. A meeting of 40,000 'loyalists' at the Exhibition Building recommended that the federal government pursue 'the suppression of all acts of disloyalty', including public processions.[96] A leading Protestant orator, the Reverend Henry Worrall stressed: 'Every effort must be made ... to resist the teachings of men like Dr. Mannix.' He concluded that Australia was a great democracy and disloyalism 'would not be tolerated'.[97] The paradox of this position – advocating free speech but denying dissent – does not seem to have dawned upon Worrall. He even recommended that those who carried the St Patrick's Day banner depicting the Easter rebels as martyrs should be gaoled. By contrast, the Australian Catholic Federation and various Irish national societies voiced their support for Mannix and their concern at 'interference with the right of freedom of speech and action'.[98]

Meanwhile, Brookes approached Hughes with a suggestion that Sinn Féin be declared a 'disloyal', and thus an illegal, organization. The Prime Minister agreed: he had already used the Wartime Precautions Act to arrest leaders of the Industrial Workers of the World,[99] and viewed Sinn Féin in a similar manner.[100] On 28 March 1918 'special regulations of the Wartime Precautions Act' were gazetted, these making it an offence for anyone to be involved with Sinn Féin or to display its emblems. Also illegal were 'advocacy of the independence of Ireland', and expressions of 'disloyalty or hostility to the British Empire'.[101] But the legislation was not retrospective and, although Mannix was a prime target of the Hughes initiative, he was not connected with Sinn Féin or the INA in any direct way. 'Loyalist' hopes that Mannix would be deported were not realized,[102] although arrests of leading INA members were made in Sydney, where the republican organization was more prominent than in Melbourne.[103]

There was also urgency within the Melbourne City Council to respond to the 'disloyalism' of the 1918 procession. The display of Sinn Féin symbols had embarrassed Melbourne's Lord Mayor, and he was determined to exercise greater control over future parades. In the meantime, Mannix counselled restraint and 'cool heads' from Catholics: 'They should walk calmly, discreetly, and fearlessly, and keep their minds and sentiments to themselves.'[104] The latter point was hardly characteristic of the Mannix style of politics. Unfortunately, although the archbishop improved the assertiveness and sense of purpose of many of his followers, particularly working-class Catholics, the stridency of his speeches also served to alienate Catholics within a wider polity dominated by Protestants. His support for the church in Australia and his criticisms of the troubles in Ireland were usually framed to antagonize opponents, not to persuade them to think differently. An outcome was that many Catholics were made scapegoats for the Mannix bandwagon, this resulting in new Protestant boycotts against Catholic tradesmen and workers.[105]

For advocates of an Irish republic, 1918 finished on a positive note. The December election for the British House of Commons witnessed the virtual collapse of the old Irish party, and a political victory for Sinn Féin. An Irish republic was symbolically announced with a de facto national assembly, Dáil Éireann, convened in Dublin. Significantly, the republic proclaimed by the rebels of 1916 was ratified, and the parliament was separate to Westminster, defiantly so. But if supporters of Sinn Féin in Melbourne planned a celebration on St Patrick's Day, 1919, it soon became obvious that this would best be done in private. William Whyte Cabena was the new Mayor of Melbourne. He was a Londonderry-born Protestant, 'one of the city's leading Orangemen', and determined that there should be no repeat of 'disloyalism' in the St Patrick's Day procession.[106] Cabena wanted assurances from the secretary of the St Patrick's Day Celebration Committee, L. Egan, that there would be no banners, flags, or any other emblems relating to 'Sinn Féin or Republican principles'.[107] Furthermore, in order to make the procession appear patriotic to empire, Cabena demanded that both the Australian flag and the Union Jack were to be carried unfurled at the head of the marchers, and 'God Save the King' had to be played at the beginning and conclusion of the parade. The mayor also advised that, as on St Andrew's Day, the Union Jack would be flown from the top of the Town Hall on St Patrick's Day.[108] Cabena had received advice from the city solicitors that Section 10 of the Unlawful Assemblies and Processions Act (1915) could have been applied to the 1918 procession. This stated, in part: 'if the procession exhibit[s] any flag or is accompanied by any music calculated to provoke animosity between His Majesty's subjects of different religious persuasions it would be an unlawful assembly'.[109] Marchers could, under these circumstances, be asked to disperse. If they refused to do so within fifteen minutes the 'Riot Act' would be read and arrests made.[110] It was also the opinion of the city solicitors that the lord mayor (or in his absence the town clerk) could 'refuse consent to anyone to hold a street procession without assigning any reason'.[111]

Cabena declared that permission to hold the St Patrick's Day parade was not forthcoming, and he was prepared to confront organizers over the issue. But nothing of this kind eventuated. The parade committee announced that influenza restrictions had made it 'difficult' to organize public events associated with St Patrick's Day. Therefore, the procession and sports carnival would not be held this year.[112] The influenza pandemic began in January 1919 and was not taken lightly by authorities. Schools were closed and many public activities were cancelled.[113] But the files of the town clerk contain no references to influenza restrictions imposed on St Patrick's Day organizers. So the pandemic seems to have been used as a convenient explanation by the committee in order to save face, particularly as council permission to hold the procession had not been granted. Moreover, the Eight Hours Day procession went ahead in April, and the influenza pandemic was not mentioned as an obstacle.[114]

On the other hand, the annual Irish National Concert was still held, as usual, in the Melbourne town hall. While the mayor had put paid to a public Irish celebration, he did not have the nerve to cancel their festivities held behind closed doors. But he would not have been pleased with the outcome, for the *Argus* reported that 'large numbers in the hall' waved Sinn Féin flags.[115] Indeed, Mannix amused the audience by asking where the

Union Jack could be found in the building, and if there were 'any anti-Irish germs clinging about'.[116] In a more serious tone he remarked that 'certain obstacles' had impeded this year's celebrations, but it 'was fortunate, perhaps, for all concerned that the ... influenza epidemic made it futile to have the issue tried out to the end'.[117] This silence, however, was not to be misinterpreted as submission by Irish Catholics. Mannix warned: 'They were quite ready to abide by any reasonable conditions that were laid down equally with others.' But Irish Catholics would not 'submit tamely to studied and deliberate insult. (Applause). The end of the chapter would be written next year. (Laughter).'[118] But it was to be no laughing matter.

The Catholic hierarchy and Irish national associations attended the Irish Race Convention of November 1919 in Sydney. The symposium affirmed Ireland's right of self-determination and pledged support to Eamon de Valera as leader. This signalled that the Home Rule movement, which had long attracted clerical support, was effectively doomed. But it also suggested that if republicanism was the way ahead, then Australian clergy wanted to control its more militant local advocates. The Anglo-Irish war was raging by this time, which made talk of Irish independence seem as 'disloyal' as it had during the First World War, particularly as Australian newspapers offered vociferous support of Britain in this latest conflict.[119] Hence, 'loyalist' opposition to the forthcoming St Patrick's Day march could again be expected. Indeed, soon after Egan applied for permission to conduct the parade,[120] a group of 'loyalist' bodies represented by the ubiquitous Dr Leeper urged the mayor not to consent to it.[121]

The difference with the previous year was that a new Lord Mayor, John Aikman, held office. Dunstan describes him as 'a fair-minded former draper'.[122] He was certainly determined to be even-handed in a time of pro-tracted sectarian and political divides. Aikman hoped to reconcile such con-flicts through negotiation and compromise, but faced a daunting task. The timing of his mayoralty was critical in a further way: the Prince of Wales was scheduled to visit the city in April 1920, so Aikman wanted 'to give a united and enthusiastic welcome to the Heir of the Throne'.[123] This would best be achieved by playing down sectional hostilities and encouraging all groups to welcome the prince. To the pragmatic Aikman this was a better approach than antagonizing and marginalizing so-called 'disloyal' Irish Catholics. However, while the mayor was prepared to defend their right to stage the St Patrick's Day procession, he demanded concessions to placate 'loyalist' opponents of the parade. This was a better option, Aikman con-sidered, than an unregulated showdown between militantly opposed forces.

The 'loyalist' deputation headed by Leeper stressed that the character of the St Patrick's Day procession had fundamentally changed. It was no longer a benign celebration of St Patrick and Irish cultural traditions, for the display of Sinn Féin flags in 1918 meant that it had now become a 'disloyal' demonstration in 'open sympathy with His Majesty's enemies'. The 'loyalist' representatives reminded the mayor that republican forces were murdering British police in Ireland: the forthcoming St Patrick's Day procession was 'in support of that', and intended 'to show their sympathy with them'.[124] Dr Mannix was, as usual, a special focus of 'loyalist' animosity. The deputation argued that because of the archbishop's advocacy of an Irish republic, he was 'threatening the existence of the British Empire and Australia'.[125]

There were rumours that if the march went ahead then a violent response from 'loyalist' opponents was likely. Of course, members of the deputation claimed to be innocent of such motives themselves, but they stressed that actions of their more militant colleagues could not be underestimated.[126] Leeper concluded: 'We warn you, my Lord Mayor, that the consequence of allowing a hostile demonstration against the Empire will be such as you will deplore for the rest of your life.'[127] The Australian Women's National League also made predictions of civil conflict. One member emphasized that with so many returned soldiers in the streets likely to be offended by the 'disloyal' parade then 'anything may happen'. Another member argued that if the procession went ahead, then 'slaughter and strife' were likely outcomes.[128]

Mayor Aikman also received letters warning of 'dire consequences' should the parade be permitted. A message artfully signed 'A Loyal Roman Catholic' (no name supplied), dubbed St Patrick's Day marchers as 'unworthy citizens' who were 'wounding the feelings of the majority of Melbourne citizens' who, incidentally, were Protestant. The letter warned the mayor that if he allowed the parade to proceed he would 'be a party to the BIGGEST RIOT this City has ever seen'. The author concluded: 'I know of arrangements being made to smash up any procession which may attempt to start, and any bloodshed resulting from the same will be upon your shoulders as a mark of disgrace for all time.'[129] This inflammatory rhetoric had become familiar to Aikman and, aware that comments by the loyalist deputation might be used as public propaganda to try to sway his decision, he excluded the press from their meeting. Leeper protested, but Aikman would not be swayed. He was intent on minimizing public controversy over the issue, and was concerned that media reports of their discussion might be taken out of context or used to exacerbate existing hostilities.[130] When the mayor met with members of the St Patrick's Day Committee on the same day, the press was also barred from that meeting.[131]

Upon receiving Egan and his colleagues, Aikman demanded an assurance that no 'disloyal' symbols would be displayed during the parade. Egan replied that the marchers would not carry any flags or emblems that might be offensive to other citizens. He insisted that the 1918 episode was an 'aberration', for the carrying of 'disloyal' symbols had not been sanctioned by the committee and, in fact, was the work of an 'unauthorized minority' beyond their control.[132] This was a doubtful claim because processionists had assembled at St Patrick's Hall before the 1918 parade, many of them clutching Sinn Féin flags. Moreover, police on duty were asked if they saw any groups joining the procession after it had started, presumably in a clandestine manner. Their reply was uniformly negative.[133] But the mayor was not interested in apportioning blame for problems associated with the 1918 march. He was concerned about how the forthcoming parade might be regulated by the St Patrick's Day Committee, particularly as it claimed to not have control over so-called 'disloyal' elements in 1918. Egan and his colleagues informed the mayor that they would ask police to patrol the procession route and urge them to confiscate any offensive flag or emblem. Aikman was pleased with these assurances, but warned that they must be followed to the letter. Otherwise the future of the parade would be in jeopardy, as would his position as Melbourne's 'custodian of the peace'. The mayor advised the committee that he would make a decision about a permit for the march next week, but reminded them of his difficult role: 'I want to do best for the citizens. I want to be fair to both sides but of course know I cannot give satisfaction to everyone.'[134]

On 5 February Aikman advised the St Patrick's Day Committee that the parade could proceed under the conditions discussed during their meeting of 30 January.[135] The mayor defended his decision in the press, arguing that he had received 'definite assurances' from the organizers that there would be nothing in the procession that might be considered offensive to loyal citizens.[136] Aikman explained that he had been 'much impressed' that among the St Patrick's Day Committee deputation were returned soldiers. Indeed, one of them, Sergeant Buckley, had been awarded the Victoria Cross. This distinguished soldier advised the mayor that 600 of his former classmates from the Christian Brothers' School had volunteered to fight for country and empire. He stressed that they had regularly marched in St Patrick's Day parades before they went to war; why should they be prevented from doing so now after serving abroad with bravery and distinction?[137] Aikman was taken by this argument: 'Apart from all assurances, I think the presence of these brave returned men in the procession is a guarantee that the procession may be permitted without any fear of a display of disloyalty.'[138]

But a second deputation by 'loyalist' bodies wanted concessions from the paraders. It argued that the 'mere absence of symbols expressive of violent antagonism to Britain and the Empire are not enough'.[139] The deputation urged the mayor to insist that 'loyalist' symbols – notably the Union Jack and Australian flags – should be carried in the Irish procession, and that 'God Save the King' be played by the marching bands.[140] As indicated previously, these had long been features of St Patrick's Day parades before 1918, but the context in which the celebration was now being staged was very different. 'Loyalists' demanded that Irish Australians publicly declare allegiance to empire and throne. To them, silence on the question of loyalty did not suggest consent. Instead, it was deemed to imply recalcitrance.[141]

On 17 February the town clerk asked the St Patrick's Day Committee for information about what would appear on procession banners, and a guarantee that this would not be changed on the day of the march. Egan replied that tableaux would focus on the Irish patron saint, as well as the patriot Daniel O'Connell. The Irish national societies would march with green sashes 'fringed with gold'.[142] No mention here of the Easter Rising, Irish republicanism, or the Sinn Féin tricolours. Egan assured the town clerk that the Union Jack would be 'emblazoned on the leading banner'.[143] Councillors were advised thus: 'The Union Jack was going to be carried at the very front of the procession, or there would be no procession at all.'[144] The mayor then asked the press to publish a letter from Mannix confirming the benign manner of the planned parade. In part it read: 'the demonstration will come off successfully without giving any occasion for soreness in any quarter'.[145] Indeed, returned soldiers wanting to march in the St Patrick's Day procession had been granted official permission to wear AIF uniform.[146]

Kiernan describes the 1920 St Patrick's Day procession as 'the most impressive ever held in Melbourne'.[147] Some 20,000 people took part in the parade, including 6,000 returned soldiers and sailors, 2,000 boys from Christian Brothers' schools, and members of Irish national societies and Catholic parishes.[148] The parade was therefore very lengthy: the *Catholic Press* timed it to have taken one hour and twelve minutes to pass a given point on the route.[149] The *Argus* acknowledged that the crowd, which was assembled behind wooden barriers in the streets and in elevated positions on buildings, was a record for St Patrick's Day. The Victorian police were prepared for trouble during the procession: 440 foot police lined the route, armed with batons and handcuffs, while 100 mounted police joined the march. But there was no disturbance.[150] There was, indeed, an absence of so-called 'disloyal' references to Sinn Féin or republicanism. The *Argus* alluded to 'one or two isolated individual cases' of 'disloyal' emblems, but admitted that the parade was not unlike previous benign celebrations.[151]

Yet the *Argus* was most annoyed that the 'promised' Union Jack had not appeared at the front of the march. The imperial symbol did not emerge until the parade had been in progress for over half an hour. Even then, the paper complained, 'it was not calculated to attract much attention', for it was 'tucked away' in a corner of the St Patrick's Society banner. Although this measured at least 10 by 12 feet in size, the Union Jack was only some 12 inches by 15 inches in diameter. The Australian flag appeared on the same banner but was nearly three times larger than the British flag, and the rest of the tableau was a representation of St Patrick.[152] The first big flags to appear in the procession were two Australian flags, one carried by a returned soldier and the other by a returned sailor. Later in the parade the green harp flag of Ireland was carried by a file of four soldiers, on a corner of which appeared a small representation of the Union Jack. With undisguised pride the *Catholic Press* noted that following behind were 'multitudes of the green harp flag'.[153] Aikman had expected that a British symbol would lead the parade, but had not insisted that it be the flag itself. Indeed, a few days before the march Mannix told the *Catholic Press* that 'the present Lord Mayor, unlike his predecessor, has not attempted to impose any humiliating condition as to the route of the procession or the flags to be carried in it'.[154] But the St Patrick's Day Committee had not fulfilled Aikman's expectation that a Union Jack icon would clearly head the march.

That said, the virtual non-appearance of the Union Jack was rather incidental to a wider impression of civic virtue arising from the parade. The participation of thousands of returned soldiers was a public reminder that Irish Australians had voluntarily served the empire in a time of crisis. Moreover, a personal bodyguard of fourteen Victoria Cross winners escorted Mannix's procession car; this was intended to counter accusations of 'disloyalty' against the archbishop himself.[155] But it was somewhat of a triumph of artifice because John Wren, a wealthy promoter of Catholic causes in Melbourne, had 'persuaded' the VC holders to march with Mannix. Indeed, most of these fourteen soldiers were not even Catholic![156]

So the 1920 parade did not exacerbate tensions between 'loyalists' and Irish Australians, and no violent outbursts emerged, despite dire predictions. Indeed, the initiatives of Wren and Mannix in helping to stage a somewhat benign, albeit triumphal procession, was likely to help restore public acceptance of St Patrick's Day, even in the eyes of the Melbourne City Council. Together with the St Patrick's Day Committee, Mannix and Wren had tempered an urge among Irish national societies to display republican symbols. Even the staunchly republican INA had produced a suitably ambiguous banner which read 'Angel of Light Give Ireland Her Right'.[157] These republican sentiments persisted privately, but the Irish-Catholic leadership now warned against their public display. For the alternative was even greater censorship by state authorities. That said, a film of the 1920 procession was released by Wren and shown at Melbourne's Princess Theatre. He gave it the title *Ireland Will Be Free*.[158]

After the 1920 parade Mannix praised Aikman as 'a man with a big mind . . . a man of sanity'.[159] But a change of city council procedure meant that councillors would now vote on next year's street march; the mayor no longer had sole jurisdiction. Sensing an opportunity, 'loyalists' lobbied the council to refuse permission for the imminent 1921 parade, but they were unsuccessful.[160] Instead, the town clerk notified J.H. Kennedy, the new secretary of the St Patrick's Day Celebration Committee, that the council had given approval for the march, albeit subject to conditions. Namely: the Australian and Union Jack flags had to be carried 'at the forefront of the procession attached to poles', and they had to measure 6 feet by 3 feet.[161] The now usual disclaimer of no 'disloyal' emblems was also added. For parade organizers, there seemed no way to avoid it this year; the flag of Britain would have to lead their march, and at a time when much of Ireland was at war with British forces.

There was disquiet about the council's parade rules. A meeting of the Irish National Foresters (INF) on 8 March 1921 moved that 'the society take no part in the procession' as a response to the council's 'discriminating' requirement. However, despite misgivings, the INF participated in the march as usual.[162] The most virulent critic was a recently formed local branch of the Irish Republican Army. The IRA not only opposed the council edict, it accused those who would comply with it as being unrepresentative of Irish ideals. The IRA appealed 'to all Irishmen and women to do their utmost to prevent it being ever [r]ecorded ... that the Irish people of Australia should ever submit to the will of an alien Government'.[163] The group warned that 'any attempt to carry the flag (while the blood of our countrymen is not yet dry on the scaffolds of Mountjoy and Cork prisons) will be met with armed resistance to-day'.[164]

The IRA was not the only Irish national group to consider direct action to rid the parade of signs of patriotism towards Britain. In the days leading up to the march, Kennedy heard rumours that various attempts would be made to 'bring down' the Union Jack. In response, he asked police for protection for flag-bearers, so 'a special picked Force of two sub-officers and 20 constables' was given that responsibility.[165] Apparently, a plan was also under way by a group of 'young Republicans' for a Union Jack doused with petrol to be carried at the head of the procession. The strategy was for the flag 'to be lit at a suitable moment', with the flag-bearer making a sprint down Queen Street to Queen's Bridge, where he was expected to dive into the Yarra River, making good his escape.[166] But the protest was poorly orchestrated. The St Patrick's Day Celebration Committee had appointed two flag-bearers. At the start of the parade a dense crowd had formed, and at the expected time a man holding the Australian flag came forward, met with cheers. He was soon followed by another flag-bearer with the Union Jack in hand, who received jeers.[167] The congested assembly and presence of a strong police contingent prevented 'rebels' from intercepting the Union Jack before it appeared.[168] To make matters worse for dissenters, the British flag was unfurled for all to see at the intersection of Bourke and Queen Streets. This was too much for a couple of the 'rebels'. They ran towards the flag-bearer, struck him a blow, and then ran away with the Union Jack, soaking it with petrol. This attracted the attention of police, who quickly apprehended and arrested the protesters.[169] They didn't even have time to light a match.

Ironically, the rebels had nearly put paid to a protest by the St Patrick's Day Committee itself. Parade organizers had followed council instructions that large British and Australian flags were to head the parade. The Union Jack, which is of sole concern here, was not carried by an Irishmen, or indeed anyone connected with St Patrick's Day.[170] It was borne by an old man, described by police as a vagrant, 'dirty in appearance and attire'.[171] The

Committee paid him 15 shillings to carry the Union Jack, and his dishevelled look and awkward manner were not calculated to inspire respect for the British flag.[172] On the contrary, this satirical ploy was a comical method of dissent, poking fun at council authority.

A subsequent police report mentioned verbal protests against the Union Jack throughout the march. Sub-inspector Grange described these as 'hostile comments, groans and hoots'. They were directed at both the flag and its bearer, who bore the brunt of spectator ridicule: 'See the animal they have got to carry it', 'He is a Chinaman', 'He is a Jap', amidst other mocking and racist terms. Grange reported that the 'hostile demonstrations were mostly from women, youths and children of both sexes'. Not that adult male protestors were passive bystanders. On the contrary, Grange notes that at various points along the procession route men attempted to rush from the crowd to seize the Union Jack, but they were driven back by police. Some protestors made their way onto the road but they were unable to penetrate a police cordon that had formed around the old man carrying the Union Jack.[173]

There was also jubilation from Bishop Phelan who, in Mannix's absence abroad, made a St Patrick's Day speech at the Exhibition Building after the procession was completed. He was 'proud' that no Irish Australian carried the Union flag, arguing that although the council had attempted to humiliate Irish people, it 'really fell on the other side to-day'. Phelan noted that opponents of the parade, by imposing a condition that the British flag would lead the march, had hoped that the procession would not be conducted. As the bishop saw it, the 'Union Jack stood for unparalleled crimes in Ireland'. It was the flag flying for the Black and Tans, who were the 'hired assassins of the British Government' in the Irish homeland.[174] He concluded that 'he was glad to see that the spirit of Irish Australians could never be extinguished and *that day they had danced on the Union Jack*'.[175]

The city council received numerous protests against 'disloyal' speech and conduct in the St Patrick's Day parade of 1921.[176] What particularly disturbed some councillors was that critics questioned their capacity to regulate street processions. The Loyal Orange Lodge warned that because of the inability of authorities to control the St Patrick's Day parade, if another march was staged next year 'loyalists' would themselves take action 'to protect the Flag of the Empire from insult and abuse'.[177] Even the usually staid *Argus* forecast that if the city council did not ban the parade then 'the public will look elsewhere for the safeguards necessary against any repetition of the St Patrick's Day outbreak'.[178] There were, indeed, calls to 'prohibit all street processions of a religious, sectarian, or sectional character',[179] but it was apparent that the council needed a new by-law to do so.[180]

In April 1921 the city solicitor advised the town clerk that in his opinion the council could introduce a by-law to prohibit street processions. It had been previously suggested that such legislation be limited to certain types of marches – so-called 'sectional' parades of an 'objectionable' nature. But the solicitor advised that it would be 'practically impossible' to frame legislation which consistently determined whether a procession was politically acceptable under the law. Therefore, if a by-law was introduced to prohibit street processions, then for practical purposes it should apply to *all* such gatherings. However, the city solicitor also warned that the legality of such a measure was 'by no means free from doubt'.[181] After heated debate in the following weeks, a majority of councillors proposed the introduction of a by-law to prohibit all street marches other than for funerals or military processions.[182] But the council was soon inundated with letters of protest and deputations, particularly from people associated with St Patrick's Day and Eight Hours Day processions.[183] Although the daily press generally supported moves to eliminate 'disloyal' street parades, there were anxieties about the breadth of the proposed legislation. The Melbourne *Herald* viewed the Eight Hours Day march as a national, rather than sectional demonstration, so thought it should not be affected by restrictive legislation.[184] There was even a murmur of support for St Patrick's Day in the tabloid press. The *Sun* remarked that those 'who want to emphasise their loyalty by acts of suppression ... are not strengthening the Imperial tie, but weakening it'. The *Sun* stressed that liberty of expression should be encouraged in a democracy, providing that it stopped short of 'sedition or blasphemy'. This was clearly the *Sun*'s view of the St Patrick's Day procession, for the paper described it as 'a harmless parade'.[185]

The council eventually passed by-law no. 162 (amending by-law no. 142) on 13 October 1921. In the following February, the St Patrick's Day Celebration Committee applied for council authority to stage its parade. By a majority of 17 votes to 11, the council ruled that permission would not be granted.[186] However, on 20 February 1922, two weeks after the council refused to allow the St Patrick's Day parade, it gave permission for a forthcoming Eight Hours Day procession.[187] To Kennedy and his colleagues, only bigotry could explain the fact that trade unionists could celebrate Eight Hours Day with a procession, yet Irish men and women were told that their parade must not be held.[188]

Predictably, the council decision met with the approval of 'loyalist' groups.[189] The town clerk was inundated with letters of support, particularly from Protestant groups and branches of the Loyal Orange Lodge.[190] But Irish national associations and Catholic groups were even more prolific in forwarding protests against the council decision.[191] Importantly, many letters of discontent pledged support to the St Patrick's Day Celebration Committee, including a commitment to follow whatever response it considered appropriate.[192] In fact, it was already known publicly what that would be. Kennedy told the press that his committee had adopted the motto 'Business as usual on St Patrick's Day'. He declared that the council's 'ridiculous attitude' would only serve to 'ensure the success of the demonstration',[193] because Irish Australians would now march in greater numbers than ever before.[194] Various Irish societies and Catholic groups voiced support for this united stand.[195] There was no turning back now.

The council saw no reason to change its stand, warning the St Patrick's Day Celebration Committee that if the parade went ahead marchers would each be liable to a fine of up to £10.[196] There had been a suggestion in council that police stop a march by reading the Riot Act as it applied to the Unlawful Assemblies and Processions Act (1915).[197] This view was put after legal advice from the city solicitor.[198] As a consequence, the town clerk notified the St Patrick's Day Celebration Committee that an unauthorized procession would breach the Police Offences Act, as well as council by-laws.[199] But a subsequent opinion from the crown solicitor contradicted this view. It stated that even if Sinn Féin flags were flown during the procession, this would not be an offence in law. The unlawful assemblies legislation applied only to symbols or music that produced hostility between different *religious* groups. Sinn Féin was a political group without denominational affiliation.[200] Moreover, the fact that Irish national societies included both Catholics and Protestants suggested that the procession was not intended to be sectarian. What *had* caused offence to 'loyalists' during the 1918 St Patrick's Day march was support for Irish republicanism. 'Loyalists' were also disgusted by attempts to desecrate the British flag in the 1921 procession. The fact that most St Patrick's Day marchers were Catholic was not the main issue. It was the *political* allegiances and actions of some Irish Australians that had disturbed 'loyalists'.

The crown solicitor's ruling was a disappointment to Mayor Swanson and his supporters. They had failed in a bid to end the St Patrick's Day parade by banning all street marches. The adoption of by-law no. 162 meant that the council was obliged to consider all applications for processions, which had resulted in some being allowed while others were refused. It therefore exposed the council to allegations that it discriminated against some groups while favouring others. Ironically, it was this political turmoil that Swanson had wanted to avoid. It was much simpler, as he saw it, to simply rule by decree. An announcement that the St Patrick's Day procession would proceed in defiance of a council ruling was all the more annoying to the mayor, because police had now received legal advice that the Unlawful Assemblies and Processions Act (1915) did not apply in this case. The crown solicitor also advised the chief commissioner of police that a breach of by-law no. 162 did not constitute an offence under the Police Offences Act. Therefore, police could not legally stop the procession, read the Riot Act, *or* arrest marchers. The only action they could take under by-law no. 162 was to record the names of persons marching 'without the consent of the local authority', and to advise them that they were liable to a council fine for their actions.[201]

Despite a realization by the council of its weakened control over street marches, it continued to talk tough with intending marchers. There was a determination that the by-law should be rigorously applied in this case, so the town clerk and city solicitor conferred on the subject of bringing fines against processionists. The solicitor emphasized that in order to substantiate the council case it would have to show 'proof of combination' among the marchers. People were entitled to walk the streets, but it was the organization of a *collective* gathering that required council permission. He therefore recommended that the names of parade marshals and anyone else 'giving orders' should be taken. This would demonstrate that the procession was a co-ordinated assembly.[202] There was also co-operation among civic authorities. After discussions with the town clerk, the acting chief commissioner of police agreed that his officers would take down 'the names and addresses of twenty to twenty-five of the ring-leaders' who led the St Patrick's Day parade.[203] To assist them in this task, the superintendent of police invited a council representative to his office on the morning of the procession. This would guide police to record names of individuals that the council *particularly* wanted to prosecute under by-law no. 162.[204] It was hoped that this would make a public example of them.

But the council was not united in this view. Councillors Dobson, Collins and Stack declared that they would march in the St Patrick's Day procession in protest against the council ruling, and in support of the rights of Irish Australians.[205] Alderman Deveney announced that he would join them carrying an Irish flag, promising that no man would prise it from his grasp.[206] A meeting of sympathetic returned servicemen and women also declared that they would march in unison.[207] This raised the ire of fellow war veterans, one of whom argued that the meeting represented 'only a small section' of the RSSILA, with these soldiers and sailors being 'in no way connected with the official body'.[208] There were also conflicts over the participation of Commonwealth public servants and members of the armed forces in an unauthorized procession. By convention, personnel who desired a half-day's leave to take part in the St Patrick's Day parade were allowed time off.[209] But the Prime Minister's Department advised that leave would not be granted in Melbourne this year because of the council's ban. However, personnel elsewhere were still entitled to the customary St Patrick's furlough.[210]

Police in Melbourne were also told that any leave for 18 March was cancelled, for extra officers were required to monitor the St Patrick's Day procession.[211] But Superintendent Evans of the Melbourne Police District played down any police expectations of conflict or disorder associated with the parade. He stated, misleadingly, that no special arrangements had been made by police in relation to this event.[212] For obvious reasons Evans did not reveal police plans to take the names of the procession's ringleaders, or to position six constables to monitor the activities of marchers as they neared the town hall.[213]

The St Patrick's Day Celebration Committee counselled restraint from all involved. The *Advocate*, too, declared: 'we urge the necessity of non-participation in any conduct that may even remotely be regarded as unruly or riotous'.[214] Melbourne's other leading Catholic newspaper, the *Tribune*, stated: 'Nothing would give greater pleasure to our enemies than that some form of riot would eventuate as a result of the procession.'[215] Importantly, 'loyalists' also called for calm. The Reverend T.E. Ruth made an 'appeal to all patriots to assist the police on Saturday by keeping away from the streets used for an illegal procession ... Riots must be avoided at all costs.'[216] Similarly, Mr Snowball MLA, argued that it was 'unthinkable that any Protestant worthy of the name would interfere with the procession'.[217] Both leaders trusted that the actions of police and the courts would provide a sufficient deterrent to any repetition of the unauthorized parade.[218]

But the St Patrick's Day Celebration Committee had received legal advice to support its claim that the council's ruling was not valid in law.[219] The committee assured marchers that 'nothing more fear-some is likely to happen than the issue of some summonses by the City Council some days after the event'.[220] Mannix confirmed that if the council launched a prosecution, it would be tested in the courts 'to the last ditch'.[221] He described the attempt to prohibit the procession as a great advertisement for Irish Catholics. This was because, as he put it, the 'eyes of all Australia' would now be upon Melbourne on 18 March.[222]

'SEE THAT YOU MARCH IN THE PROCESSION'.[223] The headline said it in a nutshell. Every supporter of St Patrick's Day worth their salt was expected to be there, whether marching behind a banner or cheering among the crowd. The *Advocate* was exultant. The paper reported that 'tens of thousands of people lined the streets or occupied vantage points on balconies and verandahs'.[224] They witnessed the most imposing St Patrick's Day march ever held in Melbourne. It was over seven miles in length, taking more than an hour and twenty-five minutes to pass the intersection of Bourke and Elizabeth streets.[225] A former officer of the AIF led the parade on horseback, carrying the Australian flag.[226] Mannix followed next in an open motor car, flanked by a bodyguard of returned soldiers.[227] Then came an army of marching Catholic schoolchildren, Irish national groups, and friendly societies, as well as clergy from various Catholic parishes.[228]

Two features of the parade deserve comment. First, Catholic newspapers claimed that 10,000 returned soldiers and sailors marched in the parade.[229] As instructed by organizers, they wore civilian attire, but the men were recognizable as war veterans by their service badges and medals.[230] The *Argus* numbered the marching returned soldiers and sailors as only 2,000.[231] Such a discrepancy of estimates can be put down to competing political perspectives. Second, a large body of men marched behind a bannerette reading, 'Other Creeds and Nationalities Record Their Protest'.[232] The *Catholic Press* described it as 'a battalion, thousands strong, of non-Catholic sympathisers'.[233] But the *Argus* reckoned that only 'about 120 persons' marched behind the bannerette.[234] It was evident that some support for the parade had been made by both returned veteran soldiers and non-Catholic sympathizers. What remained in dispute was the extent of this backing. Importantly, both the president of the Eight Hours Anniversary Committee, and the secretary of the Australian Labor Party in Victoria, marched in the St Patrick's Day parade. Council had already approved their trade union procession, but they were committed to a general defence of street marches. As promised, the four 'rebel' city councillors also took part, and two state parliamentarians, Messrs Prendegast and McNamara joined them.[235] So while the *Argus* reported that procession organizers expressed 'delight ... at having so flagrantly flouted the law',[236] the fact that they were supported by returned sailors and soldiers, as well as civic and political leaders, made it less of a rebellious act than otherwise might have appeared.

But we need to be cautious about overstating strategies to defuse hostility towards the procession. This is because it was a march of defiance *against* authority, a showdown between opposed forces that promised to be settled in the courts. Indeed, Sinn Féin colours and flags were sprinkled liberally among marchers and spectators.[237] The 1920 and 1921 parades had been conducted without overt references to Irish republicanism, but that was because the city council had demanded this as a condition of both processions. Ironically, by refusing to allow the usual march (with restrictive conditions applied), the council had in fact lost influence over the manner in which St Patrick's Day was now celebrated. Yet the council still hoped that prosecutions under by-law no. 162 would swing the power struggle back in its favour. As planned, police took down the names of people they considered to have led the procession. There were twenty-six in all, including Mannix, Kennedy, the rebel councillors and Prendegast.[238] Alderman Deveney and his colleagues were in an unusual situation, facing a possibility of charges against a council by-law they had opposed within council. But aside from the fact that the procession was unauthorized, there was nothing else to concern police on the day. The acting chief commissioner of police advised that there had been no disturbances, including any disorderly conduct in the vicinity of the town hall.[239] This was supported by the observations of by-law officers stationed at various points along the procession route. They reported that the crowd was 'very orderly' and the march 'well conducted'.[240] The *Advocate* was delighted with the behaviour of the marchers and their supporters, expressing relief that 'no disorder or incident' had marred the procession.[241] But, according to the *Argus*, credit for this resided with 'the law-abiding people of Melbourne' who, despite their opposition to the law being flouted, showed 'grim tolerance' and 'admirable restraint' in avoiding conflict with the marchers.[242] In a more alarmist tone, the Reverend Henry Worrall thundered: 'but for the restraint of the British people there would have been a bursting up of homes and drenching of the city streets with blood'.[243] On this score it seemed just as well that the courts would rule over the fate of the procession leaders.

Before any such prosecutions could be launched, a majority in council had to approve such actions. This resulted in the ludicrous situation of the four 'rebel' councillors actually voting on whether they should be charged. Mayor Swanson and his supporters had the numbers, so summonses were served upon three men – Kennedy, Father Barry and Councillor Stack.[244] They were representatives of the Irish community, the Catholic Church, and the council respectively. The town clerk advised that further summonses would be served, including one on Archbishop Mannix. But these three would serve as a beginning or, as the defendants trusted, the end. For Barry was very confident that the by-law would not stand up in court.[245] He was right. After protracted legal debate the Victorian Full Court concluded that the by-law was beyond the power of the council, and 'should be quashed on the grounds that it was not a regulation but a prohibition of processions'.[246] So ended the most dramatic series of St Patrick's Day parades in Australian history, and established, in legal terms at least, the tradition of parading in Melbourne. The whole period from 1914 had demonstrated how the competing demands of Irish freedom and empire allegiance clashed in Australia. These were played out against a backdrop of anti-Irishness, yet the whole battle was fought out specifically around the rights of Irish Australians, and others, to parade the streets of Melbourne on St Patrick's Day.

CHAPTER 5

PROCLAIMING IRELAND

Independence and empire

— ℮ℽ℄ —

Irishmen from all over the city will practice equally old and revered arts in honor of St Patrick. No son of Erin is expected to let the Day pass without wetting the whistle with a bit o' poteen, and more than one Belanger of Gagnon will join him. A sprig of shamrock and a green tie, no matter what the wearer's nationality, is a good precaution on St Patrick's Day.[1]

SHAPING THE IRISH FREE STATE

The newly formed Cumann na nGaedheal government favoured the de-Anglicization of Irish culture. English, as the dominant language in Ireland, could hardly be abandoned, but school curricula now included compulsory lessons in Irish, and a renewed emphasis on the value of traditional Irish sports, such as Gaelic football and hurling. History lessons focused on the rise to power of the modern Irish state, the significance of its revolutionary leaders, and the unfinished business of a united Ireland.[2] How would St Patrick's Day figure in this rarified political and cultural milieu? Was there now an opportunity to elevate 17 March into a day of great patriotic fervour? Would St Patrick's Day in a Catholic-dominated state be, more than ever, a partisan religious anniversary? How, in other words, was St Patrick's Day to feature in the 'invented traditions' of the newly proclaimed Irish state, this reluctant dominion of Britain?

Despite its revolutionary foundations, the government of the Irish Free State retained some of the civic customs that had emerged during the era of direct British rule in Ireland. Among them was the decision to retain 17 March as a public holiday. Subsequently, though, the Irish Government gave little thought to promoting St Patrick's Day. It remained an anniversary of religious and cultural significance, but there was no sign of 17 March being adapted or reinvented by the Cumann na nGaedheal government to promote the cause of Irish nationalism. There was merely discussion of ceremonial protocol and what role the state had, if at all, in this civic ritual. In 1926, the Minister of Telegraphs, J.J. Walsh, argued in a letter to the President, W.T. Cosgrave, that 'some Governmental or state function ought to materialize on Patrick's night'.[3] It is clear from the ensuing correspondence that Cosgrave was far from convinced that such an undertaking was government business; indeed, his first course of action was to turn the matter over to the wives of government ministers. Writing to them, he sought advice on whether a dance would be the best form of celebration, with 'costumes and dress of Irish material and workmanship to be worn'. If that was to be the case, Cosgrave reminded the ministers' wives that 'there must be a special effort made to induce people to buy and wear Irish material and that on us lies a duty to show that example'.[4] Despite any misgivings that Cosgrave may have had about the worthiness of celebrating St Patrick's Day, it afforded an opportunity to promote the government's policy of buying and promoting Irish-made goods. In the event, any plans for 1926 were abandoned owing to a lack of liaison with the necessary state services, together with an absence of money in state coffers to fund such an event. The idea of a government-organized dance was revisited in 1927, though once more abandoned. Indeed, the only official use of state resources to celebrate St Patrick's Day, outside of the annual morning church service and military parade in Dublin, was the Irish army band performing gratis on the state radio broadcaster 2RN during the evening of 17 March.[5]

The major official observance of 17 March was attendance at an Irish language mass in the Pro-Cathedral by all government ministers. This service reflected strong links between both the Irish state and the Catholic Church. The arrival of the President at the Pro-Cathedral was also part of a ceremonial military procession through the streets of Dublin. By marching through the capital on St Patrick's Day, the newly formed army of the Irish Free State was engaged in a trooping of the colours parade ceremony which, while reminiscent of Dublin Castle ceremonial under British rule on St Patrick's Day, was very different in its emphasis on public display and Irish national self-determination.[6] The route taken by the 1920s' military parade was from Collins Barracks, where Irish soldiers took part in mass and received the shamrock; then over Grattan Bridge, along North Quays, into Dame Street and on to College Green, where the biggest crowd gathered. The procession concluded on O'Connell Street.[7] This was a lengthy march before a receptive audience – a stark contrast to British ceremonial within the walls of Dublin Castle on St Patrick's Day prior to 1915.

Since the Irish state used St Patrick's Day as an opportunity to parade its army, the march was a possible target for republican dissidents to voice their disapproval of the Anglo-Irish Treaty and partition. The civil war had made enemies of former comrades, so the Irish military was well aware of the potential for violence. Consequently, military parades, including those on St Patrick's Day, were always guarded by police, and republican groups opposed to the Irish government were monitored closely. There was, nonetheless, only one significant protest during the annual military parades on St Patrick's Day. In 1935, former members of the IRA, which supported a military strategy to end partition and enforce a united Ireland, handed out leaflets denouncing both the Irish and British governments. By contrast to the tricolour flown so vividly on St Patrick's Day, these dissidents carried a black flag to mourn what they saw as the 'death' of the republican ideal in Ireland. A scuffle ensued as officers from the Garda Síochána arrested those involved. But it was not only republican sensibilities that were thwarted on St Patrick's Day, 1935. The Provost of Trinity College, Dublin, was advised by the Garda Síochána that in the interests of 'public order' the Union flag flying above the college ought to removed.[8] According to the government of the Irish Free State, neither Republicans nor Unionists had a legitimate place on St Patrick's Day.

The most significant policy of the Irish Government with respect to St Patrick's Day did much to reduce its popularity. Incredible as it might seem today, a decision was made to close all public houses and other licensed premises on 17 March. The first committee to debate the issue of a ban on drinking on St Patrick's Day came together in March 1922, thus very early on in the life of the inaugural Irish Government.[9] The temperance movement, which had a long history in Ireland, now had a significant presence among parliamentarians;[10] and, with the support of teetotallers in both Catholic and Protestant churches, important community backing. No surprise, therefore, that the Irish press commented favourably on this government initiative. In 1927 the *Irish Times*, in congratulatory spirit, was delighted to report that, 'it was a dry St Patrick's Day, since all the public houses remained closed, and not a single case of drunkenness was seen in the streets during the Day'.[11] In a similar vein, the *Irish Independent* commented that while 'in former days excessive indulgence in intoxicating liquors was a regrettable feature of St Patrick's Day, this disedifying habit has completely disappeared'.[12] The only place to get a drink on St Patrick's Day in Ireland was at the Royal Dublin Society Dog Show, which had a special alcohol licence, and was therefore always sure to attract a large crowd.[13]

The prohibition of drink sales on St Patrick's Day was, in part, a reflection of the close relationship between the Catholic Church and the Irish state. Bishops closely monitored the moral fibre of their flock, especially on occasions like the anniversary of the national apostle, when in a spirit of celebration they might be tempted to excess. A sermon by the Catholic Bishop of Cork, in 1930, went as far as deploring 'all night dances fixed on or in close proximity to the feast of St Patrick'.[14] This stance was, perhaps surprisingly, consistent with puritanical ideas about dance and festivity within the Evangelical Protestant tradition. Tellingly, though, the proscription of alcohol was avoided, where possible, by the many Irish – Catholics and Protestants – who enjoyed a drink. As one punter recalled of the 1950s: 'One of the Irishman's privileges – and favorite sport – on Saint Patrick's Day was flouting the law to get a drink. He stole into the small snack bar and drowned the shamrock with the extra pleasure that always accompanies a blow for freedom.'[15]

This closure of pubs prompted comment in newspapers overseas, where the Irish diaspora was renowned for drinking liberally on 17 March. There were no specific laws in North America or Australia to ban alcohol sales on St Patrick's Day, although prohibition was introduced in the United States in 1920, where it continued in most states until the 1930s. In 1923, however, New York was the first state to repeal prohibition laws; it also comprised a significant Irish-American electorate who were influential in this decision and most appreciative on 17 March. In 1925, a *New York Times* headline announced that the 'Free State is Dry on St Patrick's Day', then mirthfully told the story of how ' "Shamrock drowning", banned in the Free State, was indulged in by those along the border who desired, the dwellers there getting their liquor by a short walk into the Six Counties.'[16] Over the next three decades foreign papers continued to puzzle over the 'dour' Irish who, unlike those among the diaspora, seemed to have little fun on the national anniversary. In 1954 an Associated Press reporter mused that Irishmen who had spent St Patrick's Day in the United States would be 'almost homesick for a March 17 among the Irish Americans'.[17] There was, however, some local opposition to a 'dry' St Patrick's Day. In 1945, the Chairman of the Mallow Urban District Council wrote to the Taoiseach requesting that licensed premises be allowed to open on 17 March. He argued that St Patrick's Day should 'be celebrated in a free manner without any restrictions on the wishes of the people'.[18] However, it was not until 1961 that the government repealed the prohibition on alcohol. As the *Quebec Chronicle-Telegraph* reported, curiously: 'For the first time since the proclamation of the Irish republic, bars were open – legally that is – on the feast Day of Ireland's patron saint.'[19]

From the early 1920s to the late 1950s, the Irish Government had effectively strait-jacketed local observance of St Patrick's Day into a static, even staid, anniversary. Although a public holiday, St Patrick's Day was based principally on church services, its official centrepiece was a formal military procession, and, to the annoyance of many, a drink could not be taken easily as pubs were required to be closed on 17 March. In the 1950s, in particular, the constraints surrounding St Patrick's Day came in for much criticism. Ireland continued to be a highly religious nation; as such morning church services on St Patrick's Day were very welcome, but the self-denying frugality of the remainder of the day was questioned. When compared to North American and Australian celebrations on 17 March, as well as Patrician festivities in parts of Britain, the Irish seemed lacklustre on St Patrick's Day, unable to enjoy themselves, and not relishing this annual opportunity to celebrate their Irishness. The *Connaught Telegraph* of March 1952 summed up the situation:

St Patrick's Day passed off quietly and there was nothing to indicate that we were celebrating our national festival, the feast day of our National Apostle, apart, perhaps, from the services in our churches . . .

there were no band recitals, no parades in national costume ... as a contrast, in all the cities in America, of England and of every country in the world in which Irish exiles have settled in appreciable numbers, celebrations on a grand and more ambitious scale than ever before have been held ... [in Ireland] St Patrick's Day was very much like any other day, only duller.[20]

For people without a drink on St Patrick's Day, radio broadcasts were a tonic to lift flagging spirits. Ireland's state-funded radio station, 2RN, provided dedicated St Patrick's Day programming from the year of its first broadcast, 1926. By the 1930s, St Patrick's Day coverage dominated radio programmes on 17 March each year. In 1932, for example, 2RN opened at 11.45 a.m. with the sound of a carillon relayed from St Patrick's Cathedral, Armagh. This was followed by the celebration of Pontifical High Mass by His Eminence Cardinal McRory. At 2 p.m., attention switched to Dublin's Croke Park, from which the Interprovincial Hurling Championship was broadcast live. The early evening programme was dominated by religious music in honour of the life of St Patrick, until at 8 p.m. President de Valera addressed the Irish diaspora in the United States. The remainder of the day's broadcasting, until the close at midnight, was taken up by traditional Irish music, most of which was broadcast live from Feis Tighe at the Mansion House.[21] The new technology of Irish state radio allowed the national festival to be enjoyed by all those who wished to take part, and thus not solely those living in the main towns where Patrician events took place.

St Patrick's Day celebrations in Ireland were not confined solely to Dublin. In Cork there was an annual solemn High Mass at the city cathedral; in Waterford a procession of priests, students, school children, Catholic boy scouts and local bands; in Athlone a St Patrick's Day parade organized by the Gaelic League; and, in the west, Sligo hosted a military parade, while 1,000 military volunteers in Galway took part in a parade followed by an open-air mass.[22]

The brewing company Guinness recognized eight days in the calendar year as holidays, including St Patrick's Day.[23] All employees received a full day's wage while enjoying St Patrick's Day, except coopers on piece work who were paid the equivalent of an ordinary day's wages. Those who had to work within the Guinness factory on St Patrick's Day, such as the brewery policemen, received the equivalent of night-shift pay at treble rates, but without time off in lieu.[24] The day off for Guinness employees is all the more ironic given that, legally, all licensed premises were closed on 17 March!

In 1924, following the ending of the civil war in Ireland, the New York St Patrick's Day parade began to recover from the divisions of 1923. Numbers slowly picked up as New York's Irish again used St Patrick's Day to celebrate their position in American society. The 1920s were a boom decade for the US economy; in a favourable material climate, St Patrick's

Day was widely embraced by Americans from a variety of backgrounds, and thus not solely those with an Irish background. St Patrick's Day continued to have a far greater significance in America than it possessed in Ireland. In the post-war years and beyond, the parades and other celebrations were energized by the shared experiences of Irish immigrants and their descendants, and the fascination and excitement that the day's events provided the non-Irish. Not only did the numbers taking part in St Patrick's Day parades grow, especially in New York, but the variety and abundance of commercial opportunities also became an important feature of the day. In 1926, the number of souvenir sellers associated with the New York parade had grown to such an extent that the *New York Times* was forced to complain:

> there have never, it was said, been so many emblem and badge merchants on the avenue at one time before. For blocks, the sidewalks were a moving garden of shamrocks and pseudo shamrocks on the trays of hundreds of peddlars ... unscrupulous vendors were offering everything in season but oranges.[25]

Although America was badly hit by the aftershock of the Wall Street Crash, the subsequent Depression did not visibly affect support for St Patrick's Day. In 1935, the Irish tricolour officially flew over public buildings in New York in honour of Alderman Byrne from Dublin. Byrne, who was the serving Lord Mayor of Dublin at the time, was invited to New York to review the St Patrick's Day parade, and the flags were flown to honour Dublin's first citizen.[26] It also served to legitimize the Irish Free State in the eyes of many Irish Americans, and to cement links between the diaspora and its homeland. By 1936 the number of marchers taking part in the New York parade had risen to 40,000.[27]

CANADIAN EXPERIENCES IN THE INTER-WAR YEARS

The Quebec City St Patrick's Day parade, which was abandoned in 1916 owing to 'wartime pressures', was finally revived in 1921. The battle in Europe had, of course, already been over for two years; the absence of a parade during that time remains unexplained. Ironically, the Quebec City St Patrick's Day procession of 1921 was revived in the midst of another military conflict, the Irish War of Independence. The timing of the parade resumption was curious in another sense; this was the first St Patrick's Day after the Partition of Ireland, which had become law in December 1920.[28] There seemed little about the situation in the homeland to celebrate: neither Home Rule nor a sovereign republic had emerged in the wake of the fighting. So what was the impetus for the procession of 1921, which the *Quebec Chronicle* described in glowing terms as 'the most successful held for nearly a score of years'?[29] A lack of evidence means it is impossible to say. But the style of the cavalcade suggests that locals were determined to regain a sense of enjoyment on St Patrick's Day. The *Quebec Telegraph* reported fine weather and pageantry: 'the colour green was very much in evidence; even the marshals' batons were green, and youngsters waved green balloons in front of horses'.[30] This air of pleasure was, however, complicated by St Patrick's Day newspaper reports of ongoing fighting in Ireland; most editorials bemoaned the need for conflict, hoping that 'someday soon the Irish there would enjoy the same freedoms as did their countrymen in Canada'.[31] The parade itself involved some sympathy for this view; among the marchers were representatives of three branches of the Self Determination for Ireland League. Local republican organizations were, like de Valera, nonetheless disappointed with the Treaty signed nine months later. Home Rule advocates, too, had mixed feelings; their country was divided into two separate homelands, and civil war now wreaked havoc. Subsequent St Patrick's Day parades reflected diverse loyalties. In the 1926 march, 'the green, white, and orange flag of the Irish Free State predominated', but there was also a sleigh featuring the British, Irish, French and American flags.[32] Canada remained a Dominion of Britain: this was a fact that Quebec City's Irish community could not avoid, irrespective of whether they coveted or loathed that status. Inexplicably, the 1927 St Patrick's Day parade did not take place; it was considered a temporary lapse. But the following year the procession was 'dispensed with' owing to 'poor climatic' conditions during March. This explanation did not seem convincing in that parades had been held annually since 1837. Yet the decision stood. A year later the *Quebec Chronicle-Telegraph* expressed 'regret that the annual parade is apparently a thing of the past'.[33] This longstanding St Patrick's Day ritual thus faded into obscurity.

Not so in Montreal. The AOH assumed control of the parade in 1920, and was anxious to stamp its authority on the format of local festivities. In keeping with the Order's rules, the St Patrick's Day march had to be held on 17 March rather than, as was local custom, the Sunday nearest to that date. The AOH expected compliance from its members: Article 29 of its constitution deemed that this was 'a national holiday of this Order, to be celebrated by a public procession of its members, and *any member failing to parade shall be fined*'.[34] A further departure from tradition under AOH tenure of the celebrations was that St Patrick's Day mass was held at one of the smaller Catholic churches in Montreal – either St Mary's, St Gabriel's, or St Thomas Aquinas'. Previously, St Patrick's Church had convened mass to coincide with the parade; for Irish Catholics this was, after all, the largest and most historic house of worship in the city. Yet it was now out of favour as far as the AOH was concerned. It seems that the Order, which had long been unhappy with the local Catholic hierarchy's stance against militant Irish republicanism, removed the observance of mass at St Patrick's, the veritable home of the Irish-Catholic 'establishment', as a rebuke to its clerical authority. According to Regan, the priests used by the AOH to conduct its parade mass tended to be Redemptorists, often from Europe rather than Ireland.[35]

There was, indeed, a heightened emphasis on separatist politics in the Montreal parades of 1921 and 1922. The tricolour flew freely, political banners were printed in Irish Gaelic, and the march itself was described by the *Gazette* 'as one of the largest ... seen in Montreal'.[36] The parades of 1923–8 were generally well supported, though the number of participants tended to be higher when 17 March fell on a weekend rather than on regular working days. Inexplicably, and after only nine years at the helm, the AOH relinquished its organizational control of the St Patrick's Day parade and mass. A broader representative group, the United Irish Societies of Montreal (UISM), took on this responsibility in 1929, and continues to manage the St Patrick's Day festivities today. Regan's study of management of the parade found no hint in newspaper reports about the cause of this transfer of responsibility, while the records of the new organizational body, the United Irish Societies of Montreal, appear to have been lost.[37]

The 1929 parade was, nonetheless, a great success. Indeed, the event was now more 'representative' of various sections of the Irish community. Some 15,000 people marched: this included twenty-seven units from local churches and Irish societies, as well as seventeen decorated floats. Just as significantly, the AOH remained an important part of the proceedings. As was the custom, the AOH and the Hibernian Knights led the march, and the AOH even entered two floats in the procession. The Order was, nonetheless, forced to compromise: St Patrick's church again held mass to coincide with the event, and the UISM staged the parade on the Sunday nearest to 17 March.[38] At the rear of the 1929 cavalcade were local dignitaries, notably the Mayor of Montreal; and, in keeping with tradition, members of the St Patrick's Society – the original custodians of Patrician observance in Montreal – escorted them from Dominion Square to the steps of St Patrick's Basilica. Another notable participant was the Irish Protestant Benevolent Society: it was the first time for some thirty years that this group had taken part. The change signalled a simmering of sectarian tensions within Montreal's Irish community, partly as a consequence of greater political stability in Ireland itself, but also because of a return to religious pluralism in Montreal itself. Just ten years earlier it would have been almost unthinkable for Catholics and Protestants to march on the same St Patrick's Day programme; it had been difficult enough to convince Home Rulers to parade alongside militant Republicans.

During the 1930s, St Patrick's Day festivities in Montreal became even more inclusive. Patrician dinners, for example, involved not only Irishmen (and sometimes their wives) but also members of other patriotic associations. The *Gazette* insisted that 17 March was therefore no longer sectional, but instead a celebration of ethnic origins shared by other immigrant groups. The paper wrote that:

gatherings as will be held tonight in Montreal ... in honor of St
Patrick, gatherings in which the Englishman, the Scotsman, the
Welshman and the French-Canadian are proud to associate themselves,
have materially helped, and through this fraternal association will
always materially help, to dim to extinction the dividing prejudices of
nationality and cement the Canadian people in closer fraternity.[39]

There was, indeed, no denying that the St Patrick's Day parade, though still
restricted to Irish religious groups and societies, was now received as a high
point of Montreal's social calendar. Held on the Sunday nearest 17 March,
the procession wound its way through the city streets on a day primed for
public viewing. Inclement weather often threatened, but when the sun
shone huge crowds turned out to witness the spectacle of top hats, marching
bands, green paraphernalia and an escort of police motor cycles. According
to the *Gazette*, an estimated 100,000 people lined the parade route in 1937;
the march past a given point took one hour and fifteen minutes in 1938; and
'more than 20,000 sons and grandsons of Erin' paraded in 1939.[40] This
made Montreal's celebration easily the largest in Canada, and certainly one
of the most imposing in North America. Such a 'coming of age' for the local
Irish community was recognized by City Hall. Mayor Adhemar Raynault, a
French-Canadian, urged 'pride in Montreal' on St Patrick's Day, 1938, and
used the opportunity to announce that 'on the new coat of arms of the city
will appear the fleur de lys, the shamrock, the rose, and the thistle, the
national emblems of the four great races which have contributed to the
development of Montreal'.[41] Thus there was much to celebrate on St
Patrick's Day; and, in keeping with this festive spirit, the Archbishop of
Montreal gave special dispensation for Catholics observing the Lenten fast.
This was just as well because, as the *Gazette* observed, there were 'more
shamrocks shipped from Dublin, Belfast and Cork to Canada ... this year
... than ever before'. Admittedly, most would end up on lapels or in
baskets, but by the end of the day there promised to be plenty of 'drowning
the shamrock'. This was a custom, the *Gazette* noted incredulously, that was
banned on St Patrick's Day in the Irish Free State.[42] In that sense it was
better to remember Ireland from afar than to be 'dry' in the homeland on the
national anniversary.

ST PATRICK'S DAY IN AUSTRALIA: THE INTER-WAR YEARS

Melbourne's St Patrick's Day march of 1923 was much anticipated: as we
saw in Chapter 4, Catholic clergy had organized the parade of 1922 in defiance of a Melbourne City Council ban, but since then the Victorian High
Court had vindicated the church's position. Consequently, in the lead up to
the procession of 1923, Archbishop Daniel Mannix appealed to the city's

Irish-Catholic community: 'We have been at great pains to vindicate our right to hold the procession. Now that our right can no longer be challenged, we should see that our demonstration lacks nothing in either number or enthusiasm.'[43] According to press reports, Mannix had every reason, subsequently, to be pleased with the festivities. The Catholic newspaper, the *Advocate*, described the procession of 1923 as a 'complete success', with its 'former enthusiasm undiminished'.[44] Even Melbourne's conservative daily newspaper, the *Argus*, which had been critical of local St Patrick's Day parades over previous years, reported that the march was completed 'without incident' and 'the proceedings passed off smoothly'. The *Argus* considered that 'attendance was about the same as in previous years', with spectators witnessing a parade 'which took nearly an hour to pass a given point'.[45] It was smaller than the triumphal marches of 1920 and 1922, which took 72 minutes and 85 minutes respectively to complete the parade route,[46] yet it was still an imposing display. From hereon the procession was staged annually without censorship or prohibition; hence there was no longer an axe to grind with the City Council, whose repressive stance had actually inspired many Irish Australians to march. The heady years of 1918–22 had no sequel and, as might be expected, the level of public interest in the festivities lessened somewhat.

That said, the processions were still significant mass displays. According to the *Argus*, in 1925 the St Patrick's Day march took 40 minutes to pass a given point; in 1926 35 minutes; in 1927 45 minutes; and in 1928 45 minutes.[47] The 1930s Depression had a severe social and economic impact in Australia, yet there was enough organizational energy and public support to keep the St Patrick's Day march alive and kicking. The *Argus* reported that the procession of 1930 took 50 minutes to pass a given point; 42 minutes in 1931; 'over an hour' in 1936; and 65 minutes in 1937.[48] Spectator support was solid, though unspectacular from the mid-1920s through to the late 1930s. Crowd estimates were rarely offered, but the annual assembly was large enough to warrant the placing of barricades at strategic points along the route from Bourke Street to Spring Street.[49] In 1930 the *Argus* commented that the crowd viewing the procession 'was not as dense as in former years', but in 1932 the paper offered an upbeat estimate of 'more than 50,000 people' lining the procession route.[50] In subsequent years, the parade started to lose its lure as a spectacle. Although the *Argus* reported that the procession of 1939 was 'the largest for many years', involving more than 12,000 marchers, there were only '15,000 onlookers'.[51] On the eve of the Second World War, then, the sum total of paraders nearly matched the estimated number of those in attendance!

As we saw in Chapter 4, the politics of Ireland featured in the symbols and rhetoric of Melbourne's St Patrick's Day parades of 1918–22. With the genesis of the Irish Free State, would the politics of the homeland still be a key processional theme? In March 1923 the Irish civil war continued, so the political situation in Ireland found expression on St Patrick's Day. It was, as might be expected, the centrepiece of Mannix's keynote speech:

> if they believed certain pessimists they might be inclined to think that Ireland was a corpse on the dissecting table. However, as he watched the procession with great pride that day he could not convince himself that the boys and young men and the grey-haired men were marching in Ireland's funeral. Ireland's cause was just, and her cause would triumph (Applause).[52]

Mannix used his St Patrick's Day address to introduce two guests from Ireland, delegates of Eamon de Valera. The Reverend F.M. O'Flanagan and Mr J.J. Kelly announced they would be hosting a series of meetings 'open to the friends and enemies of Ireland' to 'try to convince the Australian people that the Irish Republic was right, now as it was in 1916', and that in this quest 'they did not fear the widest publicity'.[53] However, as O'Farrell has argued strenuously, Mannix was now alone within the Australian Catholic hierarchy as 'a committed republican of de Valera's stamp'. This was generally true also, writes O'Farrell, of the diaspora: 'As Irishman killed Irishman in Ireland, they also killed what remained of Australian Irish enthusiasm for Ireland's cause – whatever that was.'[54]

The symbolism of Melbourne's St Patrick's Day parade of 1923 suggested otherwise in that there was no Union Jack, while the Australian ensign and 'Sinn Féin colours' were carried in procession. Furthermore, various Irish national societies erupted into patriotic song as they marched; the *Argus* reported that 'the strain in most instances being "God Save Ireland"'.[55] Given the flag conundrum over recent years, the absence of a British ensign was par for the course; and, in the context of Mannix's high profile leadership of Melbourne's Irish-Catholic community, so too was the presence of vocal support for republicanism. But these sentiments were not matched, to the same degree, elsewhere in Australia on St Patrick's Day. There was, for instance, a general backlash against de Valera's delegates, O'Flanagan and Kelly. O'Farrell remarks that the duo 'met a discouraging reception from influential Irishmen and open hostility from most of the clergy'. Indeed, the pair's tour of Australia ended abruptly when they were arrested just five weeks after St Patrick's Day and charged with 'engaging in seditious behaviour'.[56] The envoys were deported in June 1923, a decision that elicited little opposition from prominent Irish Australians. Many of these leaders were, as O'Farrell has shown clearly, very depressed about the civil war in Ireland, and not persuaded by the political absolutism and armed militancy of the republican cause.[57]

However, the autocratic leadership style of Mannix, together with his zealous commitment to end partition, meant that Irish-Catholic support for the nationalist cause was unlikely to fade away in Melbourne. Here, as usual,

St Patrick's Day provides us with a window into diaspora politics. Mannix led the St Patrick's Day procession, but his authority was now being challenged by liberal Irish Catholics in subtle ways. In 1929, for example, Melbourne's Irish Republican Association complained to Mannix that Catholic Boy Scouts – members of an imperial organization – had been included in the annual procession for the first time.[58] Yet the boys marched and were given 'a hearty cheer'.[59] Five years later, the IRA objected to the banner of the St Patrick's Society, which included a Union Jack alongside its representation of the Australian flag (which itself already contained the Union Flag on the top left-hand corner).[60] During the annual parade, Mannix always paused to 'take the salute' of the crowd in front of Parliament House; in reciprocation, he gave the episcopal blessing to those who pressed forward.[61] He gave the appearance of a leader in total control, but his power was not absolute.

A feature of the annual procession was the thousands of marching schoolchildren representing Melbourne's Catholic schools. The parade was traditionally held on the Saturday closest to 17 March, but the students need not have felt put out by their involvement – Catholic schools in Victoria were given a holiday in the week leading up to the saint's anniversary.[62] Even here, though, we see the politics of performance on St Patrick's Day. The inter-war years were a difficult time for church-administered education: state aid to Victoria's denomination schools began in the mid-1830s, but was withdrawn in 1870. Irish Catholics, who were becoming influential in the Australian Labor Party, hoped to regain state funding for denominational education.[63] Catholic schools were cautious, therefore, of appearing too out of step, ideologically, with the Anglo-Protestant majority which lionized Australia's status as a Dominion within the British Empire. The vast majority of Catholic teachers and students were as parochially 'Australian' as their Protestant counterparts, so their country's historic link with Britain did not seem unnatural. Indeed, many schools observed both Empire Day and St Patrick's Day, while Australia's national anthem, sung universally, was 'God Save the Queen'.[64] In this context, the absence of a Union flag among marching schoolchildren on St Patrick's Day in 1923 was noticeable. However, the British ensign reappeared in 1924. The *Argus* noted, approvingly, that 'the selection of a banner remained with the individual. In one school the Irish flag and the Union Jack were about equally favoured. In another nothing was seen but the Australian flag.'[65] The following year there was an eclectic distribution of these symbols among Catholic school groups.[66] The British ensign, so despised in the Melbourne processions of 1918–22, was again on parade. Not that there was a particular reward attached to this renewed expression of loyalty: state funding of religious schools remained on the political backburner whether for Anglican, Protestant, or Catholic schools. St Patrick's Day was, in this respect, of profound significance to Catholic educators and students. This is because gate-money from the Exhibition Ground, where gymnastic displays and a sports carnival were staged annually, went directly to funding Catholic schools in Victoria, as did proceeds from the St Patrick's night concert and sale of Shamrock Day badges.[67] The overall sum of money was, at the time, significant: as examples, £2,000 in 1924 and £1,400 in 1928.[68] No wonder the Catholic schools got their young charges primed for St Patrick's Day. It helped to pay the bills.

St Patrick's Day was, nonetheless, a time for festivity and conviviality, so it gave pleasure. Families who lined up along the parade route witnessed an out of the ordinary spectacle – Irish pipers dressed in kilts, members of Irish national associations marching behind parochial banners, horse-drawn floats carrying Irish dancers and musicians, scores of horses positioned in tandem with riders carrying flags or banners, motor lorries with tableaux representing key figures and moments in Irish history, and Catholic clergy in formal dress driven by in open-topped cars.[69] There were annual competitions for the best marching group, best parade banner and the best drag (float), results of which were published in the press the following day. Prizes were competed for keenly, this helping to keep up the standard of the displays. Painstaking embroidery skills were required for the banners and flags; this was usually a job for female volunteers.[70] Women were, in addition, themselves on parade: in 1929, the *Argus* reported that 'women marched among the Irish National Foresters, as well as among the Hibernians'.[71] Processional drags also carried contingents of women from the Hibernian Society and the St Patrick's Society, each of which was decorated brightly.[72] Indeed, the *Argus* considered that the most 'artistically designed' floats and cars in the 1934 parade were 'those turned out by the women's branches of lodges'.[73] Colour was also added to the occasion by purveyors of St Patrick's Day merchandise, who sold the customary green badges, buttons, ribbons and balloons.[74]

It was a full day's entertainment. After the parade, schoolchildren massed together at the Exhibition Oval to perform choreographed movement displays. This was followed by a picnic lunch, some athletic events for the kids, and then the 'grown-up' St Patrick's Day sports went on for the rest of the afternoon. Attendances varied, but crowds of 20,000 people were fairly typical during the inter-war period. The programmes were chock-full of variety: there were sprints and middle-distance races, bicycling and motor cycling events, and even the good old Aussie favourite, wood chopping.[75] Gaelic sports occasionally made an appearance, such as in a competition to lift and hurl a ball the furthest distance.[76] But the Gaelic Athletics Association (GAA) had only a small following in Australia, and locals of Irish-Catholic descent were much more likely to be playing 'mainstream' sports like cricket, rugby and Australian Rules football than traditional Irish pastimes like hurling and Gaelic football.[77] The most 'authentic' Celtic part of the programme were the Irish dance competitions, staged concurrently with the sports carnival on site in the Exhibition Hall.[78] The resilience of sport on St Patrick's Day in Australia is a subject worth further study: even when there was no procession, a myriad of sporting events was always staged.[79] In Sydney, where the parade was cancelled back in 1896, Archbishop Moran and his successor Kelly relied on the St Patrick's Day sports carnival to draw crowds and raise money for Catholic schools.[80]

Melbourne's St Patrick's Day procession was cancelled in 1938 owing to a viral epidemic; there was a fear that attendance of children *en masse* would heighten their risk of contracting infantile paralysis.[81] However, in 1940 and 1941, with the Second World War now well advanced, the parade continued as ever. Participation remained solid: in 1941 some 9,000 boys from Catholic schools were involved, while representatives of Irish organizations totalled around 4,000 marchers.[82] Predictably, there were criticisms of the decision to parade during wartime. Mannix, while tactfully avoiding the subject of Ireland's neutral position in the conflict, responded enigmatically: 'We [Irish-Catholic Australians] are taking our part in the war side by side with other people . . . but the war should not be in our thoughts all the time . . . there were other things to think of as well.'[83] The President of the St Patrick's Day Celebration Committee, the Reverend Monsignor F.P. Lyons, was a member of the Catholic hierarchy and rode alongside Mannix in the procession. The records of this organization have not survived, but it is not difficult to imagine that the Archbishop had a profound influence over both Lyons and the deliberations of the committee he chaired. However, as argued previously, Mannix's power was not absolute. After continued public pressure, the St Patrick's Day parade was abandoned for the duration of the war. It resumed in 1946 with a smaller number of marchers than usual – just 4,500 – but any lingering suggestion that the Irish were not committed to the war effort was refuted symbolically by the presence of returned Catholic soldiers in the parade.[84] The modest number of St Patrick's Day marchers continued over the next few years.[85]

TUNING INTO THE DIASPORA: ST PATRICK'S DAY RADIO ADDRESSES

By the 1930s, communication technologies had advanced to the extent that political leaders were able to reach radio audiences over vast distances. The British monarch and American presidents had addressed their public via radio; no surprise, then, that Irish leaders now did the same. Perhaps the most exciting innovation of the time were transatlantic broadcasts. In Ireland the Athlone transmitter began operation in 1933, which allowed radio broadcasts to be relayed to the United States. With such a direct radio link between the homeland and the diaspora, St Patrick's Day soon figured as a key occasion for the Irish state to connect with Irish Americans, thus reinforcing long-standing ties between Ireland and America. The inaugural

Irish president, W.T. Cosgrave, had broadcast to America in the early 1920s, but his messages were never simultaneously available to the diaspora. It was Eamon de Valera, elected Taoiseach in 1932, who not only benefited from the opening of Athlone, but made the annual St Patrick's Day broadcast his own. In America, radio made Eamon de Valera a 'household name' among the Irish diaspora.[86] As he stated at the opening of his first broadcast in 1932:

> This is the first occasion that I have had the opportunity of speaking at the same moment to the Irish people at home and in the United States of America. The fifteenth centenary anniversary of the coming of St Patrick, the year of the Eucharistic Congress, the recent election by the people of this state of the first Fianna Fáil government, all combine to make this year's celebration of the National Festival one of unique interest in our history.[87]

De Valera used St Patrick's Day broadcasts to make links between the health, contentment and happiness of his people, and their belief in the Catholic faith and the Fianna Fáil party of government. The broadcasts allowed de Valera to project mental images of Ireland for public consumption in America; by 1936 his messages were received elsewhere across the diaspora. On St Patrick's Day, when Irishness and the fledgling Irish state were centre stage, the radio broadcasts became a metaphorical shop window for Ireland. It was a once-a-year publicity and propaganda opportunity. From hereon, St Patrick's Day radio broadcasts fulfilled a multitude of functions. They were, in part, an annual report on the state of the nation, they were an emotional appeal for political support of a united Ireland, and they helped promote the ideal that beyond the nation-state of Ireland there was an Irish-American diaspora whose primary allegiance was to 'home'. This was encapsulated at the conclusion of de Valera's St Patrick's Day speech of 1932:

> as my last word on our National Feast Day, I most earnestly appeal to all Irishmen at home and abroad to close their ranks and march forward with us. Let our desire to work for our country be our common bond, and let us be content to vie with each other for the honour of serving Ireland.[88]

The typescripts of St Patrick's Day radio addresses, preserved in the National Archives of Ireland, offer fascinating insights into the preoccupations and concerns of the Irish Government, though, particularly at this time, in the manner presented by Taoiseach de Valera. What seems striking is that references to St Patrick's Day and its celebration were limited to perfunctory remarks at either the beginning or end of the broadcast. In 1934, de Valera's message was concerned solely with the ongoing economic war between Britain and Ireland; he made no explicit reference to St Patrick's Day and failed to address the diaspora directly. Equally, while the 1935 broadcast outlined Fianna Fáil's social and economic programme, it made no reference to the significance or value of St Patrick's Day. These speeches were broadcast *on* St Patrick's Day, but they were hardly *St Patrick's Day* addresses.

Yet they were much in demand. On 17 March 1936, de Valera addressed Australia at 8.30 in the morning. At 11.00 he spoke, via the British Broadcasting Corporation (BBC), to Egypt, India, the West Indies, Canada, South Africa, New Zealand and (again) Australia. Finally, at 8.30 in the evening, he returned to the radio studio to broadcast live to both Ireland and America. The address on the BBC to the British Empire was, however, a source of some controversy. T.P. Clark, a BBC official, wrote from the BBC's Broadcasting House in London, to his counterpart in Dublin, T.J. Kiernan, of 'the Irish Free State Broadcasting Service', reminding him that 1936 was an election year in Britain, that Ireland was a sensitive issue, and the BBC's 'neutrality' in matters political was paramount. He therefore insisted that de Valera's speech 'would be essentially non-political in character, so that we may ensure that the observance of St Patrick's Day in transmissions from Daventry will follow the accepted trend of similar commemorative programmes'.[89] To guarantee that de Valera's address was non-political, the BBC requested to see the entire text of the speech a week before its transmission. Despite this affront to protocol, de Valera abided by the orders issued by the BBC. His short address offered greetings to Irish emigrant communities within Britain and her empire, and asked that they visit Ireland to renew their ties with 'the homeland of their race'.[90] He then dealt, circumspectly, with the continuing economic war, as well as issues relating to Ireland's agricultural and industrial development. De Valera's speech ended with St Patrick's Day greetings to 'the men and women of the Irish race in the United States and to all our friends of Ireland in that great land'.[91] Yet again, though, he did not explore the meaning or purpose of 17 March for Irish people: the St Patrick's Day address remained, to him, a conduit for political messages even when they were censored.

THE SECOND WORLD WAR

In 1939, with the outbreak of hostilities in Europe, Ireland chose the path of neutrality. This decision, while it disappointed world leaders committed to fighting the war, was roundly welcomed in Ireland. The Irish were, however, not alone in standing aloof to the conflict; its most powerful ally, the United States, had also adopted a policy of neutrality. In March 1940, de Valera used his St Patrick's Day radio address to explain to Americans his country's position on the war, and to discuss the ongoing issue of the partition of

Ireland. This broadcast had dual significance: not only was it the first Patrician address of the war, it was the first occasion in living memory when Palm Sunday fell on St Patrick's Day. De Valera explained the timing to his listeners: 'An old saying has it that this country will finally achieve its freedom when the Palm and the Shamrock meet – that is when Palm Sunday falls on St Patrick's Day.'[92] He therefore made a special appeal for the unity of Ireland, hoping that 'at last reason will triumph over prejudice, and even in one corner of this distracted world a peace founded on justice be established'.[93]

Obviously the meeting of the palm and the shamrock did not lead to the unification of Ireland. Paradoxically, though, the war had presented the Irish government with the potential for such a transition. This was because in 1940 the British Government had touted the possibility of ending the partition of Ireland in return for its neighbour's entry into the war on the side of the allies.[94] However, Britain had previously reneged on the promise of Home Rule; the Irish Government was, therefore, understandably wary of British assurances. Indeed, the devastating German bombing of Belfast in April 1941, which aroused widespread anger in the southern counties, prompted only minor adjustments to the Irish Government's neutrality principle: Nazi pilots stranded in the south of Ireland were interned, while Allied pilots were promptly sent to Northern Ireland.[95] In December 1941 the Japanese attack on Pearl Harbor prompted a declaration of war from America; Germany, in retaliation, announced that it was at war with America. The United States was now a key player in the Second World War; Ireland, by contrast, remained steadfastly neutral, refusing to be dragged into a 'British' conflict. This view now incensed Washington: America was, after all, fighting in both Asia and Europe.

In 1943, when Irishmen from Australia, Canada, Britain and America were fighting the war on two fronts, de Valera gave his most famous St Patrick's Day address. Commonly known as the 'dream speech', in part because of its imagery of cosy homesteads, a rejuvenated Irish language and its depiction of a rural idyll, it was effectively an assertion of Irish self-sufficiency. Whether this resolute image of a self-reliant Ireland was part of a definite plan on the part of de Valera, or merely a response to Ireland's isolationism as a result of neutrality is difficult to fathom. What is important here, is that de Valera's most famous St Patrick's Day address, if not also the best-known speech of his entire career, was not broadcast anywhere but Ireland because of the war, and failed to mention St Patrick's Day in any way at all.[96]

A year later, in another speech broadcast solely in Ireland as a result of the war, de Valera reiterated the dream of insular self-sufficiency. His 1944 St Patrick's Day address explored one of the cornerstones of Irish culture, the native language. He argued that outside of 'our national territory and our constancy in the profession of that faith which St Patrick brought us, there is nothing that is so distinctly Irish and our own as is this Irish speech'.[97] De Valera asked the Irish people that on the day when their thoughts turned to St Patrick, they should speak his language, that of Irish Gaelic, as a matter of national pride. In this speech, as with all those from 1942 until 1946 addressed specifically to the Irish nation, de Valera turned the meaning of St Patrick's Day inward. Whereas 17 March had long been a global celebration taking in Ireland and the far-flung diaspora, de Valera now narrowed the relevance of the anniversary to the Irish nation-state. In doing so he affected a change, albeit in the short term, in the way that St Patrick's Day was conceived. Emigration had made St Patrick's Day a global ritual; Irish neutrality emphasized the national significance of 17 March.

In 1946, de Valera was able to make his first St Patrick's Day speech to America since the end of the Second World War. The Irish leader was well aware of criticisms that had been made in the United States about Ireland's trenchant wartime neutrality – comments that were heightened by his decision to offer official condolences to the German ambassador in Dublin after Hitler's suicide. De Valera's St Patrick's Day address did not apologize for Ireland's neutrality; instead he queried American objections to such a policy. He argued that neutrality was the decision of a nation that had control of its own destiny. In the Irish case, this was a decision that had been driven by Britain's refusal to discuss the future prospects for a united Ireland. De Valera pleaded with Americans, who lived after all in the self-proclaimed home of liberty, to understand that until partition was ended, Ireland did not have her liberty. The speech culminated with a reminder, with respect of St Patrick, about what the division of Ireland meant:

> it is never forgotten that the territory cut off contains some of the places held most sacred by the Irish people . . . the places to which our minds inevitably turn today; the place where St Patrick, as a slave boy herded the swine, the place where he landed when he returned to preach the Christian faith to his former masters, the place where he established his Primatial See, and the place where his body was laid to rest.[98]

Put simply, de Valera was reminding Americans that without the end of partition the national apostle would never be able to represent all of Ireland. This was, however, pragmatic political posturing on the part of de Valera; in previous addresses he had shown no great interest in the life of St Patrick nor the meaning of the national anniversary.

In Ireland, the first St Patrick's Day after the end of the war was striking only in that it was mundane. Although the country had not been an active participant in the war, the first major post-war holiday of 1946 might well have been a time for people to express a sense of relief that the fighting was over. It seems, however, that the low-key nature of the day was symptomatic of the typically poor observance of St Patrick's Day in Ireland generally. Indeed, the biggest news story that accompanied the celebrations was the fact that the holiday enabled the first large-scale public use of motor vehicles since the end of the war. The *Irish Times* reported 'lines of cars parked end to end, in the streets, outside cinemas, at football grounds, race meetings, [and] showgrounds'.[99] Beyond this rediscovery of the joys of motoring, everything else seemed routine. Dublin's hotels were crowded, as usual, with many patrons drawn to an ever popular North–South football match at Dalymount Park. The biggest crowds attended the Irish Kennel Club dog show at the Royal Dublin Showgrounds, and the race meeting at Baldoyle. The longest queues, though, were for the cinema. The average wait to gain admittance to the cinema was, according to the *Irish Times*, four hours.[100] None of these attractions related specifically to St Patrick's Day. Meanwhile, the annual ceremonial drive by the Irish president to St Patrick's Day Mass at the Pro-Cathedral failed to draw a crowd. Instead the entourage merely prompted people to 'stop in the streets to watch them pass'.[101]

On St Patrick's Day, 1948, the newly elected Taoiseach, John A. Costello, called for the end of partition, pleading with Irish emigrants in America and across the British Commonwealth to work together to heal the wounds of division in Ireland. He appealed to the diaspora by reminding them how much they relished St Patrick's Day, 'the Day when the Irish, at home and abroad, wear, or should I say flaunt, in fact or fancy, the shamrock, symbol of our faith and the glory of our race'.[102] Costello closed his speech by wishing that by the following year, 'our Mother Ireland will be able to walk through all four of her beautiful green fields, and she will walk there with the walk of a queen'.[103] While such allegorical language was understandably romantic on St Patrick's Day, it was too obviously political for the BBC, so such blatant references to the ending of the link between Britain and Northern Ireland were edited out of the broadcast relayed by them to the countries of the British Empire.[104] Ireland was, by this time, symbolically flexing its growing military muscle, and St Patrick's Day, 1948 was an opportune moment for its display. One of the largest military parades ever witnessed in Ireland made its way through the streets of Dublin; the troops were then saluted from above as the Irish Air Force flew past in formation. These military manoeuvres were received warmly by large crowds. Yet St Patrick's Day still appeared lacklustre. The *Irish Times* editorial admitted that 'our national festival, indeed, well may be celebrated even more effusively abroad than at home'.[105]

In 1950, during the early stages of the Cold War, Costello used his American St Patrick's Day address to attack 'the evils of communism'. In making such a speech Costello was allying Ireland with political urgencies in contemporary America. This strategy moved Ireland beyond its position of wartime neutrality, suggesting now that it had a role in world affairs, in particular, the so-called 'free world'. The attack on communism was imaginatively related to the life of St Patrick. Costello argued that Ireland's patron saint had brought Christianity to the country, and it had acted as a safe haven for religion during the 'dark ages'. Ireland's millions of emigrants had lived in the spirit of St Patrick; they, with the support of the Irish nation and the Catholic Church, could help America find the same moral strength to defy communism and safeguard Christianity.[106] This theme was continued in 1951, when Costello sent American listeners good wishes, in a 'world overshadowed by looming war clouds'. Costello lauded America's 'courageous acceptance of responsibilities so suddenly thrust upon it for the maintenance of world peace and security'.[107]

ST PATRICK'S DAY IN POST-WAR IRELAND: THE AGRICULTURAL AND INDUSTRIAL FESTIVAL

In the early 1950s, the observance of St Patrick's Day was revolutionized by the National Agricultural and Industrial Development Association's (NAIDA) decision to annually stage an industrial pageant in Dublin. The organizers had two main objectives. First, they wanted a spectacle that would capture public interest. As such, they drew unashamedly on the successful North American model of parading on St Patrick's Day. The Irish state had, of course, honoured the national apostle in the inter-war years by staging a state procession of its armed forces, but this was not a carnivalesque parade in the North American tradition, nor was it especially popular. The second, and principal objective of the pageant, was to showcase Irish produce and industry, and thus to encourage people to 'buy Irish'. The festival was even made part of Fianna Fáil plans for economic expansion; this was evident in government programmes of 1958, 1963 and 1969. The link between Irish government policy and the staging of the pageant was clear in the message that the Taoiseach, Seán Lemass, contributed to the souvenir programme of 1959. He argued: 'Each successive annual parade should be more representative than its predecessor; in fact, each year's parade should be another milestone in the road to national and industrial prosperity, and each parade should have its own distinctive features.'[108]

The NAIDA pageant was the centrepiece of a marketing initiative called the 'Irish Week' programme. It coincided deliberately with St Patrick's Day – an opportune time for pageant organizers since 17 March was both an anniversary of national renown and a public holiday. During the week-long festival, Irish goods were promoted with missionary zeal, instilling in locals the message that wherever possible they should *only* buy Irish. The nationalistic nature of the week was further reflected by a ruling that only firms producing in Ireland and were Irish owned were eligible to take part in the industrial pageant, which was the highlight of the celebration. The pageant attracted a large number of floats from various sizes of Irish business, and the

spectacle proved, in the 1950s at least, very popular, with newspaper estimates of crowd numbers exceeding 100,000 people.[109] The cavalcade featured marching bands and decorated floats, each of which were provided by
Irish industrial and agricultural businesses. While traditional tunes and airs,
such as 'O'Donnell Abú', 'Kelly the Boy from Killan', and 'The Hills of
Pomeroy' were played, floats drifted along replete with company advertising
and smiling employees. Aside, perhaps, from the cinema this was the most
exciting show in town. As one enthusiastic observer recorded:

> the genius of the entrants excelled – with over two hundred entrants
> one glimpsed the ingenuity of craftsmanship, floral decorations, floats
> with symmetry of design and goods and commodities, from the staid
> décor of the tailored garments and home spun tweeds to the mam-
> moths of the engineering world. Every succeeding display – and they
> seemed endless – was winning for Irish industry worthy and deserving
> applause ... show boats, cottages, landscapes, modern electrical appli-
> ances, and the huge conveyances that seemed laden beyond capacity:
> Bord na Móna, CIE, Guinness, ESB – should we venture 'the big guns'
> (with respect to the others); one might say prodigious in concept, but,
> large or small, each in their own way contributed to a truly magnifi-
> cent spectacle.[110]

The observer concluded: 'it was more than a parade – it was a reflection of
the nation's endeavour to build up a strong industrial arm ... and ensure the
prosperity which has been the hope and ideal of every generation'.[111]

What is also significant from these reminiscences is that references to St
Patrick and symbols traditionally associated with the observance of 17
March were absent. The pageant was driven by economic rather than cultural considerations; it was parochial in focusing on local Irish accomplish-
ments; and it was narrow in venerating agriculture and industry over other
types of achievement. But pageant organizers were at least aware of the
global nature of St Patrick's Day celebrations and Dublin's place within
them. The programme for the pageant stressed that 17 March was 'Ireland's
feast Day the world over', and that Irishmen 'from the jungles of Africa to
the Australian Bush' would celebrate the day, 'in every land and every
clime'.[112] Most importantly, pageant organizers linked themselves explicitly
with Patrician celebrations in America, where 'the marching throngs of Irish
exiles' could be witnessed in New York, Philadelphia, Chicago, Pittsburgh
and 'almost every town and state where the Irish foregather on this Day'.[113]

The industrial pageants of the 1950s and 1960s were principally about
displaying a nexus between nationalism and modernism; they sought to venerate the commercial and technical progress of the post-war Irish Republic.
In this respect the industrial procession had more in common with the ethos
and appearance of May Day parades in the Soviet Union than it did with

St Patrick's Day parades in America. The pageant was a product of an Irish nation that was by now locked into a programme of economic development and expansion, particularly under the leadership of the Taoiseach, Seán Lemass (1959–66). The 17th of March was an annual occasion to celebrate this industrializing Irish 'new world'; hence veneration of 'old world' St Patrick was hardly its purpose or priority. Indeed, what is striking about newspaper reports and photographs of the industrial pageant is the absence of references to St Patrick and traditional Patrician symbols. Spectators were festooned with shamrocks, green ribbons and associated paraphernalia, but they were viewing an event that did not actually celebrate St Patrick's Day!

In 1965, a record sixty-five companies were represented in the industrial pageant, which, as with previous years, had its emphasis on the 'Buy Irish' campaign. The Minister for Transport and Power, Erskine Childers, reviewed the pageant from an elevated stand in front of the General Post Office on O'Connell Street, then declared himself well pleased with the event as it gave 'evidence of technological progress'.[114] While Childers looked upon the pageant as a symbol of technological advance, it was still dominated by floats that related to agriculture rather than manufacturing; indeed, the parade was headed by the world plough champion Charles Keegan and the Queen of the Plough, Eileen Brennan. Notwithstanding the increased number of floats and the enthusiasm of Childers, it is fair to say that the industrial parade, and indeed St Patrick's Day observance generally in Dublin, had become a matter of routine that failed to elicit much enthusiasm from either the public or government ministers and officials. During the 1960s, attendance at the annual High Mass at Dublin's Pro-Cathedral, once a centrepiece of the Irish state's celebration of St Patrick's Day, had become a duty of specified government ministers. In 1961, the most senior ministers attending the service were James Ryan from Finance, and Oscar Traynor from Agriculture, who represented portfolios in keeping with the industrial pageant. Such low-key attendance at the Pro-Cathedral, compared to the annual appearance of the Taoiseach and his entire cabinet during the 1920s and 1930s, demonstrated the reduced political significance of St Patrick's Day in Ireland.

The Dublin-inspired focus on industrial and economic issues on St Patrick's Day was reflected in Britain during the 1960s. Through the activities of government representatives and Irish emigrant groups, the industrial efforts of Ireland were promoted at a wide range of St Patrick's Day events. The most prestigious display was in Regent Street, London, where a showcase of Irish products was organized by Coras Trachtála, Aer Lingus and Bord Fáilte. The exhibition was the centrepiece of 'Ireland Week', which involved thirty-eight Regent Street stores, all of which participated in a window-display competition that publicized Irish goods and tourism in Ireland. The displays ranged from linens in Robinson and Cleaver's, Irish-made shoes in Mansfield's, and leprechaun dolls in Hamley's toy shop.

During Ireland Week the whole of Regent Street was decorated with tricolours, and the festivities culminated with a prize-giving ceremony on St Patrick's night.[115] Irish week was accompanied by a mass of publicity, including full-page advertisements in the British press, paid for by the Irish Industrial Development Authority, and a special supplement published by London's *Daily Mail*. The main aim of this English promotion was the same as that of Dublin's industrial pageant – to boost awareness and sales of Irish manufactured goods. But in this case the focus was on export and earning opportunities across the Irish Sea; hence the affair was hardly as provincial or parochial as in the past. Indeed, the Irish Export Centre, which was based in London, stated that one of the key aims of the week was to move from 'behind the green curtain'. This curtain, the Centre argued, was 'a sorry hotch-potch of pseudo history, movie stereotypes and newspaper sensationalism, all better forgotten'.[116] Such a statement was also significant in a Patrician context; by implication it rejected long-standing images of Ireland as simple and rural; and, given the timing of Irish Week, the contemporary relevance of the national apostle and the tradition of St Patrick's Day itself.

REPOSITIONING ST PATRICK'S DAY IN THE DIASPORA: 1940s–1960s

In the United States, explicit links between St Patrick's Day parades and the Irish homeland had diminished somewhat in the two decades after the foundation of the Irish Free State. Many Irish Americans were staunchly nationalist and so deeply regretted partition. How were they to celebrate a fractured homeland? And for Irish-American Catholics, what could they rejoice given the marginalization of their religious cohorts in Northern Ireland? St Patrick's Day, as a hallowed anniversary of Irishness, was complicated further during the war years by Ireland's policy of neutrality. Although the United States had also declined to join the Allies until 1941, once involved in the war the American government found it difficult to understand Ireland's determined neutrality; hence Washington did much to persuade Dublin to join the Allies. The active participation of Irish Americans in the war effort added to the complexities of the situation. How could emigrant Irish and their descendants, living in America, venerate the Irish homeland on 17 March when that very nation had chosen to stay on the sidelines of a world conflict? In Britain, Canada and Australia, too, tens of thousands of Irish men and women were fighting against either German or Japanese aggression. For the Irish abroad, therefore, the war years constrained their connection with Erin.

During the Second World War, St Patrick's Day in New York was recast as a local celebration of Irish-American people and their successful integration into wider society; there were few explicit references to the Irish homeland. Once the war was over, St Patrick's Day was given a new lease of life;

Irish Americans were able to celebrate an Allied victory in both Europe and the Pacific, and, in addition, the role played in this struggle by members of their own ethnic community. By 1947 the New York St Patrick's Day parade featured some 80,000 marchers and, although the weather was chilly, an estimated one million spectators.[117] A measure of the increasing 'Americanization' of St Patrick's Day in the US was the attendance in 1948 of President Harry Truman at the New York parade. He was particularly keen, on this occasion, to recognize the war efforts of Irish Americans. The parade wound its way slowly down Fifth Avenue: it again involved 80,000 marchers and a million or so spectators, but among them this time was the nation's leader, whose presence confirmed the significance and success of the Irish community in modern America, and the role of New York in that process.[118] Indeed, New York's St Patrick's Day parade was, by the late 1940s, one of the most high profile events in that city's calendar. The notorious New York writer, E.B. White, reflecting on its local importance, concluded in 1949 that 'the only event that hits every New Yorker on the head is the annual St Patrick's Day parade'.[119]

The role of politicians seeking or responding to the power of the Irish vote was never more important than in the case of Mayor Richard J. Daley of Chicago. Throughout his career, Daley courted the Irish of Chicago and ran many aspects of his administration in such a way that benefited them. It was as a result of Daley's initiative that the St Patrick's Day parade in Chicago was reintroduced as a major city event. The tradition of staging an official city St Patrick's Day parade, which began in 1843, had ceased in Chicago by 1869. The mayor's inaugural parade took place in 1956, attracting 10,000 marchers and 250,000 spectators, support that grew steadily thereafter.[120] In addition to the downtown parade, there was a Southside event that began in 1953. Started by Father Thomas J. McMahon and Jack Allen, the Southside event grew steadily in the post-war years. In 1955, the television star, Ed Sullivan led the parade, and by 1958, 250,000 spectators lined the procession route. Although competing with the downtown parade, especially during the Daley years, the Southside event has, with a few breaks, survived, and is now larger than the parade held in the city centre.[121]

St Patrick's Day parades had the widest social mix, whereas Patrician dinners and banquets were predominantly for the wealthy, powerful and famous members of Irish-American society. The importance of this latter group can be gauged by participation in St Patrick's Day banquets by those aspiring to higher office. In 1957, a young John F. Kennedy attended the dinner of the Friendly Sons of St Patrick in San Francisco, perhaps to celebrate the saint's feast day, but also, one imagines, to court those essential votes he needed for public office.

By the 1960s, the number of St Patrick's Day events across America had grown to heights that would have been unimaginable at the beginning of the century. To the far west in California, the first Los Angeles St Patrick's

Day parade had taken place in 1870, and the state had witnessed a steady growth of large- and small-scale celebrations ever since. Press coverage of 17 March in the *San Francisco Chronicle, Oakland Tribune, San Francisco Examiner* and *Los Angeles Examiner* indicates that St Patrick's Day had become a major social event in the post-war years. As the *San Francisco News* explained in a 1951 article:

> even if you don't happen to be Irish, it's hard to ignore St Patrick's Day. For the Irish are rightfully proud of being Irish, and not diffident about displaying their pride to the world. And St Patrick's Day of course gives an Irishman a special reason to boast of his ancestry, for it honours a saint who had ability and courage in considerable quality . . . Even if there was no St Patrick's Day to celebrate it would not discourage the average Irishman. He would still be an Irishman and, as all the world knows, that's cause enough for celebration.[122]

DEVELOPMENT OF ST PATRICK'S DAY IN CANADA DURING THE WAR YEARS AND AFTER

The cross-community nature of St Patrick's Day in Montreal had been evident in the 1930s by broad-based involvement in Patrician dinners, and by city-wide crowd support along the parade route. This growing sense of a shared, rather than partisan, celebration was even more pronounced in the 1940s, exemplified by the inclusion of non-Irish national societies in the annual march. The *Gazette* reported French-Canadian participation in the form of 'a large delegation of Jean Baptistes, ever ready to pay tribute to "St Patrice"'.[123] These marchers were joined by the Mayor of Verdun, Edward Wilson, who 'led a similarly large group' of English-Canadian paraders. The Caledonians, meanwhile, offered colourful musical accompaniment in the form of a marching band of Black Watch pipers.[124] Politicians, too, helped to give the event a broad stamp of civic respectability. They were situated at official viewing stands, waving on the procession: they did so, of course, in full view of prospective voters, so they were driven as much by self-interest as by munificence.

The 1940 festivities were also significant, reported the *Gazette*, because this year 'the marchers and their friends will have ladies with them for the first time at the banquet following the parade'. This was, the paper noted cryptically, 'a revival of the custom of many years ago'.[125] While it is unclear when women were included or excluded from past dinners, there was now wide support for ongoing female participation. However, as was typical in this male-dominated era, the ladies tended to be treated as adornments to the gentlemen of Irish associations like the St Patrick's Society. They added a certain grace and charm to the evening celebration, but were not given a voice during the official proceedings. It was the men who made speeches and offered salutations. Among them were clergy who, of course, were *required* to be male – irrespective of whether they represented Catholic or Protestant churches.

The decision by the United Irish Societies of Montreal (UISM) to continue with the St Patrick's Day parade at a time of war met with some opposition. Speaking at the St Patrick's night banquet of 1941, the president of the UISM, John Loye, summarized the situation:

> We were reproached for deciding to continue our parade in wartime. The reason given was not very definite, but we have a definite opinion of our own ... When a community realizes that it is under the shadow of defeat, that its cause is lost, when it becomes hapless and falls into despair, then it forgets its festivities and forgets to celebrate. In the last war the slogan was 'Business as Usual'. Why not maintain our spirit under the shadow of war unless we abandon all hope and concede we are defeated? Until such a day comes, do not expect us to abandon the St Patrick's Day parade. Let us keep our spirits up.[126]

Montreal's French-Canadian mayor, Adhemar Raynault, extended greetings to the Irish 'from other sections of the population', and added his support of the UISM stance: 'It does not hurt anyone when you celebrate with a parade ... When you love your traditions and your country so well you are good people to have in this country.'[127] The Grand Marshal of the 1941 parade, Francis Connors MLA, conceded that the march was smaller than in previous years, but this was because 'many of our Irishmen have trooped to the colors in defence of our way of life'.[128] The UISM even used the parade to remind doubters of this commitment; it included a martial float with the inscription 'Irish-Canadians fight, work, and save for victory'.[129] The end of the war in 1945, therefore, provided an opportunity for community self-congratulation next St Patrick's Day. In 1946 the *Gazette* reported a 'mile long parade' led by mounted police, with support from provincial and municipal police; these detachments were followed by 'army, navy and air force units', which 'added the military touch to the parade'.[130] This was 'the first peace-time parade in seven years', and, as the *Gazette* concluded, it 'was really going to be one to remember'.[131]

Throughout post-war Canada there was resolve to engage in joyous public festivities. In Montreal, both St Jean-Baptiste Day and Canada Day were high points on the social calendar, and so too was St Patrick's Day. In the wake of the 1950 celebrations, the grand marshal of the St Patrick's Day march, City Councillor Edward O'Flaherty, remarked triumphally: 'if parades of the calibre of yesterday's became usual in Montreal, Irishmen seeking the most in St Patrick's Day parades would be coming to Montreal instead of New York'.[132] The weather had been particularly kind, with sunshine and clear blue skies; on St Patrick's Day in previous years the snow had often to be swept from streets to allow the parade to move. The 1950 procession included a wide variety of groups, emphasizing again the cross-community nature of St Patrick's Day in Montreal. The march was headed by mounted police, then followed by the military contingent of the 6th Duke of Connaught Royal Canadian Hussars, with the Ancient Order of Hibernians bringing up third place. Other parade groups included the Innisfail Social and Sports Club, the Royal Canadian Air Force, the Royal Canadian Sea Cadets, Police Juvenile Clubs, the 79th Battery Army Cadets and the Victoria Rifles of Canada Drum and Bugle Corps, each of whom were intermingled with the 'usual' marching representatives of Irish societies and Catholic parishes.[123]

The profile of the 1955 St Patrick's Day festivities was heightened by a declaration of 'Irish Trade Week' across Canada; this was an initiative of the Irish Export Promotional Board. While local producers continued to connect themselves with St Patrick's Day, such as with the Ryan Paint Company's motto 'Let's paint the town green', Irish companies and imported Irish goods were given centre stage on 17 March in Montreal. Local department stores were inundated with products from the Emerald Isle, as the *Gazette* reported, glowingly:

> The Irish are Here! It's Irish Trade Week across Canada, and the wonderful workers of Ireland have sent us their finest merchandise – fine Irish linens, tweeds and fashions, Irish books, long-lasting Tintawn carpeting, fruit cakes, candies, famed Irish whiskey, beers, and liqueurs. Make a point this week of examining Irish merchandise in local stores. The quality is excellent.[134]

The import of Irish products coincided with local debate about the 'authenticity' of customs and practices associated with the Irish in North America. Under the heading '"Irish" Airs Not Irish', the *Gazette* reported that while Montreal's air waves were currently 'cluttered' with Irish songs, 'few realize that some of the most commonly so-called tunes are not Irish in origin at all!'. According to the *Gazette*, the ballad 'I'll Take You Home Kathleen' was written in Kentucky by a German named Westermarck in order to placate his sick wife, who had a nostalgic longing to return to her birthplace of Long Island. The well-known 'Come Back to Erin' was written by Mrs Charles Barnard of Baltimore, Maryland, in honour of Queen Victoria's visit to Ireland in 1901. Furthermore, the *Gazette* insisted, both 'Mother Machree' and 'When Irish Eyes Are Smiling' were 'pure Tin Pan Alley USA'. They were 'hands-across-the sea' salutes to Ireland, 'but not the genuine sod'. The paper concluded: 'Few really Irish airs like Danny Boy have survived the ocean crossing and the years; and of Ireland's wealth of traditionally beautiful melodies fewer still have crossed at all.'[135] The *Gazette*'s musical critique was followed, a day later, by an article complaining that hardly any Irish Canadians could effectively play the Irish bagpipes on St Patrick's Day. Even Canada's Irish Regiment, which featured a pipe band in Toronto, 'had resorted to using Scottish bagpipes'.[136] All these comments about 'authenticity' were a curious addendum to Irish Trade Week. While department stores featured local musical 'concoctions' devoted to Ireland, consumers could at least be confident of buying 'real' Irish goods on St Patrick's Day.

The cross-community nature of Montreal's St Patrick's Day festivities grew further during the 1960s. In addition to groups of Scots, English and French, local Italians and Poles now also paraded with the Irish on 17 March. This was living proof, argued the *Gazette*, 'that on St Patrick's Day, everybody is Irish'.[137] The paper reported that 'as usual, tens of thousands of smiling Montrealers watched the Pats and Mikes of all sizes and ages promenade their gay shamrocks on the main drag'. As had been the custom for eleven years, the audience for the 1960 parade included children from St Patrick's Orphanage, who had been driven there free of charge by thirty local taxi drivers – many of whom were not Irish. The *Gazette* reported 'Cohens, Kellys, Amatos, Gauthiers and Rubinskys' among the volunteer drivers, who were 'all decked out in green with their taxis' trunks loaded with goodies for the kids'.[138] It may have seemed like Christmas to the orphans, except that Santa Claus was wearing green and went by the name of St Patrick. The lead-up to Montreal's St Patrick's Day parades was, indeed, replete with pageantry and fantasy. One of the most anticipated events a couple of weeks before St Patrick's Day was the naming of the 'Pageant Queen' and her four princesses. Numerous smiling, single young girls vied for this honour, adding glamour and sex appeal to the festivities. This was an officially sanctioned part of the proceedings: the competition for the Pageant Queen was sponsored by the United Irish Societies of Montreal.[139]

DEVELOPMENT OF ST PATRICK'S DAY IN POST-WAR AUSTRALIA

By the early 1950s the Melbourne procession, after its wartime break, was in revival. Photographs printed in the *Argus* for these years indicate a return of large crowds and a lengthy parade. In 1953, for instance, the *Argus* estimated that 35,000 people lined the parade route and 14,000 marched in procession.[140] The following year, the paper suggested, 100,000 spectators were in attendance, while in 1956 some 20,000 marchers made this one of the biggest celebrations of St Patrick's Day since the early 1920s.[141] How might this renewed interest in the public observance of 17 March be explained?

The Irish nationalist cause, while it continued to fire the aged Mannix, was of comparatively little concern to most Irish-Catholic Australians. Militant expressions of Irish republicanism were, indeed, now unacceptable on St Patrick's Day. For example, at the start of Melbourne's 1959 parade, members of the St Patrick's Day Celebration Committee, with the benefit of police assistance, responded to an 'unauthorized intrusion' into the parade. A small group of marchers, apparently carrying stridently anti-British banners, had tried to join the procession; although evicted, they pushed in again later along the parade route. Bishop Fox, speaking for the Committee, described the actions of the protestors as 'unwelcome and embarrassing'.[142] The politics of Ireland were, by now, intangible to many Australians of Irish-Catholic descent. Most of them had never been to Ireland, and Australia was their natural home. When Queen Elizabeth toured the country in 1954, she was cheered by millions of her subjects. There was no contradiction, except for diehard nationalists, in Irish Australians revering the reigning monarch. She was, after all, their country's head of state.[143]

Catholics had, of course, long used the space of the streets and the spectacle of procession to self-declare their own importance in Australian society. Indeed, the 1950s were a time when the most public forms of mass worship, Blessed Sacrament and Marian processions, were staged regularly.[144] Most notably, Melbourne staged a Eucharistic Congress in 1953 without the sectarian problems that had confronted Sydney's Catholic community back in 1928, when it first hosted an International Eucharistic Congress.[145] Although Catholic–Protestant divides still affected Australian society, the sectarian bitterness of the Easter Rising, the conscription crisis and their aftermath had no peer in the 1950s.

That said, the 1950s were a politically turbulent time for Australian Catholics. The church hierarchy was on a crusade to rid the trade union movement of alleged communist sympathizers, who, according to critics, had also infiltrated the Labor Party. Mannix, speaking at a St Patrick's breakfast with the Hibernians in 1955, accused federal Labor of 'opening the door to Communism'.[146] In this view, two of the Catholic Church's traditional allies now seemed to harbour radical left-wing heretics. This diatribe against the labour movement was, for the most part, propelled by a genuine belief of imminent communist power, however unlikely that now seems. But the discourse was also a reaction to accusations by the leader of the Labor Party, Dr Evatt, that the hierarchy of the Catholic Church had mobilized its members to try to take over leadership of both the unions and their political party. The secretive Catholic 'movement', inspired by the Italian-Australian intellectual B.A. Santamaria and supported by Mannix, seemed to its zealous followers to be the last bastion of resistance against atheistic communism. Evatt, however, survived challenges to his leadership with the ongoing support of liberal-minded Catholics. Yet the ranks of the Labor Party soon thinned as a splinter group, the Democratic Labor Party, was inaugurated in 1957 with the blessing of Mannix. This had the effect of entrenching the conservative Liberal Party in power for the next eighteen years.[147] In the mid-1950s, though, there was an urgency and stridency about a quest for Catholics to wield political influence in Australia. This was expressed on St Patrick's Day in speeches by Mannix and other church leaders, and it seems no coincidence that the traditional parades in Melbourne were the largest seen since the early 1920s. Much of this support came from Catholic organizations, such as the Hibernian-Australian Catholic Benefit Society, with sixty of its branches marching in the 1953 procession.[148] Catholic schoolboys were, as usual, the largest contingent of marchers throughout the 1950s. And there was to be no reduction in the numbers of performers: in 1957 Catholic schoolgirls were also invited to parade. This was, the *Age* announced, the 'first time' in the event's history that 'girls from Catholic schools and colleges took part'.[149] If there is political symbolism in numbers, then the St Patrick's Day parades of the late 1950s were a display of latent Catholic power.

This momentum continued. The *Age* described the 1960 parade as 'one of the biggest St Patrick's Day marches ever held in Melbourne'.[150] The cavalcade took nearly ninety minutes to complete its course, and was watched by a 'huge crowd'. A spattering of well-wishers even broke through a police cordon to surround the lead car carrying the indefatigable Mannix – now ninety-six years old.[151] In 1961 some 30,000 schoolchildren marched along Bourke Street, where they were watched by a large crowd 'five-deep' in most places.[152] The 1962 parade went for nearly two hours, and, according to the *Age*, was witnessed by a crowd of some 80,000 spectators 'stretched up to 12 deep the length of Bourke Street and up to the cathedral'.[153] The highlight of the 1963 parade was the realization that this was Archbishop Mannix's 100th St Patrick's Day.[154] It was also his last; he died at the grand age of ninety-nine years.

The processions over the next few years were, as ever, dominated by around 12,000 marching children representing Catholic schools. But in the 1960s there were fewer Irish national societies on parade. In 1968 the *Age* complained that 'After the Melbourne Irish Pipe Band had passed, playing the Wearing of the Green, Ould Ireland was seen no more.'[155] This was, in part, a consequence of generational change, with fewer Irish migrants to carry the shillelagh or wear the shamrock on St Patrick's Day, and Australian-born descendants less concerned than their forebears with Irish ancestry. But the change also stemmed, it seems, from the policies of Mannix's successors towards St Patrick's Day itself. In a stinging article in the *Age*, 'Fading of the Green', Michael Ryan wrote satirically in 1968:

'SO YOU thought St Pat's Day was losing its Irishness?' said the duty priest at St Patrick's Cathedral. 'Well, 'tis no longer meant to be Irish.' Over my bewildered Begorrah! He went on, 'That's right me lad. Archbishop Knox ruled that St Patrick's Day should be an arch-diocesan event, not just an Irish national day. It was to have a new look as a Catholic festival, with emphasis on our official patron, St Patrick.'[156]

Plate 1 St Patrick's Ball, Dublin Castle, March 1848. Illustration from the *London Illustrated News*. Courtesy of Trustees National Library of Ireland.

Plate 2 50,000 men in line in the New York St Patrick's Day Parade, 1872. Illustration from the *Irish World*. Courtesy Trustees National Library of Ireland.

Plate 3 New York St Patrick's Day Parade, 1873. The grand procession marching past the City Hall, up Broadway. Illustration from the *Irish World*. Courtesy Trustees National Library of Ireland.

Plate 4 St Patrick's Day Parade, Dublin, 1905. Courtesy Trustees National Library of Ireland.

"Hello, the top of the morning to you."

MARCH 17

Plate 5 St Patrick's Day greetings card, 1909.

Plate 6 St Patrick's Day Parade, Melbourne, 1937. Courtesy of MDHC Archive, Catholic Archdiocese of Melbourne.

Plate 7 Dublin St Patrick's Day Parade, O'Connell Street, 1958. Courtesy Guinness Archives, St James's Gate, Dublin.

Plate 8 Limerick St Patrick's Day Parade, 1962. Courtesy Guinness Archives, St James's Gate, Dublin.

Plate 9 St Patrick in Chicago, St Patrick's Day Parade, 1998. Courtesy of Jim Arthur.

Plate 10 Float with an inflatable sun in the St Patrick's Festival Parade, Dublin, 1999. Courtesy of St Patrick's Festival.

Plate 11   Participants in fancy dress parading in the St Patrick's Festival, Dublin, 1999. Courtesy of St Patrick's Festival.

Plate 12   Float with an enormous green insect in the St Patrick's Festival Parade, Dublin, 1999. Courtesy of St Patrick's Festival.

Plate 13 Irish Council of County Associations Parade, London, 2000. Photo by Malcolm McNally © Malcolm McNally.

Plate 14 New York St Patrick's Day Parade, 2000. Marchers head up Fifth Avenue. Demonstrators opposed to the exclusion of gays from the event were also present along the parade route. Photo by Peter Morgan © Popperfoto/Reuters.

Even Melbourne's Catholic newspaper, the *Advocate*, had regrets. In 1970 it admitted that 'the character of the procession had altered; it had become a parade of schools'.[157]

The hyper-Catholicism of Melbourne's St Patrick's Day after Mannix's death was, in part, a product of demographic changes within the Catholic community. In a context of post-war immigration from Europe, and in particular Italy, the proportion of non-Irish Catholics had risen significantly in Australia. This was recognized by the new Catholic hierarchy, whereas Mannix had stoically revered the Irish heritage of local Catholics and an 'emerald green' St Patrick's Day. But Knox's emphasis on religion and his downplaying of Irishness, while rooted in rational argument, proved unpopular and ultimately disastrous. Parades of religious sodalities and Catholic schoolchildren had a long tradition on St Patrick's Day, but in isolation from Irish music, dance and Celtic marchers in regalia, the procession looked staid. Knox had effectively de-greened St Patrick's Day, so crowd support for the parade began to wane. In 1970 the Archbishop cancelled the annual march, announcing by way of compensation that 'he hoped that the Mass in the cathedral would become a truly diocesan celebration of the feast of the patron'.[158] Mannix, doubtless, turned in his grave.

The *Advocate* suggested that the cancellation of the St Patrick's Day procession was the fault of Melbourne's Catholic community, 'which had generally given it only minimal support during recent years'.[159] This was an intriguing admission: Knox had accentuated the Catholic character of the parade, but this was not supported by Catholics themselves. The Archbishop laid the blame squarely at the feet of the Catholic schools. He pointed out that:

> participation in the St Patrick's Day procession had dwindled over recent years. A circular had been sent to the 62 schools which had provided the bulk of participants in the past. Of 40 replies so far received, 33 schools were not in favour of continuing the procession while seven schools, with a total of about 800 children, expressed their readiness to take part. In view of these figures it was regretfully decided that the procession would not be held.[160]

It was not about to be revived. According go the *Advocate*, Knox had stated that 'Melbourne has had its last St Patrick's Day procession.'[161] The finality of the Archbishop's statement is curious; it suggests little regret about the end of the parade, and a determination to do nothing to promote its resumption. But there is another mystery in all this. Why did the Catholic schools, after decades of marching each St Patrick's Day, become reticent about their involvement? There was no hint of epidemiological concerns or physical weariness about these bronzed Aussie kids. The key factor was money. State aid to denominational schools had ended in Victoria in the 1870s; in 1963 it was reinstated, with improvements thereafter. St Patrick's Day, in that intervening period, had been a vital fundraiser for Catholic schools. Now that the state was providing funds there was no longer such a financial impetus for teachers to rally their students each year to parade. And since 17 March had been effectively 'de-greened' by Archbishop Knox, there was not much atmosphere or excitement about participating. For non-Catholics, too, there was now little to lure them to stand for a couple of hours in Bourke or Spring Streets. Whereas many Australians were comfortable with the notion of being 'Irish for a day', which gave them an excuse to drink and be merry, the same could not be said of any honorary 'Catholic for a day' status.

MARKETING AND COMMERCIALIZING
ST PATRICK'S DAY

The post-war world was a vastly transformed, as well as rapidly changing place. The collapse of the British Empire and the advent of the Cold War exerted a powerful pull on international relations. The world seemed a smaller place too. Radio, although important, was rapidly giving way to television with its accompanying visual images from across the globe, while the advent of mass air travel made emigration and return quicker and easier. The 1950s also witnessed the development of suburbs, the continued champ-ioning of the automobile and the realization, for many people, that they had disposable income. Across the western world advertising and commer-cialism boomed, as companies sought to relieve people of their money. In this climate, various festivals and celebrations became the target of market-ing experts. The already globalized celebration of St Patrick's Day now received much of their attention.

The shamrock, for example, was now readily available for international distribution. In particular, the advent of regular commercial air services across the Atlantic meant that this tiny yet precious symbol of Irishness could be transported to places where it was not easily grown in late spring, such as in bitterly cold New York and Montreal. In March 1952, to adver-tise the first direct commercial flight from Shannon airport to New York, Pan American Airlines flew 100,000 fresh shamrocks across the Atlantic for free distribution to Fifth Avenue marchers.[162] This most Irish of plants could thus be worn proudly, or provided as a gift to loved ones. Either way, Pan American Airlines got their point across: Ireland and America were now connected like never before as a tourist and trade destination. And St Patrick's Day was a key moment for both of these to take place. The market-ing of 'real' shamrock was, of course, only part of the commercialization of St Patrick's Day. More frequently, the image or symbol of the shamrock was employed artistically – adorning souvenirs, advertisements, decorations, greetings cards and clothing. This pattern was not, however, restricted to America. St Patrick's Day was also marketed in Canada and Australia, and

Irish people across the globe became accustomed to receiving small boxes full of shamrock, or else a St Patrick's Day greetings card.

By the 1950s, the United States boasted the most extensive telecommunication network of any nation. In terms of the celebration of St Patrick's Day, this meant that Patrician festivities across the country were monitored by the media. At a typical St Patrick's Day parade, local newspaper reporters and radio commentators relayed their impressions of the event, while in some of the major cities television coverage also brought moving pictures and sounds of the festivities to a very large audience. The commercial opportunities of such blanket coverage were not lost on American business, so sponsorship duly became part and parcel of the St Patrick's Day parade.[163] This also helped bring Irish performers to the United States on St Patrick's Day. In 1959, for instance, the St Laurence O'Toole Pipe Band was flown from Dublin to New York to take part in the festivities; their flight and other costs were met by sponsors, Rheingold Beer. They were the first band from Ireland to appear in a New York St Patrick's Day parade.[164]

For many Americans, television broadcasts provided a 'window' into St Patrick's Day parades around the nation. Festivities from New York and Boston were beamed into living rooms, and there were even programmes covering events in Ireland. Regional television broadcasters now made an effort to capture local celebrations. The growth of such television programming, most noticeable in the United States with its large number of broadcasters, brought a demand for addresses from the Taoiseach on St Patrick's Day, as well as programmes about the state of contemporary Ireland. In 1963, the Milwaukee station, WISN TV Channel 12, broadcast a thirty-minute film entitled *Ireland Yesterday and To-day* as part of its St Patrick's Day programme. To accompany this, WISN also wanted to show a five-minute address from the Taoiseach. The Irish Consul General in Chicago replied to the broadcaster that the Taoiseach, Seán Lemass, accepted the request because of the large local Irish population, and the impact that such a favourable coverage of Ireland might have for tourist revenue. Lemass's St Patrick's Day address of 1963, a general overview of Irish agriculture and industry, was duly filmed, then flown to WISN courtesy of Aer Lingus.[165]

The advent of sponsorship and heightened commercialism in New York's St Patrick's Day were not necessarily welcome. Many people involved in the parade, especially at the organizational and executive committee level, felt that the day should be kept as an 'authentic' celebration of Irishness in America, and thus not be sullied by marketing ploys and gaudy memorabilia. Such views were influential: in 1960 the AOH parade committee rejected offers of commercial sponsorship, and street vendors were banned from the parade route. The chairman of the organizing committee, Harry M. Hynes, argued that the 1960 parade 'was almost wholly free of novelty and commercialism'; St Patrick's Day in New York was 'not Mardi Gras', he declared.[166] His efforts, however laudable, were like King Canute trying to turn back the tide. The United States was, by the 1960s, the global centre of free-enterprise capitalism; in that sense St Patrick's Day sponsorship, commercialism and souvenir vendors could hardly be resisted in the long term. Indeed, plastic green hats, green-coloured beer, cheap souvenirs and gaudy marketing have been part and parcel of America's St Patrick's Day experience for most of the twentieth century.[167]

St Patrick's lack of a business agent and his failure to impose copyright laws meant that entrepreneurs easily appropriated his name or his anniversary to sell commercial products. The Patrician festival afforded many businesses, not solely the purveyors of plastic green hats and fake shamrocks, with opportunities to sell or promote their wares. The occasion brought together a significant volume of people in large cities and towns with time, and particularly where 17 March was a holiday, money in their pockets to spend. In Ireland, shops began to target people visiting Dublin for the industrial pageant with tempting St Patrick's Day bargains. In 1955, for instance, the footwear company Saxone offered the women of Ireland the 'Joyce' design of shoes from the California Ladies range, 'especially for St Patrick's Day'.[168] American advertisers were usually far more direct about using 17 March to promote their products. The Ballantine Ale and Beer Company, for example, produced a series of adverts in mid-March during the 1940s and 1950s: its beer was described as 'a downright pleasure' available in bottles that were the '3-Ring "handy" way to celebrate St Patrick's Day'.[169] In the drinking stakes, however, Irish brewers were just as commercially aggressive, though prone to hyperbole. The Harp advertising campaign of March 1965, for instance, portrayed a pint of the company's beer nestled in a mountain of shamrock, with the by-line: 'Celebrate this St Patrick's Day with Harp. An <u>Irish</u> drink, made with <u>Irish</u> skill from <u>Irish</u> water and <u>Irish</u> barley.'[170] The selling of goods on St Patrick's Day, although a feature of the post-war years, had its origins in the late nineteenth and early twentieth centuries. In 1898, the *Irish World* offered its readers real Irish shamrock under glass, in a brass frame, for 50 cents. By 1911, the American trade paper, *Novelty News*, carried an advert from the Miller Company, claiming it stocked 'all the latest and up to date novelties'. This was just part of 'the largest line of St Patrick's Day novelties anywhere in the world'.[171]

The most inexpensive and common form of marketing on St Patrick's Day was the ostentatious sale of virtually anything green. It seemed that any product, if emerald coloured for the day, could be sold as relevant to St Patrick's Day, irrespective of its 'authentic' relationship to Ireland. The *Irish Independent* informed readers in the homeland that green beer had become a common feature of St Patrick's Day in the United States, and there were also 'green cigarettes, green noodles and of course, millions of green ties and hair ribbons'. The paper noted that 'even bagels sold in Jewish delicatessens were green' on 17 March.[172] The most extensive and expensive commercial involvement was companies who declared themselves almost the official sponsors of St Patrick's Day. Such a tactic became easier from 1949, when American television networks began live coverage of the New York parade. In 1965, Ireland's national airline, Aer Lingus, sponsored the live four and a half hour telecast of the parade, and, as official sponsors, were able to screen advertisements featuring Ireland's attraction as a tourist centre throughout the programme.[173] It was not only Aer Lingus that benefited from this growth of live television broadcast of St Patrick's Day events. By the early 1960s, regional television channels, such as WPIX in Chicago, were broadcasting six hours of St Patrick's Day coverage, with commercial breaks throughout.[174]

This heightened commercialism notwithstanding, there were still concerns about the so-called 'paddywhackery' of 17 March in America. This included an erosion of the religious significance of St Patrick's Day, a lack of respect for the marching Irish societies and Catholic sodalities, the flaunting of cheap and garish mementoes, as well as the use of 17 March for the express purpose of drunkenness and debauchery. This change of attitude seems, as much as anything, to have had generational origins. The steady climb of many Irish Americans up the socio-economic ladder, resulting in their relentless move to suburbs outside of the ghetto, eroded the sense of Irish community that had traditionally been a feature of inner city life, and which was expressed annually on St Patrick's Day. As a result, the observance of 17 March was no longer rooted within a fixed community. It attracted the Irish and non-Irish from afar, into the domain where the parade was to be held. These areas, though traditional locations of the Irish community, had ceased to be predominantly Irish as the move to outer suburbs became commonplace. Thomas H. O'Connor, discussing his home town of South Boston, reflected on St Patrick's Day during the 1950s and 1960s:

> During the postwar years the deep pride most early inhabitants took in their Irish heritage too often seemed to take on the kind of cheap and superficial characteristics that became especially noticeable during the district's annual St Patrick's Day parade. Green derbies, make-believe shamrocks, plastic shillelaghs, Tin-Pan Alley songs, and over sized lapel buttons proclaiming 'Kiss Me, I'm Irish!', made their appearance, and old time residents complained about young people of every ethnic background from many different communities flocking into South Boston to drink, fight and turn a traditional neighborhood festivity into a blatant excuse for an ugly and embarrassing brawl.[175]

The changes in South Boston were echoed elsewhere. In the post-war era, many Irish Americans were the third, fourth and fifth generations of those who had emigrated in the post-famine era. As the years passed, many of the younger sections of the family lost the day-to-day connection with their Irish roots. While they were happy to 'celebrate St Patrick's Day once a year, to enjoy a bit of Irish music and to spend an evening with their friends at a local Irish pub', their links with a common ethnic and family background were diminishing, as were their ties with traditional Irish neighbourhoods. O'Connor concluded, wryly: 'As their fortunes brightened they gladly left the districts where their families had lived for generations and moved to new split levels and ranch houses in the suburbs.'[176]

MONITORING AND REGULATING
ST PATRICK'S DAY

The paddywhackery of St Patrick's Day in the United States and Canada was also of concern to the Irish Government. There was an understandable fear that negative connotations associated with the commercial observance of St Patrick's Day, as well as a cavalier approach to the festivities by young people – whether of Irish background or otherwise – sullied the *Irishness* of the anniversary. If the commemoration of 17 March in North America was gaudy, crass and hedonistic, this would have an impact on the image of Ireland itself. In 1960, the Irish Consul in Boston wrote to the Department of Foreign Affairs expressing concern that the celebration of St Patrick's Day in America was having an adverse effect on external perspectives of the Irish community in Boston, as well as Ireland as a nation. The Consul complained that 17 March had been celebrated in a fashion 'more akin to a hooley than a dignified salute to the patron saint ... [amidst] a plethora of shamrocks, green ties, caubeens, leprechauns and clay pipes'.[177] He dismissed the celebrations as embodying 'much of the stage Irish tradition'.[178] Nonetheless, the Consul conceded that despite his negative impressions there were positive aspects of St Patrick's Day celebrations in Boston, such as the extensive coverage of the Taoiseach's broadcast, an exhibition of Irish arts and crafts, an Irish concert and extensive promotion of Irish goods and tourism within local stores. But he concluded, with regret, that 'there is still a large element of stage Irishman connected with the festivities; much of which is deeply embedded by tradition and strengthened by commercialism'.[179]

In 1962, the Irish Ambassador to Canada had similar concerns to those of the Irish Consul in Boston. He wrote to the Department of Foreign Affairs in Dublin, complaining:

> that there is an element of clowning and buffoonery in all this is undeniable; many Irish people would find offensive the green top hats, the shillelaghs, the green carnations, green beer, green whiskey and even green traffic lanes – not to mention the festooning of everyone with shamrock.[180]

The ultimate insult for Ireland's Ambassador to Canada was the appearance at the St Patrick's Day Communion breakfast of a mace consisting of a shillelagh, and table decorations made of green top hats. Such complaints and concerns relating to the direction of North American St Patrick's Day celebrations were not limited to Irish diplomatic representatives. In 1960, the *Boston Pilot* mounted an attack on what it considered the 'offensive nature' of many St Patrick's Day greetings cards. The exchange of cards for all sorts of anniversaries had become a traditional part of North American popular culture in the second half of the nineteenth century: the first St Patrick's Day postcards emerged on the American market in 1898, and were dominated in the early years by those produced by the International Art Company and Raphael Tuck and Sons.[181] In the case of 17 March, greetings card companies began by illustrating their products with images of shamrock and St Patrick, or else idealized images of the Irish rural landscape. During the twentieth century, however, there was a dramatic increase in the volume of 'humorous' St Patrick's Day cards depicting leprechauns, pots of gold, blarney stones and the like, that trivialized and stereotyped the Irish anniversary. As early as 1910, the AOH had requested that the US Post Office destroy all St Patrick's Day postcards it considered were offensive to the Irish.[182] The *Boston Pilot* pleaded with its readers not to buy such 'offensive' cards, which ignored the holy and sacred nature of St Patrick's Day. The paper especially condemned cards that 'even when read with an Irish humour [are] insulting to normal Irish sensibilities. Nearly naked women, slobbering drunk men, cavorting pigs – all with suggestive phrases added – do nothing to promote either decent merriment or happy sentiments.'[183] The *Boston Daily Globe*, meanwhile, argued that the 'true purpose' of 17 March was to venerate and celebrate the teachings of St Patrick. The day should not be honoured, the paper argued, by 'the gyrations in South Boston . . . the green ties, verdant [and] phoney commercialized shamrock'.[184]

One of the problems for the image of St Patrick's Day celebrations in North America was that the stage Irish ideal was readily projected by newspapers, observers, commercial enterprises and also by marchers and spectators themselves. As a widely celebrated annual event that changed relatively little in content and structure, St Patrick's Day offered an easy newspaper story. At the start of spring along came the Irish, and all the old clichés could be given their yearly airing. The weather was a constant source of lame headlines. If it was good, and the sun shone, this reflected the 'proverbial luck of the Irish'.[185] If, as was more often the case, the rain or snow fell, then 'a leprechaun of a weather man played a nasty trick'.[186] The St Patrick's Day weather lottery, rather than being a product of the season, was described mystically by the *Daily News* as a result of 'evil ones who sought to put the curse on the parade of the Irish'.[187] St Patrick's Day accessories, including green ties and hats, were also cause for comment. The *New York World Telegram and Sun* reported that 'Young girls wore lapel buttons bearing this invitation in green letters: "Kiss Me, I'm Irish". A number of girls said the message did not go unanswered.'[188] Overall, then, various adornments and enticing behaviour suggested, implicitly at least, that the greeting cards the *Boston Pilot* objected to had some basis in reality.

Despite criticisms about the commercialism of St Patrick's Day, its celebration was still coveted and 17 March processions grew in size and scope. New York still claimed the most imposing annual parade which, by 1966, involved 123,000 marchers and an estimated 1.25 million spectators.[189] The AOH was aware of negative images that could be attached to St Patrick's Day, and that the appearance and conduct of the marchers helped to shape the public's perception of the Irish. To counter pejorative images and patronizing clichés about the New York parade, the AOH made considerable efforts to promote what it understood to be the authentic meaning of St Patrick's Day. Through its newspaper, the *National Hibernian Digest*, the Order reminded its members that:

> the St Patrick's Day parade in New York is a semi-religious parade, and also very Irish in character and tradition. Every marcher is a person dedicated to the honour and glory of St Patrick on March 17th. It is this state of mind that has made and keeps this parade an outstandingly worthy and glorious one, in a City that has many great parades throughout the year.[190]

To ensure that a desirable image of Irish Americans was presented on 17 March, the St Patrick's Day Parade and Celebration Committee issued 'Rules and Regulations for the Government of the Parade'.[191] Participation in the New York and other Patrician parades held under the auspices of the AOH was restricted to affiliated organizations approved by the committee. In keeping with the Irish nationalist ethos of the AOH, only patriotic Irish and American marching airs could be played by parade bands. English tunes, such as 'God Save the King' and 'It's a Long Way to Tipperary', were deemed unsuitable, and thus prohibited. Organizers also declared that no mottoes, advertisements, or signs 'that might tend to bring the parade or the Order into disrepute, or anything controversial, will be allowed'.[192] The only objects that could be carried were the official banners of each organization marching in the parade, and the American and Irish flags. Rules were even established about the appearance of marchers. While the parade committee accepted that it could not prescribe people's clothing, it would not allow 'any burlesque or dress that will look immoral or ridiculous'. Equally, the committee countered a common belief among marchers that 'sticking something on their hats like green quills, or decorations that are distasteful, if they are green in colour, are perfectly in order'. This was 'an erroneous impression', stressed the parade organizers.[193] All this, it was hoped, would help to counter press comments about cheap, tacky and tasteless forms of dress and accessory on St Patrick's Day.

Managing the New York parade was a major undertaking. The marchers, gathered into sixty separate battalions, were expected to be on time, in good order, and process smoothly around the parade route.[194] But what did such mass participation actually represent? In 1960, John M. Conway of the Irish Consulate General in New York, concluded that the parade was 'essentially a demonstration of Catholic presence, with Irish overtones'.[195] According to Conway, the symbolic power of Catholicism and Irishness at the New York parade meant that a majority of prominent people in local and state politics, particularly if they were Democrat, felt 'compelled' to be in attendance. Conway was, nonetheless, critical of much that was associated with St Patrick's Day. In particular, he singled out press coverage of the festivities. He argued that while many of the newspapers were supportive and relied on straightforward factual reporting of events, others relied on the imagery of the 'stage Irish' for the narrative basis of their stories. Conway singled out an article by Gene Knight in the *New York Journal*, which was sent in full to the Department of Foreign Affairs in Dublin. Knight had written:

> St Patrick's Day will be celebrated all over town. Folks will be singing ballads of Ol' Erin, jigs and reels will be stepped, toasts to Ireland offered in good Irish whiskey, Celtic dishes served, Gaelic poems recited. Sure EVERYBODY will be celebrating St Patrick's Day this year![196]

Equally typical of the stage Irish form of reporting was an article from *McCall's Magazine*, which was reprinted in the *New York Times*, with the headline 'Sure, and it's a darlin' day for everyone who feels Irish'.[197] The constant barrage of stereotypical images and clichés associated with St Patrick's Day in America also produced a negative reaction from the Irish press. In 1963, an *Irish Times* editorial stated:

> the shenanigans attending St Patrick's Day abroad have become more and more embarrassing to the mother country. At worst, the New York parade deserves its description as 'the cradle, matrix and ortho-centre of all paddywhackery in the United States'. At best, the St Patrick's Day manifestations express the sentimentality and condescension usually saved for poor relations or chronic drunks.[198]

In a similar vein, an *Irish Independent* editorial dismissed 'the green line down Broadway: green beer and green snow: shillelaghs, cawbeens and Mother Macree'.[199]

However, few Irish commentators appreciated that this American style of celebrating St Patrick's Day was a product of local circumstances, and certainly not intended to discredit or embarrass the Irish homeland. The *Irish Independent* conceded as much: 'It is the saga of the Irish Americans that is being celebrated as much as Ireland itself.'[200] Patrician celebrations in America reflected the historic rise to prominence of an immigrant community in an extremely competitive social and economic environment. In the 1960s, America was a multi-ethnic and racially diverse society, but ethnic groups with white skin and English as their first language were better off than, say, Hispanic immigrants with few English skills, or African Americans still agitating for their civil rights. Parades and protests were ubiquitous parts of civil society in the United States. The Irish effectively had one day each year to collectively make a song and dance about their self-importance. They lived in a hyper-commercialized society that brought the world fast food, cinema, Disneyland and nuclear weapons; so much about America was 'larger than life', and certainly more fast-paced and imposing than the Irish homeland. Little wonder, then, that Irish Americans used St Patrick's Day as a stage upon which to assert their prominence and profile. No surprise, either, that the 'stage Irishman' was part of this performance: St Patrick's Day was as much about theatre as was Hollywood.

For Irish critics to demand that St Patrick's Day should possess certain core values, wherever it was observed in the world, was both a theoretical and practical absurdity. St Patrick's Day celebrations were the historical product of their location, not a homogeneous product delivered from and arbitrated by Ireland. There was, however, a clear belief in many Irish circles that the Irish state somehow possessed ownership of St Patrick's Day. Writing from the United States under the heading 'paddywhackery in the USA', Brendan Malin argued that American St Patrick's Day celebrations were 'an insult to the nation from which it has drawn so much of its ethnic base'. He claimed that while all other national days were celebrated with 'decency and national fervour', this paddywhackery meant that 'to Ireland is reserved the public insult. And on a Day which is Christianity's most glowing milestone.' While such feelings are understandable, Malin went one step further and demanded that it was 'time for the Government of Ireland to ask: Why?'[201] But what right did the Irish Government have to control the nature of St Patrick's Day celebrations elsewhere in the world, to overrule the local and impose the national?

THE IRISH GOVERNMENT AND ST PATRICK'S DAY ABROAD

With the foundation of an independent Irish state, the whole business of St Patrick's Day became a forum for government activity. A key department in regulating and promoting St Patrick's Day outside of Ireland was the Department of External Affairs, later known as Foreign Affairs (DFA). It was through this Dublin office that overseas requests for government assistance in commemorating St Patrick's Day were received: inquirers included expatriate Irish societies, parade organizers and even Irish embassies. The records of this government department, which had a role in regulating St Patrick's Day observances abroad, provide a fascinating insight into the celebration of 17 March in different parts of the world. St Patrick's Day festivities that were approved of, or assisted by, the DFA became, in a de facto sense, events sanctioned by the Irish state. Where requests for DFA assistance were refused, Patrician programmes in the diaspora continued nonetheless; but they were considered by the Irish government to be independent and localized celebrations without official connection to the homeland. Moreover, the growing network of Irish embassies, consuls and legates across the globe were required to follow strict protocol on St Patrick's Day. Overall, there was a sense of 17 March being Ireland's national day across the whole world, and that Irish ambassadors and diplomats were expected to play a lead role in observing the anniversary in a dignified and representative manner. As the *Irish Independent* noted in 1955, the demands placed on the Irish Embassy staff in America to attend a wide range of events, across the whole of the country, meant that on St Patrick's Day 'the Irish Embassy will be virtually deserted'.[202]

The globalized nature of St Patrick's Day celebrations is well illustrated by Argentinean celebrations in 1963. To mark the Irish anniversary in that year, there were two main events. The first, on 13 March, was a banquet of the Federation of Irish-Argentinean Societies. This was followed, on St Patrick's Day itself, by an Irish-Argentinean pilgrimage to the holy site of Luján. Once in Luján, the Irish legate gave a speech about the global resonance of 17 March:

> St Patrick's Day is, perhaps, the most widely celebrated of feasts. It is the day when the Irish in New York and Dublin, in Melbourne and Buenos Aires foregather to honour the Saint who brought them the faith. His memory lives on in lands watered by the Mississippi and the River Plate, the Rhine and the Danube. In time his apostolate was to lead to the faith, and with it Europe and the centuries of our civilisation being brought by his devoted sons, the Irish, to countries and continents then unknown, across uncharted seas. The fact that we are all gathered in Luján today to do him homage is a symbol of the universality of his work and his vision.[203]

The range of officially sanctioned St Patrick's Day events involving Irish diplomats across the world, particularly in the post-war era, was considerable. In 1968, J.W. Lennon, the Irish Ambassador to Spain, attended four separate functions on St Patrick's Day. In the morning there was a diplomatic reception at the Irish Embassy for members of the Irish diplomatic corps in Spain. The ambassador then attended a special Patrician mass led by the Archbishop of Madrid, after which he visited the Sisters of Irelandesas Convent to present resident Irish nuns with gifts of shamrock. Finally, the ambassador joined the local representative of Aer Lingus for the company's presentation of a golden shamrock to General Franco, president of Spain.[204] In 1963, and with a similar full schedule, the Irish Ambassador to Canada attended the St Patrick's Day parade in Montreal, the Associated Irish Societies' banquet and concert in Toronto, a television interview in Ottawa, the Canadian St Patrick's Society's banquet in Montreal, a communion breakfast and mass in Montreal, and a reception in the Canadian Embassy. Considering how far the ambassador travelled, and how many functions he attended, his report quite properly concluded that 'Ireland's presence in Canada was, in view of our attendance at functions, more widely and effectively affirmed than previously'.[205]

For the organizers of St Patrick's Day celebrations around the world, there was often a desire to secure the attendance of a major Irish leader or political figure. As we saw in Chapter 3, American parade committees had proudly secured the participation of old campaigners from 1798 or Young Irelanders from 1848 on their review stand. After the formation of the Irish state a fascination with Irish politicians emerged, and this broadened after the Second World War to include state officials generally. The Irish government was, however, placed in a difficult situation by the volume and scope of such St Patrick's Day inquiries. Government departments in Dublin, most notably the Taoiseach's office and the DFA, received so many requests to send an official abroad that they simply could not have met them all had they wanted to. Some correspondents even asked for a donation of money in addition to, or in lieu of, the visit of an Irish official. The vast majority of requests were refused, much to the chagrin of St Patrick's Day parade committees and banquet organizers around the diaspora.

The Taoiseach's office received regular requests from the United Irish Societies of Montreal (UISM) for assistance to stage its St Patrick's Day parade. In 1965, the occasion of the UISM's 141st annual march, the association wrote to Taoiseach Jack Lynch directly, asking that an Irish policeman be sent to Montreal to lead the procession. The request was refused. In 1967, the UISM wrote once more to the Taoiseach with a plea that 'the Irish government sponsor a band, either boys and girls, for our 143rd parade'.[206] The Taoiseach's office responded: 'your request is one of many that the Government receive from many parts of the world for participation in St Patrick's Day celebrations and which it is impracticable for them to meet'.[207] Since Montreal, which boasted a significant Irish-Catholic lineage, had fared poorly in these exchanges, what hope was there for smaller, more obscure Irish communities? In 1962, Pat Flannery, the owner of a catering company in Jamaica, informed the DFA that he was holding a St Patrick's Day celebration at the Shamrock lounge in Kingston, which would feature only Irish food and drink as refreshment, and also a fifteen-minute broadcast of Irish music to be aired by the Jamaican Broadcasting Corporation (JBC). To make the occasion even more authentic, Flannery wanted the Taoiseach to record a special message for the JBC, which could be inserted at a strategic point into their programme. He also wanted the DFA to dispatch a recording of the Irish national anthem for local broadcast, since there was none available in Jamaica. The DFA decided that it was unable to assist Flannery.[208] Overall, then, the Irish state was either unwilling or unable to offer much practical assistance towards the global celebration of this most Irish of anniversaries. The government, through the DFA, was involved in regulating observances of St Patrick's Day abroad, but the funding and servicing of such occasions remained a local responsibility.

St Patrick's Day was, to many people around the world, an innocuous annual celebration of Irishness. Yet, as we have already seen, there have long been opponents who sought to deny the Irish their right to mark 17 March with a parade and patriotic symbols. For much of the 1960s, though, neither sectarianism nor politics had a noticeable impact on St Patrick's Day, largely because Irish-Catholic and Irish-Protestant communities had struck agreements about the celebration of their respective religious and political traditions. There were, however, still disputes. In Birmingham, England, the city council hoisted both the flag of St Patrick and the Irish tricolour over the Council buildings on 17 March 1965. In previous years, the flying of these ensigns had always been objected to by Birmingham's Ulstermen. As a result, city buildings, such as the town hall, had remained unadorned. Though the flags were flown on this occasion, Lord Mayor Frank Price soon backed down, removing them in response to complaints from Ulstermen who objected to the flying of 'foreign flags' in Birmingham. Despite the obvious political reasons behind the Ulstermen's criticisms, a spokesman for the lord mayor tactfully put the whole episode down to a misunderstanding of protocol relating to the flying of flags on public buildings during saints' days.[209]

In the United States, as we have seen, St Patrick's Day parades between the 1940s and 1960s tended to focus principally on Irish-American concerns; consequently there was less emphasis on commemorating the Irish homeland. That said, many within the global Irish diaspora still looked to Ireland – north and south – on 17 March; it was, after all, the spiritual home of St Patrick. Archival evidence for this transatlantic connection can be found in correspondence files of the Irish Government. In particular, the Taoiseach's position as head of state meant that numerous letters were sent directly to him – irrespective of whether the messages were of an official or diplomatic nature, or whether they were sent privately by individuals. Indeed, the average postal bag on St Patrick's Day in the Taoiseach's office consisted of official greetings from the heads of state of various countries, including Britain, America, Canada, Australia, China, Portugal and Tunisia. Messages were also sent from the heads of foreign embassies and legations situated in Dublin. An eclectic list of organizations also sent greetings to the Taoiseach, including the Supreme Council of Florida's Order of the

Moose, the Irish Musician's Association of America, the League for an Undivided Ireland, the Catholic clergy of Wolverhampton, and the Postmaster Thomas F. Flanagan of St Patrick's, Missouri – the only town in the world whose official post mark featured Ireland's patron saint. Finally, the Taoiseach was sent thousands of personal messages. Many of these, especially those from America, were sent in the form of St Patrick's Day greetings cards, about half of which featured religious images. The remainder depicted 'humorous' Irish symbols, such as shamrocks, leprechauns and shillelaghs. What is striking about many of the individual greetings is the manner in which correspondents wrote to the Taoiseach as if he were a well-known acquaintance, or even a friend. For example, Mr M. Simmons of West 34th Street in New York wrote in 1954:

> I am sending you this letter to let you know that we had a fine and great day yesterday marching up 5th Avenue on St Patrick's Day. I think the weather was with the Irish yesterday. I have not missed a St Patrick's Day parade for forty years, and next year I hope and I pray I will march again with the Irish. I think that the Irish people are the finest and greatest people I have ever seen. God Bless them.[210]

Overall, the various forms of correspondence to the Taoiseach indicate that although St Patrick's Day was being celebrated abroad, and often with a decided local focus in respect of banquets and parades, many organizations and individuals still looked to Ireland as the home of St Patrick's Day, and to the Irish nation as custodian of this observance.

In the 1950s and the early years of the 1960s, there was no portent of the Troubles that would engulf Northern Ireland from 1968. Whereas relationships between the Irish and British governments were often strained from then on, and the place of the resident Irish in Britain became increasingly difficult, relationships prior to 1968 were generally cordial. Indeed, during the 1950s and 1960s a steady stream of high-ranking Irish government ministers visited British cities on St Patrick's Day. In 1963, the Minister for External Affairs, Frank Aiken, visited London accompanied by his wife. They attended the annual banquet of the Irish Club at the Hyde Park Hotel, a diplomatic reception organized by the Irish ambassador, a church service at St Patrick's Soho, a special High Mass at Westminster Cathedral, and the National University of Ireland Club banquet at the Grosvenor House Hotel. For a three-day visit this was, indeed, a packed programme. The difficulty for Aiken and other ministers who visited the Irish diaspora on St Patrick's Day was that their time was preciously short. In the wake of Aiken's 1963 trip, the Irish Club and the National University of Ireland were warned by the Department that unless they merged their two events, they would not benefit from the presence of a minister in future, as schedules were too packed.[211] In 1964, the Taoiseach, Seán Lemass, attended the National University of Ireland gala on his St Patrick's Day visit to London.[212] A mark of how moderate Anglo-Irish relations were in the years preceding the Troubles can be found on St Patrick's Day 1965. Charles Haughey, Minister of Agriculture, was sent to Britain for the celebrations that year, and he duly attended the banquet of the Irish Club at the Hilton Hotel. Also in attendance, to mark St Patrick's Day, was the British Prime Minister, Harold Wilson. While it may not be unusual for a serving Prime Minister to attend an official dinner to mark the national day of another country, such a situation was very rare in the context of St Patrick's Day and Anglo-Irish relations. Wilson was the first serving Prime Minister to publicly attend any observance of 17 March since the Liberal, Herbert Asquith, attended a St Patrick's Day event in 1911.[213]

The sheer scale of Irish diplomatic activity on St Patrick's Day in the years between the end of the Second World War and the onset of the Troubles was impressive. Despite complaints from individual embassies and consulates that there was too much to do on 17 March, and too many events to attend, Irish diplomatic representatives abroad remained fully involved in their host nation's St Patrick's Day observances. Reports officially filed with the Department of Foreign Affairs in Dublin, that is those describing major events or observances of 17 March in the diaspora, were submitted annually by more than twenty different nations. These included countries with large Irish populations, such as America, Britain, Australia, Canada and South Africa, as well as others where St Patrick's Day was honoured despite the lack of a large Irish presence, such as South America, Sweden, Spain, Belgium, Holland, Switzerland, Iceland, the Philippines and El Salvador.[214]

BORD FÁILTE, ST PATRICK'S DAY AND IRISH TOURISM

One of the largest co-ordinated attempts to boost tourism to Ireland was the staging through the mid-1950s of An Tóstal. The aim of An Tóstal was to bring visitors from abroad to Ireland with the aim of raising the nation's income. The impetus for the An Tóstal idea was a Department of Tourism and Transport response to a Pan American Airways request that it be permitted to stage a 'Come Back to Erin' month in the weeks surrounding St Patrick's Day.[215] In the event, An Tóstal was organized by Fórga Fáilte, and was initially a month-long event that began at Easter. Those who might travel from Britain and America were specifically targeted by the organizers of An Tóstal, and they used St Patrick's Day as part of their marketing exercise. In 1953, the first year of An Tóstal, St Patrick's Day events in the United States were provided with publicity material. The marketing was thorough: 300 Tóstal lapel badges were provided by the Irish Tourist Board, Bord Fáilte, Tóstal greetings and information were placed at 'all major St Patrick's Day banquet place sittings', while forty Tóstal flags were provided on table stands for the same banquets. Finally, five large An Tóstal banners were distributed to the five biggest St Patrick's Day parades in America so that they could be carried by marchers.[216] Despite the clear opportunities afforded by St Patrick's Day as a marketing opportunity for anything Irish, especially something as relevant as tourism, An Tóstal did not include Ireland's St Patrick's Day in its list of events to attract visitors. When An Tóstal was conceived, there were debates about which major local event might induce international tourists to travel to Ireland. The representatives of Pan American Airlines suggested that St Patrick's Day was the most important event in the Irish calendar, and that An Tóstal should begin on 17 March. However, the Minister for Tourism and Transport concluded that St Patrick's Day was too early in the year to hold the promise of good weather, and it was unsuitable for expressive festivity because it occurred during the Lenten fast. He might also have added that tourists were unlikely to appreciate that pubs were closed on 17 March, and that the main parade in Dublin was a rather demure industrial pageant. Ireland's St Patrick's Day was hardly the equivalent of the conviviality of celebrations in North America. The Pan American suggestion was, nonetheless, visionary as it anticipated a re-evaluation of the tourism potential of Ireland's Patrician festivities.[217]

Official discussion about the redevelopment and repackaging of St Patrick's Day for tourists soon emerged. The most bizarre was a proposal in the 1960s to move St Patrick's Day to a time later in the year. The Taoiseach's Office conceded that the weather on St Patrick's Day in Dublin, and elsewhere in Ireland for that matter, was invariably poor in mid-March. To attract tourists to Ireland so early in the year, when the weather was so dreary, was difficult; so why couldn't St Patrick's Day be moved?[218] In an attempt to gauge whether or not this change of date was practical, a series of letters passed between T. Ó Cearbhaill of the Taoiseach's Department and F.A. Coffey from External Affairs. The aim of their discussions was to establish when St Patrick actually died, or, as Ó Cearbhaill put it, 'some information on the origin and basis of St Patrick's Day with particular reference to the fixing of the date as 17 March'.[219] It appears that if the government could cast doubt on 17 March as the date of St Patrick's death, it might be able to move the bank holiday, and hence expectations of tourist opportunities to a time of year with better weather. As the whole problem of St Patrick's precise date of death has long taxed Patrician scholars, Ó Cearbhaill's investigations soon proved inconclusive.[220]

However, the matter did not rest there. In 1962, a Commission of Inquiry was brought together to consider the re-timing of certain public holidays, including St Patrick's Day. The Commission made no firm recommendations for the repositioning of the national apostle's anniversary, but the debate did demonstrate a general dissatisfaction that Ireland's biggest public holiday fell at such a cold time of the year. Objections to retaining

17 March as St Patrick's Day centred around three key points. First, since St Patrick's Day fell within Lent it was judged 'not to lend itself to the moods and celebrations which one would associate with a national festival'. Second, predictably, was the perennial concern of inclement weather, as 'March is often harsh, making parades, outdoor demonstrations etc. unpleasant'. Third, the tourism potential of St Patrick's Day was 'presently quite limited, a fact which the Tóstal project established'.[221] The report was fully aware that any move from 17 March would be unpopular as people would cling to that date for religious and sentimental reasons, especially in North America, where, of course, it was as cold, if not colder, on St Patrick's Day. The Australians, by contrast, celebrated 17 March in typically mild, early Autumn weather. They had most to lose if St Patrick's Day was shunted to the middle of their winter. In the event, the commission recommended that St Patrick's Day be reconvened to mid-September, as this would 'be a hoteliers' Godsend, offering the prospect of a lengthening of the holiday season', and would allow for the 'shedding of the last vestiges of the reputation of alcoholism which foreigners have associated with 17 March'.[222]

Despite the lack of action resulting from the Commission of Inquiry, the idea of moving St Patrick's Day was discussed in the pages of the *Irish Independent* and the international Catholic newspaper, the *New World*, in March 1969. The latter paper reported that the Taoiseach, Jack Lynch, had recommended that 'representations should be made to Rome asking to change the feast date from 17 March to 17 April or 17 May [because of] the weather with constant rain and biting cold'.[223] The idea of moving a religious anniversary worried many people, including Mrs Josephine Clarke of Illinois, who wrote to the Taoiseach seeking an explanation. She charged the Taoiseach with trampling on Catholic tradition and seeking a change just to please tourists, politicians and businessmen. The Office of the Taoiseach responded by sending Mrs Clarke clippings from the *Irish Times* on 18 March 1969. This suggested that the idea of moving St Patrick's Day because of the weather was part of a jocular speech Jack Lynch had made during a public luncheon on 17 March. His comments were not intended to be taken seriously.[224]

In the same way that radio had transformed many people's relationship with, and observance of, St Patrick's Day, so television performed the same function. The American coverage of its parades and screening of Irish interest programmes date back to the 1950s. In Ireland, however, a national television service did not begin until New Year's Eve, 1961.[225] The state broadcaster, RTÉ, used its new service to cover the next St Patrick's Day. By the mid-1960s, Irish television, like radio decades earlier, was dedicating the bulk of its broadcasts on 17 March to programmes related to St Patrick's Day. In 1965, RTÉ screened a St Patrick's night ceilidh, which was followed by 'Patrick – A Television Opera'. The evening's programmes ended with a performance of 'The Sword and the Bell', a twelfth-century dialogue poem between the dogmatic St Patrick and the freedom-loving pagan Oisin.[226]

ST PATRICK ON THE MENU AND
THE DANCE FLOOR

A mainstay of the modern St Patrick's Day experience has been seasonal cooking. In 1930, the American magazine *Good Housekeeping* was assuring its subscribers that 'the celebration of St Patrick's Day has become a universal custom'.[227] The common awareness of St Patrick's Day had been promoted to those beyond the Irish community, in part, by women's magazines such as *Ladies Home Journal*, *Good Housekeeping*, *Delineator* and *Women's Home Companion*. Since 1906, the magazines, with a largely middle-class readership, had been encouraging women to try out different St Patrick's Day menus, and to decorate their table with an Irish theme. This tradition of advice was continued in the 1950s in particular, with mass circulation of women's magazines and the inclusion in many newspapers of a 'woman's page', where there was a focus on recipes and cooking skills at specific moments in the social calendar. In North America, especially, the development of easy to follow, but thoroughly impressive recipes was also the by-product of new kitchen technology, and the ready availability of ingredients in supermarkets. The mouth-watering dishes that emerged from suburban kitchens of Ireland and beyond were not only supposed to delight the families that consumed them, but also honour St Patrick in a stylish way. Whereas traditional St Patrick's Day fare had centred on cabbage and corned beef, the 1950s signalled a more sophisticated culinary world. The *Irish Independent* suggested that the housewives of Ireland create a three-course meal for the national festival, under the heading 'Dining of a shamrock leaf'. It began with a cream of tomato soup, followed with a roast of both chicken and ham, accompanied by creamed cauliflower and potatoes. The meal culminated with a *bavarois* of chocolate and a selection of Irish cheeses.[228] The cuisine attached to St Patrick's Day was particularly noticeable in North America. This began as early as the eighteenth century, when socially elite Irish organizations, such as the Friendly Sons of St Patrick, dined sumptuously together on 17 March.

The Irish diaspora in the United States retained the county model as a method of assembling communities of Irish men and women on an occasional basis. Expatriate county associations were one of the most important units of group solidarity within Irish-American culture. Various St Patrick's Day parades around the country included marchers drawn from the different county associations, and once the parade had been completed, the individual county groups met to celebrate in the evening with music, food and drink. Although the county associations had held formal and private dinners on St Patrick's Day since the 1880s, these groups had become far more progressive and open by the 1950s, as had American society generally. Increasingly, the county organizations moved away from the custom of a 'males only' formal dinner, now staging large-scale dances to attract men and women, both young and old. Such dances were typically held at local restaurants, bars and hotels, such as those staged by the County Claremen's and Women's Association, the County Corkmen's Association and the Kerrymen's Association in 1964. The evening's events always lasted well into the night, featuring a mix of Irish and American music. This eventually spawned a mini-industry of its own, for Irish-American newspapers were replete with advertisements for bands. Among them, in 1964, was Joe Madden and his Orchestra who promised to play 'Irish and American Music for all occasions'.[229]

PRECURSORS TO THE TROUBLES

One of the key factors that coloured and shaped St Patrick's Day in the last three decades of the twentieth century was the renewal of armed conflict in Northern Ireland. Although this will be discussed more fully in Chapter 6, it is important to emphasize that the problems that destabilized Northern Ireland from 1968 onwards were a product of long-standing social and political divides – some of which had been evident previously on St Patrick's Day.

The unionist-dominated Stormont Government, which ruled over Northern Ireland from 1920, was deeply suspicious of its Catholic population, which was overwhelmingly nationalist in outlook. The government and the police force quickly suppressed public expressions of dissent from within Catholic communities. Sectarianism, therefore, remained a potent force, and incidents, whether violent or otherwise, regularly emerged as a result of Protestant–Catholic competition in employment or housing. Given such a tense atmosphere, an event such as St Patrick's Day, which was readily acquainted in Unionist Ulster with the twin forces of nationalism and Catholicism, was an obvious flash point. Both Irish and Northern Irish papers reported numerous incidents of violence and disagreement about 'Catholic' St Patrick's Day celebrations, in particular the associated parades. In 1952, for example, the RUC police baton-charged a St Patrick's Day march in Derry that it considered was getting out of hand.[230] Northern Irish Catholics who wished to honour Ireland's patron saint faced considerable difficulties, as the *Connaught Telegraph* reported in 1951:

> in Northern Ireland the tricolour was insulted and torn to shreds, Irish men and women were dragged off to prison for daring to display the national flag. Parades were proscribed and any manifestation of patriotism was stifled by the brute force of armed B specials.[231]

The Second World War had also been a problematic time for those wishing to celebrate St Patrick's Day in Northern Ireland. While the Irish Free State remained neutral throughout the war, Northern Ireland, as part of the United Kingdom, took an active part. Although many Catholics and nationalists may have had mixed feelings about fighting a war in the name of Britain, it is clear that Northern Ireland's Catholic population played a full role in the war effort. Notwithstanding difficulties and dislocations that were caused by the war, which were bound to have an effect on normal relations in any society, the decision by the Stormont Government to cancel the St Patrick's Day and Good Friday holidays at this time seemed draconian and discriminatory. The temporary suspension of holidays in wartime was not unusual, but the targeting of holidays associated with Catholicism, when the 12th of July holiday for Protestants was still honoured, suggested a failure of parity with respect of the two populations.[232]

While taking into account the problems that accompanied St Patrick's Day in Ireland, from the foundation of the Irish state through to the outbreak of the Troubles, it is important to recognize that parades and celebrations around the country retained an ongoing political edge with regard to the partition of Ireland. The issue of the north-eastern six counties of Ireland, and the whole resonance of nationalism within Patrician observances, did not disappear with the end of the Irish civil war. As was demonstrated, the Taoiseach used his St Patrick's Day speeches to constantly revisit the partition issue, and it was something that featured in Patrician celebrations around the diaspora. A popular American St Patrick's Day greetings card in the 1950s, which depicted an Ireland divided by the border, implored the recipient to remember:

> when thinking of Ireland on St Patrick's Day remember – that the Irish nation has been partitioned by Britain against the will of the overwhelming majority of the people ... that St Patrick's See at Armagh, his grave at Downpatrick and the scenes of his boyhood on Slemish are cut off from the body of Ireland and are in the area occupied by British troops in a flagrant denial of all democratic rights. On this St Patrick's Day pledge yourself to help undo the dismemberment of St Patrick's Ireland.[233]

CHAPTER 6

MODERN TIMES, TROUBLED TIMES

— ഇൗ —

Oh it must seem so romantic
When the fighting's over there
And they're passing round the shamrock
And you're all filled up with tears
'For the love of dear old Ireland'
That you've never even seen
You throw in twenty dollars
And sing 'Wearing of the Green'

Each dollar a bullet
each victim someone's son
And ignorance kills Irishmen
As surely as if we fired the gun.[1]

BACKGROUND TO THE TROUBLES

The decades that followed the foundation of an independent Irish state and the Northern Irish parliament in Stormont were, for the most part, peaceful. There were, however, occasional IRA insurgencies, such as their attacks on English cities during the first months of the Second World War, and on customs posts along the Irish border during the 1950s. In Northern Ireland tensions between the two politico-religious communities were always high, and at times these came to a head militarily. In the early 1930s, for example, there was a prolonged period of sectarian and labour violence that led to many deaths. A major problem in Northern Ireland was discrimination against the Catholic population. This could be seen in areas such as public housing and job provision, town and city council elections, and within educational provision and opportunity. Such problems did not, however, provoke much interest outside of Northern Ireland. To the Irish diaspora, it was the ongoing partition of Ireland that provoked most interest. This narrow focus often prompted emotional responses from Irish Americans, who demanded the return of the 'fourth green field' to Mother Ireland. While such rhetoric gave life to the issue of a thirty-two county Irish Republic, it provided little in the way of practical solutions or assistance for Catholics suffering discrimination in Northern Ireland.

Given the rapid social and political changes taking place across the world during the 1960s, it was perhaps inevitable that the lid could not be kept on the wide range of problems that were present in Northern Ireland. The failed reforms of the Stormont Prime Minister, Terence O'Neill, the downturn in economic fortunes within the traditional heavy industries of Northern Ireland, together with demands made by Catholic civil rights groups, all meant that the situation had reached breaking point.[2] The period 1968–72 witnessed ever-increasing levels of violence in Northern Ireland, the emergence of powerful and active paramilitary forces within both of the major communities, the introduction of the British Army onto the streets, and the ending of the Stormont system of government by the Westminster Parliament. Concurrently, a series of major new conflicts entered the annals of British–Irish history. These included the introduction of internment, the killing of civil rights protestors by members of the British Parachute Regiment on Bloody Sunday, 1972, and countless firebomb attacks on private houses because the occupants were of the 'wrong' religion. This catalogue of events and the number of deaths that made up the history of the modern Troubles is too detailed to recount here. It is clear, however, that the ongoing tragedy of Northern Ireland, and the constant images of death, violence and destruction that were broadcast around the world had a profound effect on the Irish diaspora. The Troubles resulted in a re-questioning of notions of Irish identity, they provoked difficult questions as to whether a campaign of violence should be supported, and they understandably affected the biggest gathering of the Irish abroad, St Patrick's Day. The day became a focus for groups that wished to distance themselves from the violence in Northern Ireland, while others used the day to remind people of the events unfolding on the streets of Belfast, Derry and elsewhere. In some parts of the world, the suspicion that was aroused by Irish dissidents and their vocal support for acts of violence against Britain made for an unsavoury St Patrick's Day. In other diasporic regions the day has been a vehicle to embrace all communities in Northern Ireland. This has involved efforts to focus minds on the problems of sectarianism within that society, and in an attempt to find a lasting solution via the peace process. As through the rest of its history, St Patrick's Day reveals much about the political and social experiences of the Irish at home and abroad, and offers a window through which their competing senses of identity and loyalty can be understood.

ST PATRICK'S DAY IN IRELAND

Dublin's industrial pageant, which had been the annual parade through the city centre on St Patrick's Day, was superseded in 1969 by a parade with a general theme. It was initially organized by a voluntary committee, but was placed under the auspices of Dublin Tourism in 1970. The parade was conceived specifically as an event to boost income from tourism, and as a way of encouraging Americans to travel to Ireland. A major feature of the parade was the many American bands, drum majorettes and cheerleaders taking part. The parade organizers sent invitations to such groups, and their involvement was positively encouraged. While there was undoubtedly a desire to import American performers to make the parade a more attractive spectacle, the overarching reason behind the propagation of such links was financial. A marching band of fifty American teenagers would be accompanied by a large number of adult relatives and supporters; they would spend money flying to Ireland, staying in hotels and guest houses, as well as eating and drinking. The American inspiration for the Dublin Tourism parade was readily identified in 1970 by the Irish Consul General to America, Charles V. Whelan, who declared from the reviewing stand of the New York parade,

> there's nothing at all like this parade in New York. In Dublin they're taking a line from this one. They're bringing in the bands now. It used to be an industrial parade with floats ... Indeed, they had Judge Comerford[3] come over from New York to Dublin as the expert on this kind of thing.[4]

Dublin Tourism, as organizer of the parade, were clearly not going to admit to the financial reasoning that lay behind the event's commercial reinvention. Instead, Ruairí Brugha, the Chairman of Dublin Tourism in 1970, set out his cultural vision for St Patrick's Day:

> it is Ireland's national festival occasion – it is a focus of attraction for the people of Ireland and for our people who have settled overseas ... We intend to develop and expand the parade into a major colourful, national, cultural and industrial event which will increase in significance each year, not alone to Dublin but to Ireland and Irish people abroad.[5]

The first St Patrick's Day parade organized by Dublin Tourism was staged in 1970. The *Irish Independent* heaped praise on the organizers, calling the parade 'one of the most colourful events staged in the history of the National Festival'. The newspaper argued that Dublin Tourism should take 'credit for an exceptionally well run and sparkling parade'.[6] The first of these cavalcades featured over one hundred marching groups, as well as thirty-five bands, five of which were from America.

The Dublin Tourism parade, relying so heavily on American involvement, became an event that appeared to be trying to be more American than Irish. The banners of the marchers did not refer to places from the Irish map, but announced that they heralded from cities across America. Joseph O'Connor remembered the 'parade as a curiously American occasion'. The appearance of Americans on the streets of Dublin every 17 March was a fascinating annual event. O'Connor later wrote that he was sure that the first Americans I ever saw in the flesh were at the St Patrick's Day parade in Dublin. My brothers and sisters and I regarded these people as exotic. I remember their incredible self-confidence, their savage, cancerous suntans and lurid clothes, as they strutted down the street waving little Stars and Stripes or Tricolour flags.[7]

Irish diplomatic representatives continued to participate in St Patrick's Day events across the globe, although the Troubles affected the scope of this involvement. All Patrician events that diplomatic representatives or any touring government official might attend were closely screened. The Irish were aware that they could not afford to attend St Patrick's Day celebrations with overt republican overtones. This was especially true in America, as will be explained later. Moreover, by the 1970s many diplomats considered the duties connected with St Patrick's Day to be onerous and of questionable value. For example, the Irish Ambassador to Italy informed the Department of Foreign Affairs that on St Patrick's Day, 1973 he had attended a morning mass and reception at St Isidore's Franciscan Church, he had lunched at the Irish College in Rome, and attended an early evening mass at St Patrick's Augustinian Church. He had also hosted an embassy reception for the diplomatic circle in the late evening. The Ambassador concluded his report by complaining that the various events of the day were time-consuming, expensive, and of doubtful diplomatic use. In particular, he singled out the embassy reception as very costly, especially given the lack of central funding. It was an event that everyone within Rome's diplomatic circles expected to take place annually, but which served no obvious purpose.[8]

The Dublin Tourism St Patrick's Day parade was not immune from the politics of Northern Ireland. In 1978, during the early months of prison protests in Northern Ireland, the supporters of republican prisoners in Long Kesh used the parade to stage demonstrations. In the first incident, a man ran in front of the head of the parade and set fire to a Union flag, a clear attempt to use the backdrop of the parade to gain publicity for the republican cause. The second incident was not spontaneous. A group that had gained legitimate entry to the parade, and had dressed as the children's television characters the Wombles, converted their float as they arrived in front of the main viewing stand. Rather than being a celebration of children's favourites, the float was transformed into a protest vehicle supporting republican prisoners.[9]

By the mid-1970s, the Dublin Tourism St Patrick's Day parade had become a standard fixture within the Irish social calendar. The nature of the parade seemed never changing, and while always attracting good crowds, the media coverage of the event reduced year by year. By the 1980s, the parade appeared as a chore; something that must be endured, yet failed to really excite. This is perhaps because the main aim of the parade was, as we outlined earlier, income generation. This fact was obvious to the newspapers that reported the event, which gave full details of the visitor income balance sheet alongside the news stories of the day. A good example of this practice, appearing in the *Irish Independent* of 1975, told how

> in all almost 9,000 visitors were in the country, about 3,000 from the North, 3,000 from North America and 1,000 from Britain and Europe. To tourism it all meant a £250,000 bonanza although the hotels and pubs did not cash in as well as other years when more Americans had more money to spend freely.[10]

In 1990, the parade, which celebrated St Patrick's Day and Ireland's presidency of the European Commission, attracted a crowd estimated at 300,000 who witnessed some 6,000 participants. The decision allowing groups of visitors to parade was still well supported abroad; in 1990 there were 1,000 overseas marchers. The list of foreign visitors even included a brass band from Estonia – a symbol of the changes that were emerging after the fall of the Berlin Wall.[11] The importance of American visitors, and indeed, the whole American media market to Dublin Tourism, was demonstrated by the relaying of live coverage of the parade to thirty different television stations across America. While the parade in Dublin was watched by the Taoiseach, Charles Haughey, the majority of government ministers visited St Patrick's Day celebrations overseas. Six travelled to different events across America, while Education Minister Mary O'Rourke represented the government in London, Environment Minister Padraig Flynn travelled to Brussels, and the Junior Defence Minister, Vincent Brady visited Irish troops serving in Lebanon.[12] The lacklustre nature of St Patrick's Day celebrations in Ireland, and the government's use of foreign events as a method of promoting Ireland was, in many ways, a damning indictment of Irish government exploitation of 17 March. It seemed that the government ministers, like the spirit of celebration of the national saint, had fled Ireland to find more boisterous and important St Patrick's Day events elsewhere.

The virtually unchanging nature of the Dublin celebrations, and the media coverage of them, are clear when comparing the 1990 parade with that of 1995. In the run-up to 17 March 1995, the media suggested that the parade would attract between 300,000 and 400,000 spectators, with 6,000 participants. The overseas groups involved numbered nearly a hundred, while 6,000 overseas tourists, mostly American, were expected to accompany marching bands and cheerleading troupes. The parade would, as in years gone by, be screened by various European, Canadian and American television networks.[13] In the five years since 1990, the parade had not developed or changed in any noticeable fashion. It looked the same, attracted a similarly sized audience, and was overly concentrated on the desire to attract marchers from America and their accompanying relatives and tourist dollars. The failure of the Dublin Tourism parade to develop a new direction was beginning to lose it essential support. In 1995, An Post, Aer Lingus and other large corporations and businesses, decided against sponsoring floats in the parade as they were sceptical of the financial benefits to them of such support.

Despite the decision to re-import the razzmatazz of American parades, the Irish had, by the 1990s, failed to find anything distinctive with which to celebrate St Patrick's Day. It was to cities like New York that the Irish, and indeed most of the world, looked to on 17 March. Even Irish-based companies ran competitions so that the winner could fly to New York to witness the parade there.[14] There was a feeling that the American tradition of celebrating St Patrick's Day was long-standing and ongoing, whereas events in Ireland were poor copies. St Patrick's Day, by the late 1980s and early 1990s, was a largely nostalgic celebration – particularly in North America. By marching down Fifth Avenue, and elsewhere, Americans and Canadians with an Irish lineage renewed their ties with an Ireland they conceived as 'home'. For the Irish themselves, St Patrick's Day, so long as it sought to copy North American celebrations, would be a comparatively empty experience; how do you celebrate 'home' when you are already there? The main group that openly embraced and applauded Irish St Patrick's Day events were those Americans who flew in to take part. For them, they had succeeded in transplanting their annual march down the street from a place called Irish America to the streets of 'home'. It was evident that the Dublin cavalcade was not considered as the 'real' event. Ironically, though, North American parades were themselves sugar-coated by legend and nostalgia. Is that any more 'real'? 'Say what you like, but the Americans know all about razzmatazz. When Paddy's day comes round, we paint the town green. And I have to say folks, New York is the place to be for the parade.'[15] The argument of the writer, P.J. Hamill, an Irish American, was a clear endorsement of the New York parade as the best in the world, and an implicit rejection of events in Dublin and elsewhere as secondary. The main thrust of the article demonstrated the real confusion of the emigrant, and the emotional ties that binded them to 'home'. While Hamill embraced the New York parade as the most 'genuine' event anywhere, he conceded that the Irish-American pub was a fake representation of the ones at home; therefore, most emigrants on St Patrick's Day would be 'thinking of home and their local pub'.[16] Hamill, as with many others, looked to the New York parade as a legitimate example of 'all that is good' about Irish America, yet at the same time he preferred the pubs at 'home' as they are authentic. The comparison between parade and pub is important. The St Patrick's Day parade began in North America; hence it is an American invention and tradition. A direct copy of an Irish-American tradition does not seem to belong in Ireland. Likewise, the Irish pub only works when located in its natural environment – Ireland. Irish pubs that are located elsewhere are unlikely to appear genuine as they, like American St Patrick's Day marchers in Dublin, are in the 'wrong' place.

Another problem for the St Patrick's Day parade in Dublin was that, by the 1990s, the idea of an American-style parade was quaintly old fashioned. The great attraction of the Dublin Tourism approach to the parade, from the early 1970s, had been its new-found freshness. Gone were the tractors and ploughs of the industrial parade, which symbolized an insular Ireland, and in came the exciting, somewhat exotic, Americans. The late 1960s had a profound effect on Ireland. The ending of economic policies that had celebrated self-sufficiency, the advent of television and the slow beginnings of a secularized society, all combined to create a nation that was fascinated by the outside world. For many Irish people, the cultural aphrodisiac of the outside world was America – the land of cowboys, big cars, space walks and the nuclear age. Television provided the Irish with a ready diet of American life, and the glory and tragedy of the lives of Irish-Catholic Americans like John F. Kennedy only cemented ties between Ireland and her imposing western neighbour. The decision by Dublin Tourism to copy the American-style parade was the reason behind its initial success. The American dream was brought to life by the smiling tourists who marched down O'Connell Street. Joseph O'Connor regularly attended the Dublin Tourism St Patrick's Day parades during his childhood. As a youngster he was fascinated by all things American, and the parade was the high-point of the year because:

> The inhabitants of these transatlantic Dublins – at least, the ones who came over to see us in Ireland – really did look like they were worth getting to know. I can see them all still, these tanned and stunningly beautiful teenage girls from Dublin, Texas or Dublin, Georgia prancing and high-kicking down O'Connell Street in green and white bodices and miniskirts so short that they were actually like long sweaters. I can see them waving, blowing kisses to the crowd, grinning their orthodontically perfect grins, sashaying along to the strains of 'I'm a Yankee Doodle Dandy'.[17]

Such sights made a dramatic impact on the life of a teenage boy, but many Irish people watching the St Patrick's Day parade in the early years of the 1970s were equally captivated by its American content. In a world dominated by the Troubles in Northern Ireland, and an Ireland that was coping with the difficult processes of change and modernization, the marching Americans represented hope, or at least a welcome diversion from conflict. As the years passed, however, the Dublin Tourism parade failed to capture the imagination of locals; organizers kept delivering the brashness and wonder of Irish America on St Patrick's Day, when such images were now irrelevant to Irish people during a time of crisis. As early as 1975, the Manager of Dublin Tourism, Matt McNulty, was complaining of the lacklustre response of the crowd lining the parade route. He said, 'I'd love to see more of them cheering and waving . . . more enthusiasm generally.'[18] By the

1980s and 1990s the Dublin parade and its obsequious pandering to the American dream were anachronistic. Ireland had transformed so dramatically from the late 1960s and early 1970s, and its people had learnt so much about themselves and the outside world, that the exotic Americans marching down O'Connell Street in the 1990s appeared only as sad parodies of a remote past. The lacklustre familiarity of the annually marching Americans led Fintan O'Toole to note that St Patrick's Day marked the time of year for the 'timeless Celtic ritual of jeering good-naturedly at the high school marching band from Minnesota or Delaware'.[19] The Dublin Tourism St Patrick's Day celebrations had, by the mid-1990s, become staid. But, as we show later, it would soon be reinvented – yet again as a tourist attraction.

ST PATRICK'S DAY IN NORTHERN IRELAND

As a result of the security situation in Northern Ireland from 1968, public St Patrick's Day celebrations were rare. The 17th of March was recognized by the Stormont Parliament as a bank holiday in Northern Ireland from 1920.[20] This meant that 'banks, government and municipal offices, and schools were closed, although most shops and factories seem to have been unaffected'.[21] In addition to the partial holiday, the most obvious form of Patrician observance was the attendance, predominantly by Catholics, at St Patrick's Day church services. As 17 March had never been embraced by the Stormont Government as an event worthy of official celebration, there was little tradition of public commemoration of the day, such as by parading or festival.

One of the problems for the celebration of St Patrick's Day in Northern Ireland, irrespective of the Troubles, was that the very act of marching, especially any event with a perceived nationalist sympathy, was deemed politically contentious.[22] Since the genesis of the peace process in the 1990s, the issue of marching has become a major political concern, although the focus has normally centred on Orange Order parades. St Patrick's Day, an event that many considered a cross-community celebration, was known by its tradition, elsewhere in the world, as a day for a parade. For those in Northern Ireland who wished to celebrate St Patrick's Day, especially during the years of the Troubles, a complex question was, what form should any commemorative event take? If, as was common elsewhere, a parade of some sort was envisaged, the event would come under close and often acrimonious public scrutiny.

The Troubles and the associated problems of parading did little to help the development of a cross-community celebration of St Patrick's Day. However, the ongoing violence and associated retreat of both Catholics and Protestants into separate communities, did provide a motivation of sorts. St Patrick's Day became, as with so many other forms of celebration in

Northern Ireland, a symbol of tribal allegiance. In 1974, a St Patrick's Day parade was staged on the Falls Road in Belfast, and from 1977 a parade was staged in Derry. The commemoration of St Patrick through parading offered the nationalist communities of West Belfast and Derry their own hero and parade; it was something of a counter-weight to various William of Orange and 12 July parades held by the Orange Order. St Patrick's Day, or rather the ownership of St Patrick, thus became a symbolic battleground between the two main communities in Northern Ireland. Alongside the events in West Belfast and Derry, there were small parades across Northern Ireland organized by the Ancient Order of Hibernians, as well as town parades in smaller places like Armagh, which in 1995 attracted a crowd of 20,000.[23] Such celebrations of St Patrick's Day were the preserve of the nationalist community, and thus usually excluded Protestants and Unionists. However, in the battle for 'ownership' of St Patrick, the Protestants of Northern Ireland reawakened the pre-nineteenth-century tradition of the saint as a symbol of Protestantism. In 1985, Orangemen staged their own St Patrick's Day parade in Antrim; in 1990 there was a joint 17 March church service of the Belfast and Ballymena Orange lodges; while in 1994 the flag of St Patrick was flown from the headquarters of the Orange Order.[24] In 2000, a mural was painted by the Ulster Scots Heritage Council, which claimed St Patrick as an Ulsterman and a Protestant. The mural, which would offend many Catholics who believe that St Patrick belongs to them, was safely located within the heart of Protestant East Belfast on Ninelender Road. The Ulster Scots Heritage Council have also, since 1999, organized their own Protestant-based St Patrick's Day celebrations. The debate over the ownership of St Patrick, particularly the process that has led 17 March to be most readily associated with Catholicism, is regularly commented on by the loyalist press in Northern Ireland. In 1999, the *Orange Standard* argued:

> poor old St Patrick, how bewildered he must be by the concentration, after sixteen hundred years by Irish people here and everywhere else, on who he was, where he came from and what he did in Ireland . . . the attempt to make Patrick the pivotal figure to unite Irishmen in faith and life was doomed to fail when claims made him, for many people, the property of the Roman Catholic Church and Irish nationalism.[25]

However, not all St Patrick's Day celebrations in the period of the Troubles have sought to appropriate the saint for one or other side of the community. In 1979 there had been a cross-community committee organizing a Belfast St Patrick's Day parade. The success of such initiatives relied on the absence of party political posturing. At this time there were widespread protests in support of demonstrations by republican prisoners against the conditions of their incarceration. One group entered into the St Patrick's Day parade were intent upon preparing banners and floats which declared their support for the prisoners' campaign. While understandable in the context of the passions aroused by the prison protests, such an obvious politicization of the parade was too much for one committee member, who declared: 'I feel the St Patrick's Day parade should appeal to all sections of the community; to anyone who feels Irish.'[26] The clear problem for St Patrick's Day celebrations in Northern Ireland in the period of the Troubles was that Patrician observances could not be removed from their contemporary political context. Celebrations of a politically non-symbolic nature were a worthy aim, but given the conditions within Northern Ireland, and the entrenched feelings on both sides, such an embrace of a 'neutral' St Patrick's Day would always be difficult. Despite this, there have been many attempts at organizing celebrations that have been interdenominational, which have looked to build bridges across the community divide. Such events include a co-religious St Patrick's Day service at Down Church of Ireland cathedral in 1985, an ecumenical service in Downpatrick in 1994, and the participation, since 1994, of Protestants in the traditionally Catholic parade in Armagh. The biggest single attempt at creating consensus on St Patrick's Day, and a product of the climate engendered by the peace process, has been the attempt to stage, since 1998, a Belfast City Council St Patrick's Day parade.

The organization of such an event, through the work of Belfast City Council and the Making Belfast Work group, reflected a changing political atmosphere in Northern Ireland in the late 1990s. The staging of a St Patrick's Day event that was inclusive and intercommunity was greeted with enthusiasm by the local press:

> Belfast City centre will be awash with green on Tuesday as the City Hall prepares to welcome the St Patrick's Day parade for the first time ever. And the most important day in the calendar for Irish people worldwide, is also the perfect excuse for a fun filled children's festival, Draíocht, in West Belfast.[27]

The attendance at this 1998 event was estimated to be 80,000 people who assembled before a parade based on the theme of 'Myths, Legends and Realities', which involved hundreds of the city's young people. The symbolism of a cross-community St Patrick's Day parade through Belfast offered some evidence for the world's media that the entrenched political mind-set of people in conflict in Northern Ireland was changing. As a result, the parade gained wide coverage, especially on Irish, European and American broadcasting networks. Máirtín Ó Muilleoir argued that the 1998 celebration of St Patrick's Day in Belfast was a significant moment in the history of the city generally, and for the nationalist community specifically. He wrote that when the history of Belfast came to be written, 'St Patrick's Day 1998 will be seen as a turning point'.[28] For Ó Muilleoir, the parade was a symbol of the new Northern Ireland, a place where those tens of thousands who turned Belfast city centre black with green on Tuesday were doing more than scribbling footnotes, more than even contributing whole chapters to our history. They were shredding the pages of past wrongs, binning the Belfast of pogroms and second class citizenship, erasing the memory of too many Twelfths on the wrong side of a swagger stick.[29]

Despite the extensive media coverage and the generally positive images presented by Belfast's 1998 St Patrick's Day parade, the event did not meet with universal acclaim. Many Unionists objected to the nationalist symbolism that was attached to the parade by writers such as Ó Muilleoir, as well as the decision by parade organizers that 'all flags' would be welcome at the event. For diehard Unionists, the flying or parading of the Irish tricolour was an offensive act, which sought to identify St Patrick's Day with the forces of Irish nationalism and republicanism. Indeed, according to a government sub-committee which met to discuss the festivities, Unionists had been 'disappointed at the triumphalism which had been evident in the parade'.[30] The sub-committee concluded that such criticism by Unionists 'was seen by the public at large as petty especially given the times we are living in'.[31] Hence, despite unionist objections, a decision was made to proceed with another St Patrick's Day parade in 1999.

The 1999 parade, with the theme 'Earth, Wind and Fire', was provided with a grant of £50,000 by Belfast City Council towards organizational and staging costs. The sole condition was the event must be organized by a cross-community committee. Unionists within the City Council nonetheless attempted to block the awarding of the proposed grant; they were still concerned about the carrying of particular flags in the parade, and this was unresolved. As the planning for the 1999 parade progressed, the representatives of Protestant groups on the organizing committee withdrew. They refused to co-operate with the other committee members, and rejected every proposal to bring them back on board. Central to this intransigence was that Protestant groups opposed the ruling that allowed all flags, including the Irish tricolour, to be flown in the parade. Caitríona Ruane, Joint Chairperson of the committee, suggested that any ban would 'go against the spirit of the Good Friday Agreement [and] the ethos of a shared city', and that 'as soon as you ban any flag you will have thousands of that flag that you ban'.[32] As a result of the flag debate, the departure of the Protestant groups who had sat on the committee, and other complicating issues that surrounded the staging of the parade, none of the £50,000 grant that had been promised was paid over by January 1999. There was a belief among the parade organizers that the 'festival has been used as a political football by some elements of Belfast City Council'.[33] The fiasco was a regular cause of comment in editorial and feature columns in local newspapers. There was, it should be noted, plenty of support for the Protestant position. Eric Waugh, writing in the *Belfast Telegraph* under the heading 'The object of flaunting tricolours is to provoke', launched a stinging attack on the parading of the Irish flag on St Patrick's Day. He argued that the tricolour had nothing to do with St Patrick's Day, that its message was one of militant republicanism, and that while the flag was permitted in the parade, there 'was not the faintest hope of promoting a cross-community commemoration'.[34]

Many of the issues that related to the proposed 1999 St Patrick's Day parade were played out in Belfast City Council chambers. Such debates, though having the parade as their subject, were shaped and informed by the party politics of governing Belfast, as well as the pressures created by the Good Friday Agreement. In the wake of this document many symbolic issues, such as the flying of flags and the right to parade, became central to political debate. It was the Tourism committee of Belfast City Council that had granted £50,000 to the organizers of the St Patrick's Day parade. Unionist councillor Sammy Wilson, who argued that the Council should provide no funding or co-ordination for the parade, opposed the decision. By January 1999, the Social Democratic and Labour Party (SDLP) representatives on the Tourism committee were convinced that the whole issue of the parade was becoming counter-productive, and so withdrew their support from the decision to allocate £50,000 to the parade. The SDLP's concerns about the ongoing planning of the parade, despite the loss of the grant, resulted in amendments being placed before the Council's Development committee. The SDLP councillor, Alex Atwood, suggested that the St Patrick's Day parade be referred to the Parades Commission, the body that more normally decided on the routes of historically contentious Orange Order parades. However, the Sinn Féin councillor, Tom Hartley, argued:

> when one remembers the vast crowd of jovial and happy faces who celebrated that first '98 city centre St Patrick's Day, it is disturbing to think that a senior SDLP politician like Alex Atwood considers such a gathering a contentious parade and gives it the status of a sectarian march.[35]

The St Patrick's Day parade had been drawn into an area of debate centred on the politics of emblems and parade routes, issues that had been at the centre of many post-Good Friday disagreements in Northern Ireland. In January 1999, the Development Committee of Belfast City Council voted to not allow any funding for the parade that year, and that the council would only support the development of a cross-community event in 2000. The formal decision to withhold council funding was passed to the parade committee in February 1999, six weeks before the parade was due to take place. The decision to withhold funding was met by protests from the organizing committee of the St Patrick's Carnival. With a plea to all councillors to reverse their decision, the Joint Chairperson of the committee argued:

it is ironic that you can have a St Patrick's Carnival anywhere in the world except Belfast ... in our opinion Belfast City Council is at a crossroads. It can return to the bad old days of the past, or it can continue changing so it is fair and equitable in its dealings with all the citizens of Belfast.[36]

Without any central funding the parade committee was in an unenviable position; unless the £50,000 could be found from an alternative source, there would be no parade. The organizers approached local business leaders and other interested parties and raised the money. The parade went ahead, and was deemed a success by its committee. The theme of the parade, 'Earth, Wind and Fire', proved popular, while others took on 'the traditional look as thousands of shamrocks and saintly dress of green were content to mix with the "nouveau" ways of celebrating the day'.[37] Many Unionists construed the embrace of such traditional St Patrick's Day symbolism as representative of Irish nationalism. Despite the colour green and the shamrock being part and parcel of St Patrick's Day celebrations across the world, in a context of contested symbols and divided loyalties in Northern Ireland, their use was rejected by some sections of the unionist community. Although the parade organizers had lost many of the Protestant and unionist members of its committee, and also suffered from the withdrawal of its funding, it did confront the issue of political symbolism head on. The parade rules stated that all floats had to be registered with the committee, that no political party banners or speeches were allowed, and that no uniformed bands or those playing party tunes would be accepted.[38] However, the national flags of the Irish Republic or the United Kingdom were not banned, as any restriction on their use was considered impractical and unreasonable given that they represented the totality of states that made up the Irish isle.

Media coverage of the event was intense, though for the most part positive. The parade organizers were aware that while media interest was driven by the success of the previous year's event, it was also the product of 'the funding controversy that had been used as a political football by some politicians intent on scoring political points regardless of whose fun they were gambling with'.[39] The *Irish News*, in arguing that the 1998 Belfast St Patrick's Day celebrations had been a success, suggested that 'if Belfast wants to present an image of itself which is progressive and positive, there is no better vehicle than a St Patrick's Day Carnival'.[40]

ST PATRICK'S DAY IN BRITAIN

The celebrations of St Patrick's Day in Britain changed dramatically in the context of the Troubles. While the Irish in British society had never been openly embraced by all, and there was clearly a long history of anti-Irish mistrust and suspicion in many towns and cities, the early 1960s had offered some positive developments. As Chapter 5 demonstrated, St Patrick's Day celebrations in London were recognized by the British Prime Minister, prominent businesses and shops, and the major churches. In the post-1968 period, and more explicitly from 1974 when the IRA began its bombing campaign on the British mainland, there was an understandable, though regrettable, reaction against the local Irish. Across Britain, the Irish population suffered increased levels of abuse and discrimination; and, as a result of legislation such as the Prevention of Terrorism Act, many Irish residents were the subject of heightened police attention. As the Irish became more readily identified with a threat to the safety of British towns and cities, so St Patrick's Day ceased to be a popular public celebration. Whereas prior to the 1960s *The Times* had regularly featured reports of St Patrick's Day events across Britain, the onset of the Troubles constrained such reporting. There was a concentration on official events, such as the Queen Mother's annual presentation of shamrock to the Irish Guards,[41] or else reports of church services on St Patrick's Day, which centred around prayers for peace.[42] Increasingly, the Irish in Britain were observing 17 March only in the closed surroundings of their own sporting clubs and bars. There was now little prospect of them working, as they had done previously, with local and city councils to celebrate the day by way of a parade. The prosecution and imprisonment of Irish people living in Britain for bomb outrages such as those in Birmingham, Guildford and Woolwich, heightened British rejection of the local Irish. Equally, a gradual realization that the Guildford Four, the Maguires, and the Birmingham Six, were all the victims of miscarriages of justice, increased the sense of alienation amongst the Irish, making them increasingly anxious about their 'place' in British society.

In Britain, therefore, St Patrick's Day became a far less visible event through the 1970s and 1980s. The British press was far more likely to report the observance of 17 March by Irish Americans in New York, than it was to report on events in Birmingham or London. Celebrations like Irish Week became noticeable by their absence. Even companies such as Guinness, which in the 1990s used St Patrick's Day as a marketing tool in Britain, did not refer to the event in their British advertising during the two decades following the outbreak of the Troubles. That said, throughout the early 1980s, the Greater London Council (GLC) positively promoted the Irish community in the nation's capital, and supported special events such as St Patrick's Day. The GLC worked with the Irish Commission for Culture and Education and staged Siol Phadraig. The event was a cultural festival featuring Irish music, dance, literature and art.[43] In light of attacks on the GLC, and particularly its leader, Ken Livingstone, for the council's perceived left-wing tendencies and Livingstone's attendance at meetings with representatives of Sinn Féin, events such as Siol Phadraig were dismissed as being pro-republican. With the exception of the annual church parade in London, which was organized by the Council of Irish Counties, the only

Patrician events regularly promoted were those taking place in Irish pubs and clubs.[44] Even the church parade had fallen foul of the tensions surrounding the troubles: it was cancelled in 1972 owing to the dire political situation in Northern Ireland.[45]

By the 1990s, when open conflict in Northern Ireland had receded, clear shifts started to appear in the celebration of St Patrick's Day in Britain. The beginning of an identifiable peace process and diminishing hostility towards the Irish population in Britain produced a more open and inclusive series of St Patrick's Day events.[46] The more positive political environment of the 1990s also allowed for a steady growth of Irish celebrations across Britain on 17 March. In Manchester, for example, the first modern St Patrick's Day parade took place in 1990. Organized by the city's Irish World Heritage Centre, the event attracted only 375 participants in its inaugural year. The parade route was extended in 1993, so that the main city centre was included, and with this change the procession grew. By 1999, despite the IRA attack on the city three years earlier, it was estimated that over 15,000 participants and spectators took part in the parade, including some fifty floats and bands.[47]

The Council of Irish Counties organized the St Patrick's Day Church parade in London. This procession, which marched on the Sunday nearest 17 March from Horseguard's Parade to Westminster Cathedral to celebrate mass, featured Agnes O'Connell's London Pipe Girls Band. In 1990, Aer Lingus sponsored the event, but since the airline's band replaced that of O'Connell its 'support' proved controversial. In the same way that the advent of sponsorship had been criticized for sullying America's traditional parades in the 1950s, the dismissal of O'Connell's girls was seen as intrusive and crass. Correspondents to the letters pages of the *Irish Post* called for the reinstatement of the London Pipe Girls Band, with the familiar argument that this had 'been a traditional feature of the London parade, and much loved'.[48]

By the 1990s, concrete advances in the peace process, the global success of new Irish cultural forms, such as the music of U2, the spectacle of *Riverdance*, and the rise of a successful Irish football team, created a renewed interest in 'things Irish' abroad. In 1995, the Council of Irish County Associations held one of its biggest ever St Patrick's night dinners at the London Irish Centre, and its parade to Westminster Abbey attracted an increased number of spectators. In Coventry, a St Patrick's Day pageant was led by the city's Lord Mayor, and even the holiday camp company, Pontins, staged a residential St Patrick's Day party at its Prestatyn Sands complex in North Wales.[49] The annual Cheltenham National Hunt festival in horse racing, which often fell during St Patrick's week, was also embraced by the popular press as an 'Irish' event. A large proportion of the crowd travelled from Ireland, as did many of the trainers, jockeys and horses. While not a formal St Patrick's Day event, the Cheltenham festival, and its clear links to Ireland, were positively reported as a celebration of Irishness. This included countless headlines recounting the 'luck of the Irish' and offers of free tickets as part of promotions of Irish beer.[50] Birmingham's St Patrick's Day parade was resurrected in 1997; it had ceased in 1974 after the IRA's bombing of the city centre. In 2000, it was estimated that 80,000 people watched the Birmingham parade through the city centre streets.[51] In Coventry, Liverpool and London there were parades on St Patrick's Day that culminated in a special church mass. In Leeds, Derby, Woking, Ipswich, Harrogate, Milton Keynes, Hemel Hempstead and across London, various cultural events, dinners and dances were held. Many of these festivities, including Irish film festivals and literary events, were publicized across the whole of the community, and were not solely promoted among the Irish in Britain. Such an open celebration of St Patrick's Day in the 1990s, and, it might be suggested, the transformation of 17 March into an entertainment commodity, reflected wider socio-economic changes that had taken place in that decade. The comedian and television personality Ardal O'Hanlon wrote that in the late 1990s: 'I think it's a very good time to be Irish in Britain, speaking for myself . . . It's very fashionable to be Irish at the moment and I think everyone would like to be Irish.'[52] The profound changes that St Patrick's Day in Britain had undergone were reflected in an *Irish Post* survey of people's perceptions of what 17 March meant to them. Samuel Dunne, interviewed in 1995, argued:

> Being Irish in London, St Patrick's Day is a mark of respect of our ancestors, like an Irish Christmas day in some ways, seeing your family, reconnecting. I've lived here for twenty-seven years and every St Patrick's Day is like a cause for remembering and revisiting your Irishness.[53]

St Patrick, in this sense, seems like a green Father Christmas. Two years later, Olivia McCarthy considered that St Patrick's Day was 'a big day out basically and the religious aspect of it is forgotten by me as much as everyone else. There's the parades for the kids, but the adults just regard it as an excuse to drink.'[54] The views of Dunne and McCarthy, while snapshots, are representative of many of the Irish living in Britain. They have a deep understanding of how St Patrick's Day represents themes within the story of their community, such as emigration, national identity, family ties and religious devotion, yet they observe the day in different and very personal ways. The feeling that the parades 'are for the kids' can be understood within the context of the changing appearance of most British parades. In an attempt to attract an audience, and also to possibly make the parades non-ethnic and non-political, the various parade floats are now dominated by 'fun' entertainment figures such as the Simpsons, various Disney characters and other celebrities. The seismic shifts that have taken place with respect of British attitudes towards the Irish population, and the central place that St Patrick's

Day has within the celebration of Irishness, can also be seen among the Irish Protestant population living in Britain. One Protestant woman, from Northern Ireland, explaining why she occasionally described herself as Irish, commented that this would be done, 'if I'm not being very technically astute or very precise, or on St Patrick's Day'.[55] The world, it seemed, could be turned upside-down on 17 March, even if only for a day.

While the Irish population in Britain is large, it has no long-standing tradition of city-wide St Patrick's Day parades such as occur in North America. The Troubles have made the lives of the Irish in Britain more diffi-cult than their American counterparts. As such, St Patrick's Day does not have the same cultural fluency within the local community. Despite a resur-rection in recent years, St Patrick's Day events in Britain are still very much the preserve of the pub and the club, and are championed by beer com-panies. Celebrations of 17 March, while revealing much about the Irish in Britain, do not offer a public face of an entire community celebrating their shared, albeit different, ethnic and religious heritage. Although, as Bishop remarks, 'in recent years reticence about Irishness has diminished',[56] this may well be part of a wider process in Britain where various ethnic groups are now openly celebrating their ethnicity. While St Patrick's Day celebra-tions are steadily growing in size, and are important within the commercial sphere, the largest ethnic celebration in Britain is the Afro-Caribbean community's Notting Hill Carnival. Placed alongside St Patrick's Day, the Notting Hill Carnival, the various Asian Diwali events, Jewish New Year, and even the growth of the Highland Games, all demonstrate that ethnic festivals have been central to the gradual acceptance that Britain is a multi-cultural society.

ST PATRICK'S DAY IN CANADA

Among the diaspora, St Patrick's Day has long been a mix between celebra-tion of homeland and adopted home. Yet in Canada during the last quarter of the twentieth century, the Irish were effectively no longer an immigrant community. The majority of Canadians who self-declared as Irish had nine-teenth-century forebears from Ireland, and many of these people had never been to the ancestral homeland. Just as significantly, Irish Canadians now resided in a society that was becoming increasingly pluralistic in terms of migrant intake and linguistic practices. In 1867, when Canada confederated as a Dominion of Britain, the population was overwhelmingly of Anglo-Celtic or French descent. Around a hundred years later, immigrants were just as likely to be from other backgrounds, such as Italy, Greece, Poland, Mexico or the Philippines. As with any flourishing multicultural society, there has been significant overlap of ethnic lineage and customs. The Irish in Canada married into French and Italian families, or formed workplace rela-tionships and friendships with people from other backgrounds. Given these

changes, would St Patrick's Day still have resonance to this modern generation of Irish Canadians? And how would non-Irish family and friends
respond to the festivities?

The increased cultural diversity in 1960s Canada coincided with government initiatives to promote national unity, such as with political sanction of
state symbols and an official language. However, this evolving Canadian
nationalism had an important counterpoint in moves towards political separatism in the province of Quebec. According to French-speaking critics, late
twentieth-century Canada was, despite the rhetoric of cultural pluralism,
Anglocentric in terms of language and political power. It seemed, nonetheless, that some important changes had already taken place. In 1964, the
country was polarized by an acrimonious parliamentary debate over national
symbols. Advocates of change favoured a flag that would represent a
'modern' and 'forward-looking' Canada, while conservatives called for reten-
tion of the ensign that linked all the provinces to Britain.[57] The indigenous
Maple Leaf symbol won out; this suited French Canadians who objected to
saluting a flag with British connotations. Yet radical nationalists within the
French-Canadian community were not content with the symbolic 'neutrality' of this new national flag. Nor were they placated by the declaration, in
1969, that Canada had two official languages – English and French. Fran-
cophone activists argued that Quebec ought to have *separate* political and
linguistic status within Canada. That said, the French community in Montreal was not *isolationist*; it still engaged with English-speaking locals, many
of whom were Irish. Here, arguably, a special relationship between French
and Irish Montrealers developed, with St Patrick's Day providing a focus for
its expression.

In an article reflecting on St Patrick's Day in Montreal, the *Gazette* of 17
March 2000 argued that the French community had played a significant part
in raising the profile of the festivities over the previous twenty-five years:

> The St Patrick's parade received a new lease of life following the first
> election of the Parti Québécois in 1976. It became an occasion for
> English-speaking Montrealers to say 'we belong here too'; and for
> French-speaking Montrealers to assert their shared heritage – three
> Quebecers in seven have Irish roots.[58]

There was support for this Irish-French sense of camaraderie among
contemporaries. In 1980, a parade spectator, 46-year-old contractor, Olivia
O'Dubac, argued that:

> St Patrick's Day is so popular in Montreal because the Irish and the
> French are so alike. Both peoples love life and are, well, hot blooded.
> And the Irish blend well with the French community because they
> share the same religion.[59]

They sometimes also shared the same genes: when 22-year-old French speaker André Choquette attended the 1980 parade, replete with both shamrock and a pro-sovereignty association button affixed to his chest, he explained that his grandmother was Irish.[60] Fifteen years later, the French-Canadian Mayor of Montreal, Pierre Bourque, conceded that the St Patrick's Day festivities now outshone all others in the city: 'I've been to many parades – the St Jean-Baptiste and Canada Day parades – but this is quite special ... People came from all over the city to be here, and they're all united.' Certainly in terms of numbers the 1995 parade was imposing: 6,000 marchers, fifty floats, and thirty-seven marching bands performed before an estimated 500,000 spectators.[61] French support of St Patrick's Day, while important to the Irish festivities, could obviously not account for such broad-based public interest.

The United Irish Societies of Montreal promoted St Patrick's Day as a time for 'everybody' to be Irish. It was a message taken to heart. *Gazette* reporters found that many parade spectators made no claim to an Irish heritage, yet they each felt part of the festivities – many even wearing green top hats, ribbons and buttons as tributes to the day. In 1980, two-year-old Irene Hwang attended her first march, perched on her father's shoulders. Paul Hwang, a thirty-year-old neurology specialist from Singapore had been in Canada ten years, and was yet to miss a parade. 'I love it,' he said. 'It's not just for the Irish. It's the most multicultural event of the year.'[62] This view was confirmed by another Asian immigrant, Takoon Janmanee, who remarked in 1995: 'I've been to the last 10 parades ... I like it because it's non-political and everyone is welcome – not only the Irish.'[63] Perhaps the most significant vote for a feeling of inclusion came from a native Canadian, Kahnawake Grand Chief Joe Norton. Perched on the review stand, sipping Irish coffee, he explained his presence: 'They want everybody to participate – that's why I enjoy it ... I think we can add to the parade by being here. This is a day when all nationalities can be Irish.'[64] There was certainly enough diversity in the parade itself to reinforce the Chief's impression. Overall, there were 168 groups in the procession, including marching bands, majorette corps, church parishes and Irish societies. Scattered among them were entries that, as the *Gazette* put it, 'were not strictly Irish'. Yet this seemed to be a cause for celebration: there was plenty of applause for the 'Montreal Shriners', the oriental band from the Karnak Temple. They were 'dressed as Arabs and played music more suited to a belly-dance than an Irish jig'. Just as surprising, but also well received, was a band from the Tijuana Mexican Restaurant in New York State, who played – of all things on St Patrick's Day – 'La Cucuracha'. Organizers encouraged these type of entries: indeed, the Arab troupe from the Karnak Temple won the trophy for the 'best all-round unit' in the parade.[65]

The *Gazette* of 17 March 2000 forecast yet another popular parade in Montreal, with a turnout in excess of 500,000 spectators. A factor in the festival's success, argued the paper, was its capacity to engage all: 'Inclusiveness, as in years past, will be the glue that binds this year's parade.' In keeping with this expectation, the 2000 procession featured representatives of eight ethnic minority groups, among which were Poles, Danes, Greeks and Filipinos. And, although the local gay and lesbian community was not part of the march, which conjured up images of conflicts in Boston and New York (see pp. 222–6), parade organizers in Montreal insisted that this was not a case of prejudice on their part. Rather, they had not been approached by gay and lesbian groups requesting to join the parade.[66] The theme of inclusion was apparent also in the imagination. Messages of hope for cross-community solutions in Northern Ireland were expressed during the 1995 Montreal parade, with event organizer Thomas Fitzgerald trusting that 'we're all playing a small part in promoting peace'.[67]

The act of people toasting each other with drink in bars and pubs left the scents of whiskey and beer wafting along the parade route. It was both the right and the wrong time, then, for a message of temperance. In an article entitled 'St Patrick's Crowd Has Harsh Tone', the *Gazette* reported:

> Maybe it was to be expected, given that St Patrick's Day is, well, St Patrick's Day. But as a float bearing an anti-drug and anti-alcohol slogan made its way east along St Catherine St during yesterday's 166th annual St Patrick's Day parade it was booed. And booed. And booed.[68]

While a message of sobriety was unlikely to appeal on the very day when drunkenness seemed fashionable, there were specific effects of intoxication that concerned parade organizers. Loud-mouthed, drunken youths had directed what the *Gazette* described as 'vulgar and even hateful comments towards attractive women on the parade's three dozen floats'. Police made no arrests for anti-social behaviour, but there was a widespread belief that, by comparison with previous years, the 1990 parade had attracted an inordinate number of 'jerks'. Alcohol consumption was a feature of St Patrick's Day, but if it attracted unruly drinkers, then it became an impediment to the family atmosphere and inclusive nature of the celebrations.[69] There was also the matter of economic return to consider: the Montreal Tourist Bureau billed the St Patrick's Day parade as 'a major attraction' for visitors to the city.[70]

No surprise, then, that there were calls to 'reform' the Montreal procession. Peggy Curran, writing for the *Gazette*, compared the 'old' with the 'new', finding fault and favour in each:

> Back in the days when the Montreal parade was a parochial event, it was made up mainly of men in black top coats, high hats and white silk scarves following a banner naming their church. It was a solemn

affair. Exclusive and not very flashy, but not tacky either. Now it's more cosmopolitan ... Yet for every clown and Newfie dog in a green bandana, a dozen publicity stunts must fall ... Put a lid on hucksters selling green plastic bowler hats and shots of whiskey. Ban drinking on floats. Suggest the bands know how to play at least one Irish song. And here's a final revolutionary thought. Maybe, just maybe, it's time to ask a woman to be Grand Marshal.[71]

The commercialization, secularism and hedonism of the St Patrick's Day parade prompted clerics to try to remind Montrealers that this was, in fact, a religious occasion. The Reverend Brian Boucher, Catholic chaplain at McGill University, argued that 'despite the merriment associated with St Patrick's Day weekend, there is a serious spiritual side to the event based on the patron saint of Ireland'. He conceded that 'maybe over time the social side has predominated, but the roots are highly Christian ... The foundation is faith.'[72] In light of Curran's article this seemed a message of hope more than certainty. For the only sure thing was that Montreal's cosmopolitan and inclusive St Patrick's Day had, as its foundation, feelings of fun and pleasure.

If there was a tangible spiritual awakening on St Patrick's Day it might well have surfaced with the revival of the Toronto parade in 1988. Here again, though, the foundation was amusement, with little effort to remember the life of Ireland's patron Saint. Eamonn O'Loghlin, a member of the Irish-Canadian music and cultural association Comhaltas Ceoltoiri Eireann, announced that 'the parade will have no political or religious significance. It's a fun thing. Something like the Rose Bowl.'[73] O'Loghlin concluded that 'in the past there might have been some hostility between different segments ... the old Orange and Green thing ... Today people are more willing to live and let live. Toronto as a city has matured.'[74] As far as O'Loghlin was concerned 'Irish Canadians – whether from Dublin or Belfast – are one people and want to share their traditions, customs, culture and history with fellow Canadians.'[75] Just in case his assessment was a tad optimistic, organizers brought in a rule that prevented 'partisan' groups from marching in the parade. This prevented the Irish Freedom Association from joining the procession in 1989. The *Toronto Star* noted that 'everyone in downtown Toronto had a reason to be Irish' on St Patrick's Day, not only the fifty floats and bands and 60,000-strong crowd, but even Irish wolfhounds with green scarves and a horse dyed green. The paper boasted that 'the only reminder of the religious and political differences that have torn Northern Ireland apart was a small protest by members of the Irish Freedom Association'.[76] While it was, as the St Patrick's Parade Society commented, admirable to see 'people from all parts of Ireland, of all religious denominations, walking together and having fun while doing it', they were undoubtedly restrained from making comments about the situation in

Northern Ireland, and the parade itself was said to have no religious or political connotations. This was clever stage management. But as the Deputy Irish Prime Minister, Brian Lenihan, acted as Grand Marshal for the 1989 parade, it was no wonder that the Irish Freedom Association accused organizers of double standards. Apparently Lenihan was neither a politician, nor a representative of a political party.

OBSERVANCE OF ST PATRICK'S DAY IN AUSTRALIA: 1972–2000

During the first seven decades of the twentieth century, Melbourne's St Patrick's Day parade overshadowed those in other cities. Elsewhere in Australia such processions were less noticeable; Patrician festivities tended to focus instead on sports carnivals, race meetings, the pub and church services. The demise of Melbourne's St Patrick's Day march in 1970 suggested that this parading custom might well die out. The seeds of a concerted revival were sown, surprisingly enough, in Sydney eight years later. This city had been denied an official St Patrick's Day parade ever since 1895, when Cardinal Moran – a temperance advocate – had cancelled the procession because of a tendency among marchers to gravitate to pubs afterwards. From thereafter, the St Patrick's Day Sports Carnival and various dinners, dances and musical events became standard fare in Sydney around 17 March. Why the sudden revival in 1978?

The *Irish Echo* dubs Irish expatriate Seamus Byrne as the 'founding father of the Saint Patrick's Day parade in Sydney'.[77] In the late 1970s Byrne was both President of the Gaelic Athletic Association and Secretary of the Irish National Association (INA), an Australian-based Irish republican group, in New South Wales. At INA meetings in 1977 he tried to stimulate interest in staging a St Patrick's Day parade. He recalls that the association 'weren't real keen' about the idea at this point.[78] A proposal to hold a St Patrick's Day march was also tabled in 1978 at the Irish community's Communication Council, which then involved the INA, the GAA, the Gaelic Club and Irish musicians' clubs. Bob Cunningham, who served as Grand Marshal of the Sydney parade, explains that the suggestion did not go further because that council 'collapsed'.[79] Byrne, who was still committed to getting a St Patrick's Day march going, pressed on – this time seeking support from INA president Michael Durkan. Within six weeks Byrne, Durkan and a handful of others from both within the INA and other Irish organizations, had put together Sydney's first significant St Patrick's Day procession for eighty-three years.[80]

The march began modestly enough, but by the mid-1980s had become renowned enough to attract sponsorship. A St Patrick's Day concert, too, was added to the programme of events.[81] Management of the festivities was now the responsibility of the St Patrick's Day Committee, which first assumed this role in 1980. The *Irish Exile* was impressed by the progress made: in 1989 the paper remarked that this was 'the tenth parade organised by the committee, who have watched it grow from a trickle to a stream to the river it is today'.[82] By 1991, the St Patrick's Day procession had become a feature event in Sydney's social calendar. Police put the number of people who lined the parade route at 100,000, which easily made it the biggest Patrician march in the city's history. The Parade Committee President, John Bradley, admitted to being 'overwhelmed' by the public response, which also included a crowd of 30,000 at the St Patrick's Day concert in Prince Alfred Park.[83] All this excitement had been generated by the Irish community itself; the initiative was independent of the church. A.P. Quinn, an *Irish Echo* columnist, concludes that, 'The focus [of St Patrick's Day] became social rather than political, family rather than religious.'[84]

The festivities of 1992 were also notable. Bradley was succeeded by Martin Coleman as President of the Parade Committee. To the surprise of many, he convinced Sydney City Council that the committee's annual Irish parade took precedence over the sixtieth anniversary of the opening of the Sydney Harbour Bridge. The dates for both of these events had clashed: 'the bridge lost'.[85] These were heady days. The Parade Committee, keen to bring novelty to the celebrations, unravelled what it described as the world's 'largest shamrock' – 30 feet high and 27 feet wide – which was to be a key promotion tool. Coleman announced that he was 'determined to see the Sydney parade break new ground ... So as a contribution to the environmental development of Australia, the committee is organising the planting of 50,000 trees in the next twelve months.'[86] The Irish Greening Australia project had the support of twenty-five municipal councils. The wearing of the green on St Patrick's Day was now not only a symbol for Irishness; it was also a metaphor for an environmentally sustainable city. The parade itself, which included twenty-two marching bands and more than forty floats, was again declared a success by both organizers and the media. There were even murmurs that Sydney planned to give New York a run for its money as hosting the biggest St Patrick's Day procession in the world.[87] After all, Sydney already had the biggest shamrock – it was even fluorescent!

The theme for the 1993 parade was the 100th anniversary of the formation of the Gaelic League in Ireland. One of the best floats was that entered by the INA, which depicted 'the history of the [Irish] language from the time of the druids and bards to the language today'.[88] First prize of $2,000 went to the Kildare Association, for its 'authentic re-enactment of an 18th century wedding in St Brigid's Church'.[89] So there was an effort on the part of organizers to engage with Irish heritage and culture. New entrants to the parade included 'the Sydney mounted police, vintage cars, and a special unit of 55 people from Irish clubs in San Francisco'.[90] This was all part of the Parade Committee's vision 'to challenge New York for the best Parade title'.[91] The festivities were, indeed, an unqualified success, but they hardly rivalled the parade along Fifth Avenue. Locally, though, St Patrick's Day had become both popular and respectable. The Lord Mayor of Sydney, Frank Sartor, hosted a special civic reception for the 1993 Parade Committee, Irish-Australian dignitaries, and members of the NSW parliament. The future of St Patrick's Day in Sydney looked bright indeed.

By 3 November 1993 chaos reigned within the Parade Committee. Factional disputes had been brewing for over eighteen months, and they came to a head with the resignation from the committee of Coleman and eight others, this leaving just eleven members. Included among them were each of the five INA delegates, including Denis O'Flynn, Vice-President of the Parade Committee. Coleman explained later that the resignations were 'in protest and anger at the selfish and irresponsible actions of an outside association [the INA] that wantonly meddled in the affairs of our committee'.[92] Meanwhile, Bob Cunningham concluded that owing to 'the resignations of key people who organised the parade, I as Grand Marshal had no choice but to disband that committee'.[93] A public meeting was called for 24 November 1993, which was attended by 300 members of Sydney's Irish-Australian community. A 21-member committee was elected, with Coleman returned as president, and Phil Garde, also a previous member of the committee, appointed as the new vice-president. The election was held in the midst of extraordinary scenes. INA President (and now former Parade Committee Vice-President) Denis O'Flynn challenged the validity of the meeting and its elections. He carried with him a solicitor's letter of legal opinion that the nine remaining members of the previous organizing group 'still existed' as the Parade Committee, and that this group retained sole authority to organize the 1994 parade, which O'Flynn insisted they would do, regardless of the meeting just held.[94] Just as significantly, he warned, 'any individual or group which carries on the business of the St Patrick's Day Parade committee without the authority of the INA risks being held liable under the Business Names Act and the Charitable Collections Act'.[95] In a Machiavellian move, O'Flynn had recently changed the business name of the Parade Committee so that it was registered solely to the INA.

O'Flynn also claimed that the St Patrick's Day parade had originally been revived by the INA, and that the event had been subsidized by that organization over a number of years. In this view, the publicly elected committee was guilty of trying to take over an event that the INA had conceived and nurtured. From another perspective, the INA was trying to railroad the Irish community into believing that it 'owned' the parade. Seamus Byrne, the 'founding father' of Sydney's St Patrick's Day march, agreed that the INA had 'underwritten the parade through the hard years', yet the event was not privately run. He accepted that the INA had played a key role in the Parade Committee, but the St Patrick's Day march – and its management – belonged to the Irish community of Sydney.[96] The 'two' Parade Committees were brought together on two occasions after the 24 November meeting, but the INA-backed group refused to compromise. It was, according to O'Flynn, the registered legal guardian and business proprietor of the St Patrick's Day parade. In response, the *Irish Echo* reported, 'the community elected committee decided in an effort to avoid embarrassment to the general community', that they would not press ahead with plans to organize a parade for 1994.[97] This tactic, however noble, allowed the INA to assume complete control over the forthcoming festivities. An enormous row erupted in Sydney's Irish community, with some organizations threatening to boycott the 1994 parade, while others confirmed their support for the INA.[98] By February, twelve Irish community groups had announced their withdrawal from the festivities.[99] But the show went on. It was smaller than the previous couple of years, but was still a spectacle that attracted crowds.

The Parade Committee annual general meeting of 30 September 1994 did not allow election of new officials. This infuriated Coleman and his supporters, who appealed to the Irish Ambassador to Australia, Martin Burke, to act as an arbitrator. He recommended that the 1995 parade should proceed under the current committee, but after then 'a meeting would be convened under the auspices of the Irish National Association involving all the constituted Irish Associations and Societies [of Sydney] which would democratically elect a committee membership for the 1996 parade'.[100] The political stage seemed set. But the INA was not about to be voted out of existence on the Parade Committee. At the annual general meeting in August 1995, the INA 'introduced a clause which stipulated that nominees for the three executive positions on the committee must be members of the INA and must have spent at least one year on the committee'.[101] There were objections that this was not part of the so-called 'Bankstown Agreement' initiated by the Irish Ambassador; but O'Flynn disagreed, claiming that it fell within the spirit of that agreement.[102] The INA retained its control of the Parade Committee in 1996, and continues to do so today.

The infighting eroded camaraderie within Sydney's Irish-Australian community. Yet St Patrick's Day continued, as ever. A key question, though, is had it progressed or regressed under the guardianship of O'Flynn and the INA? Crowds who turned out for the 1996 and 1997 parades were estimated by police to be 35,000 and 20,000 respectively – significantly smaller than those of the early 1990s. The parades themselves were a mixed bag of insight and nonsense. The Dublin Association won second prize for its float depicting the dove of peace – a clear reference to hopes for the future of Northern Ireland. There was no prize for the Foxtel-sponsored float featuring a huge inflatable Bart Simpson.[103] The *Irish Echo*, though hardly a neutral observer in that it had vehemently opposed the INA's control over the parade, complained that more imagination needed to go into future celebrations. Perhaps, the paper suggested, a parade theme could be promoted, such as Irish music. The *Echo* concluded: 'A couple of kids on the back of a truck or a few balloons streaming from a car cannot be said to truly represent what the Irish in Australia are all about.'[104] Stronger criticisms emerged in the wake of the 1998 parade, and from a quarter with influence – the NSW police. Senior Sergeant Peter Leenane described it as 'the worst ever'; the parade was poorly organized, with gaps of a block long. He slammed 'alcohol problems' related to the event, and suggested that the Parade Committee 'temper it a bit and become more family oriented'. An entry of a pram stuffed full of VB beer cans did not seem to show anything distinctive about St Patrick's Day. The public of Sydney were also voting with their feet. According to the police, only 5,000 spectators turned out to witness the 1998 parade.[105] And it is not as if Sydneysiders are reticent about attending public events of this kind. The Gay and Lesbian Mardi Gras, held annually, has in recent years attracted anywhere between 300,000 and 500,000 spectators.

The 1999 St Patrick's Day parade was re-routed to try to make it a better spectacle. Frank O'Connell, the INA's latest choice for President of the Parade Committee, was very pleased that the procession flowed smoothly this time. There had been plenty of effort put in to promote the event, and this paid off with a crowd of 15,000 to witness the march, and some 14,000 at the subsequent concert in the Domain. The festivities for 2000 reflected a more determined approach on the part of organizers. Levels of sponsorship increased, the presentation of floats improved, and the Sydney City Council hosted a pre-parade reception for 100 dignitaries.[106] An evergreen Kerry Murphy, 86 years old and with flowing white beard, looked the part as the float carrying St Patrick and the Celtic cross made its way through the city.[107] Police estimated the crowd that lined the procession route at 57,000 people. Sydneysiders were again voting with their feet, this time in the affirmative. The future of the parade is, however, not assured. In March 2001 the Sydney Harbour Foreshore Authority launched a 'St Patrick's Weekend Festival' at the historic and picturesque Rocks area. The event was replete with Irish music and food, and films – all of which were free. Meanwhile, the Parade Committee was hit with a total bill of A$73,000 to block off city streets for the duration of the procession, and for the cost of employing traffic wardens and security guards along the parade route. O'Connell confided to the *Australian* that 'he fears the parade may be sunk altogether next year if the parade and Rocks festival are held on the same day'.[108] But perhaps common sense will prevail.

Clearly, the mantle of Australia's most significant St Patrick's Day parade has been with Sydney for the past two decades. Patrician marches are now also staged in other capital cities in Australia, most notably Melbourne, Brisbane and Perth, but they are not on the same scale as the Sydney exhibition. The once imposing St Patrick's Day parade in Melbourne made a faltering resumption in the 1970s,[109] but struggled for public support, waxing and waning over the next two decades. In recent years the parade has attracted some 10,000 or so spectators, with a crowd of around 15,000 attending the musical concert in the evening. The public response has improved but is still modest, despite the goodwill and best efforts of Melbourne's organizers.[110] Elsewhere 17 March is observed widely, but the format tends to be music and drink at the local Irish-Australian pub, or attendance at a St Patrick's Day race meeting. In this regard, the religious symbolism of the anniversary has little or no meaning to most Australians, even among Catholics, for a majority of this group are nominal rather than practising Christians.[111] St Patrick's Day is, as ever, a great excuse to celebrate – even though what is being celebrated is not always clear to revellers. Nonetheless, a secular and fun-filled 17 March accords with the image of St Patrick's Day now promoted by parade and festival organizers. The president of Melbourne's Irish Festival Committee, Patrick O'Reilly, commented in 1996 that, 'The celebrations of St Patrick's Day in Melbourne have changed from a strong [Irish] nationalistic religious approach to a more family oriented joyful celebration.'[112] Knox purged Melbourne's parade of its Irishness during the 1960s, substituting it with an assertive Catholicism; now the march is non-partisan in terms of faith.

None of this means, of course, that the churches are unwelcome on St Patrick's Day. But religious triumphalism is a *faux pas*. In March 1997, the *Irish Echo* announced that some 3,500 children from Catholic schools would march in the Melbourne parade. Comparatively few of these students would have been born in Ireland or had parents who emigrated from Ireland, so the St Patrick's Day connection was not immediately clear. However, Kay O'Sullivan, interviewed by the *Irish Echo*, provided a context:

> It is nearly thirty years since the Catholic kids last marched on St Patrick's Day ... today's march is different to those that have gone before. There is no political agenda. Today, the traditional bearers of the Catholic faith, the Kathleens, Brendans, and Eamonns, will be marching alongside a United Nations of names like Tran, Ai-Minh and Siao ... all points of the globe will be represented. And for that reason alone, today, St Patrick's Day is a great day for the Irish, the English, the Vietnamese, the Cambodian and everyone else who cares to come to the party.[113]

To take this global argument further, though, children from non-Catholic schools ought to be welcome, should they choose to participate, in the St Patrick's Day parade. This assumes, of course, that the event is now ecumenical, as implied by festival president O'Reilly.

Finally, what does St Patrick's Day in contemporary Australia stand for? The notion of 'everyone partying' on St Patrick's Day, while laudable in a multicultural society, avoids the underlying need to grapple with the *Irishness* of 17 March. Is St Patrick's Day only about *entertainment*? If so, all that is needed is to wear something green, listen to Van Morrison or the Corrs, and then drink Guinness, Jameson's whiskey, or lime cordial. Or is it a *national festival* in Australia's ethno-religious calendar (along with Greeks, Italians, Germans, etc.)? If so, then St Patrick's Day is a time to *understand* the lives of others. It can certainly be both. Celebration, in that respect, is not only about pleasure; it also has much to do with appreciation, which involves musing, questioning and deliberating about the meaning of St Patrick's Day and Irishness.

ST PATRICK'S DAY IN AMERICA

It was the Troubles in Northern Ireland, and then a debate that centred on the rights of Irish-American gay and lesbian groups to march in parades that dominated the post-1968 history of St Patrick's Day in America. Despite such controversies, the number of St Patrick's Day parades staged across America grew year by year from the 1970s. Even towns and cities with no noticeable Irish population and no historic links to Ireland began staging an annual celebration. In the late 1990s, the Irish-American magazine, *World of Hibernia*, listed the major St Patrick's Day festivities around the United States. The largest was the parade through Manhattan, which attracted 150,000 marchers and a crowd of 1.5 million. Second came Boston with 10,000 marchers in 1999, and a crowd of a million. The most important parade of the southern states, Savannah, was third. St Patrick's Day in the capital of Georgia has been celebrated since 1824: today it is a bank and school holiday, and its four-hour parade typically attracts a crowd of some 400,000. The fourth largest parade, in Kansas City, Missouri, was founded in 1973: it now attracts a crowd of some 250,000 and around 1,200 marchers. Similarly, the Cleveland parade involves 10,000 marchers and an annual crowd of approximately 250,000. Chicago's Southside gathers 12,000 marchers and 230,000 spectators, while the seventh largest parade is across the city in Downtown Chicago, featuring 2,000 marchers and 200,000 watching from the sidelines.[114] The final two parades in the list of St Patrick's Day big draws are those in Philadelphia and Pearl River, NY. These attracted 12,000 and 10,000 marchers, and crowds of 150,000 and 90,000 respectively in the late 1990s.[115]

One of the liveliest US parades, though not the biggest, is that which takes place in New Orleans. Founded in the 1930s, the parade is held on a Sunday to avoid Lenten restrictions. It attracts marchers and spectators from across New Orleans' diverse ethnic populations, and has always had an open policy with respect of gay and lesbian participation. The celebrations, while not on the same scale as the city's most famous carnival event, are run in the manner of a Mardi Gras rather than a typical St Patrick's Day parade:

> Parades here are participatory events. Borrowing from Carnival, we don't just wave and applaud. We scramble for beads and cups and

whatever else is thrown. On St Patrick's Day we scramble for cabbages. And potatoes. And onions. Everything but the corned beef.[116]

The tradition of throwing vegetables into the crowd was developed in the 1940s, and is used to symbolize the hunger that drove many Irish emigrants away from their home nation, and the poverty that they suffered on their arrival in New Orleans. City officials periodically warn those in the parade against throwing the larger vegetables, but 'to the participants, the tossing of the cabbages is part of the fun, and the crowd cheers a strong arm, and a fine catch'.[117] Other important parades that have grown in stature in recent years include those in Dallas[118] and in San Francisco,[119] both of which featured other cultural events such as Gaelic football matches, snake races and dances. Many small towns across America also host St Patrick's Day parades. Erin, in Tennessee, began its St Patrick's Day celebrations in 1963, despite having no sizeable or identifiable Irish population, and no recent history of emigration. The various festivities, ranging from a beauty pageant to road races, are open to all.[120] St Patrick's Day events, whether in New Orleans or Erin, are an American-invented tradition. They tend not to commemorate a distant, even reminiscent Irish ancestry, instead celebrating 17 March as a local, Irish-American entertainment extravaganza.

It appears, therefore, that the continued success of St Patrick's Day parades in America lies in the psyche of the American, rather than Irish nation. If St Patrick's Day celebrations are understood, certainly by the mid-twentieth century, as supportive of American patriotism, their long-standing attraction may be better understood. As Davies has argued: 'Americans have long been a nation of joiners ... Americans have also long been ardently and aggressively patriotic ... being thus both gregarious and nationalistic, Americans have naturally turned to forming numerous patriotic societies.'[121] That said, Irish Americans have remained painfully aware of the links between their chosen home and the land of their forefathers. The parades are markers of the success of Irish enterprise, and a celebration of the liberty that was won in America. They also serve an important purpose in interpreting events back in Ireland. Parades and other forms of St Patrick's Day celebration are assertions of 'a powerful conviction that Ireland's destiny would be determined as much by what happened in America'.[122] This dual vision of Irish America, one part which looks to America, the other to Ireland, continues today.

To some Americans, though, the celebration of the Irish national day has seemed an historical anachronism, with little relevance to modern America. In the 1960s, US news was dominated by events in South East Asia, and at home by the ongoing civil rights movement. The upsurge of violence in Northern Ireland, while of concern, did not appear overwhelming compared to other trouble spots. The 'issue' of Northern Ireland was also constrained, in part, by a realization that the Irish were now part of mainstream America;

hence their sense of ethnicity, their claim of solidarity to a 'cause' in the Irish homeland was fragmented. The *Boston Globe* of March 1969 concluded wryly of St Patrick's Day:

> every year at this time, the Congressional Record becomes more bloated than usual, bulging with long Joycean sentences in praise of St Patrick, the Irish, Robert Emmet, de Valera and the rising of the moon. It is a quaint enterprise for the solidarity that made St Patrick's Day an important American institution, is gone now, anaesthetised by the Ed Sullivan Show and smothered in suburban shopping malls.[123]

St Patrick's Day, while still a significant moment on the American calendar, was by the late 1960s celebrated within an Irish-American community that had largely assimilated, climbed the social ladder and suburbanized. The nature of annual Patrician celebrations was little changed, but the previous dynamic that demanded Irish Americans be recognized by the wider society within which it lived, was now irrelevant. Irish Americans were clearly part and parcel of American society. Such assimilation also meant that celebrating St Patrick's Day was an unquestioned part of the annual fabric of American life. As Byron has put it: 'On St Patrick's Day, I wore something green to school like everyone else. It was merely something that we did without ever asking why, like exchanging cards on St Valentine's day.'[124] By the last decades of the twentieth century, it is possible to understand the American experience of St Patrick's Day, not as representing a largely distinctive Irish-American ethnic experience, as had been necessary in the past, but instead a celebration of an assimilated American-Irish identity. In the words of Byron, St Patrick's Day, is now 'a quintessentially American institution that owes relatively little to Ireland, and is Irish in only superficial ways'.[125] While, as will be shown, the politics of Northern Ireland did shape St Patrick's Day celebrations in America from the late 1960s, its predominant focus was internal (American), rather than external (Irish). The St Patrick's Day celebrations of the late twentieth century should be understood not as displays and celebrations of *ethnic* Irishness, but rather as large-scale and warm-hearted embraces of Irish *citizenship* in America. Byron concludes that to assert or to 'be Irish on St Patrick's Day is to claim membership of the fully assimilated mainstream of middle Americans who have left the cultural baggage of their immigrant origins behind them'.[126] Such themes of successful assimilation and Americanization nonetheless papered over real changes. By the 1960s and 1970s, the Irish population in America was dwindling and growing older. The attendance at Irish clubs and cultural events fell year by year, with some of these closing their doors for good. Yet the St Patrick's Day parade remained the most visible symbol of the American Irish. Indeed, the New York parade chairman argued in 1980 that 'without the parade many people wouldn't think there were any Irish in

New York'.[127] The parade thus continued, despite seeming scarcely relevant to the changing experiences of Irish Americans.

Despite its shifting internal focus, the political dynamic that reinvigorated St Patrick's Day, and which provided many Irish Americans with a renewed sense of a cause, was supplied by events in Northern Ireland. The onset of the Troubles in Northern Ireland stirred up strong emotions in America, not only among the diaspora, but across many sections of the population. The early years of the Troubles were, however, played out against the torrid debate about American involvement in the Vietnam War. From 1968, images of the violence on the streets of Belfast, Derry and elsewhere, fought for space on the television news with the unprecedented media coverage of Vietnam and associated protests in America. For many Irish Americans, the direct involvement of British troops on the streets of Northern Ireland was yet another sign of the historical suppression of Ireland by her neighbour. The fighting in Northern Ireland was shocking, though it seemed to echo upheavals taking place in various world 'trouble spots'.

From March 1969, as the scope of the Troubles was now being realized by many politicians in the United States, there was an upswing in Irish diplomatic initiatives to Washington. It was clearly important, given the Troubles and the difficulties of a close Anglo-Irish governmental relationship, that Ireland had foreign political support. America, as ever, was where the Irish turned to. On St Patrick's Day, 1969, the Irish Ambassador to America, William P. Fay, visited the White House. He made a presentation of shamrock to the First Lady, Mrs Nixon, as the 17 March was the day on which she celebrated her birthday in line with her Irish father's wishes.[128] The presentation took place during a private audience between Mrs Nixon, the President and the ambassador. On reporting to the Department of Foreign Affairs in Dublin, the ambassador suggested that 'this was certainly one of the most successful, and from the public relations point of view, most important ceremonies of its kind in which I have participated'.[129] The celebration of St Patrick's Day in 1969 was warmly embraced by President Nixon, who stated that all Americans 'are Irish for today'. Congressman Leonard Farbstein, 'whose name excludes any undue partiality for the Irish', argued that 17 March was a celebration not only of 'the spirit of the Irish ... but of the indomitable spirit of all peoples'.[130] The ambassador felt that such an endorsement of St Patrick's Day generally, and of the Irish specifically, demonstrated that the American nation was a strong and powerful ally for Ireland.

The increased profile given to events in Northern Ireland by the media, and marked by diplomatic events in the White House, was seen by many Irish Americans as an opportunity to transform the nature of St Patrick's Day celebrations. As shown in the previous chapter, the celebration of St Patrick's Day in the 1950s and 1960s had been dogged by cheap sentimentality, drunkenness and poor-quality commemorative merchandise. The celebrations in South Boston, although not alone in being renowned for their associated drunkenness, had earned a degree of infamy. An article in the *Boston Evening Globe* in 1972, argued that on St Patrick's Day 'too much booze is the problem . . . booze rated number one, and the most popular conversational ploy was "gimme another beer" '.[131] It was argued that neither civic nor business leaders wanted the South Boston celebrations, and that both Irish government officials and recent emigrants were contemptuous of 'the emotional vomit that has marked St Patrick's Day in South Boston'.[132] The article's author, Jeremiah V. Murphy, argued that the arrival of Northern Ireland on the television screens of America, the imagery of Bloody Sunday and the high level of killings, should make those celebrating St Patrick's Day stop and think. Ireland was not a mythical place of leprechauns and shillelaghs, but a place where people died. The article closed by imploring people to remember that 'getting fall down drunk on March 17 maligns the memory of brave men and women . . . [as] sloppy drunks distort and dishonour the Irish heritage'.[133] In response to such pleas, which were a common feature of writing in both American and specifically Irish-American newspapers of the 1960s and 1970s, little changed. In Boston, various members of the Kennedy family took the applause of the crowd, while local politicians met in Dorgan's for their annual lunch of corned beef and cabbage. But the high levels of drunkenness remained.

During the Troubles, the American St Patrick's Day marches became a focus for protest against the British presence in Northern Ireland. At the New York parade of 1970, four men unfurled a banner demanding 'Civil Rights for Northern Ireland'. This was done in full view of Cardinal Cooke who was watching the parade from the steps of St Patrick's Cathedral. The demonstrators were quickly arrested, and according to one news report the policemen were encouraged to 'Hit them boys! Knock their heads!'[134] During the same parade, demonstrators from the Irish National Association for Irish Justice also protested outside the offices of the British Overseas Airways Corporation, and thirty people who marched with the American Irish Committee for Freedom in North Ireland shouted 'British troops out' and 'Civil rights for Ireland now' as they walked the parade route.[135] In the same year, the British envoy's Boston offices were besieged by members of the Committee for Justice in Northern Ireland and the Irish Republican Committee.[136] In 1972, members of the Irish Republican Aid Committee preceded the main body of the Boston parade along the march route. In a protest against the British presence in Northern Ireland they carried a coffin draped in an Irish tricolour and wore black armbands. The leader of the protest, Jim Dunn, argued that, 'We don't think bands should be playing and people cheering while people are dying in Belfast and Derry.'[137] Despite the intervention of Northern Irish politics into the arena of the American parade, the St Patrick's Day celebrations were carefully monitored through the 1970s for symbols of Irishness that were deemed inappropriate. The *New*

York Times noted in 1970 that 'every effort was made to keep the spectacle free of gimmickry and comic innovation – its character is essentially martial'.[138]

On the day after the St Patrick's Day parade, newspaper reports concentrated on the number of marchers, the size of the crowds, the weather, those marchers who did something unusual or humorous, the members of the reviewing stand and the Irish roots of the Grand Marshal.[139] This helped to give the annual ritual a sense of continuity. Yet the amount of newspaper space given to reporting the St Patrick's Day celebrations across America began to reduce year by year. As a result of the fixed nature of the annual celebration, the parades themselves ceased to be significant news events. Only when controversy formed part of the day's happenings did the media turn their focus back on 17 March. Indeed, a test of reporters engaged to cover St Patrick's Day was to find an unusual story. In 1975, at the New York State Supreme Court, a defence attorney, James M. Horan, asked that the court be closed for St Patrick's Day. Justice Burton B. Roberts agreed to put the request to a vote. Before the poll, Justice Roberts reminded jurors of the story of Jeremiah T. Mahoney. In the nineteenth century Mahoney, an Irish saloon-keeper, had opposed a law that would have made 17 March a public holiday. Justice Roberts warned the jurors that if they voted to close the court they would 'have to face the fists of Jeremiah T. Mahoney'. The jurors voted to keep the court open on St Patrick's Day, but in the event were excused from duty as Horan called the court on 17 March, declaring himself sick. Justice Roberts mused that '[he] would not be surprised if St Patrick performed one of his many miracles that enabled Mr Horan to effect a speedy recovery and participate in the St Patrick's Day parade'.[140]

Outside of New York, one of the biggest parades was in Chicago. This event had been built up and encouraged by the city's long-standing mayor, Richard J. Daley. He reviewed the parade each year from the official stand, 'wearing a kelly green fedora and tie and waving a blackthorn walking stick'.[141] The parade was always a large-scale affair attracting thousands of marchers, and the city was heavily decorated with green bunting and shamrocks. Even the Chicago River was dyed green for the day. In 1975, many of the parade floats featured huge posters bearing the image of Mayor Daley. Although the number of Irish people in Chicago, and the proportion of Irish members in City Hall were in steady decline, the St Patrick's Day parade was an annual homage to the Irish-American mayor. In an era when Irish political influence in major American cities had largely ended, Daley offered a lingering example of city hall politicians embracing and using St Patrick's Day for their own aggrandizement.

St Patrick's Day has always involved the airing of Irish concerns, grievances, and hopes, but it assumed a new level of importance during the Troubles. In 1985, the Friends of Ireland, an organization of members of the US Senate and House of Representatives, used St Patrick's Day to state that 'at issue are both the quality of life in Northern Ireland – shall justice, equity and tolerance for diversity govern? – and whether the future of Northern Ireland will be decided though constitutional, democratic means'.[142] The Friends of Ireland statement may, at first glance, appear innocuous. It reads like many other St Patrick's Day greetings and messages from all over the world. It was, however, timely, as it marked the beginning of America's role in the peace process. The year 1984 had seen the release of the report of the New Ireland Forum, which although rejected by the British government and Unionist politicians in Northern Ireland, did signal an important refocusing of minds on options for the long-term future of Northern Ireland. In November 1984, the Irish Taoiseach, Garret FitzGerald and the British Prime Minister, Margaret Thatcher, met for discussions and then issued a joint statement. They agreed to the obvious: that there was a need for a joint governmental and cross-community approach to solving the Northern Ireland problem. In the various meetings that took place in 1985, which resulted in the signing of the Anglo-Irish Agreement – an important precursor to the peace process of the 1990s – American involvement became increasingly significant. The Friends of Ireland St Patrick's Day statement informed all interested parties that

> the United States stands ready to assist that process [reconciliation and compromise] through appropriate political and economic support. A delegation of Friends of Ireland led by Speaker O'Neill is currently visiting Ireland, and other political leaders there, [bringing] the American dimension to the issues of Northern Ireland.[143]

American involvement in Irish politics, which was symbolized most potently by the role of Friend of Ireland member Senator George Mitchell during the 1990s, may be described as the 'St Patrick's Day dimension'. As will be explained later, the peace process in Northern Ireland was constantly reinvigorated during the 1990s as a result of President Clinton's hosting of a St Patrick's Day party to which all the leaders of Northern Ireland's political parties were invited. America became a persuader for peace, and St Patrick's Day celebrations were an important vehicle for the attempted bridging of political differences in the north-east counties of the homeland.

The ebbing and flowing diplomatic value of St Patrick's Day celebrations had been evident from the mid-1980s. Ronald Reagan, a President who was fiercely pro-British, especially with regard to his relationship with Margaret Thatcher, claimed an Irish-Protestant heritage. To him, St Patrick's Day was an innocuous ritual, 'a time for joy and celebration'. Such a belief in the innocent virtues of 17 March was underpinned by the President's argument that the agenda and timetable of progress in the search for peace 'are not for us to set'. Reagan likewise dismissed as heretics Americans who gave 'financial or moral support to Irish terrorists'.[144] The President was comfortable with engaging in St Patrick's Day to win Irish-American votes, but he was not prepared to commit America to an interventionist policy with respect of Northern Ireland. This was despite the fact that many Irish Americans believed that this should be the President's role.

Successive Taoiseachs sought the active involvement of American politicians in Ireland during the 1970s and 1980s. Not only did they look for American input regarding the Northern Ireland issue, but also used St Patrick's Day visits to promote Irish tourism and the value of American investment in Ireland. In 1986, Garret FitzGerald travelled to America for a two-day visit centred on St Patrick's Day. He addressed a large gathering of politicians and Irish Americans who were honouring Thomas P. O'Neill's fifty years of public service.[145] The following year, the new Taoiseach, Charles Haughey, travelled to Washington DC, for a 24-hour visit on St Patrick's Day. During the short stay he appeared on ABC's *Good Morning America*, met President Reagan at a reception hosted by the Irish Ambassador, and accompanied the President to the Speaker's St Patrick's Day lunch on Capitol Hill. In his various speeches, Haughey was at pains to promote tourism, and also asked Americans to 'participate actively and profitably in our programme of economic recovery ... in particular in financial services, computer software, information technology, food processing and bio-technology, tourism, chemicals and health care'.[146]

In 1987, the Minister for Foreign Affairs, Brian Lenihan, also travelled to America for St Patrick's Day. On the evening of 17 March he was the key speaker at the dinner of the Friendly Sons of St Patrick in Washington. Lenihan's speech echoed many of the ideas put forward by Haughey. He concentrated on the need for influential Irish Americans, such as the members of the Friendly Sons, to do three things: to travel to Ireland as tourists, to invest money in and relocate businesses in Ireland, and to work with the government 'to find a lasting solution' to the Northern Ireland problem and to strive for an 'Ireland united by agreement'.[147] What is evident from the visits and speeches of FitzGerald, Haughey and Lenihan, is that it was more important for senior Irish politicians from the 1980s to attend American-based St Patrick's Day meetings, dinners and celebrations, than it was to remain in Ireland. It was in America that the foundation stones for the Irish economic success of the 1990s, the 'Celtic Tiger', were laid, and also where many of the origins of the peace process can be discovered. While many aspects of American St Patrick's Day celebrations may have been offensive to the Irish Government, particularly the parades and their associated gimmickry, it was in America that Irish politicians could use the national anniversary to win over friends with influence.

Irish Americans, perhaps understandably, became an important external component within the Northern Ireland conflict. They fulfilled a series of traditional support roles. Money was raised to finance the 'struggle' in Northern Ireland: Irish-Catholic America was a safe haven for many activists who had to leave Ireland, and they used public events in the USA to demonstrate allegiance to the nationalist community of Northern Ireland. St Patrick's Day, as ever, was the most important public occasion on the Irish-American calendar. Various events on 17 March were used to raise funds for activists in Northern Ireland, and to offer a show of support for nationalists. Clearly, such a politicization of St Patrick's Day, while nothing new within its history, was likely to pose operational problems. Many of the parade organizers, as was demonstrated in the previous chapter, carefully marshalled their celebrations so that they could not be hijacked by external political influences. While event organizers wished to show support for a nationalist Ireland, they were aware that an excessive politicization of St Patrick's Day risked changing its traditionally celebratory nature. In 1970, for instance, marchers taking part in the New York parade unfurled a banner demanding civil rights for Northern Ireland. The banner demonstrated clear support for the Northern Ireland Civil Rights Association (NICRA). This was a non-violent and non-sectarian organization – one whose demands, civil rights for a minority group, would not have been unfamiliar to people in America. However, the parade committee took the view that the banner was political, and therefore went against the spirit of the rules and regulations for those who marched. To ensure that the parade did not become the backdrop for a procession of groups carrying political banners relating to Northern Ireland, the committee announced that, from 1971, all but one specific political banner would be unacceptable. The only banner that would be carried every year, though it linked the parade explicitly with the nationalist community of Northern Ireland, read 'England Get Out of Ireland'.[148] This was traditionally carried by the Fire Department Emerald Society.[149]

Despite the attempt to constrain the use of the New York St Patrick's Day parade as a vehicle for political statements and gestures, the committee's ruling, though adhered to by the majority, could not be fully enforced. As Reimers has argued, 'the republican cause is nearly always present at the St Patrick's Day parade'.[150] In 1972, the parade took place two months after 'Bloody Sunday' in Derry. British soldiers had shot dead thirteen people taking part in a march against the policy of internment. The murders not only shocked world opinion, but heightened the emotional ties that existed between the Irish-Catholic diaspora and the nationalists of Northern Ireland. In response to 'Bloody Sunday', many of the St Patrick's Day marchers of 1972 in New York and elsewhere wore black armbands.[151]

In 1983, the parade committee in New York elected Michael Flannery as its Grand Marshal.[152] Flannery was an 81-year-old, long-standing activist within the Irish-American community. He was also the leader of the Irish Northern Aid Committee, 'a Noraid founder, civil war veteran and an outspoken supporter of the IRA'.[153] Flannery, while fulfilling essential requirements of a Grand Marshal, such as membership of the Ancient Order of

Hibernians, was criticized by the press for his leadership of the Irish Northern Aid Committee, which was understood by many as 'an IRA support group'.[154] This perception of the St Patrick's Day Grand Marshal as a supporter of a paramilitary organization led to critics demanding that the parade be boycotted. In response to such pleas, many public officials, such as Governor Hugh Carey, who had been Grand Marshal in 1976, stayed away from the review stand, or else did not take their usual place among the marchers. The Irish Government, in the form of Taoiseach Garret FitzGerald, criticized Irish Americans who gave money to the IRA, and deplored the decision of the parade committee to elect Flannery as Grand Marshal. Despite the official rejection of Flannery, the *Irish Echo* claimed that the letters it received ran heavily in favour of the appointment of the Grand Marshal.[155]

The clearest rejection of Flannery, and therefore by implication the use of violence within Northern Ireland, came from Cardinal Cooke. The Cardinal had publicly declared his opposition to Flannery, announcing that he would keep the doors of St Patrick's Cathedral closed until the parade custodian had marched past. Rather than greeting the Grand Marshal, a traditional highpoint of the day's events, the Cardinal did not emerge onto the Cathedral steps until Flannery had gone by. Perhaps as a result of the controversy, many casual observers of the parade, those who normally joined in the celebrations for innocuous entertainment, stayed away. The absence of the green hat brigade led one commentator to suggest that, 'the more serious bent of the parade seemed to have chased away most of those who came to see a Mardi Gras'.[156]

The granting of the Grand Marshal sash to Flannery led to the boycott of the parade by two of its most staunch Irish commercial backers – Aer Lingus and Bord Fáilte. In 1985, Peter King, a Noraid supporter, was elected Grand Marshal. King opened St Patrick's Day with a press conference, where he declared,

> the message we are sending is that Irish Americans are united in solidarity against British misrule in Northern Ireland … as we march up the avenue and share all the joy, let us never forget the men and women who are suffering, and most of all the men and women who are fighting.[157]

The newly installed Archbishop of New York, John J. O'Connor, although publicly stating that he could not support the use of violence in Northern Ireland, did agree that he would greet King as Grand Marshal on the Cathedral steps. Yet the Irish Government, Aer Lingus and Bord Fáilte all boycotted the 1985 parade because of the appointment of King in this role. The Irish government issued a statement that 'there cannot be any misunderstanding of the Irish Government's position on issues related to life and death in Ireland'.[158] For Aer Lingus and Bord Fáilte, the public reason for the boycott was presented in business terms. Aer Lingus argued that they were not participating because 'the ethnic business is no longer what it was', and that they were attempting to 'get business from the general tourist'.[159] Against all precedents, Bord Fáilte argued that they were not taking part as 'the parade was being held on a weekend when [our] offices are shut'.[160] The decision of two of Ireland's biggest financial concerns in America, both of which had traditionally supported St Patrick's Day, to boycott the parade signalled two important themes. First, neither Aer Lingus nor Bord Fáilte were prepared to endorse the St Patrick's Day parade when it might be construed as supporting republicanism and paramilitarism. This was especially important given that the early 1980s were one of the most violent periods of sectarian murder in Northern Ireland, and that republicanism was becoming more powerful politically in the wake of the 1981 hunger strikes. Second, the decision to boycott, or rather the reasons given, signalled that the New York parade, and indeed many St Patrick's Day celebrations across America, had become incongruous from an Irish perspective. The 17th of March still linked Irish Americans to Ireland, in imagination if not in memory. But many Irish businesses and potential sponsors were aware, as Irish diplomats had been from the 1960s, that the 'paddywhackery' themes in the celebrations were poor representations of Ireland, and may even have impeded the nation's business image in the United States.

The politics of Northern Ireland, though sometimes impinging on the New York parade in controversial fashion, were nonetheless present. In the official annual programme, the Parade Chairman routinely ended his St Patrick's Day greetings by reminding everyone: 'As we march today to honour St Patrick, let us not forget our Brothers and Sisters in North East Ireland who do not enjoy the freedom we do.'[161] The programme listed the order of the parade and explained which bands, County Associations and other Irish societies formed each marching unit. It also offered brief biographies of the main organizers, who were a mixture of Irish migrants and descendants of Irish parents. These men appeared to be political moderates, with membership of established and reputable Irish institutions, such as the Catholic Church, the AOH, the Gaelic Athletic Association and Emerald Societies. Indeed, the parade programmes of the last three decades offer a picture of highly assimilated Irish-American males who were successful in business and commerce, or loyally serving state institutions such as the police and the coast guard. The annual parade was, in this sense, an expression of Irish-American citizenship and liberal progress.

Yet the vexed issue of the politics of Northern Ireland was never far away. The parade programmes also featured support for Saoirse and other organizations that assisted Irish Republican political prisoners. The difficulties faced by Irish political prisoners, as well as the situation of republican activists from Northern Ireland who sought political asylum in America, were covered regularly in the programme literature. The case of Joseph Doherty, for example, was long supported by the St Patrick's Day parade organization. Doherty had been arrested in America in 1983, after the British applied for his extradition. Although various courts had ruled that Doherty's case for political asylum was valid, he was held in prison. Subsequently, the New York St Patrick's Day parade was used in the campaign to free Doherty. In 1990, the procession focused strongly on the Doherty case. Even Mayor David N. Dinkins, while sporting a green jacket, wore a 'Free Joe Doherty' button.[162] In 1992, the Supreme Court ruled by a majority that Doherty should be deported, and he was flown back to Belfast in February that year. The deportation was roundly criticized by the Irish-Catholic and nationalist communities in America, and a condemnation of the decision, stamped with the wording 'Justice Denied', appeared in the 1992 New York St Patrick's Day parade programme. While the organizing committee was not a political organization *per se*, its parade mirrored many Irish-American concerns about the political situation in Northern Ireland.

The St Patrick's Day programmes also celebrated events from the nationalist history of Ireland. Common among these were legends from the pantheon of Irish nationalist heroes, such as Wolfe Tone, Robert Emmet, Daniel O'Connell and the leaders of the 1916 Rising. The celebration of the 75th anniversary of the 1916 Rising was the theme of the parade in 1991. As with other commemorations of historical events by the New York St Patrick's Day parade committee, this decision illustrated the dominant ideological position of the AOH, and its claim to represent the mood of the Irish-American community. Whereas St Patrick's Day in Ireland had avoided overt political agendas, various American celebrations grasped hold of the past as a justification for firmly held, yet often simplistic readings of the Irish situation. The 1991 St Patrick's Day programme in New York, for example, contended that the silence of the Irish Government concerning the 75th anniversary of the Easter Rising was disturbing:

> normally the 75th anniversary of any occasion calls for great ceremony. Yet little has been heard from the Irish government. Silence hardly befits the occasion. Coupled with other markers of a loss or suppression of national spirit, silence suggests an inclination to ignore the anniversary, now only weeks away.[163]

The American anniversary of the Easter Rising, and its role in the New York St Patrick's Day parade, were also criticism of the Irish Government's policy with respect to Northern Ireland. The parade programme argued that Irish Governments since 1922 had failed to develop a policy to end partition, 'other than wishing the border away', and that as they were 'caught offguard by the explosion of the North in 1969 and its continuing instability since, the South has, in effect, rejected the North'.[164] This reading of the 75th anniversary of the 1916 Rising effectively located the problems of Northern Ireland in the same historical context as the events in Dublin during Easter Week. While such a narrow, linear view of Irish political history is understandably attractive to Irish-American nationalists, it unduly simplifies the complexities of the situation in Northern Ireland specifically, and of Irish history generally.[165] While the Irish nation has undoubtedly had difficulties coming to terms with its own history of violent insurrection, largely because of the ongoing struggle across its border, it is difficult to see how the lionization of a militaristic past by the New York St Patrick's Day parade did anything to advance the situation. If anything, such historical whimsy alienated contemporary Ireland from Irish America. The projection of an overly simplified nationalist history of Ireland on St Patrick's Day in America has become as alien to the Irish homeland as paddywhackery.

On 17 March, large crowds have consistently gathered across America to watch all kinds of St Patrick's Day parades.[166] The concentration of such numbers of people on a single day, and in fixed places, meant that the parades were an irresistible magnet for politicians campaigning for public office. In New York, Chicago and other big cities, the annual parade was a pivotal date on the social calendar of the city mayor and other aspiring office holders. There are a host of examples of politicians using St Patrick's Day events to boost their public image, and thus lure the Irish-American vote. Some politicians, such as Mayor Daley in Chicago, and the Kennedy brothers on both the east and west coasts of the country, were unabashed about their use of 17 March as a means of self-promotion, and as a way of affirming their ties with the Irish-American community.[167] In 1992, during the presidential race, the Democrats and Republicans both used the Chicago South Side St Patrick's Day parade as a promotional vehicle: according to the *National Review*, this was intended 'to take advantage of full and free media coverage'.[168] Subsequently, when Hillary Clinton ran for the New York senate seat in 2000, she joined marchers in the city's St Patrick's Day parade. A major issue in the campaign against Clinton was that she was an outsider, not a New Yorker. By participating in the parade, Clinton tried to appear that she belonged to the city, that by marching with Irish Americans she was someone who could genuinely represent them. Her tactic was not, however, unique; she was joined in the parade by her opponent in the senate contest, New York Mayor Rudy Giuliani.

GAY DEBATE IN USA

In 1991, a new dynamic emerged within St Patrick's Day celebrations in America. The New York parade, and others across the country, controlled as they were by the Ancient Order of Hibernians, reflected views that were Catholic and conservative. As such the parades had always been bastions of traditional family values, and those with lifestyles that were in any way 'alternative' to the teachings of the Vatican were spurned. The 1991 parade in New York witnessed the arrival of the Irish Lesbian and Gay Organization (ILGO), which emerged 'from seemingly nowhere chanting "We're here, we're queer, we're Irish"'.[169] Why did the ILGO want to march in the parade? St Patrick's Day had long served an historic purpose by expressing the pride of the Irish in America; the popularity of the parade, in particular, symbolized their acceptance, within the host community, as full and equal citizens. The successful assimilation of the Irish into American society, and the acceptance of St Patrick's Day parades as a marker of Irishness, 'highlighted the Irish contribution to America's evolving ethos of tolerance and inclusion'.[170] The ILGO campaign to be allowed to march in the parade, was therefore 'a validation of their larger efforts to gain the full measure of respect and rights they believe they deserve'.[171] In this respect, it was argued, the ILGO's use of St Patrick's Day in the 1990s was no different to that of the general Irish-American community a century earlier. Yet the response to the ILGO initiative created chasmic divides. The 'traditional', avowedly Catholic sectors of the Irish-American community opposed the ILGO's claim of a right to march. This view also indicated that conservative attitudes towards sexuality were more staid in Irish America than in the homeland. The 1980s, a time of high unemployment in Ireland, had seen the arrival of a new wave of Irish immigration into cities like New York. The new Irish immigrants came from a country, and possessed a mind-set, that was very different from established Irish Americans. The Ireland of the 1980s and early 1990s had rejected many of the stereotypes of Irishness, embraced its new-found political and economic place in Europe, had become increasingly distant from the once 'all powerful' Catholic Church, with the result that public opinion on social issues was moving from deep conservatism to progressive liberalism. While 'traditional' Irish Americans rejected the ILGO claims, many of the new Irish immigrants had no problem with public sanction of homosexuality on St Patrick's Day.

The ILGO planned to march in the New York parade, but its application was turned down by the official organizing committee. From the outset, the ILGO was widely supported by the mainstream media, which dismissed as bigots the AOH and other organizations involved in staging the parade.[172] In an effort to reach some kind of compromise, another Irish group who had been accepted into the parade, Division 7 from Manhattan, invited the ILGO to march with them. That the ILGO had been subsumed into the main body of the parade would have been frustrating enough to the parade committee, but a decision by New York's Mayor Dinkins turned the spotlight more intensely than ever on the battle between the ILGO and the custodians of the parade. Dinkins elected to march with Division 7 and the ILGO contingent, rather than in the mayor's customary position at the head of the parade.[173] While Dinkins' decision was applauded by many liberals, the traditionally conservative Irish-American supporters of the parade, which included the Catholic-dominated AOH, were displeased about the mayor's gesture. As Dinkins marched, he was booed by many in the crowd, and even shelled with beer cans. Cardinal O'Connor, although opposed to homosexuality, refused to take a public position on the mayor's action during the parade. Yet the Catholic Church's stance on gay and lesbian involvement in the parade went on to assume utmost importance in the battle between the organizing committee and the ILGO.

In 1992, the parade committee, led by Francis Beirne, took the position that no group would be granted admittance to the parade 'that has a position contrary to the teachings of the Catholic faith'.[174] As a result of the committee's decision, the ideals of the ILGO were considered contrary to the qualification rules. The ILGO was once more banned from taking a place in the parade, but also excluded from joining the march under the auspices of someone else's banner, as had already happened in 1991. The decisions taken with respect of the ILGO clearly placed the parade committee outside of the spirit of New York's human rights legislation. As a result, City Hall removed the permit to organize the parade from the division of the AOH that had been organizing the event for over a century. There was a paradox here: the parade committee and the AOH refused to allow the ILGO to participate in the parade, but over the years it had allowed known members and supporters of NI Republican paramilitary groups to march. Each time controversy had surrounded the parade with respect of the paramilitary issue, the Church had always condemned the use of violence within a political struggle, yet the committee had never thought to reverse its decision on the selection of either Flannery or King as Grand Marshal. It was clear that the AOH and others had the power to control who should march in the parade. It was an understandable responsibility given their long custodianship of its organization, yet to many outsiders their actions appeared contradictory and driven by bigotry. Indeed, in Ireland, organizers of various parades and festivals on St Patrick's Day did not exclude gay and lesbian marchers. Commenting on the situation in New York and Boston, the *New Republic* concluded that 'some Irish Americans show themselves to be narrower than their homelanders, and less festive too'.[175]

The state division of the AOH took over the role of organizing the New York parade, and was granted a permit from the city authorities. The new committee did not, however, remove the ban on the participation of the ILGO. Hence, rather than relying solely on negotiations between the city authorities and the AOH on the issue, the ILGO took their fight to the courts. A Federal Court ruled that the AOH was within its constitutional rights to deny the ILGO permission to march in the parade. The judge dismissed the New York City Human Rights Organization, which had supported the ILGO, as comparable to 'the thought police of [Orwell's] 1984'.[176] The 1992 parade went ahead with the ILGO excluded. In response, Mayor Dinkins and other prominent city officials refused to march in the

parade, and the ILGO mounted various demonstrations along the parade
route. The Dinkins' boycott was, in this case, dismissed by Cardinal O'Connor as the 'arbitrary politicization' of the parade.[177]

In the St Patrick's Day programme published for the 1992 parade,
Francis Beirne sought to explain the position of the AOH. He reminded
readers that the New York march was 'the largest civilian annual parade in
the world'.[178] It was organized by the New York County Board of the AOH,
whose duty it was to apply to the police for a permit to hold the parade, and
to form a committee to organize the day's events. It was, Beirne argued, for
the committee to send out invitations as the laws of New York State established the New York County Board of the AOH as the Host of the Parade.
Only organizations that have marching units and 'that are qualified, under
parade rules, to march', are admitted to the parade. 'Without an invitation',
he explained, 'there is no way that any organization can march.'[179] Beirne
stressed that every marching unit had to receive a fresh invitation each year,
and that the right to invite allowed the committee to eliminate any unit
that had broken parade rules the previous year. The argument appeared
straightforward: the New York St Patrick's Day parade, although taking
place on public streets, was effectively a private parade, and only those who
had been invited could join. In 1993, this image of a private parade was
reinforced when a court judged that the New York parade should remain
under the auspices and control of the AOH.[180] Subsequently, just one hour
before the 1993 parade was due to start, 200 ILGO members protesting
against their exclusion from the parade were arrested.[181]

In 1994, although the situation was unresolved and the ILGO still
banned, the new city mayor, Rudolph Giuliani, chose to march in the
parade, despite his sympathy for the gay and lesbian position. This, if anything, gave weight to ILGO demonstrations during the parade, a fact that
led the *New York Times* to comment in 1995:

> although gay and lesbian protesters were once again arrested for
> holding a pre-parade demonstration on Fifth Avenue, even that seemed
> to have become an accepted, almost institutionalized part of the
> texture of St Patrick's Day in New York.[182]

As the controversy in New York grew, gay and lesbian groups campaigned
to be included in parades and other celebrations across America. Many cities
had no objections to gay and lesbian participation; indeed, cities such as
Savannah used their open policies as a method of promoting their parades.
In other places, however, the gay and lesbian pressure groups were met with
resistance. In 1999, in both Brooklyn and the Bronx, parades that had
always refused to allow the ILGO to march, gay and lesbian protesters were
arrested for demonstrating against their exclusion.[183] In New York that year,
the ILGO's demonstration featured more than 200 gay rights activists, who

chanted, 'Two, four, six, eight, how do you know St Patrick's straight?' They also carried placards that stated, 'Twelfth July, 17th March – same bigots, different sashes', and 'Brits out of Ireland, Bigotry out of the parade'.[184] In 2000, Hillary Clinton's use of the St Patrick's Day parade as a way of appealing to liberal voters of New York was opposed by the ILGO. The continued furore over gay marchers, and their annual presence at the St Patrick's Day parade suggests that the contested definitions of Irish identity, which were fought out symbolically on 17 March in New York, are also 'central to broader battles over the entire city's vision of itself'.[185]

The exclusion of the ILGO from the New York parade was followed by similar developments in South Boston. The Irish-American Gay, Lesbian and Bisexual Group of Boston sought to enter the parade, but its organizers denied their application. The Boston dispute was as hard fought as that in New York, but rather than merely seeking a local judicial decision, the South Boston gay and lesbian activists went to the Supreme Court to obtain a ruling on who could march in the parade.[186] The Supreme Court case was officially a dispute between the South Boston Allied War Veterans' Council, the organizers of the parade, and the Irish-American Gay, Lesbian and Bisexual Group of Boston.[187] The court ruled that the parade organizers, while not being allowed to exclude gay and lesbian marchers from the parade, could deny entry of any group that it wished from marching under its own banner.[188] Effectively, the Supreme Court decision reinforced that which had been made in New York; that the ownership of the invite list to the parade belonged to the official organizers. As such, they could overlook any group that they wished.[189] In the wake of various legal decisions relating to gay and lesbian participation in St Patrick's Day parades, it is unlikely that bodies like the ILGO will be invited to walk down Fifth Avenue in the foreseeable future. Such debates do, however, reveal the ever-changing nature of the Irish diaspora in America. They reveal some of the pressures that the traditional custodians of St Patrick's Day are under as the world around them becomes increasingly fluid in terms of notions of identity, difference and morality.

THE GREENING OF THE WHITE HOUSE AND THE PEACE PROCESS

Occupants of the White House have long seen 17 March as a significant day in the Irish-American calendar. It afforded presidents an opportunity to publicly embrace the celebrations held so dear by Irish-American voters, and allowed them to welcome various visiting Irish dignitaries and officials to Washington. President Bill Clinton was a keen advocate of the Irish cause. During the presidential election campaign of 1992, Clinton formally committed himself to a policy of despatching a special American envoy to Northern Ireland. He also promised to grant American visas to the leadership of

Sinn Féin. By engaging so personally with the peace process, the work of the Northern Irish political parties, and the London and Dublin governments, Clinton inevitably used St Patrick's Day to promote his vision for the future of Northern Ireland.[190] Although the American President built on a tradition of welcoming Irish politicians to the White House on St Patrick's Day, he widened the invitation list to include representatives from across the political spectrum in Northern Ireland. Here was a diplomatic strategy that combined the positive and celebratory themes of 17 March with the broader cause of peace and reconciliation in the Irish homeland. As such, St Patrick's Day became an important annual moment for discussions of the peace process during the Clinton Presidency. It was an opportunity to concentrate American attention on the issue of Northern Ireland in a way that was unattainable during the rest of the year. As John Bruton stated in 1995:

> I think I am realistic enough to know that people in America don't wake up every morning and ask what's happening in Ireland. They think about Ireland two or three times a year in a serious way. St Patrick's Day is one of them.[191]

Clinton signalled his hands-on role in the Northern Ireland peace process most clearly in January 1994, when he granted a visa to Sinn Féin leader, Gerry Adams, so that he could visit America and address a peace conference. There is a great affinity for Sinn Féin among many Irish Americans – particularly Catholics and nationalists – so Clinton's decision was roundly applauded by many of the bodies traditionally involved in organizing and promoting St Patrick's Day.

The 1995 St Patrick's Day annual House of Congress luncheon was the venue for the first public handshake between Gerry Adams and Bill Clinton.[192] The same gathering also allowed the Secretary of State for Northern Ireland, Sir Patrick Mayhew, to hold informal talks with Adams. Such a meeting would have been difficult to stage in either Northern Ireland or Britain at this time. This was all very significant to the world of Northern Ireland politics, although the most immediate concern for Congress diners was the menu for St Patrick's Day lunch. At a moment when the leader of Sinn Féin was publicly greeted by the President of America, the *New York Times* reported that the lunch menu 'would have made any Irishman proud: boiled corned beef and cabbage, boiled potatoes, soda bread and lime sherbet'.[193] Yet this reveals a peculiar contradiction. At one level, Clinton, an astute politician, was creating history by publicly acknowledging the leader of Sinn Féin, yet he served a St Patrick's Day lunch that few, if any, people in Ireland, would expect to sit down to.

The close relationship between Clinton and the peace process was also apparent in his visit to Northern Ireland in November 1995, when he made a commitment that US Senator George Mitchell would act as facilitator in cross-party talks in the peace process. In the three years after this visit to Northern Ireland, Clinton, and most publicly Mitchell, were instrumental in keeping the peace process moving along. Concurrently, Washington's St Patrick's Day events were vital in that they provided the major stakeholders with a third party venue at which to discuss peace initiatives. The importance of the St Patrick's Day gatherings led Deaglán de Bréadún to note: 'It had got to the stage where most of the frontline political leaders departed for Washington, leaving the Belfast scene almost deserted.'[194] President Clinton hosted one of his largest St Patrick's Day gatherings in 1998. Leaders from all the main parties were in attendance: he implored them to move towards a settlement, reminding them all that 'this is the chance of a lifetime for peace in Ireland. You must get it done. You must do it for yourselves and your children.'[195] The success of the St Patrick's Day gathering, and the whole process that followed it, was marked on Good Friday 1998 with the signing of the Belfast Agreement.

This settlement has, admittedly, been dogged by difficulties ever since. In September 1998, Clinton again visited Northern Ireland. In a speech designed to encourage all those involved to make the Agreement a working success, Clinton stated:

> Courage and reconciliation were the heart of your commitment to peace. Now, as you go forward, courage and reconciliation must drive this assembly in very specific ways: to decommission the weapons of war that are obsolete in Northern Ireland at peace; to move forward with the formation of an executive council; to adapt your police force so that it earns the confidence, respect and support of all the people; to end street justice, because defining crime, applying punishment and enforcing the law must be left to the people's elected representatives, the courts and the police; to pursue early release for prisoners whose organisations have truly abandoned violence, and to help them find a productive, constructive place in society; to build a more just society where human rights are birthrights and where every citizen receives equal protection and equal treatment under the law. These must be the benchmarks of the new Northern Ireland.[196]

In 1999, ongoing difficulties with the workings of the Agreement and complex issues such as paramilitary decommissioning meant that the St Patrick's Day gathering in Washington took on extra significance.[197] The leaders of all Northern Ireland's political parties, both nationalist and unionist, as well as the Prime Ministers of Britain and Ireland, were in attendance. While St Patrick's Day itself was marked with the traditional presentation of shamrock to the President by the Irish Taoiseach, Bertie Ahern, the gathering produced a joint statement from Clinton, Ahern and British Prime Minster Blair:

A year ago, people said it was hopeless, that the sides were too far apart. But the people and political parties in Northern Ireland proved them wrong. We all persevered. People compromised. People showed courage. One year on, we can meet the deadline that has been set. More courage will be needed. But we are nearly there. The prize is very great indeed and it is now in sight. We have come too far to go back now. Let us finish the task between now and Good Friday.[198]

Clinton's last St Patrick's Day in the White House was overshadowed by a general feeling that the spirit of the Good Friday Agreement was not taking root within the institutions that it had given rise to. Nearly 800 guests attended the gathering, and, as always, the Taoiseach was on hand to present the President with a bowl of shamrock. The assembly was marked by the attendance of Seamus Heaney to read extracts of his poetry. All the leaders of the main political parties in Northern Ireland were there, and both Gerry Adams and David Trimble used the publicity opportunities afforded by St Patrick's Day to make their case on American television. Awards were presented to George Mitchell for his efforts during the peace process, and at a breakfast in his honour, Dawn Irish Gold, a firm from Newry, provided 'the first sausages and rashers exported from Northern Ireland to the US in over thirty years'.[199] Despite the positive side of St Patrick's Day in Washington, which Clinton engendered, the event was not problem free. At the traditional luncheon hosted by the British Ambassador, the atmosphere was unruly, and the Northern Ireland Secretary, Peter Mandleson, had difficulty in making himself heard. Gerry Adams, for Sinn Féin, and Ian Paisley Junior, of the Democratic Unionist Party, both refused to attend the event. The night before, at an American-Ireland fund dinner, Paisley Junior was ejected when he interrupted a speech made by Bertie Ahern. He had held aloft a banner which read 'St Patrick says keep killers out of government'.[200]

Clinton's presidency came to a close in January 2001, but before he stood down he made one last official visit to Ireland. He had made a major contribution to the peace process, so politicians on both sides of the border understandably fêted him. A key to his effort had been the politically astute use of St Patrick's Day for discussions among stakeholders. Clinton understood that 17 March was a symbolic day in the calendar for both the Irish and the American diaspora. It offered a window of opportunity for politicians to gather so that they could discuss the peace process. In a speech in Dundalk, he remembered how St Patrick's Day had been at the symbolic heart of his policy towards Ireland:

every St. Patrick's Day, the Taoiseach comes to the United States and we have a ceremony in the White House. We sing Irish songs, tell Irish stories – everything we say is strictly true, of course. In my very first St. Patrick's Day occasion as President, I said I would be a friend of Ireland not just on St. Patrick's Day, but every day. I have tried to be as good as my word. And every effort has been an honour and a gift.[201]

The importance of St Patrick's Day in Washington as a forum for the peace process was, therefore, critical. In just a few years, the Clinton administration had transformed 17 March from a day of parades and parties into a major political event. The occasion evolved into 'an elaborate, week long cotillion in which the most important players in Ireland's politics and business can network and negotiate with their American counterparts'.[202] Washington, on 17 March, offered all those involved in the Northern Ireland peace process a 'neutral' political venue on a day of national significance. The Clinton policy of using St Patrick's Day as a focus for his Irish policy transformed the political dynamic within Northern Ireland, which had previously defined the peace process as an internal Anglo-Irish affair. Clinton's imaginative use of 17 March as a political forum counterbalanced the British position, and opened 'a new channel for Irish-American lobbying in Washington'.[203] Clinton's real achievement, considering how readily St Patrick's Day is traditionally linked with the forces of Irish nationalism and Catholicism, was to engage the politicians of unionism and loyalism within his 17 March strategy. He was able to convince them that the St Patrick's Day summits were not part of a dangerous 'green' conspiracy. In the wake of the various controversies that engulfed the Clinton Presidency, his work within Northern Ireland's search for peace ought to be an enduring positive legacy. One of the most successful strategies within that policy was the use of St Patrick's Day as a symbolic meeting place for all those with an interest in the future of Northern Ireland.

CHAPTER 7

REINVENTING ST
PATRICK'S DAY

— ஐை —

In 1948 I was age five – attending a Protestant school in West London, being
asked why I was wearing watercress on my coat. I replied, 'It's shamrock'.
'Shamrock!' What's that, mate?[1]

IRELAND ON PARADE

Towards the end of the twentieth century, Irish society underwent dramatic
changes owing to the influences of modernization and globalization. Modernization of Irish social values was expressed in referenda liberalizing the
laws of abortion and divorce; modernization of the Irish economy was apparent in the diversification of local industry and the growth of the 'Celtic
Tiger'; while Irish politics were modernized by the Dáil's proactive engagement with the European Parliament, as well as the vibrant leadership of
President Mary Robinson. This growing sense of a modern, outward-looking
Ireland was bolstered by the globalization of Irish cultural practices and performances. The 1990s saw the re-emergence of both popular and traditional
forms of Irish culture onto the world stage, such as in the spectacle of *Riverdance*, the music of the Corrs and U2, the celebrated literature of Roddy
Doyle, Seamus Heaney and Frank McCourt, and popular films such as *The
Commitments*, *Michael Collins* and *Waking Ned* (released in the US as *Waking
Ned Devine*). The adoption, too, of franchised Irish pubs in various countries
has meant that Ireland's ales, stouts and whiskeys are more than just flavour
of the month. There has, indeed, been a new spirit of self-confidence in
much of contemporary Ireland. This has been aided by the slow but steady
progress in the Northern Irish peace process. The practical effects of this
Irish resurgence have been felt in two key ways: the end of large-scale migration away from Ireland, and a global enthusiasm for things Irish.[2]

The collapse in outward Irish migration has meant that, for the first time
in history, the Irish diaspora is not being renewed by the influx of large
numbers of Irish people into countries such as Britain, America, Canada
and Australia. Moreover, the relatively small volume of Irish emigrants
to these places find Irish communities that are well established, highly
assimilated and self-confident about their future. In this regard, St Patrick's
Day festivities abroad are no longer assertive markers of Irishness in
often hostile host environments, but are instead self-congratulatory events
that are both tolerated and actively embraced by non-Irish communities.

231

The long-standing profile and importance of the Irish diaspora have produced a series of St Patrick's Day celebrations that are specific to particular nations and regions. The parade in New York has its own form and character (and a belief that it is the biggest and the best!), which is the product of a long history covering over two centuries. Thus, although celebrating Ireland's patron saint, the parade is also an AOH-organized ritual designed specifically to represent Irish Americans of the New York area. The traditions of the parade in New York are different from those in Chicago, Boston, San Francisco, Savannah or elsewhere, all of which have developed their own form of celebration. These events are also different from commemorations that take place in Australia, Canada, Britain and across Ireland, all of which reflect local traditions and histories, and celebrate 17 March in unique ways.

Nonetheless, as we now discuss, there have been features common to St Patrick's Day around the world. These include broadly similar customs of observance and comparable efforts to celebrate 'Irishness' – regardless of how 'authentic' or 'tacky' they appear. We then analyse how commercial interests have influenced the celebration of St Patrick's Day, such as through 'Paddy' merchandise and the sponsorship of parades by Irish breweries. Finally, we consider how the Dublin festival, which began as an industrial pageant in the 1950s, was transformed into an American-style carnival in the 1970s, and has since been reinvented from the mid-1990s as a triumphal celebration of Irishness.

INDULGING IN ST PATRICK'S DAY

A major factor in St Patrick's Day celebrations, especially among the diaspora, has been the ongoing demographic and cultural renewal of the Irish community as a result of continued migration from the homeland. For many people of Irish descent, St Patrick's Day celebrations offered them an identifiable annual link with their ethnic heritage. However, as generations have passed by, many Irish people have married outside their 'own' community, memberships of Irish organizations have often lapsed, and so the formalized sense of an Irish identity has tended to diminish. Reginald Byron's research has demonstrated that many Irish Americans, while claiming that their sense of Irishness was important to them, could not identify 'any domestic activity or family tradition that they regarded as especially Irish, apart from those connected with the once-a-year St Patrick's Day season'.[3] Even these activities were usually limited to wearing something green or cooking a special meal. Byron also argued that by the so-called third generation, Irish absorption into contemporary American culture was complete, and only 'small vestiges, such as celebrating St Patrick's Day' remained of a specific Irish identity.[4]

It is obviously difficult to discover what St Patrick's Day means personally to different people across the globe, as well as how and why they celebrated the anniversary. How did St Patrick's Day enter their consciousness annually? Why do forms of personal or family celebration remain fixed as tradition over the years? Despite the high profile of public St Patrick's Day events, such as parades, how significant have private observances been to the global Irish? Do personal celebrations of St Patrick's Day have a demonstrable relationship with themes of 'global Irishness' and the local success of the diaspora; or are individuals more likely to focus on memories or imaginings of the Irish homeland? In an attempt to ascertain answers to these types of questions, we used newspaper letter columns, Irish and Celtic Internet list-servs, and personal contacts to reach a range of people across the world who celebrate St Patrick's Day. The responses we received were diverse – from short answers to letters – and the process of gathering them was not systematic. Yet this was a useful exercise, for we gleaned varied snapshots of people's experiences. Respondents came forward from a range of social backgrounds and ages, in various corners of the world, and each had a story about what St Patrick's Day meant *to them*. Such an appreciation of the 'personal' St Patrick's Day experience is most important; otherwise it appears that observance of 17 March is marshalled exclusively by organizations like the AOH or Dublin Tourism, and that the day itself serves only the social, economic, or political aims of such institutions. From the correspondence we received, it appears that the vast majority of people who celebrate St Patrick's Day have done so at their own behest. They may watch a parade or attend an organized event in a pub, bar, or club, but their mode of observance is a combination of individual choice, peer-group pressures and family expectations.

Many correspondents were very aware of their family history on St Patrick's Day. Marcia Abcarain, an American, has kept the ticket that her grandfather used to attend the 'very first public celebration of St Patrick's Day held in Chelmsford, Essex, England in 1904'.[5] Denis Ashe, though remembering conflict with the Orange Order in Liverpool on St Patrick's Day, stressed that continuity of family ties and kinship were central to his 17 March, particularly when he carried his daughter on his shoulders in the Liverpool parade of 2000.[6] Much family celebration of St Patrick's Day is, of course, done within the confines of the home. Kerry Bryan of Pennsylvania recalls St Patrick's Day when she was just five years old; it was memorable because her father dyed her milk green.[7] Pam Cronk, a resident of Toronto, remembers how her Scots-Dutch father would buy her Irish mother a bowl of shamrock every year, and that the whole family would enjoy a dinner together. Such family celebrations were, according to Cronk, common: there were many 'small, unpublic family kinds of events that took place' on St Patrick's Day.[8] Paul, whose family has been living in Britain since leaving Ireland thirty years ago, writes that St Patrick's Day is an opportunity 'for my family in England to get together from all four corners of the country, for a good meal and catching up with each others' lives'.[9] The family feast was also a key to Stephen Finley's St Patrick's Day. The Californian recalled, in similar fashion to other respondents, the warmth of kinship and culinary delights of 17 March: 'The most "memorable" St Patrick's Day, in a positive way, are those spent with my wife and kids. She's of Irish heritage also and cooks various Irish dishes – Irish stew, champs, Guinness, meat pie, soda bread and so on.'[10] Yet the family component of St Patrick's Day has been eroded for some. Peter Hill, from Liverpool, comments that in the 1950s and 1960s St Patrick's Day was more of a family affair but today, 'and [he says] this with some sadness, my children have not inherited a sense of Irish-ness'.[11]

St Patrick's Day may also be attached to very personal memories. Sadly, Minoa Uffelman's sister was murdered. Touchingly, a scholarship fund was established in her memory, and the Uffelman family has continued to raise money for this cause. One of the fundraising activities involved printing and selling St Patrick's Day T-shirts for their town's celebrations. The charitable purpose for producing these T-shirts remains; they have, indeed, become a well-known part of the St Patrick's Day experience in the American town of Erin.[12] By contrast, Patrick Scannell's clearest personal memory of St Patrick' Day is joyous. To celebrate his sixtieth birthday, he flew from London to New York for St Patrick's Day. He attended mass at St Patrick's Cathedral, watched the Fifth Avenue parade, shared an Irish dinner, and spent the evening at Carnegie Hall listening to the Chieftains. This was more than a 'birthday bash'; Scannell immersed himself into Irish-American culture on the anniversary of Ireland's national apostle. Doubtless he was the envy of Irish friends back in England.[13]

The church service remains a key part of St Patrick's Day observance, whether for Catholics or Protestants. Nonetheless, many of our 'older' correspondents felt that the religious aspect of St Patrick's Day was now being largely forgotten. Sister Mary Tynan of Co. Laois feels that there is 'a moving away from the faith and cultural dimension of the day'.[14] In a similar vein, Joan Moody of Texas laments that 'most people don't look at the religious side of it, and don't understand the religious implications of what Patrick accomplished in bringing Christianity to the Irish'.[15] Mrs McGrath, of London, concludes that this is part of a wider secular malaise: 'Christianity does not seem that important to young people any more. The older generation value the foundation of their Christian upbringing.'[16]

There are, of course, many secular customs associated with St Patrick's Day, though to many of our correspondents these are the most 'gimmicky' and 'tacky' aspects of the festival. Marcia Abcarain of California confirms that she has now learned much about 'the real St Patrick' and his 17 March anniversary, which is something altogether different from 'the Americanized leprechaun and the threat of getting pinched if you didn't wear something green'.[17] Ironically, while there is much paddywhackery on 17 March, schools in North America have made an effort to understand the life of St

Patrick and the purpose of the anniversary. This is in keeping with respect for the festivals of numerous ethnic groups in the United States and Canada. The emphasis is, nonetheless, as much on celebration as education. Claudia Cole, who grew up in British Columbia, remembers St Patrick's Day as a 'party day' at school. Everyone was encouraged to wear something green, the classroom was decorated accordingly, and children were presented with stickers in the shape of shamrocks and leprechaun hats. Her abiding memory is large green cookies produced in the shape of a shamrock, and being taught the words 'shillelagh' and 'begorrah'.[18] This objectification of St Patrick's Day is rejected by Elizabeth Gallagher Cardinal of New York, who believes that the anniversary is a 'day to share my Irish roots with all ... not the quirky stereotypical things – green beer etc.'[19] Nonetheless, customs learned as children, especially those that imparted innocent pleasure, are not easily forgotten, and may remain to be exploited. Claudia Cole contends that St Patrick's Day is still kept going in Canada 'by commercial interests'. This strategy succeeds, she argues, 'because we all have happy childhood memories of celebrating the day, and want to bring back the feeling, [and] maybe pass it to the children'.[20] St Patrick's Day, like Christmas and Easter, is therefore a highly commodifiable anniversary – a theme we return to later in this chapter.

As with many forms of festive celebrations, the preparation and consumption of food are an important part of St Patrick's Day. Such meals, usually held after church attendance, a drink at the pub, or viewing a parade, were an essential part of the day. Judy O'Leary Anderson recalls that her mother, an emigrant to America from Rathmore, Co. Kerry, invited a congregation of friends and neighbours for a St Patrick's Day feast in her adopted home. Anderson writes: 'Every St Patrick's Day, after the parade, we would have about thirty people squeezed into our little flat for a ham and corned beef and cabbage dinner with Irish sodabread and tea.'[21] The anticipation and enjoyment of Irish gourmet are heightened by the location of St Patrick's Day within the period of the Lenten fast. Diarmaid Casey of Leicester remembers that as a child he had to attend mass with his mother after which he was 'allowed to eat sweets'. This was the only day prior to Easter when Casey was allowed to break his Lenten promise.[22] The staple foods of St Patrick's Day appear little changed, and so-called 'traditional dishes' are a feature of celebrations in America. The main dish on a St Patrick's Day dinner table is either bacon or corned beef and cabbage, though it is common to combine vegetables so that the dinner plate features a mixture of orange (carrot) and green (peas). Indeed, in America the corned beef and cabbage dish is unrivalled as *the* meal for St Patrick's Day. This is despite New Yorker Timothy O'Sullivan's view, which is shared by many others, that Irish Americans are mistaken to maintain that 'it's an Irish dish'. He insists that 'growing up in Ireland I never heard of it – only bacon and cabbage'.[23] The quandary over what food, if any, is authentic for St Patrick's

Day can stretch the imagination, though some purveyors frankly admit that theirs is a hotch-potch effort. In Tennessee, Melissa Ford organized a St Patrick's Day tea at her college which included '"traditional" food such as scones, shortbread and Irish breakfast tea', as well as what she admits were some 'utterly unauthentic things: Irish crème flavoured coffee, a green punch, and some horrible crème de menthe brownies that someone ordered because the icing was bright green'.[24]

Drinking is, for many people, part and parcel of St Patrick's Day. While there is an obvious presence of green beer in North America, especially in bars seeking a St Patrick's Day boost to their takings, restaurants and family homes rely on imported Irish drinks such as porter and whiskey. Some people's memories of St Patrick's Day are hazy because they consumed an excess of alcohol in pubs and bars. Images of drunken revelry appear to lie at the heart of many people's perceptions of the Irish and their national day, though such behaviour is hardly restricted to the Irish. American Michael Bodart recalls that students at the University of Wisconsin Oshkosh (UWO) celebrated 17 March by visiting many of the bars within walking distance of the campus. He admits that events often 'got out of hand, with bonfires in the streets and the tipping over of cars for (drunken) entertainment'.[25] The UWO situation became so notorious that on St Patrick's night Johnny Carson would quip on his television show, 'I bet they are having fun in Oshkosh, WI right now.' To break this pattern of St Patrick's night drunkenness, the university changed the dates of the spring break so that the student body would always be away from campus whenever St Patrick's Day fell. While the pub remains very important on 17 March, many people have no interest in drinking to excess. In many ways, the stereotype of St Patrick's Day as a time to be drunk is part of a general image 'problem' for the Irish globally. As Birmingham's Carmel Girling comments: 'drink and the Irish are hard to part in people's perceptions of the Irish and there is little to dispel that'.[26] Despite negative images attached to drinking on 17 March, the pub or bar generally provides a convivial public atmosphere for St Patrick's Day celebrations. Mrs McGrath of London, defending the role of the pub, explains: 'It is a meeting place for friends and family get togethers. Good food, music and a friendly atmosphere. People who have moved on, return to spend the day with family and enjoy each other's company.'[27] The pub therefore has wider value as a location for annual gatherings of friends and families on St Patrick's Day.

Various Irish societies and sports clubs stage special contests on St Patrick's Day; some are even finals representing the culmination of a season played over preceding months. The Irish-American Club at Cleveland, Ohio, staged its annual 'Danny Boy' singing competition on St Patrick's Day. Samuel J. Thomas wrote to us proudly that his son was victorious despite the lack of an Irish heritage: 'he is an olive-skinned 100% Lebanese American, the first such ethnic to win a bit of the green'.[28] This is, nonetheless, part of a wider trend. In recent years traditional St Patrick's Day events have become more open to people from various backgrounds; they are no longer just an enclave for the Irish.

Although St Patrick's Day is intended to be convivial, the boundaries that circumscribe acceptable public behaviour are often stretched, even broken, particularly by male revellers emboldened by alcohol. Helen Bannan attended the College of St Elizabeth, a Catholic Women's College that took part in the St Patrick's Day parade through New Jersey. The pre-scribed dress for these female students was the college's cap and gown. Bannan recalls feeling embarrassed by 'catcalls from nearby bar patrons'.[29] JoAnn Castagna of Connecticut considers boorish behaviour to be part and parcel of male group behaviour on 17 March. She contends that 'St Patrick's Day has become a kind of stand in for some kind of white male solidarity, not around [the issue of] Northern Ireland or the Irish-American diaspora, but a way of white males to march together, get drunk together, be male together.'[30] Similarly, Jeanette Lugo of South Carolina concludes that St Patrick's Day in America centres on 'Beer drinking, hard partying, whiskey, whooping and hollering, etc.', and is 'aimed at men'. 'In fact', concludes Lugo, 'you hardly even see women in ads for St Patrick's Day sales ... [and] celebrations.'[31] Rick Gagne of New Hampshire confirms these views; he considers St Patrick's Day to be an opportunity for male 'Americans to act out stereotypes of drunken Irishmen'.[32] While men appear to comprise the majority of 'problem' drinkers on St Patrick's Day, a further gender-related issue is that women have been distanced from the organization of some St Patrick's Day festivities, such as those run by male-dominated Hibernian organizations. Kitty Cronin of Rhode Island feels that the AOH does 'a good job' in New York, but she resents 'the fact that women cannot be full members of the AOH – very archaic'.[33] Christine Kleinegger, a New York resident, questions the exclusion of women from certain St Patrick's Day events, most notably the dinners held by the Friendly Sons of St Patrick.[34] This view is echoed in Australia, where Mollie Murphy blasts the organizers of Brisbane's St Patrick's Day dinner for excluding women from the Irish Club's celebrations. Murphy notes, wryly, that Prime Minister John Howard was in attendance in 2000: 'What would they do', she asks, 'if Australia had a female Prime Minister in the future?'[35] It is difficult to see how women will remain on the margins of Irish organizations that stage traditional St Patrick's Day events. Not only is this discriminatory, it flies in the face of the supposedly inclusive nature of the Irish national day.

As 'the day' for Ireland internationally, St Patrick's Day is a key moment to represent and celebrate the country and its achievements. With St Patrick's Day's annual exaltation of the Irish nation, together with, in the diaspora, regional veneration of 'Irishness', it seems that worship of nation and state now overshadows religious observance. Much of this patriotism is, nonetheless, relatively innocuous. Paul McGale of Midlothian, Scotland, feels that St Patrick's Day has allowed 'many fellow Irish to feel a little bit of pride in their homeland, a little bit thankful'.[36] Joan Moody from Texas writes that 17 March 'represents the Irish nation and how the tradition passed from one generation to the next and from one country to another'.[37] From Co. Galway, Thomas Connolly feels that St Patrick's Day 'primarily and fundamentally represents the Irish nation'. He also takes pride in the diaspora:

> One of the benefits of emigration from Ireland is that St Patrick's Day is represented and indeed celebrated in virtually every corner of the earth. The Irish diaspora has had an immense effect on upholding the pride of the Irish nation everywhere they emigrated to.[38]

St Patrick's Day, including high profile events like the parade, provide Irish people with one of their few opportunities to reflect on their sense of self, about where they belong, and what they hope for. Birmingham's Carmel Girling, when asked what St Patrick's Day meant to her, replied that it was:

> A celebration of my parents and my own cultural roots. A second generation identity is difficult. You are Irish in England and English in Ireland. The parade gives you an opportunity to express and investigate how you feel about your roots and your own identity.[39]

There are many traditions and customs associated with St Patrick's Day, some of which appear universal, while others are more localized. One of the most common traditions has been the annual dispatch of shamrock to Irish family members abroad on St Patrick's Day. The packaging and sending of shamrock has been a commercialized operation since the 1950s. A South African woman remembers that at the convent school she attended near Cape Town, the nuns showed her shamrock that had been sent from Ireland.[40] Thomas Healy, who had been born in Co. Meath in the 1930s, remembers picking shamrock for his grandmother so that she could send it in the post, as a St Patrick's Day gift, to her sons and daughters living in England, America and Australia.[41] In the same vein, Mary Jennings, also born in the 1930s, recalls her family posting shamrock to relatives in America to 'remember people away on the day'.[42]

A childhood custom, especially among those of school age, has been to pinch anyone not wearing an item of green clothing on St Patrick's Day. As Jeannie Lugo of Kansas writes, 'it seemed a day of sanctioned violence'.[43] Oregon's Martha Sherwood remembers being pinched in the 1950s for not wearing green, but was also able to report that 'according to my daughter and a Japanese foreign exchange student living with us, this is still the case here in Oregon'.[44] While it was common, especially in North America, for those not wearing the green to be meddled with, the reverse was true in Britain during the 1970s, a time when Irish people were 'on the nose' owing to the Troubles. Paul remembers that when he was a child who had recently emigrated from Ireland to England, he was sent to school on St Patrick's Day with a shamrock pinned to his clothing. In response, the local children beat him up, berating him as a 'Paddy'.[45]

While St Patrick's Day is clearly linked historically with a celebration of Ireland and its diaspora, many people in North America feel that 17 March has become self-sustaining, and no longer relies on links with 'home'. David Dunning, of New York, writes that his annual get together with friends was an 'American holiday/celebration that today is no longer Irish dependent'.[46] The point is made even more strongly by Montreal's Matthew Barlow, who expresses weariness and scepticism about claims of Irish solidarity on 17 March:

> Unfortunately St Patrick's Day doesn't mean much to me anymore. St Patrick's Day in Canada, and I'm sure much of the rest of the world, has become a Hallmark card day. It's no longer a celebration about being Irish or the Irish, or anything of the sort. It's an excuse to get drunk, the day that everyone is Irish for the day.[47]

For one Irish traveller to America, Tom Jackson, St Patrick's Day in California seemed different to that normally experienced at his home in England. The locals in particular found it 'strange that [he] was not all dressed up in green and draped in artificial shamrocks'.[48] For others, however, St Patrick's Day still serves as an important marker of the success of the Irish diaspora. Catherine Donnolly-Hue, in describing the playing of Irish tunes by the New York Police Department band on Fifth Avenue, recalls that this 'never ceases to give me a lump in my throat and goose bumps ... with the tricolour and the American flag fluttering in the breeze, it says it all – yes, we've made it! We've proved ourselves.'[49] This chest thumping has also been felt in Ireland over recent years. Annie Dillon of Co. Dublin feels that St Patrick's Day is 'a day to express pride in ourselves', and that since the mid-1990s the celebrations in Ireland 'seem to include a renewed self-esteem in being Irish coinciding with our recent financial upswing'.[50] As the visibility of Irish products and services has grown in recent years, and things Irish have become fashionable, so St Patrick's Day has been celebrated more widely. In 1999, a survey conducted for the beverage producer, Ballygowan, found that 62 per cent of the British population expected to celebrate St Patrick's Day in some way. Considering how unpopular the Irish had been in Britain in the 1970s, this was a substantial turnaround. It was argued that if the Ballygowan figures were accurate, 'space in Irish pubs and clubs around Britain will be at a premium if 40 million people decide to drown the shamrock'.[51]

COMMERCIALIZING THE GREEN

St Patrick's Day has become increasingly commercialized since the end of the Second World War. It is a day when Irish goods and companies are promoted abroad, and also when the purveyors of 'paddywhackery' have their day in the sun. In addition to the greetings cards that are now such a feature of St Patrick's Day, it is possible to purchase paper plates and napkins, banners, scarves, balloons and various decorations for any given St Patrick's Day party or gathering. Novelty blackthorn sticks, ties, hats, T-shirts and costumes are also widely available. Such commercialism has not, however, been welcomed universally. Thomas Healy of Illinois writes that 'St Patrick's Day in America has become a total business and commercial event over the years'. He also complains that many of the images depicted on Patrician greetings cards are 'demeaning to the Irish'.[52] John Maxwell, a Toronto restaurateur, complains that 'green beer, green plastic bowler hats and people running about saying "kiss me I'm Irish", is all just "paddywhackery" and has nothing to do with St Patrick's Day'.[53] Mary Jennings, from Co. Galway, has a similar view about St Patrick's Day in contemporary Ireland. She feels that 'the celebrations have lost sight of what the day is about. Now the emphasis is on commercial advertising and sponsorship.'[54]

One of the most visible international Irish cultural icons is the Guinness label. First produced at the St James's Gate brewery in Dublin in 1759, the Guinness name and taste have spread across the world. When Guinness became a public company in 1886, the value of share applications was worth over £1 million. By the 1930s, Guinness was one of the seven largest companies in the world; it remains an industrial giant. Over the years the famous black pint, with its thick white head, has become a favourite drink for those celebrating St Patrick's Day. The availability of Guinness has been enhanced by the spread, from the 1980s, of the Irish replica bar across the world. Whether in Europe, North America, Australia, or now even in China, drinkers can drown the shamrock in 'virtual' Irish surrounds.

The Guinness brewing company has had a long working relationship with St Patrick's Day. It was one of the key entrants in Dublin's industrial pageant, and its floats were always keenly anticipated by spectators. Until the late 1980s, however, Guinness did not explicitly market its products outside of Ireland as a way of commemorating St Patrick's Day. But, with the expansion of Irish bars across the world, especially in Britain, Guinness began linking the consumption of its famous drink with the celebration of Ireland's patron saint. Throughout the 1990s, Guinness was successfully marketed as 'the drink' for St Patrick's Day; it has since become as much a symbol of the celebrations as shamrock, leprechauns, or shillelaghs. The marketing material used across the world by Guinness on St Patrick's Day was both varied and inventive. It consisted of two main types: advertisements for display in public places, and promotional material for use in pubs and bars. Such material was used across the world, with necessary linguistic changes made according to location. In 1997, a press advertisement for the Spanish-speaking world, which naturally featured a pint of Guinness, declared, '¿Por todos los santos, viene o no viene esa Guinness?'[55] Another sign of the global character of the Guinness product, together with its links to St Patrick's Day, was the launch on 17 March 1998, of a new larger 65cl bottle of Guinness. This took place in Gabon, Africa, where state officials and civic dignitaries were duly invited to share in the event.[56]

In 1996, all Guinness outlets in the Asia-Pacific region were sent posters depicting a leprechaun holding a crock of gold and a Guinness, bunting made of paper Guinness glasses and green shamrocks, along with white and green balloons, a large cut-out green paper shamrock, as well as packets of self-adhesive green and white St Patrick's Day stickers. To avoid any confusion as to how such decorations were to be used, an A4 page of instructions was also sent.[57] The displays may well have been a bit of blarney, but they were expected to be erected prudently. In Australia, marketing ploys have included the erection of the world's biggest aluminium can filled with Guinness draught, and the promotion of Guinness food recipes.[58] In 1997, the company promoted St Patrick's Day consumption of its product by announcing that anyone drinking a pint of Guinness had the opportunity of winning a pub. The related drip mats declared: 'Grab a pen. Win a pub. Change your commute. Happy St Patrick's Day.'[59] Following the chance to win a pub on St Patrick's Day, Guinness has since sought to convince its customers that while 17 March is the most important date in the calendar for the consumption of its products, the rest of the year should also be used. In 1999, the company's advertising proclaimed: 'One St Patrick's Day, 364 practice days.'[60]

The promotion of Guinness on and around St Patrick's Day has also encompassed a general selling of Ireland as a tourist destination. In a variety of British and North American newspapers, Guinness sponsored special St Patrick's Day colour supplements, which promoted Ireland as a holiday venue.[61] Yet it must be said that Guinness has also avoided St Patrick's Day promotional opportunities. By the mid-1980s, and in the wake of ongoing arguments about the selection of the Grand Marshal of the New York parade and its possible links with Irish republican organizations, the company withdrew its financial support. Indeed, by 1986 Guinness decided not to participate in the parade, 'and was only a token presence on the sideline'.[62] As we will now see, ten years later Guinness had an ideal local focus for its St Patrick's Day sponsorship money.

ST PATRICK'S FESTIVAL: DUBLIN-STYLE

The advent of the St Patrick's Festival in 1996 marked a significant turning point in the anniversary's history. Dublin organizers since then have effectively sought to reappropriate St Patrick's Day as a key event in the domestic

Irish calendar, and to refocus celebration on the island where the saint carried out his work. This approach is a reaction to, and in some ways in defiance of, the diaspora-based St Patrick's celebrations that have claimed virtual 'ownership' of the festivities abroad. In seeking to reinvent St Patrick's Day celebrations, the Dublin Festival has offered new ways of understanding the contemporary resonance of 17 March. The initiative also demonstrates that global traditions are only powerful when they are locally relevant. In breaking away from the North American style of celebration, Dublin has not only challenged the veracity of 'foreign' forms of observance, it has suggested 'authentic' local alternatives.

St Patrick's Day is celebrated in more countries around the world than any other national festival. Yet in Dublin, the capital of the Irish Republic, the festivities had become rather muted by the mid-1990s. It seemed that the diaspora continued to embrace St Patrick's Day in a more demonstrative fashion than did the Irish themselves. At a time of successful social and economic transitions in Ireland, the erosion of the national anniversary was not allowed to continue. The Irish Government, aware of press criticism and complaints from organizations that had taken part in Dublin Tourism's parade, announced a steering committee to investigate alternative arrangements. The committee, appointed by the Minister for Tourism and Trade, and chaired by Michael Colgan of the Gate Theatre, made four key findings: (a) the Dublin Tourism parade lacked entertainment and imagination; (b) it failed to adequately promote Dublin as a year-round tourism destination; (c) it did not reflect the culture or cultural successes of contemporary Ireland; and (d) it did not harness global goodwill towards Ireland. In November 1995, the government formed the St Patrick's Festival committee as a new group to manage and stage Dublin's Patrician celebrations. The Irish government brief identified four key functions for the new form of celebration: (a) to promote Ireland as a tourist destination; (b) to promote Ireland as a year-round destination; (c) to stage an event of such length that it made a trip to Dublin worthwhile; and (d) to present a varied range of events to attract people of all ages. The brief was refined by the Festival organizers so that they could

> offer a national festival that ranks amongst all of the greatest celebrations in the world. Create energy and excitement throughout Ireland via innovation, creativity, grassroots involvement and marketing activity. Provide the opportunity and motivation for people of Irish descent (and those who sometimes wished they were Irish) to attend and join in the imaginative and expressive celebrations. Project, internationally, an accurate image of Ireland as a creative, professional and sophisticated country with wide appeal.[63]

The St Patrick's Festival was a new departure in the history of 17 March celebrations. Whereas specific organizations or private enterprises, such as the

AOH, tourist boards, or bars and clubs, had traditionally held responsibility for organizing parades and other celebrations, the evolution of the St Patrick's Festival was a product of direct government intervention. Effectively, Ireland was to have the first state-sponsored St Patrick's Day celebrations for public consumption. While such intervention from the government was understandable, particularly given the tourism opportunities St Patrick's Day afforded Ireland, the question still remained as to whether such a venture would be successful. The resulting St Patrick's Festival offers a fascinating insight into the struggle to revitalize Patrician celebrations in Ireland.

As part of its mission to rapidly become the single most important Patrician celebration in the world, the St Patrick's Festival had to build on existing traditions of observance, yet employ new methods of promotion. A key challenge has been to combat the widespread belief, in Ireland at least, that 'the St Patrick's Day parade conjures up images of rain-soaked Americans, walking loaves of bread, and cleverly disguised haulage trucks with festive bunting'.[64] The 1996 Festival, organized with only a four-month lead-in time and a budget of IR£700,000, was hailed as a great success. The main aim of the 1996 Festival was to move the St Patrick's Day celebrations in Dublin away from being 'just a parade'. Rather than relying solely on traditional marching bands from America and industrial floats, the Festival actively encouraged the participation of professional theatrical and local community groups in the parade, together with their involvement at other venues across the city during the day. The cumulative attendance at the various Festival-organized St Patrick's Day events was estimated to be 450,000 – around double that of 1995, the last year of the Dublin Tourism parade. The Festival director, Marie Claire Sweeney, claimed an early strategic success. She saw it as her role to 'jettison the paddywhackery and shamrockery and create a vibrant, buzzing four-day international festival'.[65]

By 1997, with a full year of planning, the St Patrick's Festival had grown in size and length in an attempt to meet the criteria that had been laid down by the government. A mark of the rapid changes the parade had undergone was apparent by the inclusion of just one commercial float. Prior to the Festival, such floats had been the mainstay of the parade. It was now a much larger enterprise, backed by major corporations. Guinness, which had once entered floats in the annual parade, was now one of ten foundation sponsors of the St Patrick's Festival.[66] The free Official Festival programme, printed in the *Irish Times*, was produced in association with Guinness, and featured a whole string of advertisements for the company's products. The back cover of the programme showed a picture of a pint of Guinness with the by-line, '17.3.97 Dress Code'.[67] The expanded Festival had a focus beyond the parade on St Patrick's Day. Events were spread across three days and were focused on different areas of the city. Yet the heart of the Festival, on St Patrick's Day, was still the parade through the city centre. In the days before the parade, there was a fire parade along the River Liffey to open the Festival,

street performances in Temple Bar, a funfair for children, and musical concerts. Guinness was sponsor of the Temple Bar Fleadh, a continuous feast of
music in an area crowded with pubs and restaurants. The close of the Festival, on the night of 17 March, was marked by a monster ceilidh in St
Stephen's Green.[68] The aggregate attendance at Festival events over the three
days was estimated at 585,000. More importantly, in the context of the
government's conception of what an event like the Festival might achieve,
there was a growing global media interest in the Dublin celebrations. Coverage of the Festival was screened across more than 450 million television sets
in Europe and America, and was covered extensively by the print media in a
wide range of countries. In its broadest terms, the Festival succeeded by
repositioning the event: more than 'just a parade this was THE major
national party of the year' and by changing the perspective so that 'Dublin,
Ireland [is] perceived as THE only place to be on, and around, St Patrick's
Day'.[69]

The 'repositioning' or, it could be argued, remarketing of St Patrick's
Day in Ireland was deemed, by the Irish Government's own criteria at least,
a huge success. The 1998 and 1999 Festivals continued to achieve large
crowds. In 1998, the aggregate attendance for the whole Festival was
865,000, while 500,000 watched the parade on 17 March. The procession,
which featured 5,000 participants from around the world and over 200
community groups, ranked alongside that of New York as the most watched
St Patrick's Day parade anywhere. In matching the size and scale of the New
York parade, the Festival fulfilled one of its objectives: to promote a sense of
Irish achievement within the confines of Ireland while still appealing to
those outside. As the Festival Office put it:

> The primary aim of the Festival, is to create an annual party for the
> Irish people – a vehicle through which they can express their national
> pride and celebrate the creativity and achievements of the whole
> country. In doing so, we want to create a Festival of international
> standing which will ensure that Dublin is known worldwide as *the*
> place to be during the period around St Patrick's Day.[70]

The St Patrick's Festival was a clear commercial and entertainment success,
and was thus applauded widely by observers from across the world. The
Desert Shamrock, the newspaper for Irish Americans living in Arizona, argued
that the Festival parade had 'put New York's to shame with colourful floats,
an 80-foot dragon and Ronan Keating of Boyzone'.[71] The Irish-American
appreciation of the vitality of the Dublin St Patrick's Festival, and the
increased numbers of American visitors to Ireland during the week
surrounding 17 March, suggest that the whole enterprise had been a success.
Rather than presenting visiting Irish Americans with a simple copy of
American habits, the St Patrick's Festival has evolved an Irish series of cele-

brations that are both unique, yet familiar. This process fits in with the views offered by Byron, who has concluded that

> the commonplace, increasingly standardised and essentialised stereo-types of Irishness held by Americans, including their interpretations of the famine, have been exported across the Atlantic, along with Bagels, basketball and St Patrick's Day parades, and are now repackaged and sold back to Americans as 'heritage' when they visit Ireland.[72]

The millennium St Patrick's Festival continued to build on the successes of the previous years. The four-day festival was based on a close partnership between those running the event, the Irish Government (most markedly in the form of the Fianna Fáil Minister for Tourism, Leisure and Sport, James McDaid), and big business. The budget had increased from its 1996 level of IR£700,000 to IR£1.3 million. All the sponsors of the Festival supported the event, but most vociferous was Festival Chairman and head of the Superquinn supermarket chain, Feargal Quinn. In 2000, he pleaded with the people of Dublin to fully embrace their St Patrick's Day celebrations asking them 'not to be shy about putting on green and silly clothes. Do it just for the craic. We will have all the excitement of last year – plus a little bit more.'[73] The 2000 festival,[74] entitled 'Hullabaloo', was also deemed a success, but this time several commentators were not won over. Prior to the festival, Declan McCormack, writing in the *Sunday Independent,* argued that the event was a 'futile farce', and that it should be more honestly rebranded as 'Seven Drunken Days of Sublime Stupidity'.[75] Despite such criticism, the Festival generated much income from merchandising, television and other electronic rights. By becoming an income generator, the Festival has reduced its level of government funding from 70 per cent of total costs in 1996, to 35 per cent in 2000.

In the wake of the various socio-economic transformations in Irish society during the 1990s, it is perhaps unsurprising that the St Patrick's Festival is both a reaction to, and a mirror for, such changes. The previous industrial pageant and Dublin Tourism parade were seen as outdated and representat-ive of an old-fashioned Ireland. Black-and-white footage of old processions, which featured inclement weather and dreary floats, was used by TV3 as the opening for their coverage of the 2000 St Patrick's Festival. It conjured up images of 'old' Ireland, which was juxtaposed against colourful coverage of the modern, multi-faceted Festival in the 'new' Ireland. The themes represented by this montage, and by the Festival itself, were products of an Ireland undergoing a period of intense change. In this context, Diarmuid Ó Giolláin noted that:

> Globalisation has undermined the power of the Irish State – and every other state – to enforce cultural conformity. This has been reflected in

the less monolithic, more playful St Patrick's Day parades of late ...
the fact that St Patrick and St Patrick's Day already belong to millions
of people who aren't Irish makes them the most inclusive of Irish
symbols, and augurs well for St Patrick's continued relevance to a
changing Irish society.[76]

What, though, explains the success of the Festival in transforming Irish
observance of St Patrick's Day? The Festival built on themes of public celebration that had, it appeared, become the norm in other contexts, such as
the 1988 commemoration of Dublin's millennium, the arrival of the Irish
football team in Dublin after their exploits in the 1990 Italian World Cup
finals, and the return of gold-medal-winning Irish boxers from the Barcelona
Olympic Games in 1992. In each of these cases a carnivalesque, often spontaneous public gathering appeared on the streets of Dublin in which pride
and joy predominated. By comparison to such euphoric assemblies, the
Dublin Tourism parade on 17 March looked very staid. Hence the new St
Patrick's Festival built on larger and more expressive ceremonial practices
established in Ireland in the late 1980s and early 1990s. It was no longer
simply a spectacle packaged for the consumption of visiting Americans in
return for their tourist dollars. What replaced the Americanized version of
the Dublin Tourism parade, which had been replete with marching bands
and majorettes, was a Festival based more explicitly on the local and
parochial. It was a Festival that sought to embrace the local communities of
Dublin and Ireland, at the same time welcoming all visitors to observe and
take part in an *Irish*, rather than a repackaged American event. A key factor
in the success of the Festival, is that the whole four days of celebration are
free to attend and open to all. In an age where arts festivals, music concerts
and leisure events are important globally, the St Patrick's Festival has successfully redeveloped a week in mid-March as a multi-faceted, Irish-hosted
celebration known across the world. Whereas the Dublin Tourism parade
relied narrowly on the tourist income generated by allowing American non-
musical marching groups, such as the Irish Societies to parade, the Festival
discontinued this tradition from 1996 as such groups now provided little in
terms of entertainment value. Visitors now generally come to Ireland for
several days to celebrate St Patrick's Day, and in buoyant mood they contribute generously to the economy. Through cheap flights, the growing
familiarity of visitors with Irish culture and entertainment icons like
Temple Bar in Dublin, Ireland is now a magnet for those wishing to celebrate St Patrick's Day in its original home.[77]

With the success of the St Patrick's Day Festival in Dublin, there has
now been a clear reinvigoration of Patrician parades and festivities across
Ireland. In literally each city, town and village, something is organized for
locals to join in a revived national awareness of 17 March. There has also
been an emphasis on celebrations that are peculiar to a locality, different

from the norm, and intended to attract public attention. In 1999, the 'shortest' St Patrick's Day parade took place in Dripsey, County Cork. A crowd estimated at 3,000 gathered to watch pipe major Michael Murphy lead the parade the 25 yards from the Lee Valley bar into the Weigh Inn bar.[78] In 2000, it was estimated that over a million people attended St Patrick's Day parades across Ireland, all drawn to different towns and cities where, with the use of imagination and a touch of tradition, seemingly 'authentic' local celebrations of 17 March are being invented.

CONCLUSION

— ❧ —

There comes into my heart a sense of dismay at the approach of St Patrick's Day – our annual entry into the Green Ghetto. Choruses of shures and begorrahs pollute the air and obscene greeting cards with pugilistic leprechauns portraying the 'Fighting Oirish' are everywhere to be found. The geographically challenged Gloc-camorrah is the classic of choice on the radio. Happy St Patty's Day greetings whack our eardrums as if the man were canonized hamburger meat.[1]

At the beginning of the twenty-first century, what are the purposes of St Patrick's Day, and what meanings are attached to the anniversary? Why is it, that many centuries since his death, St Patrick still draws attention to himself?[2] The day itself provides a common focus for millions of people who claim Irish descent; it offers them both tangible and imagined connections between local and global Irish communities. Naturally, many people of Irish descent do not actively celebrate St Patrick's Day by joining a parade or attending a special luncheon or dinner. But the vast majority of the worldwide Irish are at least aware that this is 'their' day. As Roger James, writing in the *Irish Post*, has observed:

Guinness will be guzzled by the gallon, jigs will be danced and Irish eyes will be smiling (and bloodshot) in places as distant and disparate as Tokyo, Auckland and Boston. Celtophiles the world over will remember in a bewildering variety of ways a 5th century missionary who was once a lowly sheep herder in Antrim.[3]

The non-Irish, too, are hardly isolated from the 'green for a day' bandwagon. As Arizona's *Desert Shamrock* concludes: 'On St Patrick's Day everyone is a wee bit Irish. That has never been more true than in these days of supersonic travel, the World Wide Web and Guinness exports to all four corners of a steadily shrinking globe.'[4] We venture to say that every major city in the world has an Irish bar tucked away somewhere. Such places become magnets for people wanting to celebrate Ireland's national day. There are also more tangible reasons for observing 17 March in non-Celtic regions. In France, towns and villages named after St Patrick, such as Saint-Patrice de Claids or Saint-Patrice du Desert, all celebrate on 17 March. On the Caribbean island of Montserrat, which is the only place in the world other than Ireland to

248

and the romance of the armed struggle in Northern Ireland, sit
e dancing leprechauns, 'Kiss Me I'm Irish' hats, green beer and
and corned beef. America, on 17 March, creates a St Patrick's Day
rishness that is a product of its own national history. It offers, as do
ck's Day celebrations across the world and throughout history, a
through which widely held, even if poorly understood beliefs about
i, can be viewed. It serves as an annual time capsule, opened up each
ch great excitement and gusto, yet through which the same tired
pes about the Irish are trotted out shamelessly, as if St Patrick
was a Disneyland character and leprechauns were Santa's elves.
day still functions, however, as do many of the parades and other
ags, as powerful markers of the Irish presence within a diaspora
nity and their links with the politics of the 'homeland'. St Patrick's
often been, and remains, a celebration of Irish successes and achieve-
within an emigrant host society or in Ireland itself. The anniversary
rs a day in the spotlight for those Irish, be they recent emigrants or
ving at the base of the socio-economic order, whose personal histories
cked a sense of accomplishment. For them, the annual gathering of
h presents an opportunity to rise above their usual station in life, and
proclaim their presence amidst 'like' others. In this, the function of
ck's Day remains little changed from that of the nineteenth century.
respect, too much can be made of the contemporary relevance of the
Tiger economy and the worldwide success of the Irish.
the centuries, St Patrick's Day has been embraced by different
and in a variety of ways in a multitude of locations and venues. It has
l gradually from an ethnic and religious celebration of the Irish
saint, to a largely secular and commercial holiday.[9] It has often func-
as a public display for the Irish community across the world. But 17
is also underpinned by a variety of personal and private traditions. Its
rity, across all sections of society, both Irish and non-Irish alike, has
direct proportion to its use by a variety of commercial concerns –
hose making greetings cards and plastic shamrocks, to those seeking
st their beer sales. In its entirety, the day offers an opportunity to
tand how the Irish have been transformed from feckless beggars, ban-
xiles, and a people oppressed in their own land, to a group eyed with
y others for their achievements, culture and success worldwide.
2001 the St Patrick's Festival in Dublin, was, as with many other
in the Irish Republic, postponed because of concerns about the foot-
outh outbreak in Britain. The day was still widely and vociferously
ited, albeit on a more informal and personal level, proving that Patri-
bservance does not rely on a publicly organized parade or some other
civic celebration. The year also marked the first ever St Patrick's Day
g sent from a British monarch, Queen Elizabeth II, to the head of the
tate; this is a sign of the ever closer relationship between the two

celebrate St Patrick's Day as a public holiday, there are lavish celebrations
and a host of Irish events.[5] The saying that 'everyone is Irish' on St Patrick's
Day may be an exaggeration, but the festivities have been embraced,
particularly as we saw in Montreal, by many non-Irish people too. Indeed,
the success of St Patrick's Day in North America has been something of a
catalyst for other ethnic groups to celebrate their national days, and to
express their own sense of solidarity by staging street parades and other
events in the public arena.

St Patrick's Day offers an opportunity for interaction between Irish
people who, ordinarily, may be unknown to each other. Such anonymity can
be advantageous: if 'everyone' is entitled to be green on St Patrick's Day,
there is less need to divide people along religious and political lines. The
celebrations can, therefore, provide an annual sense of group cohesion.
However, such collective effervescence tends to be transitory rather than
enduring. This is because the integrative power of ceremonial and festivity
are fleeting, even though they appear potent, in our postmodern age. Indeed,
the St Patrick's Day camaraderie of smiling marchers and back-slapping
drinkers may conceal more than it actually reveals. For most of its history, St
Patrick's Day has been dominated by all-male organizations who paraded,
dined and drank together. In recent times a particular section of the Irish-
American community – gay and lesbian organizations – have been banned
from marching in both the New York and Boston parades, a decision that
has been ratified by US courts. The Belfast parade, revived in the midst of
the peace process, has been garrotted by political and sectarian divides. The
Sydney parade, while not suffering from any resentment on the part of
the host city, has struggled to survive owing to bickering among Irish-
Australian organizations about who should control the event. A further issue
of contention is that of gender discrimination. It appears that 17 March celebrations, whether in the committee rooms of the AOH, the dining rooms of
the Friendly Sons of St Patrick or in bars across the world, have traditionally
been either exclusive to men, or dictated by men. Indeed, the history of the
Patrician anniversary has to be understood within a context of male dominance and female marginalization. There are also frequent accusations that
St Patrick's Day is used as means of collecting money for continuing the
armed struggle in Northern Ireland.[6] Such conflict is, of course, hardly new:
our study has shown that both Irish and diaspora politics have long shaped
the commemoration of St Patrick's Day, whether in Montreal, New York, or
Liverpool. Such problems are likely to resurface. This is because the familial
warmth of St Patrick's Day cannot be expected to effectively counter or even
cushion long-standing sectarian, political and other divides within Irish
communities. The 17th of March may 'green over' these difficulties, or it
may take issue with them head on. Either way, St Patrick's Day cannot be
expected to rid the Irish of their problems, as if they were snakes being
chased away by the saint himself.

Yet there remains a noble dream of unity; that the self-reflection and 'come-togetherness' of St Patrick's Day will ultimately instil a belief that there is more that holds the Irish together than drives them apart. Oliver MacDonagh concedes that there is plenty of blarney on St Patrick's Day. Yet, he reminds us, 17 March is also a time for genuine vision and hope for the future:

There is no denying that much of this [celebration] was facile, smothering the unpleasant facts, idealizing the remainder, and freely dreaming comparisons of dubious validity. Yet there is a sense, I think in which things are licensed for Irish people on St Patrick's Day. It is the day of aspiration, of vision ... Let me suggest an analogy: Dickens's use of – one is tempted to say invention of – Christmas Day. You will all remember that in the *Christmas Carol* Dickens uses the day as a vehicle for his vision of how things might be – if only hearts were changed, if predatory selves were subdued, if fears and prejudice were looked on bravely in the face and forced to dwindle. May not Irish people use *their* Special Day to similar effect, to provide a glimpse of what might be in the best of all possible worlds? Of course we know that the best of all possible worlds will be forever unrealisable. But unless it is imagined – and in a sense even created for one day in the year – where is our hope to come from, and how are we to be sustained in the struggle against ancient or inveterate evils?[7]

St Patrick's Day is a special day in the annual calendar. For a few hours each year, St Patrick becomes the world's leading de facto holyman for the Irish, its diaspora and many others. Yet as we have shown, the religious roots and importance of St Patrick's Day have been largely forgotten. Across the years, 17 March has been profoundly affected by a variety of historical forces. Politics, emigration, commercialization, the industrial and transport revolutions, and a host of other influences, have all shaped how and why St Patrick's Day has been celebrated across the world. Alongside this loss of the day's religious roots, the role of Irish Protestants, in North America and elsewhere, in beginning and sustaining the traditions of dining and parading on St Patrick's Day has also been forgotten. We have shown that the history of St Patrick's Day celebrations is complex, and is not simply the story of those Catholic Irish that emigrated in the wake of the mid-nineteenth-century famine. What we have been unable to reveal in any great detail, is how the non-Catholic Irish across the world have embraced St Patrick's Day in recent decades. It is clear that there have been many incidences when anti-Catholic groups, in an attempt to undermine or attack the rights of those who wished to celebrate, have used 17 March for negative reasons. However, the majority of Americans who now claim Irish ancestry descend from Protestant and not Catholic origins. Many of these Irish Ameri-

cans wish to embrace 17 March as a day for cele[...] are obliged to observe a St Patrick's Day whose [...] lies with Catholic organizations such as the AOH[...] much more research is required to explore the Iri[...] the diaspora, as well as those Irish – whether in [...] who have no particular sense of religious commit[...] people with these types of background perceive o[...] and heritage that is largely, yet narrowly, under[...] Irish-Catholic emigration, religious affiliation and[...] 'visible' Irish-Protestant history of 17 March is not[...] lacuna. This book has dealt with the history of St [...] across a range of geographical areas and chronolog[...] is hoped that other researchers will turn their atter[...] gration that were not covered here, and thus detail[...] functioned in diverse countries like Argentina,[...] Zealand. In addition to such national surveys, ther[...] focus on the histories and meanings of parades [...] particular contexts, and to unravel key themes w[...] such as the varied effects of gender, ethnicity, natio[...]

St Patrick's Day has become, in part, an open[...] everyone can be Irish. One of the key developme[...] Patrick's Day has been its opening up to people and[...] no Irish heritage or connection.[8] In its origins and f[...] March was a day reserved for 'insiders', a ritual in [...] played their collective identity and numeric streng[...] One has to wonder, however, whether the opening [...] everyone has produced a celebration that is confus[...] may even have negative connotations. For the most [...] no longer a time for remembering the life of a [...] message or the fortunes of the Irish nation and its[...] Patrick's Day appears as an annual homage to hee[...] alcohol – a Mardi Gras without the accompanying tr[...] to its critics, St Patrick's Day appears trite, tacky and[...] of such criticisms has led to an attempted 'reinvent[...] vance in some places, most notably the Dublin [...] embrace of arts and culture. However, many of the [...] remain self-serving and excessively indulgent. Cri[...] which St Patrick's Day is observed most often emana[...] aghast at the zealous observance of St Patrick's Da[...] incongruous that so many Americans, with even the[...] 'the old country', seem to try harder than even the [...] Patrick's Day. In this light, St Patrick's Day appears [...] about Ireland that is historically simplistic and [...] Images of the sufferings of the famine Irish, the nat[...]

countries as a result of the ongoing Northern Ireland peace process. Across the Atlantic in America, Hillary Clinton, newly elected as a Senator, declined to march in the all-important New York parade, choosing to join a smaller upstate parade. Clinton's actions, a deliberate attempt to avoid involvement in the ongoing ILGO issue, reaffirmed that the issues of politics and contested identities remain an essential part of the observance of 17 March. These, and a host of other events from the first St Patrick's Day of the twenty-first century, demonstrate how the anniversary will always offer a window through which larger issues and themes within the Irish communities can be understood. In being celebrated across the Western world, St Patrick's Day 2001 proved the ongoing validity of a comment in the *Gael* from a century earlier: 'only Christmas Day is more widely observed than 17 March'.[10] St Patrick's Day will continue to develop, and the way in which the day is celebrated will continue to be transformed at local, national and global levels. It is unquestionable that the forces of globalization and commercialization will change 17 March still further, but the Irish roots of St Patrick's Day should never be forgotten. Mary McAleese, the President of Ireland, used her St Patrick's Day speech in 2001 to call for the respect of Ireland's cultural heritage, but also insisted that there is much to be gained by moving forward and creating new traditions to be proud of. Her words, on the day reserved for celebration of her nation's patron saint, summed up the contemporary position of Ireland, and offered a context for all those celebrating St Patrick's Day to understand the importance of its commemoration.

> The voice of today's Ireland speaks more of celebration than of lamentation. A new heritage of prosperity and peace is being crafted by a generation which has known more hope, more success, more opportunity than any other. The past which shaped us no longer shackles us. Ireland has moved into a new era and confidence in the future is its hallmark.[11]

In MacAleese's comments we find the central focus of this book, indeed of St Patrick's Day. The 17th of March is a day for the Irish. It offers, however, a multitude of different views about what it means to be Irish and a host of ways in which people celebrate their sense of Irishness. MacAleese looks to a present that is no longer shackled by the past, but surely every facet of human society bears the marks of its chains. St Patrick's Day in each country studied here has been different. The anniversary is, indeed, a product of the shackles of many histories: the Irish 'homeland' that has shaped it, and the setting, traditions and circumstances of local and host communities abroad. May the future bring us a world in which St Patrick's Day is celebrated everywhere peacefully.

NOTES

— ✥ —

INTRODUCTION

1 D. Leary, 'On being born Irish-American: a glossary', in M. Coffey and T. Galway (eds), *The Irish in America*, New York, Hyperion, 1997, p. 210.

2 The lack of literature relating to the history of 17 March has also been identified by M. Fitzgerald, 'The St Patrick's Day Parade: The Conflict of Irish-American Identity in New York City, 1840–1900', PhD thesis, State University of New York at Stony Brook, 1992, p. 22.

3 G.E. Aylmer, 'St. Patrick's Day 1628 in Witham, Essex', *Past and Present*, no. 61, 1973, pp. 139–48; M. Cottrell, 'St Patrick's Day parade in nineteenth-century Toronto', *Historie Sociale/Social History*, vol. 25, 1992, pp. 57–73; K.S. Inglis, *The Australian Colonists: An Exploration of Social History, 1788–1870*, Carlton, Vic., Melbourne University Press, 1974, Chap. 6, 'St Patrick's Day'; O. MacDonagh, 'Irish culture and nationalism translated: St Patrick's Day in Australia 1888', in O. MacDonagh, W.F. Mandle and P. Travers (eds), *Culture and Nationalism in Ireland, 1750–1950*, Canberra, Macmillan, 1983, pp. 69–82; S.A. Marston, 'Public rituals and community power: St Patrick's Day parades in Lowell, Massachusetts, 1841–74', *Political Geography Quarterly*, vol. 8, no. 3, 1989, pp. 255–69; T.J. Meagher, 'Why should we care for a little trouble or a walk in the mud? St Patrick's and Columbus Day parades in Worcester, Massachusetts, 1845–1915', *New England Quarterly*, vol. 58, no. 1, 1985, pp. 5–26; A. Madson, 'St. Patrick's Day in Rock County', *Southern Humanities Review*, vol. 19, no. 1, 1985, pp. 14–24; K. Moss, 'St. Patrick's Day celebrations and the formation of Irish-American identity, 1845–1875', *Journal of Social History*, vol. 29, Fall 1995, pp. 125–48; P. O'Farrell, 'St Patrick's Day in Australia: the John Alexander Ferguson lecture 1994', *Journal of the Royal Australian Historical Society*, vol. 81, no. 1, 1995, pp. 1–16.

4 J.D. Crimmins, *St. Patrick's Day: Its Early Celebrations in New York and Other American Places, 1737–1845*, New York, The Author, 1902; W.L. Fogarty, *The Days We've Celebrated: St. Patrick's Day in Savannah*, Savannah, Printcraft Press, 1980; J. Moran, *'The Land We Left Behind': The Emergence of St Patrick's Day Celebrations in Brisbane, 1862–1870*, Ashgrove, Queensland, The Author, 1989; J.T. Ridge, *The St Patrick's Day Parade in New York*, New York, New York St. Patrick's Day Parade Committee, 1988; N. Schmitz, *Irish for a Day: St Patrick's Day Parades in Quebec City, 1850–1990*, Montreal, Carraig Books, 1991; M. Fitzgerald, 'The St Patrick's Day parade'.

5 S.P. Metress, *The American Irish and Irish Nationalism: A Sociohistorical Introduction*, Lanham, MD, Scarecrow Press, 1995, pp. 17–18.

6 S.J. Connolly (ed.), *The Oxford Companion to Irish History*, Oxford, Oxford University Press, 1998, p. 19.

7 W.J. McCormack (ed.), *The Blackwell Companion to Modern Irish Culture*, Oxford, Blackwell, 1999, pp. 515–16.

8   Although not discussing St Patrick's Day in his work, Yeats did write about St Patrick in his 1889 work, *The Wanderings of Oisin*, which is based on a discussion between St Patrick and the ancient Celt Oisin and the ensuing battle over the future of Oisin's soul. First published as *The Wanderings of Oisin and Other Poems*, London, Kegan Paul, Trench & Co., 1889.

9   J. Joyce, *Dubliners*, New York, B.W. Huebsch, 1917.

10 S. O'Casey, 'St Pathrick's Day in the Morning', in S. O'Casey, *The Green Crow*, London, Virgin, 1994, p. 190.

11 P. Galvin, *Song for a Raggy Boy: A Cork Boyhood*, Dublin, Raven Arts Press, 1991; D. Healey, *The Bend for Home*, London, Harvil, 1996.

12 F. McCourt, *Angela's Ashes: A Memoir*, London, HarperCollins, 1996; F. McCourt, *'Tis: A Memoir*, London, Flamingo, 1999, pp. 235, 246–8.

13 D. Smith, *A Song for Mary: An Irish-American Memory*, New York, Warner, 1999; B. Wannan, *Wearing of the Green: The Lore, Literature, Legend and Balladry*, Melbourne, Lansdowne, 1965; B. Wannan, *The Folklore of the Irish in Australia*, Melbourne, Currey O'Neil, 1980.

14 R.B. Sheridan, *St Patrick's Day or the Scheming Lieutenant*, London, Unit Library, 1903, p. 5.

15 Ibid., p. 11.

16 N. de Mille, *Cathedral*, London, Granada, 1982.

17 F. Delaney, *Desire and Pursuit*, London, HarperCollins, 1999, p. 77.

18 E. Barth and U. Arndt, *Shamrocks, Harps, and Shillelaghs: The Story of the St. Patrick's Day Symbols*, New York, Seabury Press, 1977; S. Ziegler and G. Connelly, *Our St. Patrick's Day Book*, Chicago, Child's World, 1987; and M.J. Fallon, *The Definitive St. Patrick's Day Festivity Book*, Santa Clara, Educare, 1997.

19 For a brief summary of further internet sources, see D. Molloy, 'St. Patrick on the web', *Irish Voice*, 17 March 1998.

20 S. Barrett, 'St Patrick's Day around the world', 27 February 1999, Ireland for Visitors, www.goireland.miningco.com/travel/goireland. Other web resources are: Irelandbynet.com; Ireland On-line (www.home.iol.ie/); Irishnet (www.ceolas.org/IrishNet/); Local Ireland (www.local.ie/); Irish Abroad (www.irishabroad.com/); and Irish America Net (www.irishamerica.net/).

21 For a major discussion on the social and political origins of various civic rituals, see E. Hobsbawm and T. Ranger (eds), *The Invention of Tradition*, Cambridge, Cambridge University Press, 1983.

22 The interplay between 'invention' and 'discovery' of civic ritual is discussed in R. Ely, 'The First Anzac Day: invented or discovered?', *Journal of Australian Studies*, no. 17, November 1985, pp. 41–58.

23 The capacity of civic ritual to evoke a sense of collective belonging is discussed at length in B. Anderson, *Imagined Communities: Reflections on the Origin and Spread of Nationalism*, London, Verso, 1983; and P. Connerton, *How Societies Remember*, Cambridge, Cambridge University Press, 1989.

24 E. Durkheim, *The Elementary Forms of the Religious Life: A Study in Religious Sociology*, translated from the French by J.W. Swain, London, George Allen & Unwin, 1926, p. 427.

25 E. Shils and M. Young, 'The meaning of the coronation', *Sociological Review* (n.s.), vol. 1, 1953, pp. 72–80. For a telling critique of this article, see N. Birnbaum, 'Monarchs and sociologists: a reply to Professor Shils and Mr. Young', *Sociological Review* (n.s.), vol. 3, 1955, pp. 5–23.

26 G. Debord, 'Society of the spectacle', *Black and Red*, Detroit, Kalamazoo, 1970,

paragraphs 1–72; S. Lukes, 'Political ritual and social integration', *Sociology*, vol. 9, no. 2, May 1975, pp. 289–308.

27 E. Hammerton and D. Cannadine, 'Conflict and consensus on a ceremonial occasion, the Diamond Jubilee in Cambridge 1897', *Historical Journal*, vol. 24, no. 1, 1981, p. 113. Examples of studies with a similar theme include C.E. Martin and W.E. French (eds), *Rituals of Rule, Rituals of Resistance: Public Celebrations and Popular Culture in Mexico*, Wilmington, SR Books, 1994; D. Adair, 'On parade: spectacles, crowds, and collective loyalties in Australia, 1901–1938', PhD thesis, Adelaide, Flinders University of South Australia, 1994.

28 M. French, 'The ambiguity of Empire Day in New South Wales 1901–21: imperial consensus or national division?', *Australian Journal of Politics and History*, vol. 24, no. 1, April 1978, pp. 61–74; D. Hood, 'Adelaide's first "taste of Bolshevism": returned soldiers and the 1918 Peace Day riots', *Journal of the Historical Society of South Australia*, vol. 15, 1987, pp. 42–53; A. Howe, 'Women against Anzac Day: the personal is the political', *Peace Studies*, vol. 6, September 1984, pp. 17–19.

29 J. Horner and M. Langton, 'The day of mourning', in B. Gammage and P. Spearritt (eds), *Australians 1938*, Sydney, Fairfax, Syme and Weldon, 1987, pp. 29–36; P. Spearritt, 'Celebration of a nation: the triumph of spectacle', *Australian Historical Studies*, vol. 23, no. 91, October 1988, pp. 3–20.

30 P. Burke, *Popular Culture in Early Modern Europe*, London, Temple Smith, 1978; R.D. Storch (ed.), *Popular Culture and Custom in Nineteenth Century England*, London, Croom Helm, 1982.

31 As examples, see D. Cannadine and S. Price (eds), *Rituals of Royalty: Power and Ceremonial in Traditional Societies*, Cambridge, Cambridge University Press, 1987; C. Rearick, 'Festivals in modern France: the experience of the Third Republic', *Journal of Contemporary History*, vol. 12, 1977, pp. 435–60; C. Lane, *The Rites of Rulers: Ritual in Industrial Society – the Soviet Case*, Cambridge, Cambridge University Press, 1981.

32 As examples, see M. Kazin and S.J. Ross, 'America's Labor Day: the dilemma of a workers' celebration', *Journal of American History*, vol. 78, no. 4, March 1992, pp. 1294–323; M. Perrot, 'The first of May 1890 in France: the birth of a working-class ritual', in P. Thane, G. Crossick and R. Roderick Floud (eds), *The Power of the Past: Essays for Eric Hobsbawm*, Cambridge, Cambridge University Press, 1984, pp. 143–72.

33 E.P. Weissengruber, 'The Corpus Christi procession in Medieval York: a symbolic struggle in public space', *Theatre Survey*, vol. 38, May 1997, pp. 117–38; N.H. Murdoch, 'Salvation Army disturbances in Liverpool, England, 1879–1887', *Journal of Social History*, vol. 25, no. 3, 1992, pp. 575–94.

34 Lukes, 'Political ritual', 299.

35 See M.P. Ryan, *Civic Wars: Democracy and Public Life in the American City During the Nineteenth Century*, Berkeley, CA, University of California Press, 1997; and T.G. Fraser (ed.), *The Irish Parading Tradition: Following the Drum*, London, Macmillan, 2000.

36 For a discussion of the importance and the origins of green within the nationalist imagination, see B. Ó Cuív, 'The wearing of the green', *Studia Hibernica*, no. 17, 1977, pp. 107–19.

37 In the 1930s the Irish Blueshirt movement rejected the colour green to distinguish themselves from their Republican opponents, choosing instead St Patrick's blue as the colour for their uniform. For details of the debate and the significance, see M. Cronin, *The Blueshirts and Irish Politics*, Dublin, Four Courts Press, 1997, p. 47.

38   J. Biggs-Davison and G. Chowdharay-Best, *The Cross of Saint Patrick: The Catholic Unionist Tradition in Ireland*, Bourne End, Kensal Press, 1984, Preface.

39   For a seminal exploration of parades and their significance, see S.G. Davies, *Parade and Power: Street Theatre in Nineteenth Century Philadelphia*, New York, University of Columbia Press, 1986, pp. 1–22.

40   Key examples of this approach can be found in D. Cannadine, 'The transformation of civic ritual in modern Britain: the Colchester Oyster Feast', *Past and Present*, no. 94, 1982, pp. 107–30; and D. Cannadine, 'The context, performance and meaning of ritual: the British monarchy and the "invention of tradition"', *c.*1820–1977', in Hobsbawm and Ranger, *The Invention of Tradition*, pp. 101–64.

41   A. Brown-May, *Melbourne Street Life: The Itinerary of Our Days*, Melbourne, Australian Scholarly Publishing, 1998, p. 201.

42   D. Macfarlane and T. Asmoucha, 'Life on parade', *Canadian Geographic*, July–August 1997, vol. 117, no. 4, pp. 72, 80.

43   Ibid.

44   M. Ryan, 'The American parade: representations of the nineteenth-century social order', in L. Hunt (ed.), *The New Cultural History*, Berkeley, CA, University of California Press, 1989, p. 139.

45   The need for such official sanction of a St Patrick's Day parade is not unusual; it has long been required also for Orange parades, Labour Day parades, May Day parades, and so on.

46   For a brilliant discussion of this theme, see R.F. Foster, *Modern Ireland, 1600–1972*, London, Penguin, 1989.

47   Extensive discussions about the life and legend of St Patrick abound. See, as examples, A.B. Proudfoot (ed.), *Patrick: Sixteen Centuries with Ireland's Patron Saint*, New York, Macmillan, 1983; A. Hopkin, *The Living Legend of St Patrick*, London, Grafton Books, 1989; B. McCormack, *Perceptions of St Patrick in Eighteenth Century Ireland*, Dublin, Four Courts Press, 2000.

48   The local town of St-Patrice was later named in his honour.

49   Hopkin, *The Living Legend of St Patrick*, Chaps 1–3; Proudfoot (ed.), *Patrick*, Chaps 2–3; D. Ó Corráin, 'Prehistoric and early Christian Ireland', in R.F. Foster (ed.), *The Oxford Illustrated History of Ireland*, Oxford, Oxford University Press, 1989, pp. 9–10.

50   These are reprinted (in English) in full in Hopkin, *The Living Legend of St Patrick*, pp. 163–76.

51   K. Schermann, *The Flowering of Ireland: Saints, Scholars and Kings*, London, Victor Gollancz, 1981, p. 89.

52   For a seminal critique along these lines, see D. Binchy, 'Patrick and his biographers: ancient and modern', *Studia Hibernica*, no. 2, 1962, pp. 7–173.

53   Hopkin, *The Living Legend of St Patrick*, pp. 42–4, 58–61.

54   *The Shan Van Vocht*, vol. 1, no. 3, 6 March 1896; 'Celtic and Christian heritage sites in County Down – Part 3', accessed 9 April 2001: http://www.fjiordlands.org/strngfrd/times/Celtic3.htm#patrician/.

55   C. Doherty, 'The problem of Patrick', *History Today*, Spring 1995, p. 18.

56   Ninine, 'Prayer to Saint Patrick', *c.* eighth century AD, translated by Whitely Stokes and John Strachan, reprinted in Proudfoot (ed.), *Patrick*, p. 128.

57   Hopkin, *The Living Legend of St Patrick*, p. 36.

58   McCormack, *Perceptions of St Patrick*, p. 46.

59   Ibid., p. 39.

60   Hopkin, *The Living Legend of St Patrick*, p. 151.

61 McCormack, *Perceptions of St Patrick*, pp. 20–33.
62 Quoted in Hopkin, *The Living Legend of St Patrick*, p. 53.
63 McCormack, *Perceptions of St Patrick*, p. 118.
64 Ibid., pp. 118–19.

1 THE EVOLUTION OF ST PATRICK'S DAY

1 *Freeman's Journal*, Dublin, 18 March 1842.
2 D.O. Giollain, 'The pattern', in J.S. Donnelly and K.A. Miller (eds), *Irish Popular Culture 1650–1850*, Dublin, Irish Academic Press, 1998, p. 201.
3 G.A. Hayes-McCoy, 'War under the banner of St Patrick – Patrician symbolism, military and heraldic', *National Souvenir of the Patrician Year, 461–1961*, Dublin, Irish Times, 1961, p. 67.
4 Information received from Ciarán Ó Maoláin. Armagh.
5 M.R. Casey, 'Ireland, New York and the Irish image in American popular culture, 1890–1960', PhD thesis, New York University, 1998, p. 271.
6 For details of the ongoing Protestant celebration of St Patrick, see T.C. Barnard, 'Crises of identity among Irish Protestants, 1641–1685', *Past and Present*, no. 127, May 1990, pp. 39–83; T.C. Barnard, 'The uses of 23 October 1641 and Irish Protestant celebrations', *English Historical Review*, vol. 106, no. 421, October 1991, pp. 889–920; and C. Kidd, 'Gaelic antiquity and national identity in Enlightenment Ireland and Scotland', *English Historical Review*, vol. 109, no. 434, November 1994, pp. 1197–214.
7 K. Danaher, *The Year in Ireland*, Cork, Mercier Press, 1972, p. 265.
8 For explanation of this process in England and public ceremonies there, see Storch, *Popular Culture and Custom in Nineteenth Century England*.
9 For detailed discussion of Irish fairs, festivals and customs, see E. Malcolm, 'Popular recreation in nineteenth-century Ireland', in O. MacDonagh *et al.* (eds), *Culture and Nationalism in Ireland, 1750–1950*, Canberra, 1983, pp. 40–55.
10 P. Logan, *Fair Day: The Story of Irish Fairs and Markets*, Belfast, Appletree Press, 1986, p. 33.
11 Quoted in J. Sheehy, *The Rediscovery of Ireland's Past: The Celtic Revival, 1830–1930*, London, Thames and Hudson, 1980.
12 McCormack, *Perceptions of St Patrick in Eighteenth Century Ireland*, p. 69.
13 King David appeared on the obverse, and St Patrick the reverse, on a Dublin issue of halfpence and farthings. Moyle considers that this may be 'the earliest pictorial representation of the national emblem in its Patrician context'. In M. Dolley, 'The Irish coinage, 1534–1691', in T.W. Moody and F.X. Martin (eds), *A New History of Ireland*, Vol. III, *Early Modern Ireland, 1534–1691*, Oxford, Clarendon Press, 1976, p. 417.
14 A. Ford, 'Reformation', in Connolly, *The Oxford Companion to Irish History*, p. 476.
15 Ibid.
16 A. Ford, 'Acts of uniformity', in ibid., pp. 564–5.
17 H. Kearney, 'England' and S.J. Connolly, 'James II', in ibid., pp. 173–4 and pp. 276–7. For detailed analysis, see M.A. Mullett, *Catholics in Britain and Ireland, 1558–1829*, New York, St Martin's Press, 1998.
18 Logan, *Fair Day*, p. 70.
19 J.R. Hill, 'National festivals, the state and "Protestant Ascendancy" in Ireland, 1790–1829', *Irish Historical Studies*, vol. 24, no. 93, May 1984, p. 31; also see B. Walker, *Dancing to History's Tune: History, Myth and Politics in Ireland*, Belfast,

Institute of Irish Studies, 1996, pp. 76–80; S. Foster, 'Buying Irish: consumer nationalism in 18th-century Dublin', *History Today*, vol. 47, no. 6, June 1997, pp. 44–52.

20 For an overview of the evolution of parading traditions, see J. Kelly, 'The emergence of political parading, 1660–1800', in Fraser, *The Irish Parading Tradition*, pp. 9–27.

21 For examples of these developments and traditions, see Hill, 'National festivals', p. 31; and for details of the Order, see P. Galloway, *The Most Illustrious Order of St Patrick, 1783–1983*, London, Philmore, 1985.

22 J. Swift, 'The journal to Stella', in Frederick Ryland (ed.), *The Prose of Jonathan Swift*, Dublin, Four Courts Press, 1922, vol. II, pp. 442–3, quoted in McCormack, *Perceptions of Saint Patrick*, p. 70.

23 J. Swift, 'Swift to Chetwode, 15 March 1728/9', in F. Elrington Ball (ed.), *The Correspondence of Jonathan Swift, 1727–1733*, London, G. Bell and Sons, 1913, vol. IV, p. 65, quoted in McCormack, *Perceptions of Saint Patrick*, p. 71.

24 For an overview of Castle life, and its St Patrick's Day celebrations, see J. Robins, *Champagne and Silver Buckles: The Viceregal Court at Dublin Castle, 1700–1922*, Dublin, Lilliput Press, 2001.

25 Ibid., p. 71.

26 For full details, see *Dublin Evening Post*, 10 March 1785.

27 *Dublin Evening Post*, 18 March 1790.

28 Ibid.

29 For brief references to earlier St Patrick's Day parades in 1779 and 1780, see Kelly, 'The emergence of political parading', p. 19. For discussion of the development of parading traditions in England from the mid-sixteenth century, see D.M. Bergeron, *English Civic Pageantry, 1558–1642*, Columbia, University of South Carolina Press, 1971.

30 Unfortunately, there is no record of who the 'true patriots' were. *Dublin Evening Post*, 17 March 1785.

31 Robins, *Champagne and Silver Buckles*, p. 99.

32 *Freeman's Journal*, Dublin, 20 March 1810.

33 *Freeman's Journal*, Dublin, 18 March 1834.

34 For details see Hill, 'National festivals', p. 33.

35 Ibid., pp. 50–1.

36 Robins, *Champagne and Silver Buckles*, p. 120.

37 For discussions of pre-famine use of St Patrick's Day by various social, religious and political groupings, see N. Jarman, *Material Conflicts: Parades and Visual Displays in Northern Ireland*, Oxford, Berg, 1997, pp. 50–1; T. Garvin, 'Defenders, ribbonmen and others: underground political networks in pre-famine Ireland', *Past and Present*, no. 96, 1982, pp. 133–55; P. Alter, 'Symbols of Irish nationalism', *Studia Hibernica*, no. 14, 1974, pp. 104–23; and P. Alter, 'Symbols of Irish nationalism', in A. O'Day (ed.), *Reactions to Irish Nationalism*, Dublin, Irish Academic Press, 1987; Hill, 'National festivals', p. 33; J. Kelly, '"The glorious and immortal memory": commemoration and Protestant identity in Ireland, 1660–1800', *Proceedings of the Royal Irish Academy*, no. 94C, 1994; S.S. Larsen, 'The glorious twelfth: a ritual expression of collective identity', in A. Cohen (ed.), *Belonging: Identity and Social Organisation in British Rural Cultures*, Manchester, Manchester University Press, 1982. For a more general discussion of the problems associated with mass meetings and celebrations, see G. Owens, 'Nationalism without words: spectacle and ritual in the repeal "monster meetings" of 1843–45', in Donnelly and Miller,

Irish Popular Culture, 1998, pp. 542–69. For the experience of Belfast during this period, and for coverage of many of the same themes, see S.E. Baker, 'Orange and green: Belfast, 1832–1912', in H.J. Dyos and M. Wolff (eds), *The Victorian City: Images and Realities*, vol. II, London, Routledge and Kegan Paul, 1973.

38 D.H. Akenson, *The Irish Diaspora: A Primer*, Belfast, The Institute of Irish Studies at the Queen's University of Belfast, 1993, p. 39.

39 For a general coverage of the lives of the Irish in Britain, see R. Swift and S. Gilley (eds), *The Irish in Britain, 1815–1939*, London, Pinter, 1989; R. Swift and S. Gilley (eds), *The Irish in Victorian Britain: The Local Dimension*, Dublin, Four Courts Press, 1999; D.M. MacRaild, *Irish Migrants in Modern Britain, 1750–1922*, London, Macmillan, 1999 (especially pp. 96–8); J.M. Werly, 'The Irish in Manchester, 1832–49', *Irish Historical Studies*, vol. 18, no. 71, 1973, pp. 345–58; T. Gallagher, 'A tale of two cities: communal strife in Glasgow and Liverpool before 1914', in R. Swift and S. Gilley (eds), *The Irish in the Victorian City*, London, Croom Helm, 1985, pp. 106–29; T. Gallagher, *Glasgow, the Uneasy Peace: Religious Tension in Modern Scotland*, Manchester, Manchester University Press, 1987; M. Durey, 'The survival of an Irish culture in Britain, 1800–45', *Historical Studies*, no. 78, 1982, pp. 14–35.

40 For an appreciation of Protestant identities during this period, see I. McBride and T. Claydon (eds), *Protestantism and National Identity: Britain and Ireland, c.1650–c.1850*, Cambridge, Cambridge University Press, 1998.

41 See F. Neal, *Sectarian Violence. The Liverpool Experience 1819–1914: An Aspect of Anglo-Irish History*, Manchester, Manchester University Press, 1988, p. 58.

42 These ranged from African-American parades to citizens' militia, through to Pinkster's Day (or King's Day), and the ceremonial raising of the Liberty Pole. For details see S.P. Newman, *Parades and the Politics of the Street: Festive Culture in the Early American Republic*, Philadelphia, University of Pennsylvania Press, 1997; G. Fabre, 'Pinkster Festival, 1766–1811: an African-American celebration', in R.A. Gutiérraz and G. Fabre (eds), *Feasts and Celebrations in North American Ethnic Communities*, Albuquerque, University of New Mexico Press, 1995, pp. 13–28; A. Lorini, 'Public rituals and the cultural making of the New York African-American community', in ibid., pp. 29–46; W.J. Bell, Jr, 'The federal processions of 1788', *The New-York Historical Society Quarterly*, no. 46, 1962, pp. 5–39; L. Rigal, '"Raising the roof": authors, spectators and artisans in the Grand Federal Procession of 1788', *Theatre Journal*, vol. 48, no. 3, pp. 253–78; Ryan, *Civic Wars*, pp. 45–7; 61–74; 78–93; and B. McNamara, *Day of Jubilee: The Great Age of Public Celebrations in New York, 1789–1909*, New Brunswick, Rutgers University Press, 1997, pp. 28, 39–45. The latter two books are reviewed in S.P. Newman, 'Conflicting celebrations: the democratization of festive culture', *Reviews in American History*, vol. 26, no. 3.

43 Crimmins, *St Patrick's Day*, p. 9.

44 'Orders of the Charitable Irish Society of Boston', quoted in C.T. Burke, *The Silver Key: The Charitable Irish Society of Boston*, Watertown, Mass., 1972, unpublished manuscript, John J. Burns Library, Boston College, Boston, p. 2.

45 Ibid., p. 4.

46 Ibid., p. 6.

47 Ibid., p. 20.

48 For details, see J. Haltigan, *The Irish in the American Revolution and their Early Influence in the Colonies*, Washington, DC, Patrick Haltigan, 1908, p. 353.

49 1762 is the commonly agreed first St Patrick's Day celebration in New York, and

the one that is accepted by the Ancient Order of Hibernians. However, 1737 has also been put forward as a date for the initial celebrations. For details see J.G. Kelton, 'New York City St Patrick's Day parade: invention of contention and consensus', *Drama Review*, vol. 29, no. 3, Fall 1985, pp. 93–105.

50 Speech by Chief Justice Daily, St Patrick's night dinner, 17 March 1779, 'Friendly Sons of St Patrick Collection', American Irish Historical Society, New York, box 32, folder 1.

51 In 1771, and therefore mirroring developments in New York, the St Patrick's Society emerged in Philadelphia to celebrate 17 March. See D. Clark, *Erin's Heirs: Irish Bonds of Community*, Lexington Key, University Press of Kentucky, 1991, p. 56.

52 See J.T. Ridge, *The St Patrick's Day Parade in New York*, New York, New York St. Patrick's Day Parade Committee, 1988, p. 4.

53 Ibid., p. 5.

54 Quoted in E.G. Burrows and M. Wallace, *Gotham: A History of New York to 1898*, New York, Oxford University Press, 1999, p. 248.

55 Crimmins, *St Patrick's Day*, p. 11.

56 For details see R. Malone, *Irish America*, New York, Hippocrene Books, 1994, pp. 17–20.

57 For evidence of the sectarian violence associated with early St Patrick's Day parades, see P.A. Gilje, *The Road to Mobocracy: Popular Disorder in New York City, 1763–1834*, Chapel Hill, NC, University of North Carolina Press, 1987, pp. 125–38.

58 P. Bishop, *The Irish Empire*, London, Boxtree, 1999, p. 72.

59 See J. Bodnar, *Remaking America: Public Memory, Commemoration and Patriotism in the Twentieth Century*, Princeton, NJ, Princeton University Press, 1992, p. 66.

60 'Orders of the Charitable Irish Society of Boston', quoted in Burke, *The Silver Key*, p. 23.

61 Ibid., p. 27.

62 Ibid., pp. 35–8.

63 Ibid., pp. 35–8.

64 Burrows and Wallace, *Gotham*, p. 543.

65 J.D. Crimmins, *Irish American Historical Miscellany: Relating to New York City and Vicinity Together with much Interesting Material Relative to Other Parts of the Country*, New York, The Author, 1905, p. 219.

66 Quoted in Ridge, *St Patrick's Day Parade*, pp. 10–11.

67 P.A. Gilje, 'The development of an Irish American community in New York City before the great migration', in R.H. Bayor and T.J. Meagher (eds), *The New York Irish*, Baltimore, Johns Hopkins University Press, 1996, p. 72.

68 See S.A. Marston, 'Adopted citizens: community and the development of consciousness among the Irish of Lowell, Massachusetts, 1839–85', PhD thesis, University of Colorado at Boulder, 1986.

69 For details of all these gatherings, see 'Thomas O'Conor Papers', American Irish Historical Society, New York, box 1, folder 24.

70 *Truth Teller*, 20 February 1836.

71 *Truth Teller*, 12 March 1836.

72 Ibid.

73 *Truth Teller*, 19 March 1836. Irish-American newspapers were always keen to signal the attendance, at any function, of a veteran of the 1798 Rebellion. This was used as shorthand to reinforce the nationalist credentials of any organization attached to such persons.

74 *The Irishman*, 15 June 1821.
75 For details of the Irish wake, see A. Schrier, *Ireland and the American Emigration, 1850–1900*, Chester Springs, PA, Dufour Editions, 1997, pp. 86–93.
76 For a discussion of how local loyalties functioned, see R. Ernst, *Immigrant Life in New York City, 1825–1863*, Syracuse, Syracuse University Press, 1994.
77 D. Clark, *Hibernia America: The Irish and Regional Cultures*, New York, Greenwood Press, 1986, p. 8.
78 For a discussion of the need for success, and the overriding literary portrayal of the Irish as failures, see C. Fanning (ed.), *The Exiles of Erin: Nineteenth Century Irish-American Fiction*, Notre Dame, University of Notre Dame Press, 1987, p. 93.
79 McNamara, *Day of Jubilee*, p. 40.
80 Quoted in McNamara, *Day of Jubilee*, p. 40.
81 See Bodnar, *Remaking America*, p. 66.
82 D.H. Akenson, *Small Differences: Irish Catholics and Irish Protestants, 1815–1922. An International Perspective*, Montreal, McGill-Queen's University Press, 1988, p. 89.
83 Akenson, *Being Had*, p. 85.
84 Ibid., pp. 90–1.
85 K.J. James, 'The Saint Patrick's Society of Montreal: ethno-religious realignment in a nineteenth-century national society', unpublished MA thesis, Dept. of History, McGill University, Montreal, 1997, p. 21.
86 J.S. Moir, 'The problem of a double minority: some reflections on the development of the English-speaking Catholic church in Canada in the nineteenth century', *Histoire Sociale/Social History*, no. 4, April 1971, pp. 53–68.
87 C.J. Houston and W.J. Smyth, *Irish Emigration and Canadian Settlement: Patterns, Links, and Letters*, Toronto, University of Toronto Press, 1990, p. 170.
88 J.R. Miller, 'Anti-Catholic thought in Victorian Canada', *Canadian Historical Review*, vol. 56, no. 4, 1985, p. 479.
89 James, 'The Saint Patrick's Society of Montreal', p. 15.
90 Ibid., p. 20.
91 *Quebec Gazette*, 21 March 1765, quoted in Schmitz, *Irish for a Day*, p. 23.
92 T. Murphy, 'Introduction', in T. Murphy and G. Stortz (eds), *Creed and Culture: The Place of English-speaking Catholics in Canadian Society, 1750–1930*, Montreal, McGill-Queen's University Press, 1993, p. xxiv.
93 Ibid., p. xxiv.
94 The only exception was Newfoundland. Ibid., p. xxv.
95 D. MacKay, *Flight from Famine: The Coming of the Irish to Canada*, Toronto, McClelland and Stewart Inc., 1990, pp. 175–93.
96 C.J. Houston and W.J. Smyth, 'Orangemen in Canada', in R. O'Driscoll and L. Reynolds (eds), *The Untold Story: The Irish in Canada*, vol. II, Toronto, Celtic Arts of Canada, 1988, p. 750.
97 H. Senior, 'The orange and the green and the snow in between', in O'Driscoll and Reynolds, *The Untold Story*, p. 565; Houston and Smyth, 'Orangemen in Canada', in ibid., pp. 743–49.
98 MacKay, *Flight from Famine*, p. 166.
99 Ibid., p. 166.
100 *Gazette*, 20 March 1824.
101 Ibid.
102 Ibid.
103 The formative years were Toronto (1832), Montreal (1834), and Quebec City

(1836). See Cotterell, 'St Patrick's Day parade', p. 60; James, 'The Saint Patrick's Society of Montreal', p. 18; Schmitz, *Irish for a Day*, p. 28.

104 James, 'The Saint Patrick's Society of Montreal', p. 18.

105 Ibid., p. 26.

106 The establishment of rival *patriote* organizations was discussed, with O'Callaghan particularly keen on a Hibernian Benevolent Society, but none seem to have come to fruition. Ibid., p. 27.

107 Ibid., p. 35.

108 Ibid., p. 36. In discussing the connection between the St Patrick's Society and conservative military groups, James draws upon M. O'Gallagher, *Saint Patrick's Quebec: The Building of a Church and of a Parish*, Quebec, Carraig Books, 1981, p. 59.

109 James, 'The Saint Patrick's Society of Montreal', p. 36. Here James draws upon the article by J. Loye, 'Saint Patrick's Day one century ago', *Gazette*, 14 March 1936.

110 Cotterell, 'St Patrick's Day parade', p. 62.

111 Schmitz, *Irish for a Day*, pp. 29–30.

112 For an extended argument along these lines, see J.B. Hirst, *Convict Society and its Enemies*, Sydney, George Allen & Unwin, 1983, pp. 57–69, 79–84.

113 R. Haines, '"Shovelling out paupers?": parish-assisted emigration from England to Australia, 1834–1847', in E. Richards (ed.), *Visible Immigrants 2: Poor Australian Immigrants in the Nineteenth Century*, Canberra, Division of Historical Studies and Centre for Immigration and Multicultural Studies, Research School of Social Sciences, Australian National University, 1991, pp. 33–68; R. Haines, '"The idle and the drunken won't do there": poverty, the new Poor Law and nineteenth-century government-assisted emigration to Australia from the United Kingdom', *Australian Historical Studies*, vol. 28, no. 108, April 1997, pp. 1–21.

114 G. Sherington, *Australia's Immigrants, 1788–1988*, Sydney, George Allen & Unwin, 2nd edn, 1990, p. 24.

115 P. O'Farrell, *The Irish in Australia*, Kensington, NSW, New South Wales University Press, 1987, p. 23.

116 Sherington, *Australia's Immigrants*, p. 24.

117 By 1851 the population of New South Wales was 178,668, of which 56 per cent was male and 44 per cent female. J.C. Caldwell, 'Population', in W. Vamplew (ed.), *Australians: Historical Statistics*, Broadway, NSW, Fairfax, Syme & Weldon Associates, 1987, pp. 27–8.

118 K.S. Inglis, *The Australian Colonists: An Exploration of Social History, 1788–1870*, Carlton, Vic., Melbourne University Press, 1974, p. 88.

119 C. Price, 'Immigration and ethnic origin', and W.W. Phillips, 'Religion', in Vamplew, *Australians: Historical Statistics*, pp. 11, 421.

120 For detailed discussions, see P. O'Farrell, *Irish in Australia*; C. McConville, *Croppies, Celts and Catholics: The Irish in Australia*, Caulfield, East Vic., Edward Arnold, 1987; K.S. Inglis, 'The Australian Catholic Community', in H. Mayer (ed.), *Catholics and the Free Society: An Australian Symposium*, Melbourne, Cheshire, 1961, pp. 7–32.

121 Quoted in M. Hogan, 'Separation of Church and State: Section 116 of the Australian Constitution', *The Australian Quarterly*, vol. 53, no. 2, Winter 1981, p. 216.

122 See P. O'Farrell, *The Catholic Church and Community: An Australian History*, Kensington, NSW, New South Wales University Press, 1985; G.I.T. Machin, *Politics and the Churches in Great Britain, 1832 to 1868*, Oxford, Clarendon Press, 1977.

123 Quoted in O'Farrell, *The Irish in Australia*, p. 41.

124 Ibid.

125 *The Sydney Gazette and New South Wales Advertiser*, 17 March 1810.

126 *The Sydney Gazette and New South Wales Advertiser*, 13 March 1823. This may be the first example anywhere in the world of a bank holiday being declared in recognition of Ireland's patron saint.

127 O'Farrell, *The Irish in Australia*, p. 42.

128 Letter received by Father J.J. Therry, 27 March 1833, quoted in O'Farrell, *The Irish in Australia*, p. 42.

129 *The Sydney Gazette and New South Wales Advertiser*, 9 March 1838. Tickets for the official St Patrick's Dinner of 1843 were deemed 'not transferable'. *Sydney Morning Herald*, 15 March 1843.

130 The Anglo-Irish in Australia, as elsewhere, remains a group seriously under-researched. For a critique, see G. Forth, '"No petty people": the Anglo-Irish identity in colonial Australia', in P. O'Sullivan (ed.), *The Irish in the New Communities*, Leicester, Leicester University Press, 1972, pp. 128–42.

131 *Australian*, 19 March 1840.

132 Ibid.

133 O'Farrell, *The Irish in Australia*, p. 44.

134 *Australian*, 19 March 1842.

135 *Sydney Morning Herald*, cited in O'Farrell, *The Irish in Australia*, p. 45.

136 *Sydney Morning Herald*, 15 March 1843.

137 O'Farrell, *The Irish in Australia*, p. 46.

138 For details of Dineley's comments in his *Observations in a Voyage Through the Kingdom of Ireland*, Dublin, 1870, see K. Danaher, *The Year in Ireland*, Cork, Mercier Press, 1972, p. 58; and McCormack, *Perceptions of St Patrick*, p. 69.

139 Ibid.

140 M. Mac Lir, in the *Journal of the Cork Historical and Archaeological Society*, 1895, quoted in Danaher, *Year in Ireland*, pp. 60–1. Examples of such crosses are housed in the Irish National Museum, Dublin.

141 For a discussion of the shamrock tradition, see, among others, *Journal of the County Kildare Archaeological Society and Surrounding Districts*, no. 5, 1906–8, Dublin, Ponsonby, 1908, pp. 440–2.

142 C. Threlkeld, *Synopsis Stirpium Hiberbicum* (Dublin, 1727), quoted in Danaher, *Year in Ireland*, pp. 62–3.

143 The Reverend J.A. Dowling, 'Ireland's national emblem', *Irish Independent*, 17 March 1920.

144 For further discussions, see E. Reilly, 'Beyond gilt shamrock: symbolism and realism in the cover art of Irish historical and political fiction, 1880–1914', in L.W. McBride (ed.), *Images, Icons and the Irish Nationalist Imagination*, Dublin, Four Courts Press, 1999, pp. 99–100; and N. Colgan, 'The Shamrock in literature: a critical chronology', *Journal of the Royal Society of Antiquaries of Ireland*, no. 26, 1986, pp. 211–26; and pp. 349–61.

145 For details of the tradition of pota Pádraig (St Patrick's pot) and the wetting of the shamrock, see Danaher, *Year in Ireland*, pp. 62–5.

146 MS42, p. 157, Irish Folklore Commission, Irish Folklore Department, University College Dublin (IFDUCD).

147 MS36, p. 238, Irish Folklore Commission (IFDUCD). See also MS 296, p. 469; MS 7, p. 218.

148 MS407, p. 27, Folklore Commission (IFDUCD).

149 Schools MS1837, pp. 8–9, Irish Folklore Commission (IFDUCD).
150 MS782, p. 255, Irish Folklore Commission (IFDUCD).

2 FAMINE AND EXODUS

1 F. Douglas, 'The nature of slavery', extract from a lecture on slavery, published as *My Bondage and My Freedom*, delivered at Rochester, New York, 1 December 1850, www.eserver.org/race/bondage-and-freedom.txt/.

2 There is an enormous body of research on the famine and its impact in Ireland and, subsequently, upon the Irish diaspora. For a recent overview of this literature, see K. Kenny, *The American Irish: A History*, Harlow, Longman, 2000, pp. 89–130.

3 For a review of this debate, see M. Daly, 'Revisionism and Irish history: the great famine', in D.G. Boyce and A. O'Day (eds), *The Making of Modern Irish History*, London, Routledge, 1996. Another important study of 'history-making' in the wake of the famine is P. O'Farrell, 'Whose reality? The Irish famine in history and literature', *Historical Studies* (Aust.), vol. 20, April 1982, pp. 1–13.

4 *The Nation*, 14 March 1846.

5 L. Williams, 'Irish identity and the *Illustrated London News*, 1846–51', in S.S. Sailer (ed.), *Representing Ireland: Gender, Class, Nationality*, Gainesville, FL, University Press of Florida, pp. 72–3.

6 Ibid.

7 *The Nation*, 21 March 1846.

8 *The Nation*, 23 March 1850.

9 D. Fitzpatrick, *Irish Emigration, 1801–1921*, Dublin, Economic and Social History Society of Ireland, 1984, p. 35.

10 For an excellent overview of the Irish experience in Britain, see MacRaild, *Irish Migrants in Modern Britain*.

11 Comment and quote from M.J. Hickman, *Religion, Class and Identity: The State, the Catholic Church and the Education of the Irish in Britain*, Aldershot, Avebury, 1995, p. 147.

12 For an example of the appalling living conditions of many Irish, and the case of 'Little Ireland' in Manchester, see M.A. Busteed, 'The Irish in nineteenth-century Manchester', *Irish Studies Review*, vol. 18, 1997, pp. 1–6.

13 For a general overview of the Irish in Lancashire and Liverpool, including details of St Patrick's Day celebrations in those locations, see W.J. Lowe, *The Irish in Mid-Victorian Lancashire*, New York, Peter Lang, 1989.

14 See Neal, *Sectarian Violence*, pp. 117–19.

15 For a contemporary report on the threat of drunkenness, see J.P. Kay, *The Moral and Physical Condition of the Working Class*, London, 1833; or, more generally, L.P. Curtis, *Apes and Angels: The Irishman in Victorian Caricature*, London, David and Charles, 1971.

16 For details, see *The Nation*, 18 March 1846.

17 *The Nation*, 25 March 1854.

18 For references to St Patrick's Day celebrations in Britain during this period, see Swift and Gilley, *The Irish in Britain*; Swift and Gilley, *The Irish in Victorian Britain*; MacRaild, *Irish Migrants in Modern Britain*; Werly, 'The Irish in Manchester, 1832–49'; Gallagher, *Glasgow, the Uneasy Peace*; J. Belchem, 'Liverpool in the year of revolution: the political and associational culture of the Irish immigrant community in 1848', in J. Belchem (ed.) *Popular Politics, Riot and Labour: Essays in Liverpool History*, Liverpool, Liverpool University Press, 1992, pp. 68–97; M. Durey, 'The

survival of an Irish culture in Britain, 1800–45', *Historical Studies*, no. 78, 1982, pp. 14–35; Lowe, *The Irish in Mid-Victorian Lancashire*, esp. pp. 130–4, 158–9, 184–5.

19   MacRaild, *Irish Migrants*, p. 96; for a discussion of the politics surrounding the Irish community in Whitehaven, see D.M. MacRaild, 'William Murphy, the Orange Order and communal violence: the Irish in West Cumberland, 1871–84', in P. Panayi, *Racial Violence in Britain, 1840–1950*, Leicester, Leicester University Press, 1993, pp. 44–64.

20   O. Handlin, *Boston's Immigrants, 1790–1880: A Study in Acculturation*, Cambridge, MA, Belknap Press, 1991, p. 157.

21   Quoted in Crimmins, *Irish American Historical Miscellany*, p. 223.

22   Burke, *The Silver Key*, p. 43.

23   Ridge, *The St Patrick's Day Parade*, p. 15.

24   J. Belchem, 'Nationalism, republicanism and exile: Irish emigrants and the revolutions of 1848', *Past and Present*, no. 146, 1995, pp. 103–35.

25   H.R. Diner, 'The most Irish city in the union: the era of great migration, 1844–77', in Bayor and Meagher, *The New York Irish*, p. 104.

26   For details, see ibid., p. 99; Burrows and Wallace, *Gotham: A History of New York*, p. 828.

27   *New York Times* report quoted by Ridge, *The St Patrick's Day Parade*, p. 20.

28   Burrows and Wallace, *Gotham: A History of New York*, p. 824.

29   *New York Evening Post*, 17 March 1853.

30   See Ridge, *The St Patrick's Day Parade*, p. 29.

31   Fitzgerald, 'The St Patrick's Day Parade', p. 40.

32   McNamara, *Day of Jubilee*, p. 7.

33   See Clark, *Hibernia America*, p. 121.

34   For a summary of the campaign to erect the monument, and details of the tragedy of 1847–48, see 'The Gross-Isle Monument Commemorative Souvenir', *Quebec Daily Telegraph*, 15 August 1909.

35   Fittingly, the inscription was carved in Gaelic, English and French, thus taking in each of the key language groups associated with the Gross Isle tragedy, ibid.

36   M.W. Nicholson, 'The other Toronto: Irish Catholics in a Victorian city, 1850–1900', *Polyphony*, Summer 1984, p. 21; Cotterell, 'St Patrick's Day parade'; Houston and Smyth, *Irish Emigration and Canadian Settlement*, p. 170; Akenson, *Small Differences*, p. 89.

37   Sir Richard H. Bonnycastle, *Canada and the Canadians*, H. Colborn, London, 1849, p. 167.

38   Ibid., p. 273.

39   Houston and Smyth, 'Orangemen in Canada', in O'Driscoll and Reynolds, *The Untold Story*, p. 744.

40   Houston and Smyth, *Irish Emigration and Canadian Settlement*, p. 183.

41   Ibid., p. 183.

42   Cotterell, 'St Patrick's Day parade', p. 62.

43   Ibid., p. 62.

44   Ibid., p. 63.

45   Ibid.

46   Ibid., p. 64.

47   Ibid., p. 64.

48   *Quebec Mercury*, 21 March 1848, quoted in Schmitz, *Irish for a Day*, p. 35.

49   *Quebec Gazette*, 19 March 1849, quoted in ibid., p. 37.

50   Ibid., p. 37.

51 Ibid., pp. 37–9.
52 The following discussion draws heavily on the research of James, 'The Saint Patrick's Society of Montreal'. A summary of this study can be found in K.J. James, 'Dynamics of associational culture in a nineteenth-century city: Saint Patrick's Society of Montreal, 1834–56', *Canadian Journal of Irish Studies* (forthcoming).
53 *Gazette*, 18 March 1845.
54 Ibid., p. 58.
55 Ibid., p. 64.
56 *Gazette*, reprinted in *True Witness*, 20 February 1856.
57 *Gazette*, reprinted in *True Witness*, 20 February 1856.
58 James, 'The Saint Patrick's Society of Montreal', pp. 66–8.
59 *True Witness*, 4 April 1856.
60 Ibid.
61 Ibid.
62 James, 'The Saint Patrick's Society of Montreal', p. 83.
63 By contrast, Western Australia began taking convicts in 1850, and continued to do so until 1868. See R. Hughes, *The Fatal Shore: A History of the Transportation of Convicts to Australia, 1787–1868*, London, Collins Harvill, 1987, pp. 273–80.
64 During the 1850s the colony of New South Wales, which spanned the east coast of Australia, was divided into three sections: the south-eastern colony of Victoria was proclaimed in 1850, while the north-eastern colony of Queensland was established in 1859. Each of these colonies became self-governing, as did South Australia and Van Diemen's Land (later Tasmania), but the relatively underdeveloped colony of Western Australia was not granted responsible government until 1890. See C.M.H. Clark, *A History of Australia*, vols III–IV, Carlton, Vic., Melbourne University Press, 1973 and 1978, pp. 447–8 and pp. 135–7.
65 By the late 1850s Chinese men constituted nearly 20 per cent of all males in Victoria. C. Price, 'Immigration and ethnic origin', in W. Vamplew (ed.), *Australians: Historical Statistics*, Broadway, NSW, Fairfax, Syme & Weldon Associates, 1987, p. 11; S. Wang, 'Chinese immigration, 1840s–1890s', in J. Jupp (ed.), *The Australian People*, North Ryde, NSW, Angus and Robertson, 1988, p. 299.
66 O'Farrell, *The Irish in Australia*, pp. 63–5.
67 Ibid., p. 63.
68 Inglis, *The Australian Colonists*, p. 88.
69 O'Farrell, *The Irish in Australia*, p. 156.
70 Ibid., 157.
71 Ibid., p. 42.
72 E. Campion, *Australian Catholics*, Ringwood, Vic., Viking Penguin, 1987, pp. 25–6.
73 O'Farrell, *The Catholic Church and Community*, p. 108.
74 Campion, *Australian Catholics*, p. 26.
75 Inglis, *The Australian Colonists*, p. 90.
76 In 1847 both Sydney and Melbourne came under the auspices of the colony of New South Wales. When Victoria was formed as a separate colony in 1851, Melbourne was declared its capital city.
77 *Argus*, 13 April 1847.
78 Ibid.
79 Ibid.
80 For a full account of the work of Father Mathew, see C. Kerrigan, *Father Mathew and the Irish Temperance Movement, 1838–49*, Cork, Cork University Press, 1992 and

E. Malcolm, *Ireland Sober, Ireland Free: Drink and Temperance in 19th Century Ireland*, Dublin, Gill & Macmillan, 1986.

81 For background explanation and critique of the government's position on alcohol sales and related threats to public order, see editorial in *Freeman's Journal*, 17 March 1842.

82 For an example of Dublin Castle correspondence, see the letter to Secretary of Clonmel Temperance Society in *Cork Examiner*, 18 March 1842.

83 For details, see Williams, 'Irish identity and the *Illustrated London News*', pp. 69–71.

84 *Illustrated London News*, 13 March 1847.

85 Ibid.

86 *Cork Examiner*, 21 March 1842.

87 *Dublin Evening Post*, 19 March 1842. For similar descriptions of such parades, see *Freeman's Journal*, 18 March 1842, and *Limerick Reporter*, 20 March 1842.

88 *Freeman's Journal*, 18 March 1842.

89 For details and examples of such songs, see R.R. Grimes, *How Shall We Sing in a Foreign Land? Music of Irish Catholic Immigrants in the Antebellum United States*, Notre Dame, University of Notre Dame Press, 1996, pp. 139–43.

90 For a useful discussion of the Irish American population and its relationship with drink, see C. McDannell, 'True men as we need them: Catholicism and the Irish-American male', *American Studies*, vol. 27, 1986, pp. 19–36.

91 For details, see Ridge, *The St Patrick's Day Parade*, pp. 15–16.

92 Marston, 'Public rituals and community power', pp. 255–69.

93 *Irish News*, 7 March 1857.

94 *The Nation*, 25 March 1854.

3 VISUALIZING IRELAND: NATIONALISM AND DIASPORA

1 Editorial comment, *Freeman's Journal*, 17 March 1882.

2 *Freeman's Journal*, 19 March 1860.

3 Ibid.

4 Ibid.

5 Robins, *Champagne and Silver Buckles*, p. 147.

6 *Freeman's Journal*, 19 March 1860.

7 *Freeman's Journal*, 18 March 1870.

8 For background, see *The Nation*, 12 March 1870.

9 For general report, see *The Nation*, 26 March 1870.

10 For details of the programme, see *The Nation*, 26 March 1870.

11 See, for example, the advertisement placed by William O'Connell, Draper and Hosier, in *Freeman's Journal*, 16 March 1870.

12 See, for example, the advertisement placed by the Dublin, Wicklow and Wexford Railway, published in the *Freeman's Journal*, 17 March 1870.

13 *Freeman's Journal*, 18 March 1870.

14 Ibid.

15 For a useful nationwide description of St Patrick's day events, see *The Nation*, 26 March 1870.

16 *Freeman's Journal*, 17 March 1874.

17 Ibid.

18 *Freeman's Journal*, 18 March 1874.

19 For coverage of the various disturbances that encroached on St Patrick's Day

during this period, see Jarman, *Material Conflicts*, pp. 61–71; and for discussion of the Orange Order and their tradition of parading, see J. Loughlin, 'Parades and politics: liberal governments and the Orange Order, 1880–1886', in Fraser, *The Irish Parading Tradition*, pp. 27–43; D.M. McRaild, '"The bunkum of Ulsteria": the Orange marching tradition in late Victorian Cumbria', in Fraser, ibid., pp. 44–59.

20 Robins, *Champagne and Silver Buckles*, p. 147.
21 For full details of all the questions, and full reports from the sixty RIC districts involved, see 'Dublin Castle Records: Circular replies regarding party demonstrations on St Patrick's day 1874', CO 904/182, Public Record Office (PRO), London.
22 The figures do not include the marchers from Cookstown, Co. Tyrone. The local RIC officer returned a figure of 30,000 marchers which was questioned and subsequently discounted by Dublin Castle.
23 Report from Lurgan, Co. Armagh, PRO CO 904/182.
24 Report from Scariff, Co. Clare, PRO CO 904/182.
25 Report from Londonderry City, Co. Londonderry, PRO CO 904/182.
26 Report from Fivemiletown, Co. Fermanagh, PRO CO 904/182.
27 See final summary table of 1874 St Patrick's Day Demonstrations, PRO CO 904/182, p. 101.
28 'Party Processions', Memo written by J.H. Burke, Under-Secretary of the Ulster Office, Dublin Castle, 13 May 1874, PRO CO 904/182.
29 Memo from Sir M. Hicks, Chief Secretary, Ulster Office, Dublin Castle, to the Duke of Marlborough, 29 April 1878, PRO CO 904/182.
30 Charles Lewis, 'Speech in the House of Commons', 30 April 1878, copy held in PRO CO 904/182.
31 *Freeman's Journal*, 18 March 1880.
32 *Freeman's Journal*, 18 March 1882.
33 For details, see *Freeman's Journal*, 18 March 1882.
34 C. McDannell, 'Going to the Ladies Fair: Irish Catholics in New York City, 1870–1900', in Bayor and Meagher (eds), *The New York Irish*, p. 249.
35 See the landmark work of K. Miller, *Emigrants and Exiles: Ireland and the Irish Exodus to North America*, Oxford, Oxford University Press, 1985; and also A. O'Day, 'Varieties of anti-Irish behaviour in Britain, 1846–1922', in P. Panayi (ed.), *Racial Violence in Britain, 1840–1950*, Leicester, Leicester University Press, 1993, pp. 26–43.
36 Miller, *Emigrants and Exiles*, p. 7.
37 Ibid., p. 526.
38 *Nation*, 22 March 1862.
39 *Nation*, 22 March 1862.
40 G. Moran, 'Nationalists in exile: the National Brotherhood of St Patrick in Lancashire, 1861–5', in Swift and Gilley, *Irish in Victorian Britain*, p. 213.
41 Ibid., p. 214.
42 *Liverpool Mercury*, 18 March 1895.
43 Ibid.
44 Ibid.
45 *Liverpool Mercury*, 18 March 1905.
46 Ibid.
47 Ibid.
48 For statements defending the political autonomy of the Gaelic League, see letters

to the editor in the nationalist newspaper *Saoirse na hÉireann (Irish Freedom)*, no. 30, April 1913.

49 For discussions of the Gaelic League, see J. Hutchinson, 'Gaelic League', in Connolly, *The Oxford Companion to Irish History*, p. 215; and more extensively, J. Hutchinson, *The Dynamics of Cultural Nationalism: The Gaelic Revival and the Creation of the Irish Nation State*, London, Allen and Unwin, 1987. The classic study of the GAA is W.F. Mandle, *The Gaelic Athletic Association and Irish Nationalist Politics, 1884–1924*, Dublin, Gill & Macmillan, 1987; see also M. Cronin, *Sport and Nationalism in Ireland: Gaelic Games and Irish Identity Since 1884*, Dublin, Four Courts Press, 1999.

50 Hutchinson, *The Dynamics of Cultural Nationalism*, pp. 122–7.

51 *The Gael*, 18 March 1916.

52 *Saoirse na hÉireann*, no. 30, April 1913.

53 *New Ireland*, 17 March 1917.

54 Ibid.

55 *The Spark*, vol. 1, no. 6, 14 March 1915.

56 *Saoirse na hÉireann*, no. 17, March 1912.

57 *United Irishman*, 23 March 1901.

58 Lees, *Exiles of Erin*, pp. 234–5.

59 *United Irishman*, 23 March 1901.

60 *United Irishman*, 10 March 1900.

61 Despite the growing importance of St Patrick's day during this period, both in North America and Britain, the related celebrations have received little attention from historians. The two most important edited collections covering America and Britain both fail to mention St Patrick's Day and its celebration by the diaspora. See D.N. Doyle and O.D. Edwards (eds), *America and Ireland, 1776–1976*, Westport, CT, Greenwood Press, 1980; and Swift and Gilley, *The Irish in Britain*.

62 W.L. Joyce, *Editors and Ethnicity: A History of the Irish-American Press, 1848–1883*, New York, Arno Press, 1976, p. 114.

63 Bishop, *The Irish Empire*, p. 101.

64 A useful study of one city that explains such growth, especially the local impact of Irish organizations, is D. Clark, *The Irish in Philadelphia: Ten Generations of Urban Experience*, Philadelphia, Temple University Press, 1973.

65 Mary C. Kelly, 'Forty shades of green. Conflicts over community among the New York Irish, 1860–1920', unpublished PhD thesis, Syracuse University, 1997, p. 372.

66 Ridge, *The St Patrick's Day Parade*, p. 31. For a case study of this event, see J.A. Garland, 'St Patrick's Day, New York City 1861', *Irish Sword*, vol. 17, no. 66, 1987, pp. 26–40.

67 *Irish People*, 16 March 1867.

68 Ibid.

69 *Irish People*, 23 March 1867.

70 Ibid.

71 *Irish Citizen*, 2 March 1868.

72 Joyce, *Editors and Ethnicity*, p. 114.

73 The Irish possession and politicization of the streets on St Patrick's Day and the messages that such action sent out can be compared with the march of the workers on May Day in France in the 1880s. For details, see G.L. Mosse, *The Nationalisation of the Masses: Political Symbolism and Mass Movements in Germany from the Napoleonic Wars through the Third Reich*, New York, Howard Fertig, 1975, p. 168.

74   Marston, S.A., 'Adopted citizens: community and the development of consciousness among the Irish of Lowell, Massachusetts, 1839–85', PhD thesis, University
of Colorado at Boulder, 1986.
75   Quoted by Clark, *Hibernia America*, p. 56.
76   Ridge, *The St Patrick's Day Parade*, p. 39.
77   Burrows and Wallace, *Gotham*, p. 1005.
78   Ibid.
79   See Joyce, *Editors and Ethnicity*, p. 115.
80   Ibid., p. 116.
81   Ibid.
82   McNamara, *Day of Jubilee*, p. 44.
83   Quoted in McNamara, *Day of Jubilee*, p. 45.
84   Bodnar, *Remaking America*, p. 67.
85   Comments made by Cardinal O'Connell, quoted in D. and T. Hoobler (eds), *The
Irish American Family Album*, New York, Oxford University Press, 1999, p. 114;
see also Marston, 'Public rituals and community power', pp. 255–69.
86   *Irish World*, 28 March 1874.
87   *Irish World*, 4 April 1874.
88   Ibid.
89   *New York Times*, 18 March 1884, quoted in Ridge, *The St Patrick's Day Parade*,
p. 64.
90   Ridge, *The St Patrick's Day Parade*, pp. 67–8.
91   *Boston Pilot*, 27 March 1880.
92   *New York Times*, 18 March 1880.
93   For a general discussion of the relationship between masculinity, St Patrick's Day,
and the downturn in support for parades in the late nineteenth century, see C.
McDannell, 'True men as we need them: Catholicism and the Irish-American
male', *American Studies*, vol. 27, 1986, pp. 19–36. For a discussion of self-
improvement, rational recreation and their impact on St Patrick's day celebrations,
see T.J. Meagher, 'Why should we care for a little trouble or a walk through the
mud?: St Patrick's and Columbus Day parades in Worcester, Massachusetts,
1845–1915', *The New England Quarterly*, vol. 58, no. 1, 1985, pp. 5–26.
94   For details of the Hewitt era, see Burrows and Wallace, *Gotham*, p. 1108.
95   *Boston Pilot*, 22 March 1890.
96   D.M. Emmons, *The Butte Irish: Class and Ethnicity in an American Mining Town,
1875–1925*, Urbana, University of Illinois Press, 1989, pp. 143–4.
97   Ibid.
98   T.J. Meagher, 'Irish American, Catholic: Irish-American identity in Worcester,
Massachusetts, 1880–1920', in T.J. Meagher (ed.), *From Paddy to Studs: Irish American Communities in the Turn of the Century Era, 1880–1920*, New York, Greenwood
Press, 1986, p. 83.
99   M.G. Towey, 'Kerry Patch revisited: Irish Americans in St Louis in the turn of the
century era', in Meagher, ibid., p. 155.
100 Ibid., p. 155.
101 For examples of such pictures, see 'Friendly Sons of St Patrick Collection', American Irish Historical Society, New York, box 33.
102 1898 St Patrick's Night Dinner Programme, 'Friendly Sons of St Patrick Collection', American Irish Historical Society, New York, box 32, folder 3.
103 1895 St Patrick's Night Dinner Programme, 'Friendly Sons of St Patrick Collection', American Irish Historical Society, New York, box 32, folder 3.

104 Speech by John S. Wise, Friendly Sons of St Patrick, St Patrick's Night Dinner Programme, 16 March 1889, 'Friendly Sons of St Patrick Collection', American Irish Historical Society, New York, box 32, folder 2.

105 Cablegram read by Mr O'Donohue, President, Friendly Sons of St Patrick, St Patrick's Night Dinner Programme, 16 March 1889, 'Friendly Sons of St Patrick Collection', American Irish Historical Society, New York, box 32, folder 2.

106 Speech by O'Donohue, Cablegram read by Mr O'Donohue, President, Friendly Sons of St Patrick, St Patrick's Night Dinner Programme, 16 March 1889, 'Friendly Sons of St Patrick Collection', American Irish Historical Society, New York, box 32, folder 2.

107 Speech by Mr Richardson, Friendly Sons of St Patrick, St Patrick's Night Dinner Programme, 17 March 1879, 'Friendly Sons of St Patrick Collection', American Irish Historical Society, New York, box 32, folder 1.

108 M. R. Casey, 'Ireland, New York and the Irish image in American popular culture, 1890–1960', unpublished PhD thesis, New York University, 1998, p. 280.

109 Akenson, *Small Differences*, p. 90.

110 M.W. Nicolson, 'The other Toronto: Irish Catholics in a Victorian city, 1850–1900', *Polyphony*, Summer 1984, pp. 20–1; G.S. Kealey, 'The Orange Order in Toronto: religious riot and the working class', in O'Driscoll and Reynolds, *The Untold Story*, p. 831.

111 Nicolson, 'The other Toronto', p. 20.

112 Cotterell, 'St Patrick's Day parade', p. 65.

113 A leading advocate of the parade's cancellation was the high profile William D'Arcy McGee, a one-time Fenian now liberal-reformist Irish Catholic. His influence appears to have been telling, which did nothing for his reputation among the Hibernians.

114 Cotterell, 'St Patrick's Day parade', p. 65.

115 *Leader*, 18 March 1862, and *Canadian Freeman*, 20 March 1862, quoted in Cotterell, ibid., p. 65.

116 Ibid., p. 67.

117 Ibid., p. 68.

118 Ibid., p. 68.

119 Ibid., p. 68.

120 For debate about Lynch's role in trying to subdue the 1866 parade, see G.J. Stortz, 'The Catholic Church and Irish nationalism in Toronto, 1850–1900', in O'Driscoll and Reynolds, *The Untold Story*, pp. 873–4.

121 Cotterell, 'St Patrick's Day parade', p. 69.

122 G.M. Craig, 'A historical perspective: the evolution of a nation', in W. Metcalfe (ed.), *Understanding Canada: A Multidisciplinary Introduction to Canadian Studies*, New York, New York University Press, 1982, pp. 111–14.

123 Cotterell, 'St Patrick's Day parade', p. 69.

124 Ibid., p. 70.

125 Ibid., pp. 71–2.

126 Ibid., pp. 72–3.

127 G.S. Kealey, 'The Orange Order in Toronto: religious riot and the working class', in O'Driscoll and Reynolds, *The Untold Story*, p. 845.

128 Ibid., p. 846.

129 Ibid.

130 Ibid.

131 Ibid.

132 One study of the Jubilee Riots has already concluded that, far from showing even-handedness and moderation, the Orangemen who controlled Toronto's civic administration and police used the occasion as a public relations ploy. They remained staunchly anti-Catholic and jealous of their control of state institutions. For details of this argument, see T.E. Strauch, 'Walking for God and raising Hell. The Jubilee Riots, the Orange Order and the preservation of Protestantism in Toronto, 1875', unpublished MA thesis, Queen's University at Kingston, Kingston, 1999.

133 Kealey, 'The Orange Order in Toronto', p. 845.

134 *Irish Canadian*, 5 April 1876.

135 This act may well have been retaliation for an outrage in 1870, 'when a foolhardy Green drove his cart, bedecked with green ribbons, through the July 12 procession'. Kealey, 'The Orange Order in Toronto', p. 845.

136 Ibid., p. 843.

137 Ibid., p. 845.

138 Ibid., pp. 842, 845. Similarly, Houston and Smyth, in their study of Orangeism in Canada, conclude that during the Victorian era there were 'rare bouts of violence that disrupted a usually peaceful co-existence' between Catholics and Protestants. C.J. Houston and W.J. Smyth, 'Orangemen in Canada', in O'Driscoll and Reynolds, *The Untold Story*, p. 752.

139 M. McGowan, 'Toronto's English-speaking Catholics, immigration, and the making of a Canadian Catholic identity, 1900–30', in T. Murphy and G. Stortz (eds), *Creed and Culture: The Place of English-Speaking Catholics in Canadian Society, 1750–1930*, p. 207.

140 Nicolson, 'The other Toronto', p. 23. For wider discussion of Protestant–Catholic relations in Canada, see J.R. Miller, 'Anti-Catholic thought in Victorian Canada', *Canadian Historical Review*, vol. 66, no. 4, 1985, pp. 474–94.

141 For a study of Thomas D'Arcy McGee's funeral procession, see P.G. Goheen, 'Symbols in the streets: parades in Victorian urban Canada', *Urban History Review/Revue d'Histoire Urbaine*, vol. 18, no. 3, February 1990, pp. 237–43. For discussion about the importance of D'Arcy McGee to the Irish-Catholic community, see R.B. Burns, 'From freedom to tolerance: D'Arcy McGee the first martyr', in O'Driscoll and Reynolds, *The Untold Story*, pp. 465–80. For a St Patrick's Day oration on the life of D'Arcy McGee, see R.D. McGibbon, 'Thomas D'Arcy McGee: an address delivered before the St Patrick's Society of Sherbrooke, P.Q., March 17th 1884', Montreal, Dawson Brothers, 1884.

142 Schmitz, *Irish for a Day*, p. 40.

143 Ibid., p. 40.

144 *Morning Chronicle*, 18 March 1876.

145 Ibid.

146 *Gazette*, 18 March 1865.

147 Ibid.

148 Ibid.

149 All quotes from the *Gazette*, 18 March 1865.

150 All quotes from the *Gazette*, 18 March 1875.

151 *Gazette*, 13 July 1877, cited in E. Folke, 'Irish folk songs in Canada', in O'Driscoll and Reynolds, *The Untold Story*, p. 707.

152 'Minutes, St Patrick's Society of Montreal', 11 March 1881, Archives of Concordia University, Montreal, cited in Regan, 'Montreal's St. Patrick's Day parade'.

153 *St Patrick's Day Montreal 1890*, Herald Print, Montreal, 1890, pp. 12–13.

154 Ibid., p. 38.

155 Ibid., p. 32.

156 Ibid.

157 Regan, 'Montreal's St. Patrick's Day parade', p.14.

158 *Gazette*, 18 March 1899.

159 This is the figure offered by John O'Dea, who was commissioned to write the 'official history' of the AOH in the early 1920s. J. O'Dea, *History of the Ancient Order of Hibernians and Ladies' Auxiliary, Vol. I*, Philadelphia, National Board of the AOH, 1923, cited in Regan, 'Montreal's St. Patrick's Day parade', p.11.

160 Ibid., p. 6.

161 Ibid., p. 16.

162 *Gazette*, 19 March 1900.

163 Regan, 'Montreal's St. Patrick's Day parade', p. 17.

164 Ibid., pp. 17–18.

165 Inglis, *The Australian Colonists*, pp. 93–4.

166 *Argus*, 6 February 1861.

167 *Argus*, 29 March 1864.

168 *Argus*, 18 April 1865.

169 *Argus*, 8 August 1860.

170 *Argus*, 7 October 1863.

171 For details, see *Argus*, 4 September, 10 October, 7 November 1866; 12 November, 23–4 December 1869. Fist fights at Society meetings were, however, not unusual before the benefit fund fiasco. See *Argus*, 4 January 1860.

172 B. McKinlay, *The First Royal Tour 1867–1868*, Adelaide, Rigby, 1970, pp. 167–93.

173 Inglis, *The Australian Colonists*, pp. 102–3.

174 Ibid., pp. 99–104.

175 *Argus*, 18 March 1868.

176 Inglis, *The Australian Colonists*, p. 89.

177 Ibid., pp. 89–99.

178 McConville, *Croppies, Celts and Catholics*, p. 81.

179 Ibid., pp. 81–3.

180 C. Kiernan, 'Home Rule for Ireland and the formation of the Australian Labor Party, 1883 to 1891', *Australian Journal of Politics and History*, vol. 38, no. 1, 1992, pp. 2–7; McConville, *Croppies, Celts and Catholics*, pp. 82–4.

181 O'Farrell, *The Irish in Australia*, p. 174.

182 O. MacDonagh, 'Irish culture and nationalism translated: St Patrick's Day, 1888, in Australia', in O. MacDonagh, W.F. Mandle and P. Travers (eds), *Irish Culture and Nationalism, 1750–1950*, Canberra, Macmillan in association with Humanities Research Centre, Australian National University, 1983, p. 72; Kiernan, 'Home Rule for Ireland', p. 7.

183 MacDonagh, 'Irish culture and nationalism translated', pp. 75–9.

184 M. O'Brien and C.C. O'Brien, *A Concise History of Ireland*, London, Thames and Hudson, 2nd edn, 1973, p. 118.

185 McConville, *Croppies, Celts and Catholics*, p. 96.

186 A. Brown-May, *Melbourne Street Life: The Itinerary of Our Days*, Melbourne, Australian Scholarly Publishing/Arcadia and Museum Victoria, 1998, pp. 176–7.

187 Ibid., p. 201.

188 O'Farrell, *The Irish in Australia*, p. 246; P. O'Farrell, *The Catholic Church and Community*, p. 232.

189 O'Farrell, *The Irish in Australia*, p. 181.

190 O'Farrell, *The Catholic Church*, pp. 183–232.

191 O'Farrell, *The Irish in Australia*, pp. 238, 242–3. Moran was similarly unimpressed with the Protestant jingoism of Empire Day. He called for it to be renamed Australia Day in order to be more inclusive and less sectional. S. Firth and J. Hoorn, 'From Empire Day to cracker night', in P. Spearitt and D. Walker (eds), *Australian Popular Culture*, Sydney, Allen & Unwin, 1979, pp. 23–5.

192 O'Farrell, *The Irish in Australia*, p. 184.

193 Ibid., p. 246.

194 Ibid.

195 *Age*, 17 March 1913.

196 McConville, *Croppies, Celts and Catholics*, p. 103.

197 Ibid., pp. 100–4.

198 Sydney seems to have been the only city to abandon the St Patrick's Day procession. In Brisbane, Perth and Adelaide the annual parade remained a regular feature of the celebrations. *Southern Cross*, 20 March 1914; *Catholic Press*, 22 March 1917, 20 March 1919.

199 E. Campion, *Australian Catholics*, Ringwood, Vic., Viking Penguin, 1987, p. 125.

200 A.D. Gilbert, 'The conscription referenda, 1916–17: the impact of the Irish crisis', *Historical Studies (Australia)*, vol. 14, October 1969, pp. 55–7, 68–70.

201 Ridge, *The St Patrick's Day Parade*, p. 85.

202 For details, see ibid., pp. 84–99.

203 Speech by William Temple Emmet, President of the Friendly Sons of St Patrick, 17 March 1910, 'Friendly Sons of St Patrick Collection', American Irish Historical Society, New York, box 33, folder 13.

204 Speech by Luke Stapleton, 17 March 1910, 'Friendly Sons of St Patrick Collection', American Irish Historical Society, New York, box 33, folder 13.

205 *Irish Times*, 18 March 1902.

206 For an overview of the public holiday debate, as well as brief insights into the place of St Patrick's Day within that context, see A. Russell, *Bank Holidays: A Victorian Invention and Modern Institution*, London, Minerva Press, 2000.

207 For details of this campaign, see P. Mooney, 'A symbol for the nation: the national holiday campaign, 1901–3', unpublished MA thesis, Maynooth, National University of Ireland, 1992.

208 For details of the Bank Holiday (Ireland) Act, see *Public General Acts Passed in the Third Year of the Reign of his Majesty King Edward VII*, London, HMSO, 1903, p. A. Discussions about the Bill can be found in House of Commons debates in *Hansard* through 1902 and 1903. The key debates related to the workings of the Act, its impact on the opening hours of public houses, and whether the Act should apply to parts of Ulster.

209 *Irish Independent*, 16 March 1905.

210 *Liverpool Mercury*, 18 March 1905.

211 Comments made by Cardinal O'Connell, quoted in Hoobler and Hoobler (eds), *Irish American Family Album*, p. 114.

212 Emmons, *The Butte Irish*, p. 257.

213 Advertisement for Cantrell & Cochrance Ginger Ale, *Irish Times*, 16 March 1912.

214 *United Irishman*, 17 March 1900.

215 Ibid.

216 *United Irishman*, 24 March 1900.

217 *Irish Times*, 18 March 1902.

218 For fuller details of this incident, see *New York Times*, 18 March 1910.

219 *Gaelic American*, 23 March 1912.

220 These examples are drawn from the event in All Saint's Parish Hall, New York, on 17 March 1912; see *Gaelic American*, 23 March 1912 for fuller details. However, it is clear that the featured pieces of music, drama and literature at such events across the country were remarkably similar.

221 'AOH St Patrick's Day Souvenir, 17 March 1905, Savannah GA', in M. McCormack, *Histories of the Order*, AOH, 1989.

222 The ball did continue at irregular intervals until the First World War, but its level of importance slipped. Reports in the *Irish Times* in 1902 and 1907 still detail the finery and the elegance of the evening, but in a changing political climate the ball lacked the social impact it had in the nineteenth century.

223 Robins, *Champagne and Silver Buckles*, p. 185.

224 *Irish Times*, 18 March 1914.

225 Ibid.

226 Ibid.

227 Dublin Castle Memo, 6 March 1915. For this, and details of all ceremonial trooping of the colour events on St Patrick's Day, see 'Headquarters of Irish Command', WO 35/59, PRO.

228 For details of the letter from Norman Witter, 17 Great Brunswick Street, Dublin, 27 February 1915, see 'Headquarters of Irish Command', WO 35/59, PRO.

4 CONTESTING IRELAND:
REPUBLICANISM AND MILITARISM

1 Michael Collins addressing a crowd at Skibbereen, Ireland, on St Patrick's Day 1922; as quoted in *Boston Daily Globe*, 18 March 1922.

2 *Irish Independent*, 18 March 1915.

3 Ridge, *The St Patrick's Day Parade*, p. 101.

4 *New York Times*, 18 March 1915.

5 *Gaelic American*, 25 March 1916.

6 Ibid.

7 For details of all the 1916 parades, see 'Sinn Féin Volunteer Parades, St Patrick's day 1916', CO 904/23, part 2, PRO.

8 Batt O'Connor, quoted in T. Brown, *The American Connection: US Guns, Money and Influence in Northern Ireland*, Boulder, COL, Roberts Reinhart, 1999, p. 8.

9 Sir Roger Casement was executed for his part in the 1916 Rising.

10 *Gaelic American*, 24 March 1917.

11 For details, see D. Brundage, 'In time of peace, prepare for war: key themes in the social thought of New York's Irish nationalists', in Bayor and Meagher (eds), *The New York Irish*, p. 333.

12 *New York Times*, 18 March 1920.

13 'St Patrick: reality and symbol', *The Day: A Message for St Patrick's Day from the Cork Twenty Club*, Cork, Cork Twenty Club, 1918, p. 4.

14 *Irish Independent*, 18 March 1920.

15 Ibid.

16 Ibid.

17 See *An t Oglác*, various dates 1919–22, copies held at CO 904 24/4, PRO.

18 *Irish Independent*, 18 March 1920.

19 *Irish Times*, 17 March 1922.

20 Quoted in Ridge, *The St Patrick's Day Parade*, pp. 113–14.
21 *Boston Daily Globe*, 17 March 1922.
22 Ibid.
23 Schmitz, *Irish for a Day*, p. 73.
24 Regan, 'Montreal's St. Patrick's Day parade', p. 20.
25 *Gazette*, 16 March 1914.
26 Regan, 'Montreal's St. Patrick's Day parade', pp. 4, 20–1. A notable development in the incipient radicalization of Montreal's AOH was a parade of November 1915 when '1200 of the Order and its friends paraded to commemorate the "Manchester Martyrs"'. R.B. Burns, 'Who shall separate us? The Montreal Irish and the Great War', in O'Driscoll and Reynolds, *The Untold Story*, p. 573.
27 Ibid., p. 571.
28 Ibid., p. 574.
29 *Gazette*, 20 March 1916, quoted in ibid., p. 572.
30 Regan, 'Montreal's St. Patrick's Day parade', p. 21.
31 *Gazette*, 16 March 1917.
32 Ibid.
33 *Gazette*, 19 March 1917.
34 *Gazette*, 17 March 1917.
35 Regan, 'Montreal's St. Patrick's Day parade', pp. 21–2.
36 Ibid., p. 22.
37 *Gazette*, 17 March 1919.
38 Regan, 'Montreal's St. Patrick's Day parade', p. 23.
39 *Age*, 18 March 1914.
40 *Age*, 23 March 1914.
41 A.D. Gilbert, 'The conscription referenda, 1916–17: the impact of the Irish crisis', *Historical Studies (Australia)*, vol. 14, October 1969, pp. 58–9, 62–3; D.J. Murphy, 'Religion, race and conscription in World War I', *Australian Journal of Politics and History*, vol. 20, no. 2, August 1974, pp. 155–6.
42 *Age*, 20 March 1916.
43 Ibid.
44 *Age*, 17 March 1916.
45 *Argus*, 2 May 1916.
46 Gilbert, 'Conscription referenda', p. 60.
47 O'Farrell, *The Irish in Australia*, pp. 256–9; P. O'Farrell, 'Archbishop Kelly and the Irish question', *Journal of the Australian Catholic Historical Society*, vol. 4, no. 3, 1974, pp. 4–5.
48 *Argus*, 28 April 1916, cited in Gilbert, 'Conscription referenda, 1916–17', p. 60.
49 O'Farrell, *The Irish in Australia*, p. 259.
50 Ibid.
51 D. Keogh, 'Mannix, De Valera and Irish nationalism', in J. O'Brien and P. Travers (eds), *The Irish Emigrant Experience in Australia*, Dublin, Poolbeg, 1991, pp. 196–8.
52 Quoted in W.A. Ebsworth, *Archbishop Mannix*, Melbourne, H.H. Stephenson, 1977, p. 146.
53 Gilbert, 'Conscription referenda', pp. 61–2.
54 *Catholic Press*, 18 May 1916, cited in Gilbert, 'Conscription referenda', p. 62.
55 Murphy, 'Religion, race and conscription', p. 156.
56 Ibid.
57 *Argus*, 13, 17 July 1916.
58 O'Farrell, *The Catholic Church and Community*, p. 324.

59   I. Turner, *Industrial Labour and Politics: The Dynamics of the Labour Movement in Eastern Australia, 1900–1921*, Sydney, Hale & Iremonger, 1979, p. 106.

60   For detailed discussions, see K.S. Inglis, 'Conscription in peace and war, 1911–1945', *Teaching History*, vol. 1, no. 2, October 1967, pp. 5–25; M. McKernan, 'Catholics, conscription and Archbishop Mannix', *Historical Studies (Australia)*, vol. 18, 1977, pp. 299–314; Gilbert, 'Conscription referenda', pp. 54–72; and Murphy, 'Religion, race and conscription', pp. 155–63.

61   Gilbert, 'Conscription referenda', p. 66.

62   Turner, *Industrial Labour and Politics*, pp. 97–110.

63   B.A. Santamaria, *Daniel Mannix: The Quality of Leadership*, Carlton, Vic., Melbourne University Press, 1984, p. 81; Inglis, 'Conscription in peace and war', pp. 20–1.

64   *Catholic Press*, 22 March 1917; *Argus*, 19 March 1917.

65   *Argus*, 22 March 1917.

66   *Argus*, 19 March 1917.

67   *Argus*, 19 March 1917; *Argus*, 20 March 1916.

68   *Argus*, 22 March 1917.

69   Ibid.

70   Murphy, 'Religion, race and conscription', pp. 158–9; Inglis, 'Conscription in peace and war', p. 20.

71   Turner, *Industrial Labour and Politics*, pp. 162–4.

72   Kiernan, *Daniel Mannix*, p. 107.

73   L. Egan, General Secretary St Patrick's Day Celebration Committee to the Lord Mayor of Melbourne, 6 December 1917, Town Clerk's Files, Melbourne City Council, Series Three, Street Processions 1917–1922, PROV VPRS 3183, Unit 156. (Subsequent references to this archive will read PROV VPRS 3183, Units 155 or 156.)

74   Secretary to the Lord Mayor to Egan, 10 December 1917, PROV VPRS 3183, Unit 156.

75   Town Clerk to Egan, 15 January 1918, PROV VPRS 3183, Unit 156.

76   Santamaria, *Daniel Mannix*, p. 81.

77   *Catholic Press*, 21 March 1918.

78   *Advocate*, 23 March 1918.

79   *Catholic Press*, 21 March 1918.

80   Ibid.

81   Ibid.; *Argus*, 18 March 1918.

82   *Catholic Press*, 21 March 1918.

83   *Argus*, 18 March 1918.

84   Ibid.

85   Ibid.

86   *Catholic Press*, 21 March 1918.

87   Letter to the editor from Prenez-Garde, *Argus*, 21 March 1918.

88   *Argus*, 25 March 1918.

89   Letter to the editor from Little Shamrock, *Argus*, 21 March 1918.

90   Letter to the editor from Clement O'Brien, *Argus*, 21 March 1918.

91   Dunstan, 'The rise and fall of St Patrick's Day', *Overland*, no. 78, 1979, p. 57; R. Rivett, *Australian Citizen: Herbert Brooks, 1867–1963*, Carlton, Vic., Melbourne University Press, 1965, pp. 62–8;.

92   Ibid., pp. 62–8; *Argus*, 26 March 1918.

93   *Argus*, 20 March 1918.

94 Sub-Inspector O'Loughlin to Inspector Corby, 22 March 1918; Sub-Inspector Madigan to Inspector Corby, 22 March 1918; Sub-Inspector Parkin to Inspector Corby, 22 March 1918; and Sub-Inspector Ryan to Inspector McKenna, 22 March 1918, PROV VPRS 3183, Unit 155. Sub-Inspector Hocking was the only one to recognize Sinn Féin symbols. Hocking to Corby, 22 March 1918, PROV VPRS 3183, Unit 155.

95 For example, a letter to the *Argus* suggested that 'no processions of any kind' should be permitted 'without carrying, unfurled, the grand old Union Jack'. Letter to the Editor from H.J. Vernon, *Argus*, 26 March 1918.

96 *Argus*, 18 April 1918. For a detailed report of the 'loyalist' meeting, see the *Argus*, 10 April 1918.

97 *Argus*, 19 March 1918.

98 *Argus*, 27 March 1918.

99 Hughes introduced the Unlawful Associations Bill on 15 December 1916. For details, see V. Burgmann, 'The iron heel: the supression of the IWW during World War I', in Sydney Labour History Group (eds), *What Rough Beast?: The State and Social Order in Australian History*, Sydney, George Allen & Unwin, 1982, pp. 171–91.

100 P. O'Farrell, 'The Irish Republican Brotherhood in Australia: the 1918 internments', in MacDonagh *et al.*, *Irish Culture and Nationalism*, pp. 182–3.

101 O'Farrell, 'Irish Republican Brotherhood', p. 182.

102 When Brookes presented his petition to Hughes in front of a crowd at the Treasury building, cheers resounded as he called for Mannix to be charged with sedition and deported. Rivett, *Herbert Brookes*, p. 68.

103 O'Farrell, 'Irish Republican Brotherhood', pp. 182–93.

104 Quoted in *Argus*, 25 March 1918.

105 S. Macintyre, *The Oxford History of Australia*, vol. 4, *1901–1942: The Succeeding Age*, Melbourne, Oxford University Press, 1986, p. 187; McKernan, 'Catholics, conscription and Archbishop Mannix', p. 309.

106 Dunstan, 'The rise and fall of St Patrick's Day', p. 57.

107 Town Clerk to Egan, 25 January 1919, PROV VPRS 3183, Unit 155. See also preliminary correspondence of 6 and 18 January 1919 in this file.

108 Town Clerk to Egan, 25 January 1919, PROV VPRS 3183, Unit 155.

109 Malleson Stewart and Co. to Town Clerk, 4 February 1919, PROV VPRS 3183, Unit 156.

110 Ibid.

111 Ibid.

112 *Argus*, 18 March 1919.

113 Macintyre, *The Oxford History of Australia*, pp. 187–8.

114 Acting Town Clerk to Secretary, Eight Hours Celebration Committee, 19 March 1919; Secretary, Melbourne Eight Hours Anniversary Committee to Lord Mayor, 26 March 1919; and Town Clerk to Secretary, Eight Hours Anniversary Committee, 27 March 1919; MCCA Series 120/1 1533/1919; *Argus*, 8 April 1919; *Herald*, 2 April 1919.

115 *Argus*, 18 March 1919.

116 Ibid.

117 *Catholic Press*, 20 March 1919.

118 *Argus*, 18 March 1919.

119 O'Farrell, *The Irish in Australia*, p. 281.

120 Egan to Lord Mayor Aikman, 12 January 1920, PROV VPRS 3183, Unit 155.

121 The groups represented were the Loyalist League of Victoria, the Australian Women's National League, the Protestant Federation of Victoria, the Protestant Alliance, the Loyal Orange Institution, the Ulster and Loyal Irishmen's Association, and the British Empire Union. Leeper to Aikman, 30 January 1920, PROV VPRS 3183, Unit 155.

122 D. Dunstan, 'Rise and fall of St Patrick's Day', p. 57.

123 Memorandum, Aikman to Town Clerk, 4 February 1920, PROV VPRS 3183, Unit 155.

124 Leeper to Aikman, 30 January 1920, PROV VPRS 3183, Unit 155.

125 Ibid.

126 Notes on Loyalist Deputation, 30 January 1920, PROV VPRS 3183, Unit 155.

127 Ibid.

128 Ibid.

129 'A Loyal Roman Catholic' to Lord Mayor, 31 January 1920, PROV VPRS 3183, Unit 155.

130 Notes on Loyalist Deputation, 30 January 1920, PROV VPRS 3183, Unit 155.

131 Notes on St Patrick's Day Committee Deputation, 30 January 1920, PROV VPRS 3183, Unit 155.

132 Ibid.

133 See copies of police reports in the town clerk's files, PROV VPRS 3183, Unit 155, for 1918.

134 Notes on St Patrick's Day Committee Deputation, 30 January 1920, PROV VPRS 3183, Unit 155.

135 Town Clerk to Egan, 5 February 1920, PROV VPRS 3183, Unit 155.

136 *Age*, 5 February 1920.

137 Memorandum, Mayor Aikman to Town Clerk, 4 February 1920, PROV VPRS 3183, Unit 155.

138 Ibid.

139 Leeper to Mayor Aikman, 10 February 1920, PROV VPRS 3183, Unit 155.

140 Ibid.

141 The mayor received similar advice by mail from 'loyalist' groups. See, for example, Victorian Protestant Federation, Flemington and Kensington branch to Mayor Aikman, 23 January 1920, PROV VPRS 3183, Unit 155. For further discussions of 'loyalist' lobbying of the mayor, see the *Argus*, 9, 11 February 1920.

142 Egan to Mayor Aikman, 21 February 1920, PROV VPRS 3183, Unit 155.

143 Ibid.

144 Minutes of a meeting of the Melbourne City Council, 8 March 1920, quoted in *Argus*, 9 March 1920.

145 *Argus*, 11 March 1920.

146 *Age*, 24 February 1920.

147 Kiernan, *Daniel Mannix*, p. 135.

148 *Catholic Press*, 25 March 1920; *Argus*, 22 March 1920; *Advocate*, 8 April 1920.

149 *Catholic Press*, 25 March 1920.

150 Ibid.; *Argus*, 22 March 1920.

151 *Argus*, 22 March 1920.

152 Ibid.

153 *Catholic Press*, 25 March 1920.

154 *Catholic Press*, 18 March 1920.

155 Kiernan, *Daniel Mannix*, pp. 135–6.

156 Ibid., p. 136; H. Buggy, *The Real John Wren*, Melbourne, Widescope, 1977, p. 205.

157 *Argus*, 22 March 1920.
158 Kiernan, *Daniel Mannix*, p. 139; *Ireland Will Be Free*, 1920, Melbourne Diocesan Historical Commission, B&W silent film, 35mm, Screen and Sound Australia Archives, Canberra, Cover Title No. 11803.
159 *Catholic Press*, 25 March 1920.
160 See, for example, Secretary, Loyal Orange Institution of Victoria, Protestant Hall, to Mayor Swanson, 22 January 1921, Town Clerk's Files, Melbourne City Council Archives, Series 120/1, 1917–1922, 413/1921 (Subsequent references to this archive will read MCCA Series 120/1.)
161 See Kennedy to Mayor Swanson, 7 January 1921; and Town Clerk to Kennedy, 26 January 1921, PROV VPRS 3183, Unit 155. For a newspaper summary, see the *Age*, 2 March 1921.
162 *Herald*, 9 March 1921.
163 Statement issued by the Irish Republican Army, Melbourne Branch, 19 March 1921, cited in PROV VPRS 3183, Unit 155.
164 Ibid.
165 Sub-Inspector W.R. Grange to Superintendent of Police, Melbourne District, 19 March 1921, PROV VPRS 3183, Unit 155.
166 Brennan, *Dr Mannix*, p. 178.
167 *Herald*, 19 March 1921.
168 Brennan, *Dr Mannix*, p. 178.
169 *Herald*, 19, 21 March 1921. For a copy of the original police report, see Sub-Inspector W.R. Grange to Superintendent of Police, Melbourne District, 19 March 1921, PROV VPRS 3183, Unit 155.
170 *Catholic Press*, 24 March 1921.
171 Sub-Inspector W.R. Grange to Superintendent of Police, Melbourne District, 19 March 1921, PROV VPRS 3183, Unit 155.
172 *Age*, 21 March 1921; *Herald*, 19 March 1921; Brennan, *Dr Mannix*, p. 178.
173 Grange to Superintendent of Police, Melbourne District, 19 March 1921, PROV VPRS 3183, Unit 155.
174 *Catholic Press*, 24 March 1921.
175 Emphasis added to the original. *Age*, 21 March 1921; *Herald*, 21 March 1921.
176 For criticism of Phelan's speech, see Secretary, Victorian Protestant Federation, Bairnsdale Branch to Lord Mayor, 5 May 1921, MCCA Series 120/1 2099/1921. For opposition to the 'flag incident', see Secretary, Shire of Warrnambool to Town Clerk, 22 April 1921, MCCA Series 120/1 1927/1921.
177 Secretary, Loyal Orange Lodge, Protestant Hall Branch to City Council, 24 March 1921, PROV VPRS 3183, Unit 156.
178 *Argus*, 5 April 1921.
179 *Argus*, 7 April 1921. See also the *Herald*, 6 April 1921.
180 *Argus*, 7 April 1921.
181 City Solicitor to Town Clerk, 2 April 1921, PROV VPRS 3183, Unit 156.
182 Shorthand notes of council discussion on 34th Order of the Day, 4 May 1921, PROV VPRS 3183, Unit 156.
183 Deputation to the Lord Mayor from the St Patrick's Day Celebration Committee, 21 May 1921, PROV VPRS 3183, Unit 156; Deputation to the Lord Mayor from Melbourne Eight Hours Anniversary Committee, 'Protest Against By-Law to Prohibit Street Processions', 17 May 1921; Secretary, Melbourne Eight Hours Anniversary Committee to Lord Mayor, 19 May 1921, PROV VPRS 3183, Unit 156.

184 *Herald*, 6 April 1921.

185 *Sun*, 28 May 1921.

186 *Argus*, 10 February 1922. But this decision did not affect other parts of Victoria. In Ballarat, for example, the city council not only permitted the usual procession, but granted a half-day holiday for the event, *Argus*, 22 February 1922. Moreover, the Mayor of South Melbourne had already approved a St Patrick's Day parade. The march would traverse to Queen's Bridge Street, where a boundary between the Melbourne and South Melbourne council areas was drawn, *Argus*, 16 March 1922.

187 Kennedy to Town Clerk, 4 March 1922, PROV VPRS 3183, Unit 156; *Argus*, 10 February, 7 March 1922; *Herald*, 7 March 1922.

188 Kennedy to Town Clerk, 4 March 1922, PROV VPRS 3183, Unit 156; *Advocate*, 2 March 1922.

189 *Argus*, 16 February 1922.

190 As examples, see Secretary, Protestant Alliance Friendly Society of Australasia, Box Hill to Mayor Swanson, 4 March 1922, MCCA Series 120/1 1265/1922; and Loyal Orange Institution of Victoria, Frankston to Mayor Swanson, 26 February 1922, MCCA Series 120/1 1265/1922.

191 As examples, see General Secretary, Irish National Foresters' Benefit Society, St Patrick's Hall, Bourke Street to Town Clerk, 6 March 1922, MCCA Series 120/1 1261/1922; and General Secretary, Australian Catholic Federation to Town Clerk, MCCA Series 120/1 991/1922.

192 As examples, see Secretary, Australian Catholic Federation, Rokewood Branch to Town Clerk, 6 March 1922, MCCA Series 120/1 1265/1922; and Secretary, Catholic Young Men's Society of Victoria, Federal Executive to Town Clerk, 14 February 1922, MCCA Series 120/1 857/1922.

193 *Argus*, 8 February 1922.

194 *Argus*, 24 February 1922.

195 J.J. Keating to Mayor Swanson, 28 February 1922, MCCA Series 120/1 1175/1922. For further declarations of support, see *Advocate*, 2 March 1922.

196 Town Clerk to Kennedy, 7 March 1922, PROV VPRS 3183, Unit 156; *Argus*, 8, 22 February 1922.

197 Ibid.

198 Memorandum: Town Clerk to City Solicitor, 10 February 1922; City Solicitor to Town Clerk, 13 February 1922, PROV VPRS 3183, Unit 156.

199 Town Clerk to Kennedy, 13 February 1922, PROV VPRS 3183, Unit 156.

200 E.J.D. Guinness, Crown Solicitor to Chief Commissioner of Police, Melbourne, 6 March 1922, PROV VPRS 3183, Unit 156.

201 Ibid.

202 Conference between Town Clerk, City Solicitor and By-laws Officers, n.d., PROV VPRS 3183, Unit 156 (1922).

203 Town Clerk's Notes attached to 'Re St Patrick's Day Procession and Asking that Council Receive a Deputation re Same', PROV VPRS 3183, Unit 156.

204 Superintendent of Police to Town Clerk, 17 March 1922, PROV VPRS 3183, Unit 156.

205 *Advocate*, 2 March 1922; *Argus*, 25 February 1922. In fact councillor Dobson had never been involved in a St Patrick's Day parade, but he felt compelled to participate on this occasion. *Tribune*, 2 March 1922.

206 *Argus*, 6 March 1922.

207 *Argus*, 21 February 1922; *Advocate*, 23 February 1922.

208 See letters to the editor by 'Scotia', and 'A.Z.L.', *Argus*, 23 February 1922.

209 Postmaster General's Department, Central Administration Section, Personnel Branch, Records Section, File G1926/1304, AAVIC, MP273/1; 'St Patrick's Day Celebrations, 1916–20: Leave Arrangements', Department of the Navy, Correspondence Files, Annual Single Number Series, 1911–1921, File 19/20/1427, AAVIC, MP472/1.

210 The Prime Minister's Department had originally given approval for leave in Melbourne, but it was forced to rescind this decision after the town clerk of Melbourne pointed out that the procession was not sanctioned by the city council. Memorandum: Secretary, Prime Minister's Department to Secretary, Postmaster-General's Department, 3, 13 March 1922, AAVIC, MP273/1; Postmaster General's Department, File G1926/1304; and Memorandum: Town Clerk to Lord Mayor, 13 March 1922, PROV VPRS 3183, Unit 156.

211 *Herald*, 7 March 1922.

212 *Argus*, 16 March 1922.

213 Superintendent of Police to Town Clerk, 16 March 1922, PROV VPRS 3183, Unit 156.

214 *Advocate*, 9 March 1922.

215 *Tribune*, 16 March 1922.

216 *Argus*, 16 March 1922.

217 Ibid.

218 Ibid.

219 *Tribune*, 16 March 1922.

220 Ibid.

221 *Argus*, 16 March 1922.

222 *Argus*, 18 March 1922.

223 *Advocate*, 9 March 1922.

224 *Advocate*, 23 March 1922.

225 *Catholic Press*, 23 March 1922; *Argus*, 20 March 1922.

226 *Catholic Press*, 23 March 1922.

227 *Argus*, 20 March 1922.

228 For full details of the order of procession, see *Advocate*, 8 March 1922.

229 *Advocate*, 23 March 1922; *Catholic Press*, 23 March 1922.

230 *Catholic Press*, 23 March 1922. Returned nurses also joined in the procession, but they were transported in motor cars and not expected to march. Instructions for the participation of war veterans appears in the *Advocate*, 9 March 1922.

231 *Argus*, 20 March 1922.

232 *Catholic Press*, 23 March 1922.

233 Ibid. Another Catholic paper, the *Advocate* was more circumspect. It spoke of a 'large number' of non-Catholics constituting a 'splendid body' among the processionists. *Advocate*, 23 March 1922.

234 *Argus*, 20 March 1922.

235 Ibid.

236 Ibid.

237 *Advocate*, 23 March 1922; *Catholic Press*, 23 March 1922; *Argus*, 20 March 1922.

238 Report by M.M. O'Toole, Chief By-Laws Officer, 'St Patrick's Procession', 20 March 1922, PROV VPRS 3183, Unit 156.

239 Acting Chief Commissioner to Town Clerk, 22 March 1922, PROV VPRS 3183, Unit 156.

240 As examples, see Report by M.J. Dickens, By-Laws Officer, 'St Patrick's Procession', 20 March 1922; and Report by E.J. Bennett, Assistant By-Laws Officer, 'St Patrick's Procession', 20 March 1922, PROV VPRS 3183, Unit 156.

241 *Advocate*, 23 March 1922.
242 *Argus*, 20 March 1922.
243 Quoted in Dunstan, 'Rise and fall of St Patrick's Day', p. 59.
244 *Argus*, 30 March; *Argus*, 4 April 1922; City Solicitor to Town Clerk, 6 April 1922, PROV VPRS 3183, Unit 156.
245 *Argus*, 5, 6, 8, 10 April 1922.
246 A. May, *'Theatrum urbis*: Melbourne street processions', in G. Davison and A. May (eds), *Melbourne Centre Stage: The Corporation of Melbourne 1842–1992*, a special issue of the *Victorian Historical Journal*, vol. 63, nos. 2–3, October 1992, p. 79.

5 PROCLAIMING IRELAND:
INDEPENDENCE AND EMPIRE

1 *The Gazette* (Montreal), 17 March 1955.
2 For an overview of many of the issues attached to the revolution and the period of state building, see Tom Garvin, *1922: The Birth of Irish Democracy*, Dublin, Gill & Macmillan, 1997, and John M. Regan, *The Irish Counter-Revolution*, Dublin, Gill & Macmillan, 2000.
3 'Letter from J.J. Walsh to W.T. Cosgrave, 16 January 1926', Dept. of Taoiseach S599, NAI.
4 'Circular from W.T. Cosgrave to all minister's wives, 1 February 1926', Dept. of Taoiseach S599, NAI.
5 'Letter from J.J. Walsh to Director of 2RN, 3 March 1927', Dept. of Taoiseach S599, NAI.
6 For details of the military parades on St Patrick's Day in Dublin, see Dept. of Foreign Affairs, 433/8, NAI.
7 The most comprehensive annual coverage of the military parade was offered by the *Irish Independent*. See, for example, 17 March 1930.
8 'State ceremonies, St Patrick's Day 1935', Dept. of Justice, JUS8/404, NAI.
9 'Dáil Eireann Proceedings of first and Second Dáil and related documents', Dáil Eireann papers, DE 4/11/61, NAI.
10 The Committee that advised on the closure of licensed premises on St Patrick's Day consisted of: P. McGoldrick, TD, S. McGarry, TD, P. Hughes, TD, S. McEntee, TD, P.J. Cahill, TD and Mrs T. Clarke, TD.
11 *Irish Times*, 18 March 1927.
12 *Irish Independent*, 18 March 1930.
13 For a personal account, see B. Behan, *Brendan Behan's New York*, London, Hutchinson, 1964, p. 18.
14 *Irish Independent*, 17 March 1930.
15 *Quebec Chronicle-Telegraph*, 17 March 1961, quoted in Schmitz, *Irish for a Day*, p. 8.
16 *New York Times*, 18 March 1925.
17 *Quebec Chronicle-Telegraph*, 17 March 1954, quoted in Schmitz, *Irish for a Day*, p. 8.
18 'St Patrick's Day: closure of public houses', Dept. of Taoiseach, S892B, NAI (March 1945).
19 *Quebec Chronicle-Telegraph*, 17 March 1954, quoted in Schmitz, *Irish for a Day*, p. 8.
20 *Connaught Telegraph*, 24 March 1951.
21 For details of the programme, see *Irish Times*, 17 March 1932.
22 See *Irish Times*, 18 March 1932.
23 The other Days recognized by Guinness were Good Friday, Easter Monday, Whit Monday, Queen Victoria Day, the first Monday in August, Christmas Day and St

Stephen's Day. See Rule 14 in Guinness contracts relating to Public Holidays (1930), held in Guinness Archives, Dublin.

24 For details of Guinness employment and pay practices on St Patrick's Day, see 'Night Duty payments to employees on holidays; memo dated 18 March 1933', held in Guinness Archives, Dublin.

25 *New York Times*, 18 March 1926, quoted in Ridge, *The St Patrick's Day Parade*, pp. 119–20.

26 *Irish Independent*, 18 March 1935.

27 Ridge, *The St Patrick's Day Parade*, p. 130.

28 Foster reminds us that the *subsequent* 1921 Treaty did not enable Partition; instead 'Partition cleared the way for the Treaty'. Foster, *Modern Ireland*, p. 503.

29 *Quebec Chronicle*, 18 March 1921, quoted in Schmitz, *Irish for a Day*, p. 74.

30 *Quebec Telegraph* report of 17 March 1921, summarized in ibid.

31 Ibid.

32 Ibid.

33 *Quebec Chronicle-Telegraph*, 16 March 1929, quoted in ibid., p. 77.

34 Regan, 'Montreal's St. Patrick's Day parade', p. 16 (emphasis added to the original).

35 Ibid.

36 *Gazette*, 18 March 1922.

37 Regan, 'Montreal's St. Patrick's Day parade' p. 26. The web site of the United Irish Societies of Montreal, while providing a brief overview of local St Patrick's Day festivities since 1824, is silent about its *rise* to prominence as official organizer. http://www.ditton.net/uis/.

38 By coincidence, the first parade under UISM control was held on Sunday 17 March 1929. This suited both the new organizer and its predecessor, the latter seeing 17 March as *the* day on which to march.

39 *Gazette*, 17 March 1937.

40 *Gazette*, 17 March 1937, 21 March 1938, 20 March 1939.

41 *Gazette*, 21 March 1938.

42 *Gazette*, 17 March 1938.

43 *Advocate*, 22 March 1923.

44 *Advocate*, 23 March 1923.

45 *Argus*, 19 March 1923.

46 *Catholic Press*, 25 March 1920; *Argus*, 22 March 1920; *Catholic Press*, 23 March 1922; *Argus*, 20 March 1922.

47 *Argus*, 16 March 1925, 15 March 1926, 21 March 1927, 19 March 1928.

48 *Argus*, 17 March 1930, 16 March 1931, 16 March 1936, 15 March 1937.

49 *Argus*, 19 March 1928, 18 March 1929.

50 *Argus*, 17 March 1930, 14 March 1932.

51 *Argus*, 20 March 1939.

52 *Argus*, 19 March 1923.

53 Ibid.

54 O'Farrell, *The Irish in Australia*, p. 291.

55 *Argus*, 19 March 1923.

56 O'Farrell, *The Irish in Australia*, p. 291.

57 Ibid.

58 P. O'Farrell, *Vanished Kingdoms: Irish in Australia and New Zealand*, Kensington, NSW, New South Wales University Press, 1990, p. 229.

59 *Argus*, 18 March 1929.

60 O'Farrell, *Vanished Kingdoms*, p. 229.

61 *Argus*, 18 March 1929, 21 March 1927.

62 *Argus*, 18 March 1946. In New South Wales, too, Catholic schools observed a holiday for St Patrick's Day.

63 M. Roe, '1830–50', and T. Irving, '1850–70', in F. Crowley (ed.), *A New History of Australia*, Richmond, Vic., William Heinemann, 1974, pp. 113–14, 162–3.

64 For details, see S. Firth and J. Hoorn, 'From Empire Day to cracker night', in P. Spearritt and D. Walker (eds), *Australian Popular Culture*, Sydney, George Allen & Unwin, 1979, pp. 17–38.

65 *Argus*, 17 March 1924.

66 *Argus*, 16 March 1925.

67 *Argus*, 16 March 1931.

68 *Argus*, 17 March 1924, 19 March 1928.

69 *Argus*, 15 March 1926, 21 March 1927, 19 March 1928, 17 March 1930.

70 *Argus*, 19 March 1928, 17 March 1930, 13 March 1933.

71 *Argus*, 18 March 1929.

72 *Argus*, 16 March 1925, 18 March 1929, 17 March 1930.

73 *Argus*, 19 March 1934.

74 *Argus*, 19 March 1928, 16 March 1931, 18 March 1935.

75 *Argus*, 17 March 1924, 19 March 1928, 18 March 1929.

76 *Argus*, 18 March 1929.

77 P. O'Farrell, 'St Patrick's Day in Australia', *Journal of the Royal Australian Historical Society*, vol. 81, no. 1, June 1995, p. 14.

78 *Argus*, 19 March 1934, 15 March 1926, 21 March 1927.

79 See MacDonagh, 'Irish Culture and Nationalism Translated: St Patrick's Day, 1888', pp. 72–3; O'Farrell, *The Irish in Australia*, passim.

80 For fuller details, see 'St Patrick's Day Souvenir Programmes', Sydney, 1931–38, Mitchell Library, Sydney, ML 263.9809944105. In country areas, too, sports carnivals were the major fund-raiser on St Patrick's Day. See, for example, *Argus*, 16 March 1925.

81 *Argus*, 14 March 1938.

82 *Argus*, 18 March 1940, 17 March 1941.

83 *Argus*, 17 March 1941.

84 *Argus*, 18 March 1946.

85 *Argus*, 17 March 1947, 15 March 1948, 14 March 1949, 13 March 1950.

86 Casey, 'Ireland, New York and the Irish image', p. 125.

87 Taoiseach's broadcast 1932, Dept. of Taoiseach 97/9/354, NAI.

88 Taoiseach's broadcast 1932, Dept. of Taoiseach 97/9/354, NAI.

89 'Taoiseach's Broadcasts. St Patrick's Day 1934–51', Dept. of Taoiseach, 97/9/354, NAI.

90 Ibid.

91 Ibid.

92 Ibid.

93 Ibid.

94 For details of Churchill's offer to de Valera, see R. Fisk, *In Time of War: Ireland, Ulster and the Price of Neutrality, 1939–45*, London, Deutsch, 1983; J.T. O'Carroll, *Ireland in the War Years, 1939–45*, Newton Abbot, David and Charles, 1975; and G. Roberts, 'The British Offer to End Partition, June 1940', *History Ireland*, 9, 1, 2001, p. 5.

95 Foster, *Modern Ireland*, p. 561.

96 'Taoiseach's Broadcasts. St Patrick's Day 1934–51', Dept. of Taoiseach, 97/9/354, NAI.
97 Ibid.
98 Ibid.
99 *Irish Times*, 19 March 1946.
100 Ibid.
101 Ibid.
102 'Taoiseach's Broadcasts. St Patrick's Day 1934–51', Dept. of Taoiseach, 97/9/354, NAI.
103 Ibid.
104 *Irish Press*, 3 April 1948.
105 *Irish Times*, 17 March 1948.
106 'Taoiseach's Broadcasts. St Patrick's Day 1934–51', Dept. of Taoiseach, 97/9/354, NAI.
107 Ibid.
108 *St Patrick's Day 1959: Souvenir Ireland's Industrial Pageant*, Dublin, Frederick Press, 1959, p. 3.
109 Figure for the 1950 pageant, *Irish Independent*, 16 March 1950.
110 'We salute them', *St Patrick's Day 1959: Souvenir Ireland's Industrial Pageant*, Dublin, Frederick Press, 1959, p. 11.
111 Ibid., p. 11.
112 Ibid., p. 7.
113 Ibid.
114 *Irish Independent*, 18 March 1965.
115 For details of the week, see *Irish Press*, 14 March 1961.
116 *Irish Times*, 14 March 1961.
117 Reimers, 'An end and a beginning', in Bayor and Meagher, *The New York Irish*, pp. 419–20.
118 Ridge, *The St Patrick's Day Parade*, p. 140.
119 E.B. White, *Here is New York*, New York, Harper and Brothers, 1949, p. 15.
120 'Letter from Sean G. Ronan, Consulate of Ireland, Chicago, 22 March 1956', Dept. of Foreign Affairs, S4334/C, NAI.
121 E. McMahon, 'What parish are you from? A study of the Chicago Irish community and race relations, 1916–70', unpublished PhD thesis, Loyola University, Chicago, 1989, pp. 170–6.
122 *San Francisco News*, 17 March 1951.
123 *Gazette*, 18 March 1940.
124 Ibid.
125 *Gazette*, 16 March 1940.
126 *Gazette*, 17 March 1941.
127 Ibid.
128 Ibid.
129 Ibid.
130 *Gazette*, 18 March 1946.
131 Ibid.
132 *Gazette*, 20 March 1950.
133 *Gazette*, 17 March 1950.
134 *Gazette*, 17 March 1955.
135 All quotes from *Gazette*, 17 March 1955.
136 *Gazette*, 18 March 1955.

137 *Gazette*, 21 March 1960.
138 Ibid.
139 *Gazette*, 16 March 1970.
140 *Argus*, 16 March 1953.
141 *Argus*, 15 March 1954, 19 March 1956.
142 *Age*, 16 March 1959.
143 P. Spearritt, 'Royal progress: the Queen and her Australian subjects', in S.L. Goldberg and F.B. Smith (eds), *Australian Cultural History*, Melbourne, Cambridge University Press, 1988, pp. 138–57.
144 For further details, see D. Hilliard, 'God in the suburbs: the religious culture of Australian cities in the 1950s', *Australian Historical Studies*, vol. 97, October 1991, pp. 399–419; and K. Massam, 'The blue army and the Cold War: anti-communist devotion to the Blessed Virgin Mary in Australia', *Australian Historical Studies*, vol. 97, October 1991, pp. 420–8.
145 See D. Adair, 'Consensus and division on a spiritual occasion: the Twenty-ninth International Eucharistic Congress, Sydney, 1928', in M. Hutchinson and S. Piggin (eds), *Reviving Australia*, Sydney, Centre for the Study of Australian Christianity, 1994, pp. 202–32.
146 *Argus*, 21 March 1955.
147 For fuller discussions, see O'Farrell, *The Catholic Church and Community*, chapter 6.
148 *Argus*, 16 March 1953.
149 *Age*, 18 March 1957.
150 *Age*, 21 March 1960.
151 Ibid.
152 *Age*, 20 March 1961.
153 *Age*, 19 March 1962.
154 *Age*, 18 March 1963.
155 *Age*, 18 March 1968.
156 Ibid.
157 *Advocate*, 12 March 1970.
158 Ibid.
159 Ibid.
160 Ibid.
161 Ibid.
162 Ridge, *The St Patrick's Day Parade*, p. 144.
163 Ibid., p. 149.
164 Ibid.
165 'TV and Radio Station Milwaukee, request for St Patrick's message from the President', Dept. of Foreign Affairs, 304/25/26, NAI.
166 Ridge, *The St Patrick's Day Parade*, p. 151.
167 For example, see the American children's book by Barth and Arndt, *Shamrocks, Harps and Shillelaghs*, which insists that 'there are always novelties among the marchers ... everywhere, among the marchers and spectators alike, there are green hats, green banners and green carnations. And whether they are Irish or not, almost everybody is smiling', p. 90.
168 *Irish Independent*, 16 March 1955.
169 *Irish World and American Industrial Liberator*, 14 March 1944.
170 *Irish Independent*, 17 March 1965.
171 For details and quotes, see Casey, 'Ireland, New York and the Irish Image', pp. 281–2.

172 *Irish Independent*, 18 March 1965.

173 *Irish Independent*, 17 March 1965.

174 *National Hibernian Digest*, March–April 1961.

175 T.H. O'Connor, *South Boston: My Home Town*, Boston, North-Eastern Univ. Press, 1994, p. 107.

176 Ibid., p. 216.

177 'Letter from G. Woods, Consulate of Ireland, Boston', Dept. of Foreign Affairs, S4334/C, NAI.

178 Ibid.

179 Ibid.

180 'St Patrick's Day, Canada', Dept. of Foreign Affairs, 433/27, NAI.

181 Casey, 'Ireland, New York and the Irish Image', pp. 284–5.

182 Ibid., p. 286.

183 *Boston Pilot*, 12 March 1960.

184 *Boston Daily Globe*, 18 March 1960.

185 *New York Journal-American*, 17 March 1964.

186 *New York World Telegram and Sun*, 17 March 1964.

187 *Daily News*, 18 March 1964.

188 *New York World Telegram and Sun*, 17 March 1964.

189 Ridge, *The St Patrick's Day Parade*, p. 156.

190 *National Hibernian Digest*, March–April 1961.

191 'Rules and regulations for the government of the parade', issued by the St Patrick's Day Parade and Celebration Committee, copy in the 'Donald O'Callaghan Papers', American Irish Historical Society, New York, box 6, folder 5.

192 Ibid., p. 3.

193 Ibid., p. 3.

194 For an example of the battalion organization, and an indication of the sheer scale of the parade, see *Irish Echo*, 14 March 1964.

195 'Letter from John M. Conway, Irish Consulate General, New York, 25 March 1960', Dept. of Foreign Affairs, S4334/C, NAI.

196 *New York Journal*, 14 March 1960.

197 *New York Times*, 17 March 1960.

198 *Irish Times*, 25 March 1963.

199 *Irish Independent*, 18 March 1963.

200 Ibid.

201 *Hibernia*, April 1963.

202 *Irish Independent*, 16 March 1955.

203 'St Patrick's Day reports, 1963', Dept. of Foreign Affairs, 433/27, NAI. See also 'St Patrick's celebrations in South America', Dept. of Foreign Affairs, 433/5 Part II, NAI, for similar reports.

204 'St Patrick's celebrations in Spain, 1968', Dept. of Foreign Affairs, 433/12 Part II, NAI.

205 'St Patrick's Day, Canada', Dept. of Foreign Affairs, 433/27, NAI.

206 'Letter from the United Irish Societies of Montreal to the Office of the Taoiseach, 27 January 1967', Dept. of Taoiseach, 96/6/165, NAI. For full details of similar requests received from the same organization in this period, see the whole file, 'St Patrick's Day: celebration in US and Canada, March 1965–February 1968', Dept. of Taoiseach, 96/6/165, NAI.

207 'Letter for the Office of the Taoiseach to the United Irish Societies of Montreal, 13 February 1967', Dept. of Taoiseach, 96/6/165, NAI.

208 'Shamrock Catering Co., Jamaica. Request for St Patrick's Day message from the President, 1962', Dept. of Foreign Affairs, 304/25/28, NAI.

209 For details of the Birmingham controversy, see *Birmingham Evening Mail*, 17 March 1965, and Dept. of Foreign Affairs, 433/16 Part II, NAI.

210 For details of this letter, and of all other St Patrick's Day greetings, see 'St Patrick's Day messages to Taoiseach, 1952–9', Dept. of Taoiseach, 97/9/11181, NAI.

211 'St Patrick's Day London, 1963', Dept. of Foreign Affairs, P302/2, NAI.

212 For pictures of Lemass at the gala, and of many other post-war St Patrick's Day events in London, see F. Whooley, *Irish Londoners: Photography from the Paddy Fahey Collection*, Stroud, Sutton, 1997, p. 113.

213 'St Patrick's Day London, 1965', Dept. of Foreign Affairs, 96/2/4, NAI.

214 For details of St Patrick's Day events in these countries between the 1940s and 1970s, see Dept. of Foreign Affairs, S433/1–S433/25, NAI.

215 The Pan American Airways suggestion is discussed in 'Bórd Fáilte meeting minutes, 29 May 1958', Dept. of Tourism and Transport, TTA 12/5, NAI.

216 See 'Publicity in Connection with An Tóstal', Dept. of Tourism and Transport, TTA 855, NAI.

217 For details of the debate on the timing of An Tóstal and the possible inclusion of St Patrick's Day within the calendar of events, see 'Future of An Tóstal', Dept. of Tourism and Transport, TTA 12/5, NAI.

218 See, for example, discussion between government departments on desirability of moving public holidays, in 'Bank and Public Holidays', Dept. of Taoiseach, S6215 B/63, NAI.

219 'St Patrick's Day: Bank and Public Holidays', Dept. of Taoiseach, S10405 D/63, NAI.

220 Some definitively stated answers, albeit unproven, as to St Patrick's death date have been offered, for example, 'St Patrick died on 17 March 493, being then one hundred and twenty years of age. This is the record of his age and death which we find in the ancient chronicles', E. Leahy, *The Life of St Patrick*, Dublin, Irish Messenger, 1917.

221 Memo to Commission of Inquiry, 21 December 1962, 'St Patrick's Day, 1962–3', Dept. of Taoiseach, S10405 D/63, NAI.

222 Ibid.

223 *The New World*, March 1969, quoted in 'St Patrick's Day: Bank and Public Holiday, March–April 1969', Dept. of Taoiseach, 96/6/723, NAI.

224 Ibid.

225 For coverage of the opening of RTÉ, see Robert J. Savage, *Irish Television: The Political and Social Origins*, Cork, Cork Univ. Press, 1996.

226 For details of the 1965 St Patrick's Day television programmes, see *Irish Independent*, 17 March 1965.

227 *Good Housekeeping*, March 1930, in Casey, 'Ireland, New York and the Irish Image', p. 104.

228 *Irish Independent*, 16 March 1950.

229 *Irish Echo*, 14 March 1964.

230 'St Patrick's Day in Northern Ireland', Dept. of Foreign Affairs 433/18, NAI.

231 *Connaught Telegraph*, 24 March 1951.

232 See *Irish Independent*, 16 March 1945.

233 1950s' greetings card, Donal O'Callaghan Papers, box 7, folder 4, Irish American Historical Society, New York.

6 MODERN TIMES, TROUBLED TIMES

1 Edited and appended from *Stiff Little Fingers*, 'Each dollar a bullet', *Flags and Emblems Album*, Essential Records, 1991.

2 For an overview of the origins of the troubles, see T.P. Coogan, *The Troubles*, London, Arrow, 1996; C. Kennedy-Pipe, *Origins of the Northern Ireland Troubles*, London, Longman, 1997; S. Wichert, *Northern Ireland Since 1945*, London, Longman, 1999.

3 Judge James Comerford was the legendary organizer of the New York St Patrick's Day parade.

4 *New York Times*, 18 March 1970.

5 *St Patrick's Day Souvenir Programme*, Dublin, Irish Times, 17 March 1970.

6 *Irish Independent*, 18 March 1970.

7 *Irish Post*, 'St Patrick's week supplement', 23 March 1997.

8 The comments of the ambassador in Rome were echoed by his colleague in Lisbon, Portugal. For details of such comments, see 'St Patrick's Day in Italy', Dept. of Foreign Affairs, 433/2 Part II, NAI.

9 *Irish Times*, 18 March 1978.

10 *Irish Independent*, 18 March 1975.

11 For details of the Tartu City Brass Band, see *Irish Independent*, 16 March 1990.

12 *Irish Independent*, 19 March 1990.

13 *Irish Independent*, 16 March 1995.

14 Bernie Byrne won a 1995 competition organized by the company marketing Diet 7-Up, to fly to New York for St Patrick's Day, see *Irish Independent*, 16 March 1995.

15 P.J. Hamill, 'And our national pleasures of the pub', *Irish Independent*, 17 March 1995.

16 Ibid.

17 J. O'Connor, *Sweet Liberty: Travels in Irish America*, London, Picador, 1996, p. 11.

18 *Irish Independent*, 18 March 1975.

19 *Irish Times*, 17 March 2000.

20 A bank holiday differs from a public holiday in that not all businesses, shops, factories and offices are closed. On a bank holiday only state and financial concerns, such as banks, civil service offices and schools, are closed.

21 Walker, *Dancing to History's Tune*, p. 81.

22 See for example the various chapters in Fraser, *The Irish Parading Tradition*; D. Bryan, 'Ireland's very own Jurassic Park: The mass media, Orange parades and the discourse on tradition', in A.D. Buckley (ed.), *Symbols in Northern Ireland*, Belfast, Institute of Irish Studies, 1998, pp. 23–42.

23 For details of the Armagh parade, see *Irish Independent*, 18 March 1995.

24 For details of these events, see Walker, *Dancing to History's Tune*, p. 85.

25 *Orange Standard*, March 1999.

26 *Belfast Telegraph*, 17 March 1979.

27 *Andersontown News*, 14 March 1998.

28 Máirtín Ó Muilleoir, 'Glorious green gridlock', *Andersontown News*, 21 March 1998.

29 Ibid.

30 'Minutes of Development (Tourism and Promotion of Belfast) Sub Committee, Wednesday 13 May 1998', Linen Hall Library Northern Ireland Political Collection.

31 'Meeting convened by the Lord Mayor, David Alderdice, Re: St Patrick's Day

parade. 11 January 1999', Linen Hall Library Northern Ireland Political Collection.

32 Ibid.

33 Ibid.

34 Eric Waugh, 'The object of flaunting tricolours is to provoke', *Belfast Telegraph*, 6 February 1999.

35 'Memo from Belfast Sinn Féin Council leader Tom Hartley, 8 February 1999', Linen Hall Library Northern Ireland Political Collection.

36 'Letter from Caitríona Ruane, Joint Chairperson, St Patrick's Carnival Committee, to all Belfast City Councillors', Linen Hall Library Northern Ireland Political Collection.

37 'Carnabhal Naomh Phadraig 1999', Linen Hall Library Northern Ireland Political Collection.

38 'Guidelines for participation in the Belfast St Patrick's Day parade, 1998'; and 'Carnabhal Naomh Phadraig 1999', Linen Hall Library Northern Ireland Political Collection.

39 'Carnabhal Naomh Phadraig 1999', Linen Hall Library Northern Ireland Political Collection.

40 *Irish News*, 3 February 1999.

41 For example, see *The Times*, 18 March 1972, 18 March 1976, and 18 March 1978.

42 For example, the service held at Westminster Cathedral, *The Times*, 16 March 1978.

43 For details of Siol Phadraig, see *Irish Post*, 9, 16, and 25 March 1985.

44 For examples, see the *Irish Post* of the 1970s and 1980s for those weeks either side of St Patrick's Day.

45 *Daily Telegraph*, 10 March 1972.

46 This is not to dismiss the continuation, right through the 1990s, of immigration to Britain by men predominantly employed within the construction business. Such shifting labour was supported culturally by a network of pubs, clubs, accommodation and Irish service industries. For details of this community and their relationship to St Patrick's day, see *The Economist*, 16 March 1991, p. 52.

47 *Irish Post*, 'Manchester Irish Festival supplement', 21 March 1997.

48 *Irish Post*, 24 March 1990.

49 For details of these and other events, see *Irish Post*, 11 March 1995.

50 For a general assessment of the Irish at the Cheltenham festival, see R. Smith, *One Day as a Lion*, Dublin, Sporting Books, 1997.

51 Figure supplied by parade organizers, letter received 16 March 2000.

52 *Irish Post*, 'St Patrick's Week supplement', 15 March 1997.

53 *Irish Post*, 23 March 1995.

54 *Irish Post*, 15 March 1997.

55 M. Kells, 'I'm myself and nobody else: gender and ethnicity among young middle class Irish women in London', in P. O'Sullivan (ed.), *Irish Women and Irish Migration. Volume 4: The Irish World-Wide. History, Heritage, Identity*, London, Leicester University Press, 1995, p. 205.

56 Bishop, *The Irish Empire*, p. 159.

57 For fuller details, see B. Fraser, *The Search for Identity: Canada, 1945–1967*, Toronto, Doubleday, 1967, pp. 234–47.

58 *Gazette*, 17 March 2000.

59 *Gazette*, 17 March 1980.

60 Ibid.

61 *Gazette*, 20 March 1995.
62 *Gazette*, 17 March 1980.
63 *Gazette*, 20 March 1995.
64 Ibid.
65 *Gazette*, 17 March 1980.
66 *Gazette*, 17 March 2000.
67 *Gazette*, 20 March 1995.
68 *Gazette*, 19 March 1990.
69 Ibid.
70 *Gazette*, 20 March 2000.
71 *Gazette*, 17 March 1995.
72 *Gazette*, 18 March 2000.
73 *Toronto Star*, 17 March 1987.
74 Ibid.
75 Ibid.
76 *Toronto Star*, 20 March 1989.
77 *Irish Echo*, vol. 8, no. 20, 19 October 1995–1 November 1995, p. 15.
78 Ibid.
79 Letter to the editor from Bob Cunningham, St Patrick's Day Grand Marshal, *Irish Echo*, vol. 7, no. 1, February 1994, p. 13.
80 *Irish Echo*, vol. 8, no. 20, 19 October 1995–1 November 1995, p. 15; *Irish-Australian*, vol. 1, no. 2, 'St Patrick's Day supplement', 1995.
81 Cunningham, *Irish Echo*, February 1994, p. 13.
82 *Irish Exile*, vol. 2, no. 1, March 1989, p. 10.
83 *Irish Exile*, vol. 4, no. 3, April 1991, p. 18.
84 *Irish Echo*, vol. 8, no. 4, 9 March 1995–22 March 1995, p. 10.
85 *Irish Exile*, vol. 5, no. 2, March 1992, p. 17.
86 Ibid.
87 *Irish Echo*, vol. 5, no. 3, April 1992, p. 13; *Irish Exile*, vol. 5, no. 2, March 1992, p. 17.
88 *Irish Echo*, April 1993, p. 19.
89 Ibid.
90 *Irish Echo*, March 1993, p. 20.
91 Ibid.
92 *Irish Echo*, vol. 6, no. 11, December 1993, p. 3.
93 Cunningham, *Irish Echo*, February 1994, p. 13.
94 *Irish Echo*, vol. 6, no. 11, December 1993, p. 3.
95 Ibid.
96 *Irish Echo*, vol. 8, no. 20, 19 October 1995–1 November 1995, p. 15.
97 *Irish Echo*, vol. 7, no. 1, February 1994, p. 13.
98 *Irish Echo*, vol. 7, no. 2, March 1994, p. 3.
99 *Sydney Morning Herald*, 8 February 1994.
100 *Irish Echo*, vol. 8, no. 16, 24 August 1995–6 September 1995, p. 3.
101 *Irish Echo*, vol. 8, no. 20, 19 October 1995–1 November 1995, p. 15.
102 *Irish Echo*, vol. 8, no. 16, 24 August 1995–6 September 1995, p. 3.
103 *Irish Echo*, vol. 9, no. 6, 28 March 1996–10 April 1996, p. 14.
104 *Irish Echo*, vol. 10, no. 6, 27 March 1997–9 April 1997, p. 9.
105 *Irish Echo*, vol. 11, no. 7, 9 April 1998–22 April 1998, pp. 1, 9.
106 *Irish Echo*, vol. 12, no. 6, 25 March 1999–7 April 1999, p. 3.
107 Murphy makes occasional references to St Patrick's Day in his published

reminiscences. See K. Murphy, *Kerry Murphy's Memoirs: The Diaries of an Irish Immigrant*, Sydney, Walla Walla Press, 1998.

108 *Weekend Australian*, 17 February 2001.

109 Fergus Shiel of the *Irish Echo* informs us that the parade was resumed in 1974. *Irish Echo*, vol. 6, no. 3, April 1993, p. 14.

110 For discussion, see *Irish Echo*, vol. 11, no. 4, 26 February 1998–11 March 1998, p. 13; G. Henderson, 'Irish have made their mark', *Age*, 19 March 1996.

111 *Age*, 20 February 1999.

112 *Irish Echo*, vol. 9, no. 6, 28 March 1996–10 April 1996, p. 16.

113 *Irish Echo*, vol. 10, no. 6, 27 March 1997–9 April 1997, p. 11.

114 For background on the Chicago parade, see M.G. Holi and P.M. Green, *Chicago: A View From City Hall*, Chicago, Arcadia, 1999.

115 *World of Hibernia*, Spring 1998, vol. 3, no. 4, p. 22.

116 For details of the New Orleans parade, see *New Orleans Magazine*, March 1998, vol. 32, no. 6, p. 20.

117 *World of Hibernia*, Spring 1997, vol. 2, no. 2, p. 114.

118 See *Dallas Magazine*, March 1986, pp. 15–19.

119 See *Sunset*, March 1985, pp. 10–11.

120 Details received from Minoa Uffelman, Tennessee, America, 22 March 2000.

121 W.E. Davies, *Patriotism on Parade: The Story of the Veterans and Hereditary Organisations in America, 1783–1900*, Cambridge, MA, Harvard University Press, 1955, p. 1.

122 Holland, *The American Connection*, p. 9.

123 M.F. Nolan, 'Little to excite Irish on this March 17', *Boston Globe*, 16 March 1969.

124 R. Byron, *Irish America*, Oxford: Clarendon Press, 1999, p. 3.

125 Ibid., p. 16.

126 Ibid.

127 L.D. Almeida, 'From Danny Boy to Bono. The Irish in New York City, 1945–85', PhD thesis, New York University, 1996, p. 127.

128 Mrs Nixon had actually been born on 16 March, but had always celebrated her birthday on 17 March.

129 'St Patrick's Day: Presentation of shamrock to Heads of Foreign States etc.', Dept. of Taosieach, S15291, NAI.

130 Ibid.

131 *Boston Evening Globe*, 16 March 1972.

132 Ibid.

133 Ibid.

134 *New York Times*, 18 March 1970.

135 Ibid.

136 *Boston Evening Globe*, 17 March 1970.

137 *Boston Globe*, 20 March 1972.

138 Ibid.

139 See, for example, *New York Times*, 18 March 1975.

140 *New York Times*, 18 March 1975.

141 Ibid.

142 'Friends of Ireland St Patrick's Day Statement 1985', Consulate General of Ireland Collection, box 3, folder 10, American Irish Historical Society.

143 Ibid.

144 'Statement by President Reagan at the White House on March 17, 1986', 'Consulate General of Ireland Collection', American Irish Historical Society, New York, box 3, folder 10.

145 'Remarks of Taoiseach, Dr Garret FitzGerald, TD, at the dinner to honour the Speaker, Thomas P. O'Neill, Jr, as he celebrates fifty years of public service, Washington, DC, 17 March 1986', 'Consulate General of Ireland Collection', American Irish Historical Society, New York, box 3, folder 10.

146 'Remarks by An Taoiseach of Ireland, Mr C.J. Haughey, TD, at a luncheon on Capitol Hill hosted by Speaker Wright, 17 March 1987', 'Consulate General of Ireland Collection', American Irish Historical Society, New York, box 3, folder 11.

147 'Remarks by Tanaiste and Minister for Foreign Affairs of Ireland, Friendly Sons of St Patrick dinner, 17 March 1987', 'Consulate General of Ireland Collection', American Irish Historical Society, New York, box 3, folder 12.

148 Ridge, *The St Patrick's Day Parade*, p. 160.

149 The links between the civil services, such as the Fire Department and the Irish are longstanding. Of the first 414 men recruited to the New York Fire Department in the 1860s, 194 of them were Irish. See Fitzgerald, 'The St Patrick's Day parade', p. 111.

150 D. Reimers, 'An end and a beginning', p. 437.

151 Ridge, *The St Patrick's Day Parade*, p. 161.

152 For a report of Flannery on parade day, see *US News and World Report*, 28 March 1983.

153 Reimers, 'An end and a beginning', pp. 435–6.

154 R. O'Hanlon, *The New Irish Americans*, Boulder, Roberts Rinehart, 1998, p. 134.

155 Reimers, 'An end and a beginning', p. 436.

156 Ridge, *The St Patrick's Day Parade*, p. 170.

157 Ibid.

158 *New York Times*, 17 March 1985.

159 *Irish Post*, 16 March 1985.

160 Ibid.

161 See, for example, programmes for *230th Saint Patrick's Day Parade, March 16, 1991*; and *231st Saint Patrick's Day Parade, March 17, 1992*.

162 For details of the 1990 parade and the focus on the Doherty campaign, see *New York Times*, 18 March 1990.

163 Eoin McKiernan, 'What anniversaries tell us', programme for *230th Saint Patrick's Day Parade, March 16, 1991*.

164 Ibid.

165 In 1997, the St Patrick's Day parades were used to commemorate the 150th anniversary of the Irish Famine, an event that was politicized and history mobilized as a weapon for controlling a past that located the British as the pursuers of a policy of genocide in mid-nineteenth-century Ireland. For an example of such press coverage, see *US News and World Report*, 24 March 1997.

166 For an illustration of parades and events across the Southern States, see *Southern Living*, March 1992, vol. 27, no. 3, p. 34.

167 In 1998, Mayor Daley was alleged to have referred to an Irish-Italian queen of the Chicago St Patrick's Day parade, as a 'dago'. Although the allegation was denied, it produced a lively discussion relating to the ethnic basis of 17 March celebrations in the city. See *Chicago Tribune,* 30 March 1998; *Editor and Publisher*, 4 April 1998.

168 J.R. Coyne Jr, 'Saint Pat's, booze and ballots', *National Review*, 13 April 1992, vol. 44, no. 7, p. 26.

169 O'Hanlon, *New Irish Americans*, p. 136.

170 E.T. O'Donnell, 'Parade gave expression to many cultures, parades bring US diversity to main street', *Salt Lake Tribune*, 17 March 2000.

171 Ibid.
172 For a general discussion of press responses, see C. Michaud, 'Columnists line up to back marchers in parade dispute', *The Advocate*, 23 April 1991, no. 575, p. 25.
173 For a discussion of the reaction to the Dinkins decision to march with the ILGO, see editorial in *The New Republic*, 22 April 1991, vol. 204, no. 16, p. 8; also *National Review*, 1 February 1993, p. 18.
174 Quoted in Reimers, 'An end and a beginning', p. 432. The question as to whether gay and lesbians were contravening Church teachings was a vexed issue, and one frequently debated. See, for instance, D.E. DeCosse, 'The Catholic case for inclusion', *America*, 8 May 1993, vol. 168, no. 16, p. 15.
175 *New Republic*, 4 April 1994, p. 8.
176 For extensive coverage of the legal debate, and strong support for the decision to exclude the ILGO, see J.P. McCarthy, 'St Patrick's war', *National Review*, 12 April 1993, vol. 45, no. 7, p. 26.
177 *National Review*, 1 February 1993, vol. 45, no. 2, p. 18.
178 F. Beirne, 'St Patrick's Day parade 1992 greetings', *231st St Patrick's Day Parade Programme*, p. 3.
179 Ibid.
180 For explanation and discussion of the ruling, see *Wall Street Journal*, 4 March 1993.
181 Paul Baumann, 'Sodom and begorra', *Commonweal*, 9 April 1993, vol. 120, no. 7, p. 5.
182 *New York Times*, 18 March 1995.
183 *New York Times*, 15 and 22 March 1999.
184 *Irish Times*, 18 March 1999.
185 R.H. Bayor and T.J. Meagher, 'Introduction', in Bayor and Meagher, *The New York Irish*, p. 7.
186 Explanation of the decision to go to the Supreme Court can be found in C. Bull, 'Courting trouble', *The Advocate*, 21 February 1995, p. 31.
187 For coverage of the case, see D.T. Wackerman, 'Mind's eye', *America*, 15 July 1995, p. 5.
188 For the most detailed discussion of the legal debate relating to control of St Patrick's Day parades, see P. Walkowski and W.M. Connolly, *From Trial Court to US Supreme Court*, Boston, Branden Publishing, 1996.
189 For a legal explanation of the rulings, see H.A. Silverglate, 'Gays, St Patrick's Day and cultural war', *The National Law Journal*, 27 March 1995, p. 21.
190 For a general discussion of the Clinton Presidency and the peace process, see T. Birney and Julian O'Neill, *When the President Calls*, Belfast, Guildhall Press, 1997; S. Farren and R.F. Mulvihill (eds), *Paths to a Settlement in Northern Ireland*, London, Colin Smythe, 2000; J.E. Thompson, *American Policy and Northern Ireland. A Saga of Peacebuilding*, Westport, CT, Praeger Publishers, 2001; D. de Bréadún, *The Far Side of Revenge. Making Peace in Northern Ireland*, Cork, Collins Press, 2001; T. Hennessey, *The Northern Ireland Peace Process*, Dublin, Gill & Macmillan, 2000.
191 *New York Times*, 17 March 1995.
192 For a critique of such moves, see C.C. O'Brien, 'The wearing of the greenbacks', *National Review*, 17 April, 1995, p. 26.
193 *New York Times*, 17 March 1995.
194 De Bréadún, *The Far Side of Revenge*, p. 33.
195 *Irish Times*, 18 March 1998.
196 President Clinton, keynote address, Waterfront Hall, Belfast, 3 September 1998.
197 For an overview of the day's events and gatherings, see *Irish Times*, 18 March 1999.

198 Joint statement issued by President Clinton, Taoiseach Ahern and Prime Minister Blair, Washington, 18 March 1999.
199 *Irish Times*, 18 March 2000.
200 Ibid.
201 Speech by President Clinton, Courthouse Square, Dundalk, 12 December 2000.
202 C.M. Cannon, 'Blessed (and feted) are the Peacemakers', *National Journal*, 20 March 1999, p. 763.
203 *Irish Times*, 18 March 1998.

7 REINVENTING ST PATRICK'S DAY

1 Questionnaire received from Mike Cronin Senior, Surrey, England, March 2000.
2 For a brief discussion of the popularity of the Irish, see C. Boylan, 'If you're Irish, come into the Casbah ... there's a welcome there for you', *Irish Independent*, 17 March 1995.
3 Byron, *Irish America*, p. 225.
4 Ibid., p. 110.
5 Letter received from Marcia Abcarain, America, March 2000.
6 Letter received from Denis Ashe, Britain, March 2000.
7 Questionnaire received from Kerry Bryan, America, March 2000.
8 Letter received from Pam Cronk, Canada, March 2000.
9 Letter received from Paul, March 2000.
10 Questionnaire received from Stephen Finley, America, March 2000.
11 Questionnaire received from Peter Hill, Britain, March 2000.
12 Questionnaire received from Minoa Uffelman, America, March 2000.
13 Questionnaire received from Patrick Scannell, Britain, March 2000.
14 Questionnaire received from Sister Tynan, Ireland, March 2000.
15 Questionnaire received from Joan Moody, America, March 2000.
16 Questionnaire received from Mrs McGrath, Britain, March 2000.
17 Letter received from Marcia Abcarain, America, March 2000.
18 Letter received from Claudia Cole, Canada, March 2000.
19 Questionnaire received from Elizabeth Gallagher Cardinal, America, March 2000.
20 Questionnaire received from Claudia Cole, Canada, March 2000.
21 Judy O'Leary Anderson, quoted in Hoobler and Hoobler (eds), *Irish American Family Album*, p. 115.
22 Questionnaire received from Diarmaid Casey, Britain, March 2000.
23 Questionnaire received from Timothy F. O'Sullivan, America, March 2000.
24 Questionnaire received from Melissa Ford, America, March 2000.
25 Letter received from Michael Bodart, America, March 2000.
26 Questionnaire received from Carmel Girling, Britain, 2000.
27 Questionnaire received from Mrs McGrath, Britain, March 2000.
28 Letter received from Samuel J. Thomas, America, March 2000.
29 Letter received from Helen M. Bannan, America, March 2000.
30 Questionnaire received from JoAnn Castagna, America, March 2000.
31 Questionnaire received from Jeanette Lugo, America, March 2000.
32 Questionnaire received from Rick Gagne, America, March 2000.
33 Questionnaire received from Kitty Cronin, America, March 2000.
34 Letter received from Christine Kleinegger, America, March 2000. See also *Sunday Gazette*, 17 March 1991, and *Sunday Times Union*, 11 March 1990.
35 Letter received from Rosalie 'Mollie' Murphy, Australia, March 2000.

36 Questionnaire received from Paul McGale, Britain, March 2000.

37 Questionnaire received from Joan Moody, America, March 2000.

38 Questionnaire received from Thomas Connolly, Ireland, March 2000.

39 Questionnaire received from Carmel Girling, Britain, March 2000.

40 Letter received, South Africa, March 2000.

41 Questionnaire received from Thomas Healy, America, August 2000.

42 Questionnaire received from Mary Jennings, Ireland, March 2000.

43 Letter received from Jeannie Lugo, America, March 2000.

44 Letter received from Martha Sherwood, America, March 2000.

45 Letter received from Paul, March 2000.

46 Questionnaire from David Dunning, America, March 2000.

47 Questionnaire received from Matthew Barlow, Canada, March 2000.

48 Questionnaire received from Tom Jackson, Britain, March 2000.

49 Questionnaire received from Catherine Donnolly-Hue, America, March 2000.

50 Questionnaire received from Annie Dillon, Ireland, March 2000.

51 *Irish Post*, 11 March 2000.

52 Questionnaire received from Thomas Healy, America, August 2000.

53 *Gazette*, 15 March 1995.

54 Questionnaire received from Mary Jennings, Ireland, March 2000.

55 'For the love of St Pat, are you bringing that Guinness or not?', 1997 St Patrick's day advertisement, GCC/MK02/0026, held by the Guinness Archives, Park Royal, London.

56 Invitation cards for launch of large 65cl bottle of Guinness in Gabon, GOL/MK03/GAB/0001, March 1998, held by the Guinness Archives, Park Royal, London.

57 Asia-Pacific region merchandising pack, GOL/MKO3/SIN/0020–21, March 1997, held by the Guinness Archives, Park Royal, London.

58 Guinness Australasia 1999, GOL/MK09/AUS/0001, held by the Guinness Archives, Park Royal, London.

59 Win your own pub in Ireland promotional material, GOL/MK03/USA/0127–32, March 1997, held by the Guinness Archives, Park Royal, London.

60 One St Patrick's day, 364 practice days campaign 1999, GPR/MK03/0421, held by the Guinness Archives, Park Royal, London.

61 See, for example, *The Observer*, 16 March 1997, featuring a Guinness-sponsored supplement entitled 'Life in Ireland'.

62 Sponsorship video, New York St Patrick's day parade 1986, GOL/MK07/0981.01, held by the Guinness Archives, Park Royal, London.

63 St Patrick's Festival brief, www.stpatrick'sday.ie/history/.

64 *Business Contact*, March 2000.

65 Ibid.

66 The other foundation sponsors were Aer Lingus, Aer Rianta, An Post, Baileys, Guardian Insurance, Irish Ferries, the National Lottery and Telecom Eirann.

67 *Irish Times*, 'St Patrick's Festival Programme', 12 March 1997.

68 For details of all the different events during the Festival, see *Irish Times St Patrick's Festival Programme*, 12 March 1997.

69 St Patrick's Festival, 'The Evolution of the Parade', June 1998, memo held by the Festival Office, Dublin.

70 Ibid.

71 *The Desert Shamrock*, March/April 1999.

72 Byron, *Irish America*, p. 297.

73 *The Mirror*, 3 January 2000.

74 For details of the programme, see *Irish Times Festival Supplement*, 11 March 2000.
75 *Sunday Independent*, 6 February 2000.
76 *Irish Times*, 17 March 2000.
77 The assistance of Marie Claire Sweeney (Festival Director, 1996–2000) and Maria Moynihan (Festival Director, 2000–) was invaluable in understanding the contemporary importance of St Patrick's Day in Ireland.
78 *Irish Times*, 18 March 1999.

CONCLUSION

1 Malachy McCourt, 'St. Patrick's Day? Bah, humbug!' *Irish Voice*, 17 March 1998.
2 For recent discussion of this issue, see O'Hanlon, *New Irish Americans*, p. 43.
3 M. Rogers, 'Clover all over', *Irish Post*, 'St Patrick's week supplement', 14 March 1997.
4 *The Desert Shamrock*, March/April 1999.
5 Montserrat's celebrations are a legacy of the forcible settlement of the island by Irish immigrants in the seventeenth century. For brief details, see Rogers, 'Clover all over', *Irish Post*, 'St Patrick's week supplement', 14 March 1997.
6 For an example of the 'loyalist policing' of St Patrick's Day and the associated fund-raising activities, see 'In the United States of America The Dark Side . . . Terrorism, Racism, Hate!' http://toad.net/~sticker/pat.htm/.
7 O. MacDonagh, 'St Patrick's Day, 1983', The Aisling Society of Sydney, talks delivered to the society, 1956–1983, March 1983, Mitchell Library of New South Wales, ML MSS 6653 (2).
8 The best example of an 'open door' policy with respect of who is permitted to parade, can be found at the Queen's, New York, St Patrick's Day Parade and Fair. For further details, see http://www.stpatsforall.com/paradefotos.html/.
9 See Casey, 'Ireland, New York and the Irish image in American popular culture, 1890–1960', PhD thesis, New York University, 1998, p. 268.
10 *Gael*, March 1900.
11 *Irish Emigrant*, 16 March 2001.

SELECTED BIBLIOGRAPHY

— ‿‿ —

ARCHIVES

American Irish Historical Society, New York.
Australian Archives of Victoria, Melbourne.
British Library, London.
Centre for Migration Studies, Ulster American Folk Park.
Guinness Archives, Park Royal, London.
Guinness Archives, St James's Gate, Dublin.
Irish Folklore Commission, Dublin.
John J. Burns Library, Boston College, Boston.
Melbourne City Council Archives, Melbourne.
Mitchell Library, Sydney.
National Archive of Ireland, Dublin.
National Library of Australia, Canberra.
National Library, Dublin.
National Library Photographic Archive, Dublin.
Northern Ireland Political Collection, Linen Hall Library, Belfast.
Northern Ireland Public Record Office, Belfast.
Public Record Office, London.
Public Record Office of Victoria, Melbourne.
Screen and Sound Australian Archives, Canberra.

NEWSPAPERS

Advocate (Melbourne).
Age (Melbourne).
Andersonstown News (Belfast).
Argus (Melbourne).
Australian (Sydney).
Belfast Telegraph.
Boston Daily Globe.
Boston Evening Globe.
Boston Pilot.
Bulletin (Sydney).
Catholic Press (Sydney).
Chicago Tribune.
Connaught Telegraph (Galway).
Cork Examiner.
Daily News (New York).
Daily Telegraph (London).
Dallas Magazine.

Dublin Evening Post.
Freeman's Journal (Dublin).
Freeman's Journal (Sydney).
Gael (Dublin).
Gael (New York).
Gaelic American (New York).
Gazette (Montreal).
Herald (Melbourne).
Hibernia (New York).
Irish Australian (Sydney).
Irish Citizen (New York).
Irish Echo (New York).
Irish Echo (Sydney).
Irish Exile (Sydney).
Irish Independent (Dublin).
Irishman (New York).
Irish People (New York).
Irish Post (London).
Irish Press (Dublin).
Irish Times (Dublin).
Irish Voice (Sydney).
Irish World (New York).
Irish World and American Industrial Liberator (New York).
Limerick Reporter.
Liverpool Mercury.
Los Angeles Examiner.
Mirror (London).
Nation (Dublin).
National Hibernian Digest.
New Ireland (Dublin).
New Orleans Magazine.
New York Journal.
New York Journal-American.
New York Times.
New York World Telegram and Sun.
Oakland Tribune.
Observer (London).
Orange Standard (Belfast).
Quebec Daily Telegraph.
Salt Lake Tribune.
San Francisco Chronicle.
San Francisco Examiner.
San Francisco News.
Saoirse (Belfast).
Saoirse na hÉireann (Dublin).
The Shan Van Vocht (Belfast).
Southern Cross (Adelaide).
Spark (Dublin).
Sun (Melbourne).
Sunday Independent (London).

Sunday Times (London).
Sydney Gazette and New South Wales Advertiser.
Sydney Morning Herald.
Toronto Star.
Tribune (Melbourne).
Truth Teller (New York).
United Irishman (Dublin).
US News and World Review (New York).
Wall Street Journal (New York).

THESES

Adair, D., 'On parade: spectacles, crowds, and collective loyalties in Australia, 1901–1938', PhD thesis, Adelaide, Flinders University of South Australia, 1994.

Almeida, L.D., 'From Danny Boy to Bono: the Irish in New York City, 1945–85', PhD thesis, New York University, 1996.

Bric, M.J., 'Ireland, Irishmen and the broadening of the late 18th century Philadelphia polity', PhD thesis, Johns Hopkins University, 1991.

Casey, M.R., 'Ireland, New York and the Irish image in American popular culture, 1890–1960', PhD thesis, New York University, 1998.

Corcoran, the Reverend W.T., 'The reassertion of Irish ethnic identity after World War II in Chicago', unpublished PhD thesis (in progress), University of Loyola, Chicago, 2001.

Fitzgerald, M., 'The St Patrick's Day Parade: the conflict of Irish-American identity in New York City, 1840–1900', PhD thesis, State University of New York at Stony Brook, 1992.

Gleeson, D.T., 'The Irish in the South, 1815–77', PhD thesis, Mississippi State University, 1997.

Gordon, M.A., 'Studies in Irish and Irish-American thought and behaviour in gilded age New York', PhD thesis, University of Rochester, 1977.

Irvine, J.A., 'Aspects of identity: evidence from the Irish American press, 1871–1925', PhD thesis, University of Pittsburgh, 1994.

James, K.J., 'The Saint Patrick's Society of Montreal: ethno-religious realignment in a nineteenth-century national society', unpublished MA thesis, Department of History, McGill University, Montreal, 1997.

Kelly, M.C., 'Forty shades of green: conflict over community among New York's Irish 1860–1920', PhD thesis, Syracuse University, 1997.

Knobel, D.T., 'Paddy and the Republic: popular images of the American Irish, 1820–60', PhD thesis, Northwestern University, 1976.

McCarron, E.T., 'The world of Cavanagh and Cottrill: a portrait of Irish emigration, entrepeneurship and ethnic diversity in mid-Maine, 1760–1820', PhD thesis, University of New Hampshire, 1992.

McGivern, E.P., 'Ethnic identity and its relation to group norms: Irish Americans in metropolitan Pittsburgh', PhD thesis, 1979.

McMahon, E.M., 'What parish are you from? A study of the Chicago Irish parish community and race relations, 1916–70', PhD thesis, Loyola University of Chicago, 1989.

Marston, S.A., 'Adopted citizens: community and the development of consciousness among the Irish of Lowell, Massachusetts, 1839–85', PhD thesis, University of Colorado at Boulder, 1986.

Mazzaroli, L.A., 'The Irish in New South Wales, 1884–1914: some aspects of Irish sub-culture', PhD thesis, University of New South Wales, 1980.

Moloney, M., 'Irish music in America: continuity and change', PhD thesis, University of Pennsylvania, 1992.

Nolte, W.M., 'The Irish in Canada, 1815–67', PhD thesis, University of Maryland College Park, 1975.

O'Kane, D.F., 'The myth of Irish identity', PhD thesis, Drew University, 1982.

Regan, P., 'Montreal's St. Patrick's Day parade as a political statement: the rise of the Ancient Order of Hibernians, 1900–1929', BA (Hons) thesis, History Department, Concordia University of Montreal, 2000.

Smith, H.R. Jr, 'From stereotype to acculturation: the Irish American's fictional heritage from Brackenbridge to Farrell', PhD thesis, Kent State University, 1980.

Strauch, T.E., 'Walking for God and raising Hell: the Jubilee Riots, the Orange Order and the preservation of Protestantism in Toronto, 1875', MA Thesis, Queen's University at Kingston, 1999.

Zbiek, P.J., 'Ethnicity, assimilation and community development in a rural society: Eastern Sullivan County, Pennsylvania, 1815–70', PhD thesis, Kent State University, 1987.

SECONDARY SOURCES

Adair, D., 'Consensus and division on a spiritual occasion: the Twenty-ninth International Eucharistic Congress, Sydney, 1928', in M. Hutchinson and S. Piggin (eds), *Reviving Australia* (Sydney, Centre for the Study of Australian Christianity, 1994, pp. 202–32).

Adams, W.F., *Ireland and the Irish Emigration to the New World from 1815 to the Famine* (New Haven, CT, 1932).

Akenson, D.H., *Small Differences: Irish Catholics and Irish Protestants, 1815–1922. An International Perspective* (Montreal, McGill-Queen's University Press, 1988).

—— *The Irish Diaspora: A Primer* (Belfast, The Institute of Irish Studies at the Queen's University of Belfast, 1993).

Alter, P., 'Symbols of Irish nationalism', *Studia Hibernica*, vol. 14, 1974, pp. 104–23.

—— 'Symbols of Irish nationalism', in A. O'Day (ed.), *Reactions to Irish Nationalism* (Dublin, Irish Academic Press, 1987).

Anderson, B., *Imagined Communities: Reflections on the Origin and Spread of Nationalism* (London, Verso, 1983).

Anon, *St. Patrick's Day and the Religious Crisis in France* (Dublin, 1907).

Aylmer, G.E., 'St. Patrick's Day 1628 in Witham, Essex', *Past and Present*, no. 61, 1973, pp. 139–48.

Baker, S.E., 'Orange and green: Belfast, 1832–1912', in H.J. Dyos and M. Wolff (eds), *The Victorian City: Images and Realities*, vol. II (London, Routledge and Kegan Paul, 1973).

Barnard, T.C., 'Crises of identity among Irish Protestants, 1641–1685', *Past and Present*, no. 127, May 1990.

—— 'The uses of 23 October 1641 and Irish Protestant celebrations', *English Historical Review*, vol. 106, no. 421, October 1991.

Barth, E. and Arndt, U., *Shamrocks, Harps, and Shillelaghs: The Story of the St. Patrick's Day Symbols* (New York, Seabury Press, 1977).

Bayor, M.P. and Meagher, T.J. (eds), *The New York Irish* (Baltimore: Johns Hopkins University Press, 1996).

Beckett, J.C., *Anglo-Irish Tradition* (Ithaca, NY, Cornell University Press, 1976).

Belchem, J., 'Liverpool in the year of revolution: the political and associational culture of the Irish immigrant community in 1848', in J. Belchem (ed.), *Popular Politics, Riot and Labour: Essays in Liverpool History* (Liverpool, Liverpool University Press, 1992), pp. 68–97.

—— 'Nationalism, republicanism and exile: Irish emigrants and the revolutions of 1848', *Past and Present*, no. 146, 1995, pp. 103–35.

Bell, R., *Description of the Condition and Manners of the Peasantry of Ireland* (London, The Author, 1804).

Bell, W.J. Jr, 'The federal processions of 1788', *The New-York Historical Society Quarterly*, no. 46, 1962, pp. 5–39.

Bennett, W., *Narrative of a Recent Journey . . . in Ireland* (London, Charles Gilpin, 1847).

Bergeron, D.M., *English Civic Pageantry, 1558–1642* (Columbia, University of South Carolina Press, 1971).

Biggs-Davison, J. and Chowdharay-Best, G., *The Cross of Saint Patrick: The Catholic Unionist Tradition in Ireland* (Bourne End, Kensal Press, 1984).

Binchy, D., 'Patrick and his biographers: ancient and modern', *Studia Hibernica*, no. 2, 1962, pp. 7–173.

Birnbaum, N., 'Monarchs and sociologists: a reply to Professor Shils and Mr. Young', *Sociological Review* (n.s.), vol. 3, 1955, pp. 5–23.

Birney, T. and O'Neill, J., *When the President Calls* (Belfast, Guildhall Press, 1997).

Bishop, P., *The Irish Empire* (London, Boxtree, 1999).

Blessing, P., *The Irish in America: A Guide to the Literature and the Manuscript Collections* (Washington, DC, Catholic University of America Press, 1992).

Bodnar, J., *Remaking America: Public Memory, Commemoration and Patriotism in the Twentieth Century* (Princeton, NJ, Princeton University Press, 1992).

Bolger, S.G., *The Irish Character in American Fiction, 1830–60* (New York, 1976).

Breen, M.P., *Thirty Years of New York Politics up to Date* (New York, author, 1899).

Brennan, N., *Dr Mannix* (London, Angus and Robertson, 1965).

Brookfield, H.C., 'Microcosm of pre-famine Ireland: Mallow District, 1775–1846', *Journal of the Cork Historical and Archaeological Society*, 57, 1952.

Brown, T.N., 'Origins and character of Irish-American nationalism', *Review of Politics*, 18, July 1956.

—— *The Irish Diaspora in America* (Washington, DC, Catholic University of America, 1984).

—— *The American Connection: US Guns, Money and Influence in Northern Ireland* (Boulder, COL, Roberts Reinhart, 1999).

Brown-May, A., *Melbourne Street Life: The Itinerary of Our Days* (Melbourne, Australian Scholarly Publishing/Arcadia and Museum Victoria, 1998).

Bryan, D., 'Ireland's very own Jurassic Park: the mass media, Orange parades and the discourse on tradition', in A.D. Buckley (ed.), *Symbols in Northern Ireland* (Belfast, Institute of Irish Studies, 1998, pp. 23–42).

Buckley, A.D. (ed.), *Symbols in Northern Ireland* (Belfast, Institute of Irish Studies, 1998).

Buggy, H., *The Real John Wren* (Melbourne, Widescope, 1977).

Burgmann, V., 'The iron heel: the supression of the IWW during World War I', in Sydney Labour History Group (eds), *What Rough Beast?: The State and Social Order in Australian History* (Sydney, George Allen & Unwin, 1982), pp. 171–91.

Burke, C.T., *The Silver Key: The Charitable Irish Society of Boston* (Watertown, MA, 1972, unpublished manuscript, John J. Burns Library, Boston College, Boston).

Burke, P., *Popular Culture in Early Modern Europe* (London, Temple Smith, 1978).

Burrows, E.G. and Wallace, M., *Gotham: A History of New York City to 1898* (New York: Oxford University Press, 1999).

Busteed, M.A., 'The Irish in nineteenth-century Manchester', *Irish Studies Review*, vol. 18, 1997, pp. 1–6.

Buttmore, J., *Holiday Law in Ireland* (Dublin, Blackhall, 1999).

Byron, R., *Irish America* (Oxford: Clarendon Press, 1999).

Campion, E., *Australian Catholics* (Ringwood, Vic., Viking Penguin, 1987).

Cannadine, D., 'The transformation of civic ritual in modern Britain: the Colchester Oyster Feast', *Past and Present*, no. 94, 1982, pp. 107–30.

—— 'The context, performance and meaning of ritual: the British monarchy and the "invention of tradition", *c.*1820–1977', in E. Hobsbawm and T. Ranger (eds), *The Invention of Tradition* (Cambridge, Cambridge University Press, 1983, pp. 101–64).

Cannadine, D. and Price, S. (eds), *Rituals of Royalty: Power and Ceremonial in Traditional Societies* (Cambridge, Cambridge University Press, 1987).

Carr, J., *Stranger in Ireland* (London, Richard Phillips, 1806).

Casey, D.J. and Rhodes, R.E., *Modern Irish American Fiction: A Reader* (Syracuse: Syracuse University Press, 1989).

Clark, C.M.H., *A History of Australia*, vols III–IV (Carlton, Vic., Melbourne University Press, 1973 and 1978).

Clark, D., *The Irish in Philadelphia: Ten Generations of Urban Experience* (Philadelphia, Temple University Press, 1973).

—— *Irish Relations: Trial of an Irish Immigrant Tradition* (East Brunswick, NJ, 1981).

—— *Hibernia America: The Irish and Regional Cultures* (New York, Greenwood Press, 1986).

—— *Erin's Heirs: Irish Bonds of Community* (Lexington Key, University Press of Kentucky, 1991).

Coffey, M. and Golway, T., *The Irish in America* (New York, Hyperion, 1997).

Cohen, A.P., *The Symbolic Construction of Community* (London, Anthony Paul, 1985).

Colgan, N., 'The Shamrock in literature: a critical chronology', *Journal of the Royal Society of Antiquaries of Ireland*, no. 26, 1986, pp. 211–26, 349–61.

Comerford, V., *The Fenians in Context* (Dublin, Wolfhound, 1985).

Connell, K.H., *Irish Peasant Society* (Oxford, Clarendon Press,1969).

Connell, P., *Changing Forces Shaping a 19th Century Irish Town* (Maynooth, St Patrick's College, 1978).

Connerton, P., *How Societies Remember* (Cambridge, Cambridge University Press, 1989).

Connolly, S.J., *Priests and People in Pre-Famine Ireland* (New York, St Martin's Press, 1982).

—— (ed.), *The Oxford Companion to Irish History* (Oxford, Oxford University Press, 1998).

Coogan, T.P., *The Troubles* (London, Arrow, 1996).

Cotterell, M., 'St Patrick's Day Parade in nineteenth century Toronto', *Historie Sociale/Social History*, 25, 1992, pp. 57–73.

Crimmins, J.D., *St. Patrick's Day: Its Early Celebrations in New York and Other American Places, 1737–1845* (New York, The Author, 1902).

—— *Irish American Historical Miscellany: Relating to New York City and Vicinity Together with Much Interesting Material Relative to Other Parts of the Country* (New York, The Author, 1905).

Cronin, M., *The Blueshirts and Irish Politics* (Dublin, Four Courts Press, 1997).

—— *Sport and Nationalism in Ireland: Gaelic Games and Irish Identity Since 1884* (Dublin, Four Courts Press, 1999).

Cronin, S., *Washington's Irish Policy, 1916–86* (Dublin: Anvil Books, 1987).

Curtis, L.P., *Apes and Angels: The Irishman in Victorian Caricature* (London, David and Charles, 1971).

Daly, M. 'Revisionism and Irish history: the great famine', in D.G. Boyce and A. O'Day (eds), *The Making of Modern Irish History* (London, Routledge, 1996).

Danaher, K., *The Year in Ireland* (Cork, Mercier Press, 1972).

Danaher, K. and Lysaght, P., 'Supplement to a Bibliography of Irish Ethnology and Folk Tradition', *Béaloideas*, 48–9, 1980–1, pp. 206–27.

Dauwer, L.P., *Boston's St. Patrick Day Irish* (Boston: The Author, 1980).

Davies, S.G., *Parade and Power: Street Theatre in Nineteenth Century Philadelphia* (Berkeley, University of Columbia Press, 1986).

Davies, W.E., *Patriotism on Parade: The Story of the Veterans and Hereditary Organisations in America, 1783–1900* (Cambridge, MA, Harvard University Press, 1955).

De Blacam, H., *St Patrick Apostle of Ireland* (Milwaukee: Bruce Publishing).

Debord, G., 'Society of the spectacle', *Black and Red* (Detroit, Kalamazoo, 1970, paragraphs 1–72).

De Bréadún, D., *The Far Side of Revenge: Making Peace in Northern Ireland* (Cork, Collins Press, 2001).

Delaney, F., *Desire and Pursuit* (London, HarperCollins, 1999).

De Mille, N., *Cathedral* (London, Granada, 1982).

Diner, H.R., *Erin's Daughters in America: Irish-American Women in the Nineteenth Century* (Baltimore: Johns Hopkins University Press, 1983).

—— 'The most Irish city in the union: the era of great migration, 1844–77', in R.H. Bayor and T.J. Meagher (eds), *The New York Irish* (Baltimore, Johns Hopkins University Press, 1996).

Doherty, C., 'The problem of Patrick', *History Today*, Spring 1995, p. 18.

Dolan, J.P., *Immigrant Church: New York's Irish and German Catholics, 1815–65* (Baltimore, Johns Hopkins University Press, 1975).

Donnelly, J.S. and Miller, K. (eds), *Irish Popular Culture, 1650–1850* (Dublin, Irish Academic Press, 1998).

Doyle, D.N., *Irish Americans, Native Rights and National Empires, 1890–1901* (New York, Arno Press, 1976).

—— *Ireland, Irishmen and Revolutionary America* (Cork, Mercier Press, 1981).

—— 'The Irish in Chicago', *Irish Historical Studies*, vol. 26, no. 103, 1989, pp. 293–303.

Doyle, D.N. and Edwards, O.D. (eds), *American and Ireland, 1776–1976* (Westport, CT, Greenwood Press, 1980).

Drudy, P.J. (ed.), *The Irish in America: Emigration, Assimilation and Impact* (Cambridge, Cambridge University Press, 1985).

Duggan, D., 'Judge Comerford and the politics of the parade', *New York*, 13 March 1972, p. 38.

Durey, M., 'The survival of an Irish culture in Britain, 1800–45', *Historical Studies*, no. 78, 1982, pp. 14–35.

Durkheim, E., *The Elementary Forms of the Religious Life: A Study in Religious Sociology*, translated from the French by J.W. Swain (London, George Allen & Unwin, 1926).

Ebsworth, W.A., *Archbishop Mannix* (Melbourne, H.H. Stephenson, 1977).

Edelstein, T.J., *Constructing the Political Spectacle* (Chicago, University of Chicago Press, 1988).

—— (ed.), *Imagining an Irish Past: The Celtic Revival, 1840–1940* (Chicago, University of Chicago Press, 1992).

Ely, R., 'The First Anzac Day: invented or discovered?', *Journal of Australian Studies*, 17, November 1985, pp. 41–58.

Emmons, D.M., *The Butte Irish: Class and Ethnicity in an American Mining Town, 1875–1925* (Urbana, University of Illinois Press, 1989).

Erie, S.P., *Rainbow's End: Irish-Americans and the Dilemmas of Urban Machine Politics, 1840–1985* (Berkeley, CA, University of California Press, 1988).

Ernst, R., *Immigrant Life in New York City, 1825–1863* (Syracuse, Syracuse University Press, 1994).

Estyn E. E., *Irish Folk Ways* (London, Routledge and Kegan Paul, 1957).

Fabre, G., 'Pinkster Festival, 1766–1811: an African-American celebration', in R.A. Gutiérraz and G. Fabre (eds), *Feasts and Celebrations in North American Ethnic Communities* (Albuquerque, University of New Mexico Press, 1995, pp. 13–28).

Fallon, M.J., *The Definitive St. Patrick's Day Festivity Book* (Santa Clara, Educare, 1997).

Fallows, M.R., *Irish Americans: Identity and Assimilation* (Englewood Cliffs, NJ, Prentice-Hall, 1979).

Fanning, C. (ed.), *The Exiles of Erin: Nineteenth Century Irish-American Fiction* (Notre Dame, University of Notre Dame Press, 1987).

Farren, S. and Mulvihill, R.F. (eds), *Paths to a Settlement in Northern Ireland* (London, Colin Smythe, 2000).

Fielding, S., 'The Catholic Whit Walk in Manchester and Salford, 1890–1939', *Manchester Region History Review*, 1, 1987.

—— *Class and Ethnicity: Irish Catholics in England, 1880–1939* (Milton Keynes, Open University Press, 1993).

Firth, S. and Hoorn, J., 'From Empire Day to cracker night', in P. Spearritt, and D. Walker (eds), *Australian Popular Culture* (Sydney, Allen & Unwin, 1979).

Fisk, R., *In Time of War: Ireland, Ulster and the Price of Neutrality, 1939–45* (London, Deutsch, 1983).

Fitzpatrick, D., *Irish Emigration, 1801–1921* (Dublin: Economic and Social History Society of Ireland, 1984).

—— 'That beloved country, that no place else resembles: connotations of Irishness in Irish-Australasian letters, 1841–1915', *Irish Historical Studies*, vol. 27, no. 108, 1991, pp. 324–51.

Fogarty, W.L., *The Days We've Celebrated: St. Patrick's Day in Savannah* (Savannah: Printcraft Press, 1980).

Forth, G., '"No petty people": the Anglo-Irish identity in colonial Australia', in P. O'Sullivan (ed.), *The Irish in the New Communities* (Leicester, Leicester University Press, 1992, pp. 128–42).

Foster, R.F., *Modern Ireland, 1600–1972* (London, Penguin, 1989).

Foster, S., 'Buying Irish: consumer nationalism in 18th-century Dublin', *History Today*, vol. 47, no. 6, June 1997, pp. 44–52.

Foster, T.C., *Letters on the Condition of the People of Ireland* (London, Chapman and Hall, 1847).

Fraser, B., *The Search for Identity: Canada, 1945–1967* (Toronto, Doubleday, 1967).

Fraser, T.G. (ed.), *The Irish Parading Tradition: Following the Drum* (London, Macmillan, 2000).

French, M., 'The ambiguity of Empire Day in New South Wales 1901–21: imperial consensus or national division?', *Australian Journal of Politics and History*, vol. 24, no. 1, April 1978, pp. 61–74.

Friendly Sons of St. Patrick, *The Charter, Constitution, By-laws, Officers, Committees, Roll of*

Members &c., of the Friendly Sons of St. Patrick in the City of New York (New York, Dempsey and Carroll, 1899).

Gailey, A., 'Scots element in North Irish popular culture', *Ethnologia Europaea*, 8, 1, 1975.

Gallagher, T., 'A tale of two cities: communal strife in Glasgow and Liverpool before 1914', in R. Swift and S. Gilley (eds), *The Irish in the Victorian City*, London, Croom Helm, 1985, pp. 106–29).

—— *Glasgow, the Uneasy Peace: Religious Tension in Modern Scotland* (Manchester, Manchester University Press, 1987).

Galloway, P., *The Most Illustrious Order of St Patrick, 1783–1983* (London, Philmore, 1985).

Galvin, P., *Song for a Raggy Boy: A Cork Boyhood* (Dublin, Raven Arts Press, 1991).

Garland, John A., 'St Patrick's Day, New York City 1861', *The Irish Sword*, vol. 17, no. 66 (1987), pp. 26–40.

Garvin, T., 'Defenders, ribbonmen and others: underground political networks in pre-famine Ireland', *Past and Present*, no. 96, 1982, pp. 133–55.

—— *1922: The Birth of Irish Democracy* (Dublin, Gill & Macmillan, 1997).

Gilbert, A.D., 'The conscription referenda, 1916–17: the impact of the Irish crisis', *Historical Studies (Australia)*, vol. 14, October 1969, pp. 55–7, 68–70.

Gilje, P.A., *The Road to Mobocracy: Popular Disorder in New York City, 1763–1834* (Chapel Hill, NC, University of North Carolina Press, 1987).

—— 'The development of an Irish American community in New York City before the great migration', in R.H. Bayor and T.J. Meagher (eds), *The New York Irish* (Baltimore, Johns Hopkins University Press, 1996).

Gillespie, R. and Kennedy, B.P. (eds), *Ireland: Art into History* (Dublin, Town House, 1994).

Giollain, D.O., 'The pattern', in J.S. Donnelly and K.A. Miller (eds), *Irish Popular Culture 1650–1850* (Dublin, Irish Academic Press, 1998).

Good, P.K., 'Irish adjustment to American society: portrait of an Irish-Catholic parish, 1863–86', *Records of the American Catholic Historical Society of Philadelphia*, vol. 86, 1975.

Gordon, M.A., *The Orange Riots: Irish Political Violence in New York City 1825–1963* (Ithaca, NY, Cornell University Press, 1997).

Green, A.S., *Irish National Tradition* (London, Macmillan, 1923).

Green, E.R.R. 'Ulster emigrants' letters', in E.R.R. Green (ed.), *Essays in Scotch-Irish History* (London, Routledge and Kegan Paul, 1969).

Grimes, R.R., *How Shall We Sing in a Foreign Land? Music of Irish Catholic Immigrants in the Antebellum United States* (Notre Dame, University of Notre Dame Press, 1996).

Haines, R., '"Shovelling out paupers?": parish-assisted emigration from England to Australia, 1834–1847', in E. Richards (ed.), *Visible Immigrants 2: Poor Australian Immigrants in the Nineteenth Century* (Canberra, Division of Historical Studies and Centre for Immigration and Multicultural Studies, Research School of Social Sciences, Australian National University, 1991, pp. 33–68).

—— '"The idle and the drunken won't do there": poverty, the new Poor Law and nineteenth-century government-assisted emigration to Australia from the United Kingdom', *Australian Historical Studies*, vol. 28, no. 108, April, 1997, pp. 1–21.

Haltigan, J., *The Irish in the American Revolution and their Early Influence in the Colonies* (Washington, DC, Patrick Haltigan, 1908).

Handlin, O., *Boston's Immigrants, 1790–1880: A Study in Acculturation* (Cambridge, MA, Belknap Press, 1991).

Hannan, D., 'Kinship, neighbourhood and social change in Irish rural communities', *Economic and Social Review*, vol. 2, 1972.

Hayden, M. and Moonan, G.A., *A Short History of the Irish People* (Dublin, Talbot Press, 1921).

Hayes-McCoy, G.A., 'War under the banner of St Patrick – Patrician symbolism, military and heraldic', *National Souvenir of the Patrician Year, 461–1961* (Dublin, Irish Times, 1961).

—— *A History of Irish Flags from Earliest Times* (Boston, G.K. Hall, 1979).

Healey, D., *The Bend for Home* (London, Harvil, 1996).

Healy, J.N. (ed.), *Irish Ballads and Songs of the Sea* (Cork, Mercier, 1967).

Hennessey, T., *The Northern Ireland Peace Process* (Dublin, Gill & Macmillan, 2000).

Hickman, M.J., *Religion, Class and Identity: The State, the Catholic Church and the Education of the Irish in Britain* (Aldershot, Avebury, 1995).

Hill, J.R., 'Nationalism and the Catholic Church in the 1840s', *Irish Historical Studies*, vol. 19, 1975, pp. 371–95.

—— 'National festivals, the state and "Protestant Ascendancy" in Ireland, 1790–1829', *Irish Historical Studies*, vol. 24, no. 93, May 1984, pp. 30–51.

Hilliard, D., 'God in the suburbs: the religious culture of Australian cities in the 1950s', *Australian Historical Studies*, vol. 97, Octtober 1991, pp. 399–419.

Hobsbawm, E. and Ranger, T. (eds), *The Invention of Tradition* (Cambridge, Cambridge University Press, 1983).

Holi, M.G. and Green, P.M., *Chicago: A View from City Hall* (Chicago, Arcadia, 1999).

Holland, J., *The American Connection: US Guns, Money and Influence in Northern Ireland* (Boulder, CO, Roberts Rinehart, 1999).

Hoobler, D. and Hoobler, T. (eds), *The Irish American Family Album* (New York, Oxford University Press, 1999).

Hood, D., 'Adelaide's first "taste of Bolshevism": returned soldiers and the 1918 Peace Day riots', *Journal of the Historical Society of South Australia*, vol. 15, 1987, pp. 42–53.

Hopkin, A., *The Living Legend of St Patrick* (London, Grafton Books, 1989).

Horner, J. and Langton, M., 'The day of mourning', in B. Gammage and P. Spearritt (eds), *Australians 1938* (Sydney, Fairfax, Syme and Weldon, 1987, pp. 29–36).

Houston, C.J. and Smyth, W.J., *Irish Emigration and Canadian Settlement: Patterns, Links, and Letters* (Toronto, University of Toronto Press, 1990).

Howe, A., 'Women against Anzac Day: the personal is the political', *Peace Studies*, vol. 6, September 1984, pp. 17–19.

Hughes, R., *The Fatal Shore: A History of the Transportation of Convicts to Australia, 1787–1868* (London, Collins Harvill, 1987).

Hughes, T.J., 'Society and settlement in 19th century Ireland', *Irish Geography*, vol. 5, 1965.

Hutchinson, J., *The Dynamics of Cultural Nationalism: The Gaelic Revival and the Creation of the Irish Nation State* (London, Allen and Unwin, 1987).

Inglis, K.S., 'The Australian Catholic community', in H. Mayer (ed.), *Catholics and the Free Society: An Australian Symposium* (Melbourne, Cheshire, 1961, pp. 7–32).

—— 'Conscription in peace and war, 1911–1945', *Teaching History*, vol. 1, no. 2, October 1967, pp. 5–25.

—— *The Australian Colonists: An Exploration of Social History, 1788–1870* (Carlton, Vic., Melbourne University Press, 1974).

Jarman, N., *Material Conflicts: Parades and Visual Displays in Northern Ireland* (Oxford, Berg, 1997).

Jarman, N. and Bryan, D., *From Riots to Rights: Nationalist Parades in the North of Ireland* (Coleraine, Centre for the Study of Conflict, 1998).

Joyce, J., *Dubliners* (New York, B.W. Huebsch, 1917).

Joyce, W.L., *Editors and Ethnicity: A History of the Irish-American Press, 1848–1883* (New York, Arno Press, 1976).

Kay, J.P., *The Moral and Physical Condition of the Working Class* (London, James Ridgeway, 1833).

Kazin, M. and Ross, S.J., 'America's Labor Day: the dilemma of a workers' celebration', *Journal of American History*, vol. 78, no. 4, March 1992, pp. 1294–323.

Kells, M., 'I'm myself and nobody else: gender and ethnicity among young middle class Irish women in London', in P. O'Sullivan (ed.), *Irish Women and Irish Migration. Volume 4: The Irish World-Wide. History, Heritage, Identity* (London, Leicester University Press, 1995).

Kelly, J., '"The glorious and immortal memory": commemoration and Protestant identity in Ireland, 1660–1800', *Proceedings of the Royal Irish Academy*, no. 94C, 1994.

Kelton, J.G., 'New York City St Patrick's Day Parade: invention of contention and consensus', *Drama Review*, vol. 29, no. 3 (1985), pp. 93–105.

Kennedy-Pipe, C., *Origins of the Northern Ireland Troubles* (London, Longman, 1997).

Kenny, K., *The American Irish: A History* (Harlow, Longman, 2000).

Keogh, D., 'Mannix, de Valera and Irish nationalism', in J. O'Brien and P. Travers (eds), *The Irish Emigrant Experience in Australia* (Dublin, Poolbeg, 1991).

Kerrigan, C., *Father Mathew and the Irish Temperance Movement, 1838–49* (Cork, Cork University Press, 1992).

Kidd, C., 'Gaelic antiquity and national identity in Enlightenment Ireland and Scotland', *English Historical Review*, vol. 109, no. 434, November 1994.

Kiernan, C., 'Home Rule for Ireland and the formation of the Australian Labor Party, 1883 to 1891', *Australian Journal of Politics and History*, vol. 38, no. 1, 1992, pp. 2–7.

Kimball, S.T., *Family and Community in Ireland* (Cambridge, MA, Harvard University Press, 1968 edn).

Lane, C., *The Rites of Rulers: Ritual in Industrial Society – the Soviet Case* (Cambridge, Cambridge University Press, 1981).

Larsen, S., 'The glorious twelfth: a ritual expression of collective identity', in A. Cohen (ed.), *Belonging: Identity and Social Organisation in British Rural Cultures* (Manchester, Manchester University Press, 1982).

Leahy, E., *The Life of St Patrick* (Dublin: Irish Messenger, 1917).

Le Chevalier de La Tocnaye, *Frenchman's Walk Through Ireland, 1796–97* (Belfast, 1917 edn).

Leerseen, J., *Remembrance and Imagination: Patterns in the Historical and Literary Representation of Ireland in the Nineteenth Century* (Cork, Cork University Press, 1996).

Lees, L.H., *Exiles of Erin: Irish Migrants in Victorian London* (Manchester, Manchester University Press, 1979).

Legg, M., *Newspapers and Nationalism: The Irish Provincial Press, 1850–1892* (Dublin, Four Courts Press, 1999).

Levin, B., *A Walk Up Fifth Avenue* (London: Sceptre, 1989).

Leyburn, J.G., *The Scotch-Irish: A Social History* (Chapel Hill, NC, University of North Carolina Press, 1962).

Loftus, B, *Mirrors: Orange and Green* (Dublin, Picture Press, 1994).

Logan, P., *Fair Day: The Story of Irish Fairs and Markets* (Belfast: Appletree Press, 1986).

Lorini, A., 'Public rituals and the cultural making of the New York African-American community', in R.A. Gutiérraz and G. Fabre (eds), *Feasts and Celebrations in North American Ethnic Communities* (Albuquerque, University of New Mexico Press, 1995, pp. 29–46).

Lowe, W.J., *The Irish in Mid-Victorian Lancashire: The Shaping of a Working-Class Community* (Ithaca, NY, Peter Lang, 1989).

Lukes, S., 'Political ritual and social integration', *Sociology*, vol. 9, no. 2, May 1975, pp. 289–308.

McBride, I. and Claydon, T. (eds), *Protestantism and National Identity: Britain and Ireland, c.1650–c.1850* (Cambridge, Cambridge University Press, 1998).

McBride, L.W. (ed.), *Images, Icons and the Irish Nationalist Imagination* (Dublin: Four Courts Press, 1999).

McCaffrey, L.J., *The Irish Diaspora in America* (Washington, DC, 1984).

—— *Textures of Irish America* (Syracuse: Syracuse University Press, 1992).

McCarthy, J., 'The Gra-a-and Parade', *American Heritage*, February, 1969, p. 55.

McCartney, C. and Bryson, L., *Clashing Symbols? A Report on the use of Flags, Anthems and Other National Symbols in Northern Ireland* (Belfast, Institute of Irish Studies, 1994).

McConville, C., *Croppies, Celts and Catholics: The Irish in Australia* (Caulfield, East Vic., Edward Arnold, 1987).

McCormack, B., *Perceptions of Saint Patrick in Eighteenth Century Ireland* (Dublin: Four Courts Press, 2000).

McCormack, W.J. (ed.), *The Blackwell Companion to Modern Irish Culture* (Oxford, Blackwell, 1999).

McCourt, F., *Angela's Ashes: A Memoir* (London, HarperCollins, 1996).

—— *'Tis: A Memoir* (London, Flamingo, 1999).

McDannell, C., 'True men as we need them: Catholicism and the Irish-American male', *American Studies*, vol. 27, 1986, pp. 19–36.

MacDonagh, O., 'Irish culture and nationalism translated: St Patrick's Day in Australia 1888', in O. MacDonagh, W.F. Mandle and P. Travers (eds), *Culture and Nationalism in Ireland, 1750–1950* (Canberra, Macmillan, 1983).

McDowell, R.B. (ed.), *Social Life in Ireland* (Dublin, 1957).

Macfarlane, D. and Asmoucha, T., 'Life on parade', *Canadian Geographic*, July–August 1997, vol. 117, no. 4, pp. 72, 80.

Machin, G.I.T., *Politics and the Churches in Great Britain, 1832 to 1868* (Oxford, Clarendon Press, 1977).

Macintyre, S., *The Oxford History of Australia*, vol. 4, *1901–1942: The Succeeding Age* (Melbourne, Oxford University Press, 1986).

MacKay, D., *Flight from Famine: The Coming of the Irish to Canada* (Toronto, McClelland and Stewart Inc., 1990).

McKernan, M., 'Catholics, conscription and Archbishop Mannix', *Historical Studies (Australia)*, vol. 18, 1977, pp. 299–314.

McKinlay, B., *The First Royal Tour 1867–1868* (Adelaide, Rigby, 1970).

Mac Lir, M., in the *Journal of the Cork Historical and Archaeological Society*, 1895.

McNamara, B., *Day of Jubilee: The Great Age of Public Celebrations in New York, 1789–1909* (New Brunswick, Rutgers University Press, 1997).

MacRaild, D.M., *Culture, Conflict and Migration: The Irish in Victorian Cumbria* (Liverpool, Liverpool University Press, 1998).

—— 'William Murphy, the Orange Order and communal violence: the Irish in West Cumberland, 1871–84', in P. Panayi, *Racial Violence in Britain, 1840–1950* (Leicester, Leicester University Press, 1993), pp. 44–64.

—— *Irish Migrants in Modern Britain, 1750–1922* (London, Macmillan, 1999).

Madson, A., 'St. Patrick's Day in Rock County', *Southern Humanities Review*, vol. 19, no. 1, 1985, pp. 14–24.

Malcolm, E., 'Popular recreation in nineteenth-century Ireland', in O. MacDonagh,

W.F. Mandle and P. Travers (eds), *Culture and Nationalism in Ireland, 1750–1950* (Canberra, Macmillan, 1983).

—— *Ireland Sober, Ireland Free: Drink and Temperance in 19th Century Ireland* (Dublin, Gill & Macmillan, 1986).

Malone, R., *Irish America* (New York, Hippocrene Books, 1994).

Mandle, W.F., *The Gaelic Athletic Association and Irish Nationalist Politics, 1884–1924* (Dublin, Gill & Macmillan, 1987).

Mannion, J.J., *Irish Settlements in Eastern Canada* (Toronto, 1974).

Marston, S.A., 'Public rituals and community power: St Patrick's Day parades in Lowell, Massachusetts, 1841–74', *Political Geography Quarterly*, vol. 8, no. 3, 1989, pp. 255–69.

Martin, C.E. and French, W.E. (eds), *Rituals of Rule, Rituals of Resistance: Public Celebrations and Popular Culture in Mexico* (Wilmington, SR Books, 1994).

Massam, K., 'The blue army and the Cold War: anti-communist devotion to the Blessed Virgin Mary in Australia', *Australian Historical Studies*, vol. 97, October 1991, pp. 420–8.

May, A., '*Theatrum urbis*: Melbourne street processions', in G. Davison and A. May (eds), *Melbourne Centre Stage: The Corporation of Melbourne 1842–1992*, a special issue of the *Victorian Historical Journal*, vol. 63, nos 2–3, October 1992.

Meagher, T.J., 'Why should we care for a little trouble or a walk in the mud? St Patrick's and Columbus Day parades in Worcester, Massachusetts, 1845–1915', *New England Quarterly*, vol. 58, no. 1, 1985, pp. 5–26.

—— (ed.), *From Paddy to Studs. Irish-American Communities in the Turn of the Centruy Era, 1880–1920* (New York, Greenwood Press, 1986a).

—— 'Irish American, Catholic: Irish-American identity in Worcester, Massachusetts, 1880–1920', in T.J. Meagher (ed.), *From Paddy to Studs: Irish American Communities in the Turn of the Century Era, 1880–1920* (New York, Greenwood Press, 1986b).

Metress, S.P., *The American Irish and Irish Nationalism: A Sociohistorical Introduction* (Lanham, MD, Scarecrow Press, 1995).

Miller, J.R., 'Anti-Catholic thought in Victorian Canada', *Canadian Historical Review*, vol. 56, no. 4, 1985, pp. 474–94.

Miller, K. and Wagner, P. (eds), *Out of Ireland: The Story of Irish Emigration to America* (London: Aurum Press, 1994).

Miller, K.A., *Emigrants and Exiles: Ireland and the Irish Exodus to North America* (Oxford, Oxford University Press, 1985).

Miller, K.A., Boling, B. and Doyle, D.N., 'Emigrants and exiles: Irish cultures and Irish emigration to North America', *Irish Historical Studies,* 22 September 1980, pp. 97–125.

Moir, J.S., 'The problem of a double minority: some reflections on the development of the English-speaking Catholic church in Canada in the nineteenth century', *Histoire Sociale/Social History*, no. 4, April 1971, pp. 53–68.

Molloy, D., 'St. Patrick on the web', *Irish Voice*, 17 March 1998.

Moody, T.W. and Martin, F.X. (eds), *A New History of Ireland*, vol. III, *Early Modern Ireland, 1534–1691* (Oxford, Clarendon Press, 1976).

Mooney, J, *Holiday Customs of Ireland* (Philadelphia: Macalla and Co., 1889).

Moran, G., 'Nationalists in exile: the National Brotherhood of St Patrick in Lancashire, 1861–5', in R. Swift and S. Gilley (eds), *Irish in Victorian Britain: The Local Dimension* (Dublin, Four Courts Press, 1999).

Moran, J., *'The Land We Left Behind': The Emergence of St Patrick's Day Celebrations in Brisbane, 1862–1870* (Ashgrove, Queensland, The Author, 1989).

Moss, K., 'St. Patrick's Day celebrations and the formation of Irish-American identity, 1845–1875', *Journal of Social History*, vol. 29, Fall 1995, pp. 125–48.

Mosse, G. L., *The Nationalization of the Masses: Political Symbolism and Mass Movements in Germany from the Napoleonic Wars through the Third Reich* (New York: Howard Fertig, 1975).

Mullett, M.A., *Catholics in Britain and Ireland, 1558–1829* (New York, St Martin's Press, 1998).

Murdoch, N.H., 'Salvation Army disturbances in Liverpool, England, 1879–1887', *Journal of Social History*, vol. 25, no. 3, 1992, pp. 575–94.

Murphy, D.J., 'Religion, race and conscription in World War I', *Australian Journal of Politics and History*, vol. 20, no. 2, August 1974, pp. 155–6.

Murphy, R.C. and Mannion, L., *The History of the Friendly Sons of St Patrick in the City of New York* (New York: J.C. Dillion, 1962).

Murphy, T. and Stortz, G. (eds), *Creed and Culture: The Place of English-speaking Catholics in Canadian Society, 1750–1930* (Montreal, McGill-Queen's University Press, 1993).

Neal, F., *Sectarian Violence. The Liverpool Experience 1819–1914: An Aspect of Anglo-Irish History* (Manchester, Manchester University Press, 1988).

Newman, S.P., *Parades and the Politics of the Street: Festive Culture in the Early American Republic* (Philadelphia, University of Pennsylvania Press, 1997).

O'Brien, M. and O'Brien, C.C., *A Concise History of Ireland* (London, Thames and Hudson, 2nd edn, 1973).

O'Carroll, I., *Models for Movers: Irish Women's Emigration to America* (Dublin, Attic, 1989).

O'Carroll, J.T., *Ireland in the War Years, 1939–45* (Newton Abbot, David and Charles, 1975).

O'Casey, S., 'St Pathrick's Day in the Morning', in S. O'Casey, *The Green Crow* (London, Virgin, 1994).

O'Clery, C., *The Greening of the White House* (Dublin, Gill & Macmillan, 1996).

—— *Daring Diplomacy: Clinton's Secret Search for Peace in Ireland* (Boulder, CO, Roberts Rinehart, 1997).

O'Connor, T.H., *South Boston: My Home Town* (Boston, Northeastern University Press, 1994).

—— *The Boston Irish: A Political History* (Boston, Back Bay Books, 1995).

Ó Corráin, D., 'Prehistoric and early Christian Ireland', in R.F. Foster (ed.), *The Oxford Illustrated History of Ireland*, Oxford, Oxford University Press, 1989.

Ó Cuív, B., 'The wearing of the green', *Studia Hibernica,* vol. 17, 1977.

Ó Danachair, C., *A Bibliography of Irish Ethnology and Folk Tradition* (Dublin, Mercier, 1978).

O'Dea, J., *History of the Ancient Order of Hibernians and Ladies' Auxiliary*, vols. I–III (Philadelphia, National Board of the AOH, 1923).

O'Driscoll, R. and Reynolds, L. (eds), *The Untold Story: The Irish in Canada*, vol. II (Toronto, Celtic Arts of Canada, 1988).

O'Fahey, C.J., 'Reflections on the St Patrick's Day orations of John Ireland', *Ethnicity*, 2, 1975, pp. 244–57.

O'Farrell, P., 'Archbishop Kelly and the Irish question', *Journal of the Australian Catholic Historical Society*, vol. 4, no. 3, 1974, pp. 4–5.

—— 'Emigrant attitudes and behaviour as a source of Irish history', *Historical Studies,* 10, 1976.

—— 'Whose reality? The Irish famine in history and literature', *Historical Studies* (Aust.), vol. 20, April, 1982, pp. 1–13.

—— 'The Irish Republican Brotherhood in Australia: the 1918 internments', in O. MacDonagh, W.F. Mandle and P. Travers (eds), *Culture and Nationalism in Ireland* (Canberra, Macmillan, 1983).

—— *The Catholic Church and Community: An Australian History* (Kensington, NSW, New South Wales University Press, 1985).

—— *The Irish in Australia* (Kensington, NSW, New South Wales University Press, 1987).

—— *Vanished Kingdoms: Irish in Australia and New Zealand* (Kensington, NSW, New South Wales University Press, 1990).

—— 'St Patrick's Day in Australia: the John Alexander Ferguson lecture 1994', *Journal of the Royal Australian Historical Society*, vol. 81, no. 1, 1995, pp. 1–16.

O'Gallagher, M., *Saint Patrick's Quebec: The Building of a Church and of a Parish* (Quebec, Carraig Books, 1981).

O'Hanlon, R, *The New Irish Americans* (Boulder, CO, Roberts Reinhart, 1998).

O'Neil, T., *Life and Tradition in Rural Ireland* (London, J.M. Dent, 1977).

Osofsky, G., 'Abolitionists, Irish immigrants and the dilemmas of romantic nationalism', *American Historical Review*, vol. 80, 1975, pp. 889–912.

Ó Súilleabháin, S., *A Handbook of Irish Folklore* (Dublin, Mercier, 1942).

—— *Irish Folk Custom and Belief* (Dublin, Mercier, 1967).

O'Sullivan, P. (ed.), *Irish Women and Migration. The Irish Worldwide: History, Heritage, Identity*, Vol. 4 (Leicester, Leicester University Press, 1995).

Owens, G., 'Nationalism without words: spectacle and ritual in the repeal "monster meetings" of 1843–45', in J.S. Donnelly and K. Miller (eds), *Irish Popular Culture* (Dublin, Irish Academic Press, 1998, pp. 542–69).

Perrot, M., 'The first of May 1890 in France: the birth of a working-class ritual', in P. Thane, G. Crossick, and R. Roderick Floud (eds), *The Power of the Past: Essays for Eric Hobsbawm* (Cambridge, Cambridge University Press, 1984, pp. 143–72).

Plumptre, A., *Narrative of a Residence in Ireland During 1814 and 1815* (London, 1817).

Potter, G., *To The Golden Door: Story of the Irish in Ireland and America* (Westport, CT, Greenwood Press, 1973).

Proudfoot, A.B. (ed.), *Patrick: Sixteen Centuries with Ireland's Patron Saint* (New York, Macmillan, 1983).

Rearick, C., 'Festivals in modern France: the experience of the Third Republic', *Journal of Contemporary History*, vol. 12, 1977, pp. 435–60.

Regan, J.M., *The Irish Counter-Revolution* (Dublin, Gill & Macmillan, 2000).

Reid, T., *Travels in Ireland in the Year 1822* (London, 1823).

Reilly, E., 'Beyond gilt shamrock: symbolism and realism in the cover art of Irish historical and political fiction, 1880–1914', in L.W. McBride (ed.), *Images, Icons and the Irish Nationalist Imagination* (Dublin, Four Courts Press, 1999, pp. 95–112).

Ridge, J.T., *Erin's Sons in America: The Ancient Order of Hibernians* (New York: Ancient Order of Hibernians, 1986).

—— *The St Patrick's Day Parade in New York* (New York: New York St. Patrick's Day Parade Committee, 1988).

Rigal, L., '"Raising the roof": authors, spectators and artisans in the Grand Federal Procession of 1788', *Theatre Journal*, vol. 48, no. 3, pp. 253–78.

Rivett, R., *Australian Citizen: Herbert Brooks, 1867–1963* (Carlton, Vic., Melbourne University Press, 1965).

Roberts, G., 'The British offer to end partition, June 1940', *History Ireland*, vol. 9, no. 1, 2001, p. 5.

Robins, J., *Champagne and Silver Buckles: The Viceregal Court at Dublin Castle, 1700–1922* (Dublin, Lilliput Press, 2001).

Russell, A., *Bank Holidays: A Victorian Invention and Modern Institution* (London, Minerva Press, 2000).

Ryan, M.P., 'The American parade: representations of the nineteenth-century social order', in L. Hunt (ed.), *The New Cultural History* (Berkeley, CA, University of California Press, 1989).

—— *Civic Wars: Democracy and Public Life in the American City During the Nineteenth Century* (Berkeley, CA, University of California Press, 1997).

Sailer, S.S. (ed.), *Representing Ireland: Gender, Class, Nationality* (Gainesville, FL, University Press of Florida, 1997).

Samuel, R. (ed.), *Patriotism: The Making and Unmaking of British National Identity* (London: Routledge, 1989).

Santamaria, B.A., *Daniel Mannix: The Quality of Leadership* (Carlton, Vic., Melbourne University Press, 1984).

Savage, R.J., *Irish Television: The Political and Social Origins* (Cork, Cork University Press, 1996).

Schermann, K., *The Flowering of Ireland: Saints, Scholars and Kings* (London, Victor Gollancz, 1981).

Schmitz, N., *Irish for a Day: St Patrick's Day Parades in Quebec City, 1850–1990* (Montreal, Carraig Books, 1991).

Schrier, A., *Ireland and the American Emigration, 1850–1900* (Chester Springs, PA: Dufour Editions, 1997).

Shannon, W., *The American Irish* (New York, Macmillan, 1963).

Shea, A.M. and Casey, M.R., *The Irish Experience in New York City: A Select Bibliography* (New York: New York Irish History Roundtable, 1995).

Sheehy, J., *The Rediscovery of Ireland's Past: The Celtic Revival, 1830–1930* (London, Thames and Hudson, 1980).

Sheridan, R.B., *St Patrick's Day or the Scheming Lieutenant* (London, Unit Library, 1903).

Sherington, G., *Australia's Immigrants, 1788–1988* (Sydney, George Allen & Unwin, 2nd edn, 1990).

Shils, E. and Young, M., 'The meaning of the coronation', *Sociological Review* (n.s.), vol. 1, 1953, pp. 72–80.

Smith, D., *A Song for Mary: An Irish-American Memory* (New York, Warner, 1999).

Smith, R., *One Day as a Lion* (Dublin, Sporting Books, 1997).

Spearritt, P., 'Celebration of a nation: the triumph of spectacle', *Australian Historical Studies*, vol. 23, no. 91, October 1988a, pp. 3–20.

—— 'Royal progress: the Queen and her Australian subjects', in S.L. Goldberg and F.B. Smith (eds), *Australian Cultural History* (Melbourne, Cambridge University Press, 1988b, pp. 138–57).

Stivers, R., *Hair of the Dog: Irish Drinking and American Stereotype* (University Park, Pennsylvania State University Press, 1976).

Storch, R.D. (ed.), *Popular Culture and Custom in Nineteenth Century England* (London, Croom Helm, 1982).

St Patrick's Day 1959: Souvenir Programme Ireland's Industrial Pageant (Dublin, Frederick Press, 1959).

Swift, R. and Gilley, S. (eds), *The Irish in Britain, 1815–1939* (London: Pinter, 1989).

—— *The Irish in Victorian Britain: The Local Dimension* (Dublin, Four Courts Press, 1999).

Thelan, D. (ed.), *Memory and American History* (Bloomington: Indiana University Press, 1990).

Thompson, J.E., *American Policy and Northern Ireland. A Saga of Peacebuilding* (Westport, CT, Praeger Publishers, 2001).

Trillin, C., 'American chronicles: democracy in action', *New Yorker*, 21 March 1988, pp. 85–99.

Turner, I., *Industrial Labour and Politics: The Dynamics of the Labour Movement in Eastern Australia, 1900–1921* (Sydney, Hale & Iremonger, 1979).

Vamplew, W. (ed.), *Australians: Historical Statistics* (Broadway, NSW, Fairfax, Syme & Weldon Associates, 1987).

Walker, B., *Dancing to History's Tune: History, Myth and Politics in Ireland* (Belfast, Institute of Irish Studies, 1996).

Walkowski, P.J. and Connolly, W. M., *From Trial Court to United States Supreme Court. Anatomy of a Free Speech Case. The Incredible Inside Story Behind the Theft of the St. Patrick's Day Parade* (Boston, Branden Publishing, 1996).

Wannan, B., *Wearing of the Green: The Lore, Literature, Legend and Balladry* (Melbourne, Lansdowne, 1965).

—— *The Folklore of the Irish in Australia* (Melbourne, Currey O'Neil, 1980).

Weissengruber, E.P., 'The Corpus Christi procession in Medieval York: a symbolic struggle in public space', *Theatre Survey*, vol. 38, May 1997, pp. 117–38.

Werly, J.M., 'The Irish in Manchester, 1832–49', *Irish Historical Studies*, vol. 18, no. 71, 1973, pp. 345–58.

Whooley, F. *Irish Londoners: Photography from the Paddy Fahey Collection* (Stroud, Sutton, 1997).

Wichert, S., *Northern Ireland Since 1945* (London, Longman, 1999).

Williams, L., 'Irish Identity and the *Illustrated London News*, 1846–51', in S.S. Sailer (ed.), *Representing Ireland: Gender, Class, Nationality* (Gainesville, FL, University Press of Florida, 1997), pp. 59–94.

Wilson, A. J., *Irish America and the Ulster Conflict, 1968–95* (Washington, DC, Catholic University of America Press, 1995).

Wittke, C., *The Irish in America* (Baton Rouge, Louisiana State University Press, 1956).

Wright, R.L. (ed.), *Irish Emigrant Ballads and Songs* (Bowling Green, Ohio, 1975).

Ziegler, S. and Connelly, G., *Our St. Patrick's Day Book* (Chicago, Child's World, 1987).

INDEX

— ༀ —